MEDIEVAL
AND
RENAISSANCE
DRAMA
IN ENGLAND

Editorial Board

MEDIEVAL AND RENAISSANCE DRAMA IN ENGLAND

Volume 16

Edited by
John Pitcher

Associate Editor
Robert Lindsey

Book Review Editor
Susan Cerasano

Madison • Teaneck
Fairleigh Dickinson University Press
London: Associated University Presses

Associated University Presses
2010 Eastpark Boulevard
Cranbury, NJ 08512

Associated University Presses
Unit 304, The Chandlery
50 Westminster Bridge Road
London SE1 7QY, England

Associated University Presses
P.O. Box 338, Port Credit
Mississauga, Ontario
Canada L5G 4L8

The paper used in this publication meets the requirements of the American National Standard for Permanence of Paper for Printed Library Materials Z39.48-1984.

International Standard Book Number 0-8386-4000-1 (vol. 16)
International Standard Serial Number 0731-3403

All editorial correspondence concerning *Medieval and Renaissance Drama in England* should be addressed to Dr. John Pitcher, St. John's College, Oxford OX1 3JP, United Kingdom. Orders and subscriptions should be directed to Associated University Presses, 2010 Eastpark Boulevard, Cranbury, New Jersey 08512.

Medieval and Renaissance Drama in England disclaims responsibility for statements, either of fact or opinion, made by contributors.

Contents

6 CONTENTS

Reviews

Foreword

Volume 16 contains several archival studies, with new findings and conclusions about the place of drama in the provinces, the design of the Swan Theatre, and the financing and presentation of an Elizabethan entertainment. One of the essays is devoted to the career of a Jacobean actor. Other contributors focus on, among other things, the function of laughter and blasphemy in the theater, the representation of women in shops on the early modern stage, and the date and the topicality of the Jacobean tragedy *The Insatiate Countess.*

JOHN PITCHER

Contributors

JOHN H. ASTINGTON is Professor of English and Drama at the University of Toronto. He is the author of numerous articles on the pre-Restoration theater, and of *English Court Theatre 1558–1642*.

HARRY BERGER, JR. is Professor Emeritus, Literature and Art History at Cowell College, University of California, Santa Cruz. He is the author of *Fictions of the Pose: Rembrandt Against the Italian Renaissance* and *The Absence of Grace: Sprezzatura and Suspicion in Two Renaissance Courtesy Books*.

ILONA BELL is Professor of English at Williams College. She is the author of *Elizabethan Women and Poetry of Courtship,* as well as essays on Elizabethan women and Renaissance poetry.

CURTIS BREIGHT is an Associate Professor of English and Film Studies at the University of Pittsburgh. He has published a book entitled *Surveillance, Militarism and Drama in the Elizabethan Era* (1996), and is currently writing a book on Shakespeare and cinema.

CHARLES CATHCART, an independent student who lives in Blackburn in the U.K., is interested, chiefly in early modern drama in England.

CYNDIA SUSAN CLEGG is a Distinguished Professor of English Literature at Pepperdine University. Her recent publications include *Press Censorship in Elizabethan England.*

PHILIP D. COLLINGTON, Assistant Professor of English at Niagara University, has published on Shakespeare in *English Literary Renaissance* and *Shakespeare Quarterly.*

VIVIANNA COMENSOLI is a Professor of English at Wilfrid Laurier University in Ontario, Canada. She is the author of *"Household Business": Domestic Plays of Early Modern England* and co-editor of *Enacting Gender on the English Renaissance Stage.*

9

KEVIN CRAWFORD is completing his doctorate as a Hudson Strode Fellow of Renaissance Studies at the University of Alabama; he was previously a Lecturer in English and Literature at Florida Atlantic University.

INDIRA GHOSE, is Assistant Professor at the English Department of the Free University, Berlin. Her publications include *Women Travellers in Colonial India: The Power of the Female Gaze,* and *Memsahibs Abroad: Writings by Women Travellers in Nineteenth Century India.*

JOAN OZARK HOLMER is Professor of English at Georgetown University is the author of *"The Merchant of Venice": Choice, Hazard and Consequence.*

WILLIAM INGRAM, University of Michigan, has published extensively on the Elizabethan stage in its social and economic contexts.

W. DAVID KAY is an Emeritus Professor of English at the University of Illinois at Urbana-Champaign. He is the author of *Ben Jonson: A Literary Life* and the editor of John Marston's *The Malcontent.*

MARGARET MAURER is Professor of English at Colgate University. She is engaged in a study of Shakespeare's comedies, particularly *The Taming of the Shrew.*

C. EDWARD MCGEE teaches English at St. Jerome's College, University of Waterloo. He has co-edited the *Records of Early English Drama: Dorset and Cornwall.*

ROBERT S. MIOLA teaches at Loyola College of Maryland as the Gerard Manley Hopkins Professor of English. He has just completed *Shakespeare's Reading* and the Revels edition of Jonson's *Every Man In His Humour.*

JUNE SCHLEUTER, Charles A. Dana Professor of English at Lafayette College, is co-author of *Reading Shakespeare in Performance: King Lear* and co-editor of *Shakespeare Bulletin.* She has published several books on modern drama.

ALAN SOMERSET is Professor of English at the University of Western Ontario. He is the editor of *Shropshire* for *Records of Early English Drama* and *The Stratford Festival Story.* He is currently completing his edition of Staffordshire and Warwickshire for REED.

FRANCES TEAGUE is a Professor at the University of Georgia. She has published several books on early modern drama, as well as books about early women writers and many articles.

LESLIE THOMSON is Professor of English at the University of Toronto. She has recently co-authored *A Dictionary of Stage Directions in English Drama, 1580–1642.*

MARGARET THICKSTUN teaches seventeenth-century English and American literature at Hamilton College. She has published on dissenting women's use of Scripture and the authority to preach.

BRIAN WALSH teaches English at Rutgers University, New Brunswick.

GEORGE WALTON WILLIAMS, Emeritus Professor of English, Duke University. He is Associate General Editorof the Arden Shakespeare Edition (The History Plays) and co-editor, MLA Variorum *Henry V.*

MICHAEL WINKELMAN teaches at the University of Texas-Pan American, in Edinburg, Texas. He is currently writing a book on marriage relationships in Tudor political drama.

MEDIEVAL
AND
RENAISSANCE
DRAMA
IN ENGLAND

Articles

"Mysteries End": EDAM, REED, and the Midlands

ALAN SOMERSET

FOLLOWING upon the publication of Harold C. Gardiner's seminal book, *Mysteries End,* scholars for over a half century have sought to refine upon that book's conclusions and to chart the course of Reformation, economic change, iconographic tradition, and the revolution in religious practices. Two large international projects, launched over twenty-five years ago, supply the acronyms that form part of my title. EDAM (Early Drama, Art, and Music) was founded by Clifford Davidson, and REED (Records of Early English Drama) by Alexandra Johnston. Both have investigated, surveyed, analyzed, and compared different bodies of evidence: EDAM has focused upon iconographic and musical representations and REED has surveyed manuscript and early printed evidence. But they have worked toward common goals: to gather and present that evidence, to interpret its significance, and thereby to deepen our understanding of medieval and early modern ceremony, art, and ritual. This paper was originally delivered at a session of the Kalamazoo International Medieval Congress, organized to honor Clifford Davidson on his retirement and to commemorate EDAM as its work concludes. It gave me an opportunity to review EDAM and REED's labors in an area with which I am most familiar, the Midlands, to try to show how the researches of the two projects illuminate each other, and to suggest how our understanding has been deepened by them.

My approach is to reflect upon the value for me, the Warwickshire REED editor, of *The Early Art of Coventry, Stratford-upon-Avon, Warwick and Lesser Sites in Warwickshire,* by Clifford Davidson and Jennifer Alexander.[1] How does the book help the researcher to "lift the veil," to gain some appreciation of local traditions and practices that were in many cases obliterated or fundamentally altered by the Reformation, and/or were obscured by the loss of documentary material? This is a question I can appreciate because I previously dealt with another Midlands county's records (Shropshire's) without the benefit of an EDAM survey of the county. I kept having the frustrating experience of being told that I should look at this or that church because it contained interesting and/or relevant art, but when I did find time to make a side trip to investigate I usually found that the building was locked, or that my informant had been mistaken.

I want to look at the value for me of *The Early Art of Coventry* in three ways, first by looking at the iconographic remains from three village parishes, near Stratford-upon-Avon, with which I have some personal associations (they weren't quite a "random" selection). Second, looking at larger towns, I will investigate "riding" ceremonies at Coventry, Stratford, and Warwick, and speculate about their place in local traditions. Finally, I wish to look at representations of St Catharine of Alexandria, across the art of Warwickshire, speculate about the play of St Catharine that was mounted in Coventry in the "Little Park," and suggest some comparisons to Shrewsbury. This is a speculative survey, and I promise no conclusions.

My Warwickshire research follows in the wake of Reginald Ingram's REED edition of the Coventry records, and hence my work has taken me into smaller boroughs and parishes, where the documentary evidence is often scanty.[2] There are no churchwarden's accounts from any of the rural parishes in Warwickshire that predate the sixteenth century, only two that begin before 1550, and a further six that survive from the later sixteenth century.[3] We are presented, then, with virtually a blank wall; *pas de documents, pas d'histoire.* There is nothing here that could shed light on how parishioners and priests organized their religious lives, how they financed their churches and activities, or how their religious art was created. We may only have some evidence about how and when their religious artifacts were damaged, destroyed, or obliterated. In fact, the only way to gain some insight into the lives of these places before the Reformation is through the art within their parish churches. Or perhaps I should say, the remains of art that have escaped destruction or obliteration either at the hands of iconoclasts or through the effects of time.

Now to my three parish churches, all of which are located in tiny villages. First, Wootten Wawen, a village on the A3400 some six miles north of Stratford, has an excellent pub (The Bull) which provides a pleasant stopping place on the journey to Birmingham. Its parish church, St Peter's, has a noteworthy collection of art, details of which are found in the EDAM volume. First, there is painted glass from the fourteenth century; these are representations of the heads of angels, in six panels across the top of the east window, some of which are now incomplete. But most remarkable are the wall paintings found in the south chapel. These were discovered under whitewash in 1918, were described in 1919 by Pierre Turpin in an article in *The Burlington Magazine,* but are now largely faded and indecipherable.[4] Paradoxically, Reformation attempts to obliterate these wall paintings has led to their preservation, because wall paintings fade and disappear naturally over time unless they are "fixed" by overpainting, as occurred here and elsewhere. These paintings comprise two rows of quatrefoils, and include paintings of the Birth of the Virgin; the Annunciation; two paintings of John the Baptist (one of him preaching to people who are kneeling and the other showing him preaching in the wilderness); the Harrowing of Hell; the Angel and the three Women at the Tomb; the Ascension; two scenes from the life of St Catharine of Alexandria (her trial before Emperor Maximus and his fool and her martyrdom and execution by beheading before the same king and fool); and finally a series of depictions of Pride, Sloth, Avarice, and Lechery. On the east wall of the same chapel is a painting of the Coronation of the Virgin. In all, this is a remarkable and concentrated collection of wall paintings.

My second location is Wolverton, a tiny hamlet about four miles north of Stratford. I attended my best friend's wedding there, in the church of St Mary. Artifacts that I did not notice that day, as the happy couple took their vows, include an Easter Sepulchre, at the right of the altar (much defaced), and painted glass in some of the windows. In the tracery of the east window there are fragments of a depiction of Doomsday, including a standing angel in white alb, blowing a trumpet, with three fragments of nude figures presumably arising from tombs. (This is not in its original location.) In the fourth window on the north side there is a fragmentary head of St Michael (possibly) with cross, diadem, and sword. (Some glass is misplaced.) In the second panel of the same window there is a depiction of St Anthony, with a modern face inserted (his hand holds a crutch with a bell attached), and a fragment of boar's head with a bell on the collar.

Third, to Halford, another tiny hamlet, six miles southeast of Stratford, on the Fosse Way. It is the home of another good friend, and its church is also devoted to St. Mary. I have not visited this church, which is remarkable for its sculptures. Not in its original location, there is a depiction of a tumbling trick (apparently a backward somersault) being performed by man with three faces, one bearded and two clean-shaven; there are also two smiling faces of onlookers. On a capital on the north doorway there is a sculptured figure from the early twelfth century, a man holding what appears to be a club in his right hand and the head of an animal (perhaps a cow) in his left hand. The figure has a painted and girdled tunic gathered in loose folds below the waist. In a niche above the string-course at the right side of the chancel arch there is a sculpture of the Crucifixion; it may be the figure of St. John pointing at the cross, or perhaps the Virgin (it is defaced and not positively identifiable). Most remarkable, on the tympanum of the north doorway there is an early twelfth-century bas-relief sculpture of an angel, a front view, holding a long narrow scroll. This is described by Deborah Kahn as "the best piece of Norman sculpture in the country."[5] High praise for Halford's tiny church!

What do we make of these three churches, with their widely differing types of art? The internal coherence of each collection bespeaks decisions, planning; lacking churchwardens' accounts we cannot be sure who the planners were (or who supplied the money to hire the artists), but in the case of Halford Deborah Kahn makes an interesting suggestion. She notes that the churches in nearby Whatcote and Idlicote likely were built by the masons responsible for Halford, and suggests that a local branch of the Giffard family was the driving force behind the construction and decoration. These churches provide evidence of organized and thriving local communities, whose other ceremonial and celebratory activities we can only guess at. Their art provided a matrix of visual devotional experience for local people, and this may help to explain the choices of subjects for other representations made by "impresarios" (to use the word loosely) in larger boroughs in the county.

I want to look next at riding ceremonies in the larger boroughs in Warwickshire, and this leads me to consider St George, one of the most popular saints in the period and one who is well represented in the art of Coventry, Stratford, Warwick, and many smaller parishes. Quickly to survey the smaller parishes first, St George is known to have existed at Coleshill, represented in painted glass from the fourteenth century but now destroyed. He wore mixed chain and plate armor, and was depicted thrusting his spear into the head of the dragon. At Wroxall the saint survives in painted glass, in the tracery of the east window, dating from the fifteenth century; he is wearing full armor with helmet and lance, and has the dragon under his feet. Finally, at Baddesley Clinton a representation in painted glass in the east window; from the early sixteenth century, was a gift of the Ferrers family; it is now destroyed.

As well as being depicted in art, the saint was the subject of popular devotional "ridings" in Coventry and Stratford, and perhaps at Warwick as well. Looking first at Coventry, the supposed birthplace of St George, the list of iconographic representations includes:

1. St Michael's Cathedral had a fourteenth-century sculpture, now lost; it was formerly on the tower until it was replaced in 1880s; it depicted a standing figure with a spear thrust into the mouth of the dragon.
2. Holy Trinity Guild formerly had an image on a cup, recorded in 1441, now lost.
3. St Mary's Cathedral Priory had an image with a relic of the saint; this was noted in its pre-Reformation list of relics but is now lost.
4. The Chapel of St George, Gosford Gate has a sculpture on horseback in full armor, with the horse trampling the dragon which has the saint's spear grasped in its claw (the rest of the spear is missing), dated c. 1470–90.
5. St Mary's Hall has a tapestry dating from about 1510, showing the saint in armor with nimbus, holding a staff with a banner containing the cross of St George.

Moving from art to theater (loosely defined), an annual St George procession was held in Coventry and is recorded in 1498, 1518 (in which year the cross was borne in procession on St. George's Day, Ascension, Pentecost, and Corpus Christi), and 1539. As well, a pageant of St George was staged for royal entries in 1474 and 1498, at the conduit in Cross Cheaping. Both times he is "killing the dragon" and in 1474 the *mise-en-scène* was fully described:

seint George Armed and a kynges doughter knelying a fore hym with a lambe and
the fader & the moder beying in a toure a boven beholding seint George savyng
theire doughter from the dragon//and the Condite rennyng wyne in iiij places and
mynstralcy of Orgonpleyinge and seint George havyng this speche under wryttyn

> O mythty god oure all socoure celestiall
> Wich this Royme [d] hast geven to dowere
> to thi moder and to me George proteccion perpetuall
> hit to defende from enimies ffere and nere
> And as this mayden defended was here
> Bi thy grace from this Dragon devoure
> So lorde preserue this noble prynce and euer be his socoure[6]

It is not hard to imagine the source of St George's appeal; however before
drawing conclusions let us turn next to Stratford, where in Holy Trinity
Church St George is represented in a wood carving, a misericord, on the
south side. This is dated between 1430 and 1440, and shows St George with
the dragon having George's spear thrust into his mouth. Coming from the
early sixteenth century, a wall painting on the west wall of Guild Chapel, on
the north side, shows St George in plate armor, on horseback, swinging his
sword. The dragon has wings and claws, and a serpent's tail. The saint's
horse has a single horn, with which he is also spearing the dragon; the saint's
audience includes a lady leading a lamb. This was whitewashed over and
damaged in the late 1560s, while John Shakespeare (father of William) held
civic office. However, as at Wootten Wawen the attempt to obliterate paradoxically caused the wall painting to be preserved, although its original colors
are faded. It is a very elaborate depiction. When we turn to the Stratford records we discover St George in the streets, in an annual procession on Ascension Day, recorded in the records of the town's Bridge Wardens. These
accounts begin in 1524 (although there must have been wardens to maintain
the Clopton Bridge and its predecessor from much earlier). The wardens received income from an annual Bridge Ale, and mainly spent their money on
paving stones and gravel. But from 1542 until 1547 and 1553 until 1557 they
also supported an annual Saint George ceremony: I won't go into all the details from the records but I wish to highlight a few salient points, chief of
which are records of the maintenance of the "harness" (armor) worn by the
doughty saint. This was scoured in 1542–43, 1543–44, 1545–47, and in
many other years, indicating that the armor must have become scuffed and
soiled, in order to make necessary this scouring to restore it to gleaming
brightness. It also required "leathering" or points, in several years, by which
I understand that its buckles, straps, and flexible parts needed renewal. In
sum, this was a set of working armor, a costume for an actor, not just a ceremonial prop. Saint George rode on horseback, while the payments for "bearing the dragon" indicate that it was carried on the ground, by two men

(hence, we may assume that it was a big dragon). The dragon required mending or dressing, indicating (as we should expect) that the costume sustained damage during the annual performance. The purchase of two dozen bells and gloves in 1553–54 perhaps indicates that St George was accompanied by dancers or jesters. Most spectacularly, in 1553–54 and 1555–56 gun powder was purchased, suggesting that the dragon was a fire-breathing serpent; this may also suggest why the armor came to need scouring. The Bridge Wardens obviously wanted to put on a good show, and these details (along with the artistic representations of Saint George, already detailed) indicate the source of the saint's appeal. Saint George was a man of action, and any presentation of him naturally concentrated upon his defining moment, the battle with the dragon. There was no interest in the saint's whole life, but a concentration on the spectacle. This is what we should expect—if you think about it for a moment, we don't encounter many representations (on walls, or in the streets) of, say, the meditations of St Bonaventure. A contemplative would not "play" well at all. This thought came to me when I looked at the famous Fouquet representation of the Martyrdom of St Appollonia, a field day for dentists; we will return to it in a moment when considering St Catharine of Alexandria.

I turn next to Warwick, and become a little speculative. Saint George was represented there in three ways. First, there survives a seal from the church of Trinity St Mary and St George, showing the saint in armor with a shield marked with the cross, stepping on the dragon and piercing its head with his lance. In the church there was a banner depicting the saint; it was inventoried in 1463, but is now destroyed. In the Beauchamp chapel there formerly was a sculpture; this was on a reredos dated between 1450 and 1464, and it was destroyed in 1642 by Colonel Purefoy. There was a guild of St George and the Holy Cross in the town, which was responsible for the upkeep of the bridge over the River Avon.[7] We know a little about a late manifestation of a Midsummer riding at Warwick because of some very strange evidence arising from a lawsuit in the Court of Exchequer over rights to mill grain. Robert, Lord Brooke, sued Thomas and Henry Bewfew over what he took to be infringement of his rights, as the owner of the Castle Mill, to have the monopoly over grinding corn within his manor (which included the town of Warwick). Mills owned by the Bewfews at Guy's Clife, as well as mills at Emscote and within the grounds of the old priory, had been competing for business, and Brooke wanted to put a stop to it. One of the ways the millers touted for business from small farmers was to use a loader and a "load horse," a huge animal capable of carrying heavy loads in panniers across its back. The loader, leading the horse, would pick up smaller loads of grain (less than wagonloads) and redeliver the milled results. How could Brooke prove that his miller, loader and load horse should have preeminent rights in Warwick? His lawyers produced a set of interrogatories, and depositions were taken from the oldest inhabitants that could be found in the town, about customs and practices as far back as anyone could remember. Deponents of great antiquity were found; one was fifty, and a second was fifty-eight (we remember that Shakespeare died at the age of fifty-two). The two oldest deponents, aged "fourscore years or thereabouts," were able to recall practices back into the 1570s. The strangest part of this suit is that Brooke's case rested partly on the customs of the annual Midsummer riding through Warwick. What was the order of procession, which was the leading horse, and why? The evidence on this point alone fills over three single-spaced pages and, like legal evidence the world over, is wearyingly repetitious. But here is a sample, a description (by the fifty-eight year old) of the annual riding, responding on behalf of Lord Brooke:

> To the eighth Interrogatorye this deponent saithe That there is, & hath beene an ancient Custome during the whole time of this deponents remembrance, & as hee hath heard for many years before, for the seuerall loaders of the aforesaid Castle Mills, Priory Mills, GuyesClifte Mills & Emscotte Mill to ride yearely & euerye yeare on Mydsommer daye on theire seu[er]all loade horses vp & downe the Towne of Warwicke in manner followeinge, that is to saye, The loader of the Castle Mills goinge on his loade horse with his bells for his musicke, The loader of the Priorye Mills on his loade horse havinge with him for his musicke a taber & a pipe, The loader of GuyesClifte Mills on his loade horse havinge for his musicke a paire of bag pipes, the loader of Emscott Mills rydinge on his loade horse & havinge for his musicke a fiddle: and further saith, that the loaders of the three mills, called Priory Mills, Guyes Clifte Mills, & Emscott Mills doe then vsuallye come & repayre on their loade horses, & musicke vnto the said Castle Mills, to call the loader of the said Castle Mills, who continuallye rideth foremoste vppe & downe the towne togeather wth the said other loaders, who afterwardes doe bringe home the said loader of the said Castle Mills vnto the said Mill, & there commonlye leave him & thence departe, & further saith, That he hathe been credibly informed, That if any of the loaders of the Priory Mills, GuyesClifte Mills, & Enscott Mill shall faile in the performance of this Ceremonie, & to ride vp & downe the aforesaid towne of Warwicke, with the loader of the Castle Mills, & to call the said loader as aforesaid, That then such loader soe makinge Defaulte ought to haue noe priveledge or libertie of loading within the said towne for one whole yeare next followeinge, & alsoe saith, he hath heard that the reason of such ridinge of the said loaders is to continue a remembrance that noe loader belonginge to any other mill ought to bee privileged to loade or fetche & carrye any griste from the saide towne of Warwicke.[8]

This takes us back into the 1570s, but I am sure that there is an earlier history than this. The riding as described seems to me to be a secularized, post-Reformation version of an annual ritual whose earlier history would probably have had some religious signification and connection. But beyond that speculation it would be reckless to go, fascinating though it is to think about this local custom in Warwick.

I turn now to the final aspect I wish to consider, the representation of St Catharine of Alexandria in Warwickshire. She was ranked with St Margaret and St Barbara as one of the fourteen most helpful saints in Heaven; St Catharine was the most widely venerated female martyr in northwest Europe. Her reputed office as one of Joan of Arc's spiritual mentors boosted her esteem in France—in fact, in France her feast was celebrated until the beginning of the seventeenth century in several dioceses as a holy day of obligation, whose splendid ceremonial outdid the feasts of some of the Apostles.[9] Catharine's cult was also widespread in England, and certainly in Warwickshire. What was the source of her popularity? I believe it was her martyrdom, because it had all the stuff of high drama and possibilities for spectacular depiction, like the martyrdom of St Appollonia. As a young virgin of eighteen, St Catharine denounced the Emperor Maximus for his persecution of Christians. Imprisoned, and confronted with the most learned scholars that Maximus could assemble, Catharine vanquished them all; they became Christians and were immediately put to death. The empress, intrigued by Catharine's power, visited her in prison, was converted, and also faced execution. Tried and condemned, Catharine was sentenced to die on the wheel, but at her touch this gruesome instrument of torture shattered spectacularly. One would expect this parade of miracles to change Maximus's mind, but no; he had Catharine beheaded, whereupon angels conveyed her body to Mount Sinai.[10] Thus far extends her legend, embellished by hagiographic enthusiasm. What about her representation in Warwick art?

Examination of the index of saints in *The Early Art of Coventry* shows that St Catharine was very popular indeed. I hesitate to name her the most popular saintly subject of representation because of the destruction of so much evidence, but she certainly earns that position in the surviving art in the county. I will first survey "other locations"—small parishes and localities where usually there is a single representation—and give brief descriptions. At Weoley Castle, Birmingham, there is a pewter plate dating from 1300 to 1350; Catharine has a wheel studded with knives in her left hand and a sword in her right. At Bulkington there was painted glass from the early fourteenth century, now lost; it was described as depicting her crowned and standing holding her wheel, whose edge was studded with knives, in one hand. At Tysoe, a sculpture on the font, dating from the fourteenth century, depicted her crowned with her wheel in one hand and a sword in the other. At Ufton a sculpture on a churchyard cross, now lost, dating from the fourteenth century, depicted her with her wheel in her right hand. At Wroxall, there is painted glass in second north window, third panel, dating from the fourteenth century, which is mostly a modern restoration. At Caldecote there is a depiction in painted glass in the seventh south window, first panel, dating from the early fifteenth century, which shows her with her sword and a book. At Haseley, painted glass in the tracery of the west window (originally perhaps in the north window), dating from the fifteenth century, depicts her with her wheel. At Newton Regis, painted glass in the north chapel, fourth window, first panel, depicts her with her wheel and sword. At Solihull there was an image, now lost, but noted in the churchwardens' accounts from 1534 to 1535, because there were payments for a light yearly before her. I include Warwick in this list, because there is only a single representation of St Catharine there. In the Beauchamp chapel there is a sculpture, dating between 1450 and 1460 (when the chapel was built and decorated), depicting Catharine with her sword and a book. Remembering Catharine's reputation as a spiritual mentor to Joan of Arc, we are perhaps surprised to find her in the chapel devoted to the man who tried and executed Joan of Arc. Finally, at Wootten Wawen there is the series of wall paintings, already noted, two of which depict scenes from the life of St Catharine, including her trial before Emperor Maximus and his fool, and her martyrdom and execution by beheading before the same king and fool. This is quite an array of material, and it is notable for its concentration upon Catharine's martyrdom. With the exception of Caldecote (where we see a book as well as the wheel) and Warwick (where her sword and a book are shown), her instruments of torture are featured, not her faith or knowledge. Although Catharine was patroness of female students and young maidens, doubtless because of her ability to confute pagan scholars, the wheelwrights also claimed her as patroness, and appear to win the day here because the saint was evidently associated, in popular devotion, with her spectacular martyrdom. Recalling the martyrdom of St Appollonia, one can easily envision the possibilities for spectacle.

In larger boroughs, where the presence of schools should have kindled interest in Catherine's learning, one might expect greater variety among the representations, but one does not find it in Coventry. There was reportedly a relic of the saint in St Michael's Cathedral, but it is of course not extant. Representations there include a wood carving from the decorated ceiling of St Mary's Hall's council chamber, probably originally from a reredos, depicting Catharine with her sword and wheel. She was a patroness of the guild of Holy Trinity, St Mary, St John the Baptist, and St Catharine; naturally there was an image in Chapel of Guild in the Cathedral, now destroyed, but noted in 1457. In the chapel there was also a wood carving, on a misericord, now destroyed, but described about 1465. A tapestry in St Mary's Hall, executed about 1510, shows the saint with her sword and wheel. Finally, painted glass was reported in 1719 to exist depicting Catharine, in some rooms beyond the Mayoress's parlor. It is now lost, and no description is extant. Again, you note that whenever details are available, it is the sword and wheel that are depicted. What, therefore, would we expect to see in a representation by living persons? We know that St Catharine was included the Corpus Christi proces-

sion in 1539–42 and 1544–45 when the Corpus Christi guild paid "Kateryn & margret" fourpence in wages. No props (wheels, swords, or whatever)
are specified, nor is the saint's absence from the procession lists explained in
1543 or other years.

Finally, and most intriguingly, the Coventry City Annals record a playing
place associated with a St Catharine play. In 1505, the annalist tells us, "Iohn
Dadsbury In his year as the Play of St Christian played in the Little Park."
Evidence given in Chancery in 1528 indicates that this performance actually
took place at Pentecost, 31 May 1506, and recounts that "a great play called
'Saint Christian's Play' was held and put on in a field near the aforesaid city
of Coventry called Little Park, in the time of John Dudsburye, then mayor."
This tells us a little about the scope of activities that could be accommodated
in the (otherwise unidentified) Little Park. In 1491, the analist informs us "A
Play of St Katherine in the Little Parke."[11] That is all the evidence that survives for this performance. This is the case with another record naming St
Catharine, at London in 1393, and the earliest allusion to a "ludum de Sancta
Katarina" at Dunstable, about 1100. Can we penetrate this wall of silence,
about what a "play" of St Catharine might include?

From our survey of the way St Catharine is depicted in the religious art of
Warwickshire, I think we can be reasonably confident that any representation
would concentrate upon her trial and martyrdom. This is confirmed, I think,
by two pieces of evidence from other Midlands localities. First, the Mayor's
Book at Hereford records, in 1503, a list of the pageants for the procession
of Corpus Christi—"pageants" here no doubt refers to tableaux, perhaps carried or wheeled through the streets. The list of twenty-seven pageants generally represents the topics of plays in the craft cycles (York, Chester,
Towneley), with some oddities, particularly the last four, which follow the
Passion, Crucifixion, deposition, burial and laments-of-the-three-Marys sequence: "Milites armati custodes sepulcri" refers to the soldiers guarding the
tomb, and if it is a Resurrection pageant it is strange that that event is not
named. "Pylate cayfas annas & mahounde" may be misplaced, but it remains
a puzzle, as does the next, "Knyghtes in harnes." This last may be a mistaken
repetition of the "milites armati," or it may refer to an unknown subject. The
final pageant is the biggest mystery of all; the journeymen Cappers were to
be responsible for "Seinte keterina with [ij] *(corrected to)* Tres Tormentors."
As David Klausner says, this saint pageant "clearly has no place in a Creation
to Doomsday cycle," and he goes on to note that there was no church in
Hereford dedicated to St Catherine.[12] (Nor is there one, by the way, in Coventry.) Her appearance in this pageant list presumably is evidence, from beyond
Warwickshire, of devotion to her. That she appears with two (corrected to
three) tormentors is once again evidence of fascination with Catharine's trial
and martyrdom—one can be reasonably sure that a complete description of
the pageant would include a wheel and a sword.

And finally, as promised, I turn to Shrewsbury, where we find the fullest evidence about staged representations of St Catharine, again in a town that, like Coventry and Hereford, had no church dedicated to the saint. But in 1526, in Trinity Term (11 June–30 July), the town put on "Saynt Kateryn is play" and the accounts for this are at the same time maddeningly lacking in detail, filled with puzzles, and wonderfully detailed.[13] First, for the maddening lack of detail. The accounts list a number of payments, thirteen of which were made by three of the "Six Men" (minor town officials elected in a given year) to various people "by bill." This implies that the individuals paid in this way had submitted bills of particular expenses, salaries, and so forth, and were paid. We have some of these bills from various activities in other years, and they can be wonderfully detailed, but for 1526 we have only the accounts I am outlining. Therefore, we have no way of knowing for what the thirteen claimants had submitted bills; it follows that a lack of a payment for a particular item that we might expect (such as a reward to a player playing Maximus or Catharine) does not mean that somebody was, or was not, paid for such activities.

As regards puzzles, it is evident that the accounts as we have them are incomplete and/or inaccurate. On 25 April the Aldermen agreed that each of them should contribute individually toward the play, but the amount of these contributions is not recorded. On 26 April, the Mercers, Ironmongers, and Goldsmiths company met "to know of the company wither that they wilbe wylling to have any sport or play at Penticost [i.e., 20 May] next foloying or not." Their decision is not recorded; however when these requests for support came from the bailiffs and aldermen, usually some big production was in the wind, and usually such appeals were positively entertained. As well, it is likely that other guilds were canvassed for support, but their records do not survive to tell us. In the borough's account books, there are two summary (inclusive) payments that might seem to establish the budget for this production. First, Richard Atkis (one of the Six Men) received a lump-sum payment: "Item in Redy money by thandes of Master bailly hosior for to pay for the play v li.' This looks straightforward—a play with a budget of £5, whose expenses should be detailed in payments "by bill." However, this £5 payment on folio 150v of the records manuscript is succeeded by another payment, on folio 157; this payment is once canceled, and then entered again: "Item paid to dyuers persones for the play as aperith by particular parcelles iiij li. xvj s. viij d." So, were the costs of the play £4. 16s. 8d., £5, or (adding the two sums together) £9 16s. 8d.? When you add up the total of the particular payments "by bill" the situation is further confused. The total of these particulars is £5 6s. 3d., an amount that agrees with neither of the summary payments recorded. We also note that one Thomas Cooper is paid "opon the rest of his bill" but there is no other payment to Thomas Cooper, so obviously we don't have a complete list of the particular payments. What is going

on here? These accounts are too early to have been audited by Arthur Ander-
sen! Are we dealing with cost overruns, familiar to anyone who has worked
with production budgets? The point is, we will never know whether the play
cost £5, or £5 6s. 3d., or £9 16s. 3d., or some other sum; the only thing we
do know, from all this, is that the town appears to have spent a lot of money
on the St Catharine play!

It is notoriously difficult to estimate the present value of sums of money in
records from this period, but when you consider that a skilled laborer in 1600
in London would receive about £1 for four weeks' work, we realize that considerable inflation has occurred. We might safely say that Shrewsbury spent
something between £1000 (= £5) and £1950 (= £9 16s. 3d.) on the St Catharine play in 1526. Looking at Shrewsbury productions from other years gives
some comparative levels of expenditure, although the records of expenditures
are similarly incomplete or puzzling. In 1555–56, the next year a civic play
is recorded, the assembly agreed to spend no more than £5 on their play,
besides contributions from the guilds (no guild records survive from this
year). In 1560–61 a "Passion of Christ" production is mentioned in town
annals, but there are no accounts whatsoever. In 1563–64 Mr Ashton, the
schoolmaster, planned a production; the assembly prudently decided to can-
vass the guilds first, and the Mercers agreed to contribute £2 to the play (there
is no record of what the town contributed, or any of the other guilds). Finally,
in 1568–69 the town contributed £10 and the Mercers £2 toward Mr Ashton's
final production.[14] So, a sum, in 1525–26 between £5 and £9. 16s. 3d. is certainly within the limits of normal expenses for large-scale civic productions
in Shrewsbury.

After the incompleteness, and the puzzles over the accuracy of the accounting, we come to the wonderful details that the records afford: payments for
particular series and good that let us glimpse at some aspects of the production of the St Catharine play, with the help of the religious art of Warwickshire. I won't weary you with the details of all the detailed payments—for
example, "for mosse to a woman ij d." doesn't tell us much, because we
don't know for what the moss might have been used (I have a speculation,
which will appear in its proper place). We are intrigued by large payments to
one William Edwards, one for 24 pence 'opon the rest of a bill of parcelles"
(the bill of parcels, or particulars, is lacking); there is a second payment to
Edwards for his reward: 26s. 8d.—the largest single payment in the lists. Was
Edwards the producer or director? Another payment intrigues us: "to Richard
Glasier for beyng lord of mysrule & other his labor vj s. viij d." Glasier was
a local man who was paid on two other occasions for being the Abbot of
Marham in a town game in 1520 and 1542–43. We might wonder about his
role here, but the Wootten Wawen wall paintings, in which St Catharine is
tried before Emperor Maximus and his fool, and later is executed in the presence of the same persons, might provide fuel for fruitful speculation. Moving

on, there are some "Costes for the play" recorded on f 156v of the records, and here we find that "iij hedes of herre ij berdes with a desertes hed & berd" cost 4s. 10d. Was the dizard's head and beard for Richard Glasier? Other properties purchased indicate a desire for a very colorful show: a dozen silver papers, a dozen gold papers, a dozen synaper (i.e., crimson) and green papers, a pound of Arsedine (a gold-colored alloy of copper and zinc), and a dozen gold foil. Sound is indicated by a payment to a minstrel of 5s. and by the purchase of six dozen bells. Finally, very spectacular pyrotechnics are indicated by the purchase, for 2 shillings, of four pounds of gunpowder, and by the expenditure of 2 pence for camphor and saltpeter. These are not large quantities when one compares them to the ordnance collected for large royal or aristocratic fireworks displays, particularly if staged upon water; however for a local civic play, this is an impressive quantity of gunpowder![15] An ounce or two, properly packed, would be enough to blow off your hand, so four pounds would be enough, properly placed, to create some very large explosions or other effects. Together with the camphor and saltpeter these explosives would produce quite a show. The *OED* supplies an illuminating example, from Francis Bacon's *Sylva Sylvarum* (1626): "Brimstone, Pitch, Champhire, Wildfire . . . make no such fiery wind, as Gunpowder doth." Saltpeter is, of course, an ingredient of gunpowder, but its separate purchase, along with camphor, indicates that a special color or type of pyrotechnic was desired. Camphor burns with a "white, pale, or milky-coloured fire," which might give some idea of the special effect intended.[16]

But, you are doubtless asking, what has all this to do with a play of St Catharine in Shrewsbury in 1526? Here we must again launch ourselves into speculation. You will recall that in legends of St Catharine her wheel, which was to be the instrument of her torture, is almost universally to be found in early artistic representations. To be broken on a wheel studded with knives, a hideous torture, involved the systematic breaking of all the victim's long bones before death was allowed to take place. According to legend, St Catharine's wheel of execution disintegrated spectacularly at her touch, forcing the Emperor Maximus to have her martyred by the sword (decapitation, I imagine, was seen as far quicker and less painful death). I wish to suggest that the high point of this play, the disintegration of the wheel, was accomplished through a spectacular pyrotechnic display, smoke, and explosions. I remind you of the firework known in North America as a "pinwheel" (you nail it by its center to a support so that it can revolve. When you light it, it whizzes around and around, casting sparks and smoke in all directions and making wonderful noises.) These fireworks have been known in England, for centuries, as "Catharine wheels." As Philip Butterworth points out, these wheels were more correctly referred to as "girandoles"; he describes them as "larger wheels mounted vertically or horizontally and fired by linked rockets around the periphery." Butterworth supplies a description by Robert Norton, an

early pyrotechnical specialist, that gives some idea of the effects that could
be obtained, and also suggests a use for the various colored papers that were
purchased at Shrewsbury in 1526:

> The Worckes may be framed . . . either vpon great woollen spinning Wheeles,
> Coach Wheeles, or other Wheeles, made of purpose easie to runne around, and the
> greater the better shew . . . Tyres of coloured Fires, Serpents, breakers, or shewers
> of Gold [may be placed between the rockets] as you shal think with time between
> them fitted, that the Wheele may moue from the ending of euery Rocket, vntill the
> beginning of the next, with a Sulpher match betweene them."[17]

This is admittedly speculative, but I wonder if there was a huge "Catharine
wheel" girandole firework at Shrewsbury in 1526, fixed to disintegrate after
it had spun spectacularly for a time. If not, why buy all that gunpowder, camphor, and saltpeter? And perhaps the moss was used, soaked in a solution of
saltpeter and then dried, to make the wicks connecting the various rockets,
so this could all be done safely.

I can speculate no further. I hope I have been able to show a few ways in
which having the details of the religious part of a particular region can help
to illuminate some aspects of the dramatic and representational activities that
occurred there. And, if you were to conclude that I wished, and wish, that
there had been an Early Drama, Art, and Music volume for Shropshire before
and while my research there was underway, you'd be right.

Notes

1. Clifford Davidson and Jennifer Alexander, *The Early Art of Coventry, Stratford-upon-Avon, Warwick, and Lesser Sites in Warwickshire,* Early Drama, Art and
Music Reference Series, 4 (Medieval Institute Publications, Western Michigan University, Kalamazoo, Mich., 1985).

2. Reginald Ingram, ed. *Coventry,* Records of Early English Drama (Toronto: University of Toronto Press, 1981).

3. The early survivals are listed in Ronald Hutton, *The Rise and Fall of Merry
England: The Ritual Year 1400–1700* (Oxford: Oxford University Press, 1974), appendix, pp. 289–90. They are: Solihull (1534–43), St Nicholas Warwick (1547),
Rowington (1554–89), Great Packington (1557–1631), Kingsbury (1572–87), Bide-
ford (1582–97), Southam (1582–1647), and Shipston (1593–1617).

4. Pierre Turpin, "Ancient Wall-Paintings of the Charterhouse, Coventry," *Burlington Magazine* 35 (1919): 246–53.

5. Deborah Kahn, "The Romanesque Sculpture of the Church of St Mary at Halford, Warwickshire," *Journal of the British Archaeological Association* 133 (1980):
64–73.

6. *Coventry,* 54–55.

7. *The Victoria History of The County of Warwick,* edited by H. Arthur Double-day and William Page (London: Constable, 1904–69), 2: 151.

8. Quoted from evidence in a suit regarding watermills, in the Warwick County Record Office: WCRO; CR 1886/7543 (1633).

9. *Catholic Encyclopaedia* Online *http://www.newadvent.org/cathen/03445a.htm.* Date visited: 20 February 2002.

10. *Catholic Encyclopaedia* Online.

11. *Coventry,* 100, 128 (translated 536), 74.

12. David N. Klausner, ed., *Herefordshire/Worcestershire,* REED (Toronto: University of Toronto Press, 1990), 116, 11.

13. All the evidence is found in my edition, *Shropshire,* REED, 2 vols (Toronto: University of Toronto Press, 1994) 1:183–4.

14. *Shropshire,* 1:205, 207–8, 211–12.

15. Philip Butterworth, *Theatre of Fire: Special Effects in Early English and Scottish Theatre* (London: Society for Theatre Research, 1998), appendix 2, lists firework accounts for Edinburgh displays in 1566 and 1617, and Kenilworth in 1572. This comprehensive account contains many helpful details about early pyrotechnics.

16. Butterworth, *Theatre of Fire,* 213.

17. Ibid., 111–13, quoting Robert Norton, *The Gvnner Shewing the Whole Practise of Artillerie . . . Together with the making of Extraordinary Artificial Fireworkes . . .* (London, 1628).

The Real Misfortunes of Arthur; Or, Not Making it on the Elizabethan Stage

WILLIAM INGRAM

A Heroicall Poem may be founded somewhere in Alfreds reigne
—*Trinity ms, p 38*

. . . OR in lots of other places as well, if the list in the Trinity *ms* is any indication of the range of Milton's reading and thinking on the matter. He noted possibilities in such subjects as "Harold slaine in battel by William the norman" or "Edmund Ironside murder'd," or even "Hardiknute dying in his cups" as "an example to riot" (p 38). He listed other, earlier, events as well, under the heading of "British Troy," such as "the massacre of the britains by Hengist," "the life of offa," even "the slaughter of the monks of Bangor" (p 37). He even considered reworking "Scotch stories or rather brittish of the north parts," including "Macbeth" and "the matter of Duncan" (p 41).

But the piece of British history that most held his fancy as a potential subject for a Heroicall Poem was the story of Arthur. In *Mansus* (1639) he mused that he would "some day recall in song" his country's "native kings," especially Arthur, "shatter[ing] the Saxon phalanxes" (80–84). A year later the resolve seemed even firmer. "For my part, I am resolved to tell . . . of the chiefs, Brennus and Arviragus, and of old Belinus, and of the Armorical settlers who came at last under British law. Then I shall tell of Igraine pregnant with Arthur by fatal deception" and so on (*Epitaphium Damonis,* 162–71).

In professing such an interest in the figure of Arthur, Milton showed himself more a Spenserian than a Shakespearean. Though he professed to revere the "honour'd Bones" of "my *Shakespeare*" he was not temperamentally inclined to follow Shakespeare's taste in historical subjects. Like Sir Guyon, Milton was more drawn to the "auncient booke, hight *Briton moniments*" full of stories from Brutus to Uther Pendragon and on to Gloriana. Milton's own list of topics suggests that he found uncongenial the stories accumulated around the various Edwards and Henrys and Richards and Johns that characterized the Elizabethan history play, whether Shakespeare's or another's. Though Milton's own public and professional life was intimately bound up with the very issues dealt with in those plays, the ebb and flow of daily poli-

32

tics in the Commonwealth must have seemed to him accidental trappings, mere contingencies alongside the real stories, the "stories of Britain" and especially of Arthur that he would one day relate (*Ep. Dam.,* 171).

Milton's sense of priorities in these matters constitutes a curious reverse-image of the attitudes prevalent a generation earlier, in the heyday of the English history play, when the story of Arthur was barely attended to by playwrights and—we may perhaps conjecture by analogy—little demanded by audiences. Plays about legendary British history did periodically make their appearance, plays about King Leir or Locrine or Edmund Ironside, but virtually none about Arthur. One can point to only a single surviving example, the Senecan *Misfortunes of Arthur* put together by Thomas Hughes and other "Gentlemen of Grayes-Inne" and played before the queen at Greenwich on 28 February 1588. In addition to this, we know from Henslowe's *Diary* the titles of two plays now lost—an anonymous *Uther Pendragon* from 1597 and a play by Richard Hathway called *Arthur King of Britain* from 1598—but aside from that one occasional and decidedly private work and these two free-floating titles there is nothing to fasten upon for the remainder of Elizabeth's reign; indeed, the record reveals more plays about Robin Hood than about Arthur in this period. If one looks backward to the earlier Tudors as likelier sponsors of plays on Arthurian themes, given their supposed espousal of a "Tudor myth," one finds instead plays like *Albion Knight* or *Respublica* or *Kynge Johan,* whose focus is on other matters entirely. It may well be, of course, that there were numerous early Tudor plays on Arthurian themes that have not survived; if so, they must have passed out of the common consciousness even by the 1580s, as there seems to be little evidence of nostalgia for such material among Elizabethan playwrights or patrons. And if there really were such early Arthurian plays, their disappearance would suggest that, to the extent that early Tudor history plays were in the service of any agenda—and thus candidates for preservation—the agenda was likelier to have been the Reformation than the Tudor lineage.

It's curious that the Wars of the Roses, as seen from the vantage point of the 1630s, should have struck Milton as void of poetic interest; the topic had appeared fruitful enough for poets four decades earlier. In 1595 the first part of Daniel's *Civill Wars* made its appearance, and Drayton's *Mortimeriados* and *England's Heroicall Epistles* followed in short order. These works, arriving as the theatrical interest in such matters was cresting (perhaps even waning), contended in the marketplace with other works like William Warner's *Albions England,* a Trojan-myth historical poem first published in 1586, whose ponderous fourteeners had passed through four editions by the time the Daniel and Drayton works appeared. But even Warner's devotion to the mythological past did not extend wholeheartedly to Arthur:

> His *Scottish, Irish, Almaine, French,* and *Saxone* Battels got,
> Yeeld fame sufficient; these seeme true, the rest I credit not. (p. 90)

Eventually the *Civill Wars* and the *Epistles* managed to rival Warner's poem in popularity, though one might argue that the taste for stories and poems about the Edwards and Henrys and Richards which those poems satisfied had first been awakened by the then-current success of such accounts in the theater.

But, unless one posits an inherently greater chauvinism among playwrights, one is hard pressed to explain why dramatic poets should have been so much more strongly attracted to their nation's recent dynastic struggles than they were drawn to the rich antiquarian romanticism of "Brennus and Arviragus, and of old Belinus" that continued to engage their nondramatic poetic brethren. Holished furnished material for both kinds of interests, but was as skeptical as Warner about one part of it, noting that "Of this Arthur manie things are written beyond credit" (I.574). The various contributors to the successive editions of the *Mirour for Magistrates* aimed for a similar range of coverage, but centered their meditations upon moments of reversal and recognition in the lives of their several subjects rather than on the full sweep of historical events, thus allowing themselves greater scope for the rhetorical exploration of ethical dilemmas and for the kind of self-reflection that results in useful maxims for posterity. The *Mirour* was conceived as extending forward from "the comming of Brute . . . unto this presente time"; in pursuit of that goal the 1574 edition by John Higgins featured lives of Albanact, Humber, Locrine, Bladud, and Ferrex and Porrex, among others, while Thomas Blenerhasset's continuation in 1578 included such lives as Guidericus, Vortiger, and Uther Pendragon.

But the dramatists of the 1580s and 1590s who looked into the *Mirour,* like those who dipped into Holinshed, found other lives more to their liking: Mortimer, Gloucester, Mowbray, Suffolk, Clifford, Northumberland, Buckingham, Richard II, Henry VI, Edward IV, Richard III. We've all been taught how the *de casibus* tradition embodied in the *Mirour* was an influence on those playwrights, but nobody has told us why the opening set of stories about the early Britons and their falls from eminence exercised so much less influence upon their thinking, or at least upon their writing, than did this other, later, group of stories.

Might the playwrights have intuitively understood something about the different subject matter requirements of a "historical play" and a Heroicall Poem, or a historical poem, or even a biographical poem, something that is no longer intuitive to us? Our own modern formulation might be that in the strict sense a "historical poem" is a kind of oxymoron, a contested ground in which the truth claims of historical accounts are belied by the imaginative scope expected of poetry; but we would have to say the same of a historical play, except perhaps in the case of legendary history where truth claims are less insistent. Spenser, who saw much virtue in the earlier stories, and especially in an Arthur story, knew there was a difference, affirming in his Letter

to Ralegh that "the Methode of a Poet historical is not such as of an Histori-
ographer" because the latter person "discourseth of affayres orderly as they
were done, accounting as well the times as the actions" where the former
"thrusteth into the middest." It's difficult to see which of these categories
better describes what the writer of a historical play was doing, though Spenser's suggestion seems to be that playwrights, to the extent they were Poets
Historical, would have preferred the same texts other poets preferred.

But the evidence is that they did not. Arguably they were aware of differing
complexities, differing susceptibilities to the demands of form and rhetoric,
though it may have been no more than a presumed distinction between the
theatrical potential inherent in legendary history as against more recent, more
"factual" history. Or the theatrical poets may have been less concerned with
writing stories that might attract patronage than were the narrative poets. Or,
to take another tack, perhaps the playwrights were simply the automatic in-
heritors of a Reformation tradition of dramatic subject matter that purposely
(sometimes seditiously) engaged the dilemmas of contemporary life by ex-
ploiting parallels in the events of the recent rather than the remote past. Arthur Ferguson saw a distinction between these two pasts, and suggested that
in the 1580s and 1590s "poetry was simply separated from history" and "its
claim to a superior interpretive function" was "confined to the legendary
past"; thus, "in the long run, the entire body of legendary history came to be
relaxed to poets and romancers, leaving the documentable past to the unquestioned jurisdiction of historians."[1] And to the writers of history plays, though
he does not say so.

Of course the writers of history plays would have understood that legendary history was also a usable quarry, that one needn't be restricted to Edwards and Johns and Richards when alluding to contemporary events; they
would remember the example of Thomas Sackville (a principal architect of
the *Mirour*) who presumed rightly that Ferrex and Porrex were perfectly ade-
quate vehicles for dramatizing the problem of succession. But surviving evidence suggests that the playwrights of the 1580s and 1590s elected not to
replicate Sackville's example, either in subject matter or in structure. And
we, for our part, cannot remember that Queen Elizabeth ever said "know ye
not that I am Gorboduc?" One is forced to conclude that the playwrights
of the 1580s and 1590s, for reasons difficult to reconstruct at our distance,
understood that their best and most promising materials lay in the stories
from the recent past, "the documentable past" in Ferguson's terms.

One might prefer the heritage of the Reformation dramatic tradition, and
the example of Bale, as a possible explanation for the preponderance of recent rather than legendary history in the surviving English history plays of
the 1580s and 1590s; if so, one would then have to account somehow for the
survival into that period of a tradition whose roots lay in the theological and
political disputations of a half century earlier. The range of humanist assump-

tions about the moral and prudential values of history that characterized the final decades of the century were different in kind from the narrow political didacticism that informed its use, or its exploitation, by dramatists in the 1530s and 1540s. Nonetheless, issues of religion may in some sense inform the whole range of sixteenth-century dramatic writing; one might be tempted to ask (as some political commentators do today in another context) whether any political or economic or historiographic thought can be independent of religious concerns.

Surely all these notions were fused in the heyday of the Reformation. A play performed somewhere in Suffolk on May Day 1537, about which we know nothing other than that it "was of a kinge how he shuld Rulle his Realm," so troubled the duke of Suffolk that he wrote to Thomas Cromwell about it, urging that such plays be suppressed.[2]

We don't know which King was represented in the play, or whether the complaints embodied in the play were theological or economic or social; the duke of Suffolk, in reporting the incident, apparently didn't think such details mattered ("it's all one," he might have muttered). No doubt there were many such plays in the 1530s, about many kings, some legendary, some recent, all provoking calls for suppression from various members of the establishment. The climate of reception in the 1580s and 1590s was different, however, and plays about how a king should rule (or, more commonly, about how he should not) were no longer deemed objectionable as a class, but that is not enough in itself to suggest why plays about recent history were preferred in the 1580s and 1590s over other kinds of history.

Peter Clark has recently argued that the post-Reformation church's growing identification with a ruling élite during the closing years of the sixteenth century resulted in the decline of the parish church as a meeting ground for the entire community, and the correlative rise in importance of the alehouse as a venue for popular entertainment, for minstrelsy, and for concerned if inebriated discussion about the body politic.[3]

One might well imagine that for such a clientèle, events of "the documentable past" were likelier to form a ground for such discussion than stories of "Brennus and Arviragus, and of old Belinus." We have, of course, no way of knowing what kinds of conversations actually took place in such alehouses, though it has been conventional to presume that alehouse customers were likelier to turn up in playhouses than to buy the writings of Poets Historical.

Elizabethan assumptions about the historical process, and about the lessons to be extracted from it, have been interrogated by more recent schools of enquiry, and we have been instructed in the past few years about a good many of the complexities in the texts that have come down to us, involving principally the Henrys, but also some Richards and Edwards and Johns. But the labeling process itself, and the attendant erasures and exclusions it creates in the record, have been subject to less persistent questioning than the topic would seem to invite. We know that the plays assembled for the First Folio were divided into three groups, with the group called Histories comprised of the ten plays (one John, two Richards, seven Henrys) that we have continued to list in this category. But there are six other plays in the Folio on historical subjects; three on Roman history, one on Scottish history, and two on legendary British history. In some sense understood by Heminges and Condell, and probably by Jaggard as well, these latter six were not considered to be History Plays.

The distinction has troubled later commentators. M. M. Reese imagined all Renaissance historiography as properly concerned with the life of the state, proposing that when a play on such a subject "directed attention to the purely human drama that governed great events" it moved in the direction of tragedy, but that a play could be properly called a history play "wherever the serious political issue was allowed to dominate."[4] Irving Ribner approved of this definition;[5] but I find it too easy a distinction. I have difficulty excluding any of Shakespeare's "history" plays from the former group, or some of his "tragedies" (like *Julius Caesar*) from the latter. And I would be equally perplexed about the proper classification, under this scheme, of *The Massacre at Paris* or *The Battle of Alcazar* or *The Wounds of Civil War* or *Jack Straw* or even *Locrine*. This last play, attributed on its title page to one "W.S." (and actually included in the Third Folio on those grounds) is a piece of legendary history about the son and heir of Brute the founder, not only the kind of story Milton preferred but a story he particularly turned to. The play's closing scene shows Locrine's daughter Sabren drowning herself to avoid being murdered by her stepmother. Milton, in his retelling, recounted how she

> flying the mad pursuit
> Of her enraged stepdam *Guendolen,*
> Commended her fair innocence to the flood

and his invocation to her "under the glassy, cool, translucent wave" prepares for the climax to one of his best-loved works.

But even in the theatrical environment of the 1580s and 1590s where plays about legendary British history could achieve success—though not as great success as plays about more recent history—there were, to the best of our knowledge, hardly any plays about Arthur. We can't know, of course, whether this paucity is merely the random result of unrelated individual preferences among playwrights or whether it represents a consensus judgment. A colleague of mine has suggested that the Arthur story (or stories) would have been a poor choice for any Elizabethan writer seeking a vehicle for commentary on his own times, principally because the tales about Arthur are finally and inescapably romances and thus unfit ground for discourse about the body politic. This is a promising notion, though one might observe that parts of the Arthur story are no more romantic than many parts of Holinshed, and that a playwright who wished to explore the national heritage by focusing on issues of fidelity and betrayal in high places, of patriotism and self-interest, of misplaced idealism, of the entropy endemic to human activity, or of the working-out of designs beyond the power of monarchs to alter, might find much to use in the Arthurian narrative. The English history plays that have come down to us are surely full of Mordred-types, Gawain-types, Guinevere-types, and Arthur-types; the best and most inclusive gallery for showing off such figures—certainly for dealing with all the above themes—is perhaps Shakespeare's *Henry VI* triptych. But for all its similarities, *Henry VI* is not an Arthur play; in the late 1580s Shakespeare, a young playwright working on his first grandly conceived project, clearly preferred the Henry story; no Milton he.

Nor has Shakespeare left us any manuscript musings about the kinds of historical narratives he might have contemplated working on. No matter, some critics would say; we have little need of such evidence, for in his case we have the plays themselves, sixteen of them, history plays (in the broadest sense) on a variety of topics from legendary, classical, and recent history, though mostly the last. Yet he, too, seems to have known what his colleagues in the playhouse knew; namely, that on the stage—even if not on the page— the Edwards and Henrys and Richards and Johns were in, and Arthur was out.

Notes

1. Arthur B. Ferguson, *Clio Unbound: Perception of the Social and Cultural Past in Renaissance England* (Durham: Duke University Press, 1979), 36.

2. P.R.O., S.P.1/120 fol. 100^v–101^r. Suffolk was not opposed to playing in general; he had a troupe of his own, which played at York three years after this incident, in 1540 (REED *York* i.269).

3. Peter Clark, *The English Alehouse: A Social History 1200–1800* (London: Longmans, 1983), 153–54.

4. M. M. Reese, *The Cease of Majesty: A Study of Shakespeare's History Plays* (London, 1961), 66.

5. Irving Ribner, *The English History Play in the Age of Shakespeare* (New York, 1965), 12.

The Presentment of Bushell's Rock: Place, Politics, and Theatrical Self-Promotion

C. E. McGEE

ON 23 August 1636, King Charles I and Queen Henrietta Maria visited Mr. Thomas Bushell at his estate near Enstone, about seven miles northwest of Woodstock in Oxfordshire. Bushell had discovered there a "rarity of nature," "a natural curiosity," a rock, which the king had seen in the fall of 1635 and judged worthy to be not only "preserved," but also "ornated with groves, walks, fish ponds, gardens, and waterworks."[1] Having proceeded with that work, Bushell prepared a series of theatrical devices for the entertainment of the royal couple when he learned of their intention to view the rock late in the summer of 1636. Occasioning a royal visit, Bushell's rock provided him with a splendid opportunity not only to ingratiate himself with the king and queen, but also to promote political and economic interests of moment. Bushell seized the opportunity. While deploying various customary tropes of praise, loyalty, gratitude, and good wishes, he used the entertainment of the royal couple both to achieve precise, immediate objectives and to further, though by indirection, what appears to be, in retrospect, his very life's work.

Bushell published an account of his shows for the royal couple in a souvenir booklet entitled *The Severall Speeches and Songs, at the presentment of Mr Bvshells Rock to the Qveenes Most Excellent Majesty* (appendix A). As set forth in this little book, Bushell's entertainment had five parts proceeding from words of welcome, through the interpretation and presentation of the rock, to a farewell song. Coherent in its overall design, the entertainment included the following:

(1) a speech of welcome by a fictive hermit, who met the king, queen and their attendants at the entrance to the underground space containing the rock and related the story of Bushell's reformation and the hermit's liberation;

(2) a "contemplation" upon the rock, nature's "maister-peece" (101), apparently by Bushell himself, during which speech he ushered the visitors into the presence of the rock and pointed out impressive aspects of it;

(3) "A Sonnet within the pillar of the Table at the Banquet," a sonnet, or song, inviting the royal couple to partake of the first fruits of the estate laid out on the table before them;

(4) a dialogue with Echo by which Bushell, while loyally praying for the well-being of the king, the queen, and their family, formally presented the rock to the queen;

(5) a farewell song, expressing thanks for the royal visit, sadness at the king and queen's departure, and hope that the entertainment had pleased them.

Bushell himself may have been the author of these several speeches and songs,[2] which he had published by the nearby Oxford stationer, Leonard Lichfield. The music he attributes to Simon Ives, one of the composers of *The Triumph of Peace* and a musician with some cachet at court in 1636.[3]

Focusing on Ives and on speeches that he implied are his own, Bushell ignored the contributions made by other artists. John Aubrey claimed that a "Goodall of Christ Church Oxford" composed music for the show and a student from there, whose name he could not recall, sang.[4] More important, Bushell failed to mention in his published account of the entertainment another speech that was probably part of it, that of the Red Bull actor, member of the King's Revels, and relentless self-promoter himself, Thomas Jordan.[5] In *Wit in a Wilderness of Promiscuous Poetry,* Jordan published the speech of Calliope, "composed, and spoken by the Author to the late King," he claims, "at The Dedication of Mr. Tho. Bushel's Rock at Enston in Oxon" (appendix B).[6] This speech is not inconsistent with other aspects of the entertainment. In it Calliope explains that news of "a strange Rock discover'd under ground" (15) brought her to Bushell's estate, where she has found such waters, walks, and woods that it shall be the Muses' "everlasting home" (60). Taking up a question posed in Bushell's "Contemplation"—"Where are the Muses, that were wont to sing / Their well tun'd note about *Parnassus* spring?" (108–9)—Calliope's speech calls attention to beautiful physical features and natural amenities of the estate as developed by Bushell in accordance with the king's wishes. Whereas Bushell's devices focused on subterranean developments, Jordan attended to those above ground. Taken together, the songs and speeches of the entertainment celebrated both what geography had bestowed upon Thomas Bushell at Enstone and what the host had done to enhance it—celebrated, as it were, "Nature to advantage dressed" by art and technology.

What nature had bestowed upon Bushell on the north bank of the River Glyme at Enstone was a craggy mass of stone, ten feet tall and ten feet across, carved by the flow of subterranean springs (fig. 1). The fictive hermit who delivered the first speech, noting the rock's conjunction of opposites, its density and delicacy, pointed out the wonder of it—"solid ROCK that various streames hath spun / Even into strings as small as smallest wyre" (133–34). By the time of the king and queen's visit in 1636, Bushell had created an underground grotto of which the rock formed one wall.[7] Behind it was a cellar "for keeping Liquors cool, or placing Musick, to surprise the Auditors."[8]

Figure 1. Interior Prospect of Bushell's Rock, following its restoration by Lord Edward Henry, Earl of Lichfield. Copperplate engraving published in Robert Plot, *The Natural History of Oxford-shire, Being an Essay toward the Natural History of England* (Oxford: The Theatre, 1676), facing p. 238. Courtesy of the Thomas Fisher Rare Book Library, University of Toronto.

Nature had *given* Bushell what King James I had had to purchase. In the mid-1620s, he paid Isaac de Caus and his men "for making a Rocke in the vaulte under the [Whitehall] banquetting house" and, a year later, for adding shell-work to the rock face.[9]

Bushell also enhanced his natural "maister-peece" (101) at Enstone. He raised its "curl'd head" (149) to a height of about thirteen feet and placed a fountain there.[10] Tapping a spring up the hill to the northwest, en route to Chipping Norton (fig. 2), Bushell increased the volume of water flowing to the site and, more important, the water pressure there, so that various kinds of waterworks could operate effectively.[11] One held a silver ball aloft on its "ascending Streame";[12] another suddenly enclosed visitors in a fence of water, to the amusement, and sometimes to the titillation, of others as when "fair Ladies [who] cannot fence the crossing" are caught "flashing and dashing their smooth, soft and tender thighs and knees";[13] a third produced a canopy of rain in which "a man (in the Showers full Carreere) may stand dry,

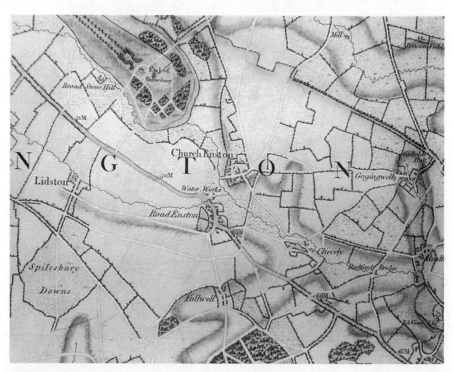

Figure 2. Mr. Bushell's "Water Works." "A New Map of the County of Oxford," drawn by Richard Lewknor and engraved by J. Cary (1793, 1794), shows the location of Bushell's estate to the east of the highway on the north bank of the River Glyme until 1857. The building closest to the river is probably the banqueting house built by Bushell over his rock. Courtesy of the Library of Congress.

which with the reflection of the Sunne at high Noone, makes appeare to our fancies Rainbowes and flashings like Lightning."[14] Bushell also installed cisterns to store water and leaden shelves to modulate its flow over the rock face. He added devices to produce various sound effects, seemingly coming from within the rock, and adorned the outside with artificial songbirds. In his "Contemplation vpon the Rock," Bushell drew attention to this particular feature as an image of the natural harmonies of the place: "The fountaines times doe keepe to birds that sing, / And on the plaine song utter'd by each spring / The ayerie Choristers division run" (130–32). But these "natural" harmonies were, of course, produced not by nature but by hydraulic mechanisms, like those described in John Bate's *Mysteryes of Nature and Art,* first published in 1634 and reissued in 1635 with a new section devoted to mechanisms by which to mimic the songs of birds.[15] Twenty-three years later Bushell recalled that he had "beautyfied" the place with "artificial Thunder and Lightning, Rain, Hail-showers, Drums beating, Organs playing, Birds singing, Waters murmuring, the Dead arising, Lights moving, Rainbows reflecting with the beams of the Sun, and watry showers springing from the same Fountain."[16] Contemporary visitors reported his use of mirrors on the wall opposite the rock face to create a visual echo of the auditory ones produced naturally in the grotto and his installation of a small pool in which moved figures of Neptune, a duck, and a spaniel.[17]

Over the grotto, Bushell built a banqueting house (fig. 3). The decorations of the main room included another rock, one in the shape of a bear's head from which another fountain welled up and into which its waters mysteriously returned.[18] Through a grate in the floor, one could see the grotto below.[19] Above was a ceiling painted with biblical stories on the theme of water: the woman encountered by Christ at Jacob's well (John 4:6–28); the angel that led Hagar and Ishmael to water (Genesis 21:8–21); Susannah and the elders who secretly watched her bathing (Daniel 13). Bushell's banqueting house served him as a hermitage, for adjacent to the main room he had two small rooms: a study draped in black and a bedroom adorned with pictures on cloth of the birth and the Passion of Christ. When Lieutenant Hammond visited in September 1635, he took the décor of the study as "representing a melancholly retyr'd life like a Hermits."[20] He reinforced this impression of Bushell when he concluded his account of Enstone with a reflection on the place and the man:

> the whole length of the foresayd Garden, House, Rocke and Walkes is a most pleasant, sweet and delightsome Place; yet did it seeme strange to me that a Gentleman should be so strangely conceited and humour'd, as to disburse and lay out so much Money as he has done, in planting, framing, contriuing and building vpon another Mans Freehold, to reare a Paradise and then to loose it. A man gim-cracke sure, yet hereditary to these Hermiticall and Proiecticall Vndertakers.[21]

Figure 3. Exterior Prospect of the Banqueting House, 1676. Copperplate engraving in Plot, *The Natural History of Oxford-shire* (1676), facing p. 240. Courtesy of the Thomas Fisher Rare Book Library, University of Toronto.

Although *The Presentment of Bushell's Rock* does not allude to all of these enhancements of it, most of them were in place for the king and queen's visit in 1636, and all but one of them—"the Dead arising" being the strange and notable exception[22]—could have been seen (or heard) by John Aubrey when he visited the site in 1643.

When Charles and Henrietta Maria visited Enstone, Bushell's immediate and explicit hope was simply for a favorable response to his entertainment of them. The entire piece ends with a song asking them to, "Let him know you are pleas'd / That his heart may be eas'd / Or this Rock or this cave / Is his Tombe or his grave" (285–88). Like a number of other shows, this one tried to force the principal figures in the audience to show their hand.[23] A positive response to that appeal would have given Bushell some assurance that he would also achieve his secondary aim, a political one, which the hermit made explicit:

> Vouchsafe a blessing, such a one as may,
> Preserue this ROCK, my mansion from decay.
> For envie would expell me from my home,
> And sinck me in the ruines of my owne. (76–79)

However wonderful Bushell's project seemed to some, it had met with resistance from others, especially from locals who objected to "disposing of a highway to another place."[24] An order of 7 June 1637 from the council to Sir Robert Jenkinson and John Martin, justices of the peace for Oxfordshire, listed the obstacles thrown in Bushell's way. Some copyholders of the manor "out of a malignant disposition . . . [have] fined Bushell for having turned the said highway, some have cut down trees planted for beautifying the said rock, and others have presumed to forbid his workmen employed in setting up a wall for preserving the groves and works, not at all regarding his Majesty's direction."[25] The king ordered the Earl of Danby to deal with opposition to the project in 1635, but clearly, Danby had not been altogether successful. Consequently, in 1637 the council went on to order that the justices arrest those acting in contempt of the king's wishes, facilitate the construction of a wall about the estate, and compensate neighbors appropriately. Bushell's entertainment had been effective: as this order implies, the hermit's petition had been granted, royal protection for the rock secured. And the royal couple were sufficiently pleased with the site, its development, and their entertainment there that the queen commanded that the rock "be called after her owne / Princely name / Henrietta" (16–19).

Thomas Bushell, however, had more removed, ambitious, and potentially profitable aspirations. Of these, *The Several Speeches and Songs* made no direct mention; instead the entertainment, in presenting the rock and its development, provided an analogue for the project Bushell hoped to undertake.

At the same time that he was developing the rock at Enstone, he was negotiating with Lady Elizabeth Middleton for control of her late husband's lease of the silver mines in the north of Wales. Sir Hugh Middleton had profited handsomely from these mines; paying an annual fee of £400 for the Cumsumblock mine, he reaped a profit of £24,000 per year.[26] Many Welsh mines, however, could no longer be worked because of flooding and Middleton's own were in neglect by the time of his death in 1631. Bushell, drawing on ideas he attributed to Bacon, planned to use adits to drain the pits so as to gain access to the mineral resources there.[27] By October 1636, he had arranged to take over the lease from Elizabeth Middleton in return for a payment of one year's rent. This deal was subject to government approval, which the Privy Council gave, subject to Bushell satisfying "the Lord Treasurer and Lord Cottington that the works should go on," on 25 January 1637.[28]

The entertainment for King Charles and Queen Henrietta Maria the preceding summer seems to have facilitated these negotiations, for the transformation of the rock of Enstone stood as an analogue for what was possible in Wales. Bushell used the development of that site as a precedent, model, and justification for the development of mineral resources elsewhere. A project worthy of the queen's name, "Henrietta's Rock," might be matched (and duly outdone) by one in her husband's name elsewhere.[29] As in Oxfordshire, so in Cardiganshire, the earth needed human intervention to deliver its riches. The same ideology that authorized applying human arts and technology to the natural resources of Bushell's rock—and the manifest success of doing so—justified similar enterprises in Wales. And Thomas Bushell was clearly the man to oversee these projects, for he had demonstrated at Enstone his readiness to do the king's bidding, his ability to work an underground site, his knowledge of hydraulic technology needed to drain the silver mines of Wales, and his commitment to realize the potential of what nature had bestowed upon them.

In his theatrical devices Bushell made no explicit mention of his plans for the Welsh mines, but he may have encouraged Charles I to see the connection when the king paid his first visit to Enstone in 1635. Bushell recalled, twenty-three years later, that on that occasion the king "conceived me capable . . . to do him some more acceptable service in Mineral discoveries (for the Honour of the Nation)" because of "my then discourse in commemoration of my old Master [Sir Francis Bacon]." Or Bushell may have used a gift rather than words to encourage the monarch to see the work at Enstone in Welsh terms. In the same account Bushell goes on to say that he made the king "a collation . . . *of his own native silver,* upon his second visiting that Rock the year following," that is, in 1636.[30] Bushell may or may not have shaped the reception of his entertainment by these means, but he himself certainly connected his entertainment of the royal couple with mining projects. In fact, he interpreted the speech of the hermit "ascending out of the ground, as a prophetick preludium to the practical discovery of Mineral Treasures, and all mysterious Arts."[31] Thomas Broadway, Bushell's "True Friend and Servant," conjoined the two projects with a third metaphorical rock, in a letter expressing his confidence "that as your desires are set on the material rocks of *Wales* and *Enstone,* so will your better affections be firmly grounded upon the rock *Christ Jesus.*"[32] Nor did King Charles fail to see the parallel between the rock in Oxfordshire and the rocks in Wales. In a letter of 12 June 1643, he concluded his thanks to Bushell for various services in the civil war with the assurance that he would restore Bushell to his lands and clear his debts "to the end that you maye enjoy your desires at Enston rocke and the rocks in Wales, which your own industrie and Gods providence hath helped you unto."[33]

To argue his political and economic case more strongly, Bushell used *The Presentment of Bushell's Rock* to promote a certain idea of himself—that of a prodigal son, a sinner reformed. He offered the fullest version of this self-representation in a confessional book published in 1628, *The First Part of Youth's Error.* The pious figure in the picture facing the title page of this volume (fig. 4) marks how far Bushell claimed he had come since the wasteful days when he was dubbed "buttoned Bushell."[34] Asked to carry the seal at the installation of Sir Francis Bacon as lord chancellor, Bushell appeared at court in a gold suit, trimmed with gold lace and adorned profusely with gold buttons.[35] In *The First Part of Youth's Error* however (and repeatedly in his later writings), Bushell confessed to his profligacy as a young man. Later he also admitted that his self-indulgence and corruption, like that of other servants of the lord chancellor, contributed to Bacon's demise in 1621.[36] After his fall, Bushell went into retreat, first on the Isle of Wight, then on the Calf of Man, "where he late had an hermiticall life in ye cave of a hollow rock." To atone for his "former debauchedness," he lived on "a parsimonious diet of herbs, oil, mustard, and honey, with water sufficient, most like to yt [of] our long liv'd fathers before the flood."[37] Bushell followed that regime strictly, so he says, "until divine providence call[ed] him to a more active life."[38]

Enstone was the site for that more active life. In the first speech of the entertainment, the hermit pretended to mistake King Charles for Christ and his visit for the Last Judgment. The hermit's defense of Bushell arose logically from this "mistake," and so he summed up the story of his master's conversion as follows:

> A Prodigall profuse in vast expence,
> That nothing studied, but to please his sense,
> Trimming a glorious outside, whil'st within
> He cherisht nought, but propagating sinne,
>
> . . . .
> God of his mercy pleased was at last

Figure 4. Mr. Thomas Bushell, 1628. This woodcut, which faces the title page of *The First Part of Youth's Error* (London, 1628; BL shelfmark 851. f. 38), is published by permission of The British Library.

A gratious Eye vpon his soule to cast,

.   .   .   .

What followed next must be conceau'd of course,
Confession, contrition, and remorse,
These guides to heauen he happily persu'd,
View'd his past life, and that againe review'd:
And to that end he purchas'd at a price
This field, then sterill, now his Paradise;
Where he as man of old, by God being bound
With Adam, wrought, and dig'd, and drest the ground.

                                    (40–43, 46–47, 52–59)

In contrast to this story, John Aubrey reported that Bushell's rock was dis-covered by a laborer hired "to clear some boscage which grew on the side of the hill and also to dig a cavity in the hill to sit, and read or contemplate."[39] Robert Plot gave an even more practical explanation, noting that Bushell found the rock when "cleaning the spring then called *Goldwell,* though quite over-grown with bryars and bushes, to place a *Cistern* for his own drink-ing."[40] Bushell's hermit, however, (like Bushell himself) represented the dis-covery as the culmination of Bushell's moral transformation and a consequence of striving to live in accordance with God's dictates to Adam. What's more, Bushell would, so the hermit said, continue in his pious ways. If King Charles would preserve the rock from those threatening to destroy it, then the "true Possessor" of it, "to whom heauen / For pure devotion-sake this place hath giuen" will "Build Altars here, and daily offerings pay / For his preseruers health" (80–84).

In his "Contemplation upon the Rock," Bushell invoked similar values: "virgin silence" (128), music to charm "the chastest eare" (129), and a har-mony of sound like the "choice Hymnes" that "holy virgines" sing out on "holy-dayes" (136–37), "So that devotion here is kept on wing, / And rather rais'd, then checkt by whispering / Of springs with ROCKS, or ROCKS with light heel'd streames" (138–40). The "Sonnet within the pillar of the Table" varies the same theme by portraying the "first fruits" (169) of the estate as a "humble sacrifice" (162) and the place itself as an Eden, but an Eden without Adam, Eve, or serpent (165–66). The concentration of religious language throughout the songs and speeches is part of a rhetorical strategy designed by Bushell to establish himself as devout, virtuous, and trustworthy. No longer the man whose corruption helped to sink Bacon, he is now a man whom a merchant might trust with wares, an investor with savings, and a king of England with the silver mines of Wales. Bushell would later try to raise venture capital by minting a gold medal which, in its design, co-opts the authority of Sir Francis Bacon, portrays Bushell himself as a hard-work-ing man among rocks, and represents his enterprise as the work of God (fig. 5).[41]

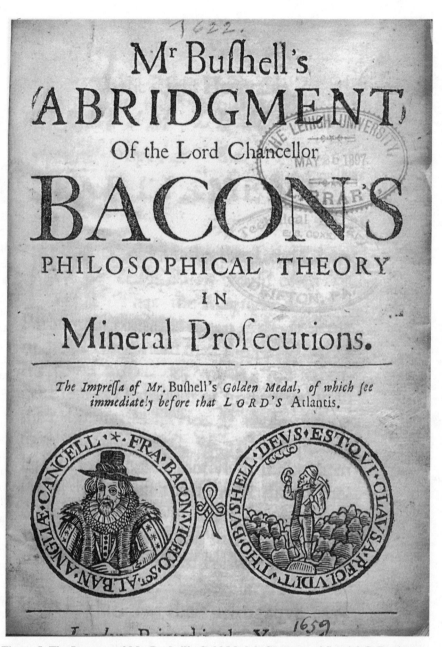

The Impressa of Mr. Bushell's Golden Medal, of which see immediately before that LORD'S Atlantis.

Figure 5. The Impresa of Mr. Bushell's Gold Medal. Courtesy of Special Collections, Linderman Library, Lehigh University, from the title page of its copy of *Mr Bushell's Abridgment of the Lord Chancellor Bacons Philosophical Theory in Mineral Prosecutions* (London, 1659).

The language of faith and morals found in *The Several Speeches and Songs at the Presentment of Bushell's Rock* recurs throughout Bushell's efforts to promote his enterprises. In these efforts, he was relentless, as his letters from prison reveal. When incarcerated for debt, he worte and later published a letter to his "Fellow-sufferers in restraint," inviting the "Condemned men for Petty-Felonies, to work in the Mines of their own Country, rather than be banished to Slavery in Forein parts."[42] He told again the story of his "licentious Prodigality" and moral transformation and, using his own case as a precedent, argued that their reformation would add strength to their work in the mines. Bushell also wrote "To My Fellow-Prisoners for Debt, in Mind and Body," relating again how God "out of this depth of desolation graciously called me to the publick service of my Country, in the innocent way of a Miner."[43] He then offered his fellow prisoners jobs in the mines where they would receive material benefits and spiritual instruction as well. Bushell aimed not only to prove the efficacy of Bacon's theories concerning mineral resources, but also to establish on that material foundation a community modeled on Solomon's House in Bacon's *New Atlantis*.[44]

Unfortunately Thomas Bushell's moral reformation seldom extended to financial dealings with other individuals. The evidence that survives concerning his development of the mines in Cardiganshire, Devon, Cornwall, and Somerset along with his establishment of a royal mint at Aberystwyth is a mass of monopolistic maneuvers, petitions to gain access to others' mines, bad debts, unpaid bills, arrests, imprisonments, orders protecting him from arrest, orders forbearing prosecution, and pardons.[45] According to one petition, by 1642 "Bushell took himself into the King's quarters, where he has ever since remained."[46] Thomas Bushell's alleged moral reformation, crucial rhetorically to the prosecution of his schemes, seems so irrelevant to his treatment of other people that shortly after his death in 1674, John Aubrey summed him up as "the greatest arts-master to run in debt (perhaps) in the world." "He had," Aubrey goes to say, "the strangest bewitching way to draw in people (yea, discreet and wary men) into his projects that ever I heard of. His tongue was a chain and drew in so many to be bound for him and to be engaged to his designs that he ruined a number. . . . He died one hundred and twenty thousand pounds in debt; and lived so long that his debts were forgotten, so that they were the great-grandchildren of the creditors."[47]

In his use of drama, Thomas Bushell seems to be a throwback to the Elizabethan period, when regular progresses gave towns and aristocratic families a royal audience. In manor house shows and in civic pageants, pride of place was often as important rhetorically as praise of the monarch. This celebratory mode did not silence discussion of political and economic issues that might divide host and visitor; on the contrary, it offered a conventionally safe mode of discourse for families and boroughs to further their interests. By the time King Charles and Henrietta Maria visited Bushell's rock however, the masque had largely displaced other forms of drama both at court and in the country homes of the nobility. Thomas Bushell proceeded nevertheless as if a royal visit required theatrical devices, devices both celebrating the natural beauties and amenities of the place as well as the owner's enhancement of it and serving political purposes. What seems important about *The Presentment of Mr. Bushell's Rock* is the extremity of the case, an impression created perhaps by the oddity of such an entertainment in the reign of Charles I. At Bushell's rock the geography truly was indispensable to the show: nature's masterpiece was the centerpiece of the drama. There Bushell capitalized on the king and queen's brief tour of his estate by honoring them, aggrandizing himself, and promoting his political and economic projects—promoting them as if they were royal couple's own, not to mention God's. And there Bushell's self-promotion, dressed up in a bold, materialistic, sincere, and mystifying rhetoric of spiritual values and moral reformation, proved to be exceptionally efficacious.

Appendix A

I: Note on the Text

This edition of *The Severall Speeches and Songs, at the presentment of Mr Bvshells Rock* uses the British Library copy as its copy text, collated with the six other extant copies of the book, those at the Bodleian Library; Balliol College, Oxford; Queen's College, Oxford; the University of Durham; the Folger Shakespeare Library; and the Houghton Library, Harvard University. Both W. W. Greg in *A Bibliography of the English Printed Drama to the Restoration* and the *Short-Title Catalogue* divide these copies into two groups. The copies at the Bodleian, the Folger, and Durham University lack the line identifying the bookseller on the title page; as a result, the title page ends with "Printed by LEONARD LICHFIELD." followed immediately by the year of publication, as follows: "M.DC.XXXVI." This group of copies also includes the catchwords "Of" and "Harke" on sig. B1 and sig. B1v respectively. Within this group, the Bodleian copy represents the earliest state of the text, for it alone includes an error in the spelling of the queen's name on the title page: "HENRETTA" FOR "HENRIETTA." The copies that make up the second group (Balliol, Queen's, British Library, and Harvard) lack the catchwords on B1 and B1v noted above and alter several features of the title page. The printer has substituted a comma for the period after "LICHFIELD," deleted the period after the "M" in the year of publication, and added the name of the bookseller in a new line above the date, "*and are to be sold by* Thomas Allam." Apart from these items noted, there are no other variants or stop-press corrections in the seven extant copies of *The Sev-*

erall Speeches and Songs, at the presentment of Mr. Bvshell's Rock. Although crowding within lines of the speeches often occurs, the book itself is attractive, with ornaments that frame the title page and set off the speeches and songs from one another.

Very little is known about Thomas Allam, an Oxford bookseller recorded in the *Short-Title Catalogue* from 1636 until 1639. Presumably his business connections with Leonard Lichfield, rather than the suitability of *The Severall Speeches and Songs* to his stock, led to their collaboration in this case, for of the five books for which he is know in the *STC,* four of them were printed by Lichfield. Leonard Lichfield's business appears to have been of a different order. Recorded in the *STC* as publishing about fifteen titles each year from 1637 to 1641, Lichfield traded largely in scholarly texts, religious treatises, sermons, and official documents for the university and the church. While such works constituted the bulk of his list, *The Severall Speeches and Songs* would not have been out of place there, since he also printed, regularly if not frequently, books of occasional verse, plays, and other entertainments, most notably *The King and Queen's Entertainment at Richmond,* also in 1636. Throughout the second half of the 1630s, Oxford University paid Lichfield both for publishing several collections of occasional verse, some copies of which were specially bound for presentation to members of the court, and for carrying letters to the queen (*The Life and Times of Anthony Wood, antiquary, at Oxford 1632–1695, described by Himself, Volume IV: Addenda,* collected by Andrew Clark [Oxford: Oxford Historical Society at the Clarendon Press, 1895], 56–57).

Thomas Bushell published the songs and speeches presented in 1636 on two later occasions. He appended the first two speeches of the entertainment to *Mr Bushell's Abridgment of the Lord Chancellor Bacons Philosophical Theory in Mineral Prosecution* (London: Thomas Newcombe, 1659), "Postscript," 24–27. A year later, in *An Extract by Mr. Bushell of his late Abridgment of the Lord Chancellor Bacons Philosophical Theory in Mineral Prosecutions* (London: Thomas Leach, 1660), he again published that postscript along with a copy of the songs and speeches from the 1636 show in their entirety ("Postscript," 33–40). Both these volumes were clearly attempts on the part of Bushell to ingratiate himself with those in power: Parliament in 1659, King Charles II in 1660. Whereas his *Abridgment* began with a dedicatory epistle to the Right Honorable William Lenthal, Speaker of Parliament, *An Extract* began with an epistle to the "Dread Sovereign," who had brought the interregnum formally to an end on 29 May 1660, and whose picture now appeared on the verso of the title page. In both works, Bushell provided a summary of the main ideas set forth in Bacon 's *New Atlantis* and added a postscript explaining what had obstructed his efforts to apply Bacon's mineral theories and realize his social vision. Bushell discussed aspects of his relationship with King Charles I more fully in this postscript than in any of his other writings. Besides parts of the text of *The Presentment of Bushell's Rock,* he included evidence of the late king's support for his mining projects and the monarch's memory of his entertainment at Enstone. He described some of the improvements he made to the rock and its setting as well as his proposal to Lord Saye and Sele that Charles I, then at Carisbrook Castle, remain under a kind of house arrest at Enstone. That proposal being rejected however, Bushell himself "declined the recesses of that solitude" (21/31). Along with many other documents from his past, documents rearranged for each successive republication but seldom revised, the entertainment that had served Bushell well in 1636 served once again in its published forms in 1659 and 1660 to promote him and his projects.

In transcribing the text, I have preserved the spelling, capitalization, punctuation, type faces, line breaks, and general format of the original. The locations of ornaments and typographical lines that separate speeches and songs have been noted rather than reproduced. Emendations appear in caret brackets.

II: The Text

THE
SEVERALL
SPEECHES AND
Songs, at the presentment of
5   Mr BVSHELLS ROCK
TO THE
QVEENES
Most Excellent Majesty.
Aug. 23. 1636.
10   HER HIGHNESSE
being Gratiously Pleased to
Honour the said ROCK, not
only with HER
ROYALL *Presence;*
15   BVT
COMMANDED THE SAME
to be called after her owne
Princely name
HENRIETTA.

20   OXFORD,
Printed by LEONARD LICHFIELD,
and are to be sold by Thomas Allam.
MDC. XXXVI.

The *Hermits* speech ascending out of the
25   ground as the KING entred the Rock.

WITH bended knees thus humbly doe I pray,
You blessed powers, that glorifie this day,
And to my frozen lipps haue vtterance giuen,
Speak, O speak the Commands you bring from heauen!
30   For by times Embleme that since Noahs flood,
I thus haue grasp'd, my soule hath vnderstood,
The world no farther Iorney hath to saile
Then is betwixt this Serpents head, and taile.   Holding a
If then before the Earths great funerall,   serpent in hi\<s\>
35   Most glorious SIR, you hither come to call   hand.
The Inmates of this solitarie place
To strict accoumpt, for Heauens sake daigne the grace
To lend your patience, and a gentle eare
To what I ought to speak, and you may heare:
40   A Prodigall profuse in vast expence,
That nothing studied, but to please his sense,
Trimming a glorious outside, whil'st within
He cherisht nought, but propagating sinne,
That multiplied so fast, there was no place
45   Allow'd for virtue, or for sauing grace;
God of his mercy pleased was at last
A gratious Eye vpon his soule to cast,
Which being so neere a finall rack as now
His only care, his studie is, but how
50   He may redeeme the yeares he lost in sinne
And liue as he to liue did now beginnne.
What followed next must be conceau'd of course,
Confession, contrition, and remorse,
These guides to heauen he happily persu'd,
55   View'd his past life, and that againe review'd:
And to that end he purchas'd at a price
This field, then sterill, now his Paradise;
Where he as man of old, by God being bound
With Adam, wrought, and dig'd, and drest the ground:
60   Here are no Riuers such as Eden had,
Nor were these banks with trees or flowers clad
T'invite a stay, the Owle, not Philomell
Within this solitarie place did dwell.
And I, the Genius of this obscure Caue
65   Since the great deluge, liu'd as in a graue,
Chain'd to this ROCK, my Toumb-stone in dispaire
Of freedome, or to view such beames, as are
Shot from your Virtues: All my dayes were night,
Vntill the humble Owner brought to light
70   These eyes of mine, and forc'd great nature show
This master-peece, a grace she did not owe

To any age before, and sooth to say,
I thinke it was created 'gainst this day.
If then you be the God of Brittaines earth,
75   And rule this Ile, (as sure you are by birth)
Vouchsafe a blessing, such a one as may,
Preserue this ROCK, my mansion from decay.
For envie would expell me from my home,
And sinck me in the ruines of my owne.
80   But let the true Possessor, to whom heauen
For pure devotion-sake this place hath giuen,
Let him in peace enioy it, that he may
Build Altars here, and daily offerings pay
For his preseruers health grant this, and then
85   I that liu'd long with stones, will liue with men:
And thinke the golden age is now begunne,
In which no injuries are meant or done:
Such Innocents as yet remaine with vs
That doe inhabit here, and humbly thus
90   We meane to liue, having no other fare
Then uncurst water, uncorrupted aire.
Vouchsafe to enter, and you here shall find
Nothing but what may please a displeas'd mind.
    My bold Commission's done, and I returne
95   Downe to my humble graue, my peacefull urne.

Mr BVSHELL his Contemplation
vpon the Rock.

Great nature, had I not a Soule, that spies
A greater power enthron'd aboue the skies,
100   I should adore thee, and should Idolize
This maister-peece of thine, and sacrifice
The fat of Bullocks to thy memorie,
But we forbidden are to deifie
What may be seene; since that it is reveal'd
105   The face of what's divine must be conceal'd
From mortall eyes, untill that greatest light
Be quite put out that severs day from night.
Where are the Muses, that were wont to sing
Their well tun'd note about *Parnassus* spring?
110   Where is that Master-peece of Poets now
That had a Lawrell wreath to crowne each brow?
Where are those paper-spoylers, that can part
With many sheetes to paint out painted Art
In praising faces, features such as be
115   In beautie poore, if once compar'd to thee?
Shall I not thinke the world on's death-bed lyes,

And summon'd to his funerall obsequies,
The soules departed hence, when thus I see
Nature unlocke her richest treasurie.
120 And in this doting age discover more
Then in six thousand yeares that past before<?>
You, that can sequester your selves from men,
And buried be alive, in Caue, or den,
In hollow ROCK, or in a desart groue,
125 That the sad note of murmuring water love;
Ile bring you to a ROCK, that for it's pleasure
The Indies cannot purchase with their treasure,
Where none but virgin silence liveth there
And sweetest Musicke charmes the chastest eare
130 The fountaines times doe keepe to birds that sing,
And on the plaine song utter'd by each spring
The ayerie Choristers division run;
The solid ROCK that various streames hath spun
Even into strings as small as smallest wyre,
135 Seemes to consort, and so make up a quire
Such as the holy virgines sweetly raise
When <they> choice Hymnes doe sing on holy-dayes.
So that devotion here is kept on wing,
And rather rais'd, then checkt by whispering
140 Of springs with ROCKS, or ROCKS with light heel'd streames
Night swimmes away in rest, the day in dreames,
So that the watchfull HERMIT needs no clock,
There are perpetuall Chymes within this ROCK,
That will not let his contemplation sleepe,
145 Would he be sad, there he may learne to weepe
Of every object offer'd to his eye;
The humble pavement never shall be dry,
But moystened still, with teares that there are shed,
From the rich fountaine of the ROCKS curl'd head.
150   This my Propheticke soule foretells shall be,
        ENSTON, the honour, that shall dwell with thee.

A Sonnet within the pillar of the
Table at the Banquet.

1.

155 *Come away blest soules<,> no more*
Feede your eyes with what is poore.
'Tis enough that you haue blest
What was rude; what was undrest,
And created in a trice
160 *Out of Chaos paradise.*

Come away and cast your eyes
On this humble sacrifice.

2.

We no golden apples giue,
165   *Here's no Adam, here's no Eve:*
Not a Serpent dares appeare,
Whilest your Majesties stay here.
Oh then sit, and take your due,
Those the first fruits are that grewe
170   *In this Eden, and are throwne*
On this Altar as your owne.

3.

Set a chaire for earth's Jove,
Bring another for his love.
175   *Come away, vouchsafe to taste*
What was gathered up in haste,
If we live another yeare
By your grace and favour here,
Italy, and France, and Spaine
180   *Of their fruits shall boast in vaine.*

Mr BVSHELL presenting the *Rock* by
an Eccho sung to the KING and
QVEENES *Majesty.*

The Eccho.

185	ECCHO	ECCHO
	I charge thee answere me to what I aske,	*aske*
	Hath ought presented to these Princes pleas'd?	*pleas'd*
	Pleas'd<!> O gentle Eccho speak that word againe,	*againe*
	How haue they lik'd our Rock, our Caue, our Well?	*well*
190	Well! proud would their Host be should I tell him	*tell him*
	Tell him Eccho, I will that he dispaire not	*spare not*
	What shall we giue them by way of thankfulness?	*thankfulnes*
	That, like thee, is aire; we would giue what's reall	*all*
	All, why all that we haue is but this Rock,	*this Rock*
195	Giue them this poore Rock, Eccho meane you so?	*so*
	To which of them, to'th King or to the Queene?	*the Queene*
	What to the King, if this be giuen the Queene?	*the Queene*
	The Queene, there's nought more pretious: 'tis true:	*true*
	Can nothing more be added to his blisse?	*blisse*
200	Blisse, the blisse of Heauen Eccho you meane sure;	*sure*
	Sure be't to them both as this our blessing;	*sing*

Sing gentle Eccho, is that thy desire?   *desire*
Then blessed be this paire
On the earth, in the aire,
205   Blessed in their lasting ioyes,
Blessed in their Girles, and Boyes,
Let them live to heare it told,
Their grand-Grandchildren are growne old.
Let her beauty ever last,
210   And his vigor neuer wast.
Let the sea, that bounds these Isles,
Ebbe at least ten thousand miles:
And returne no more, but leaue
New kingdomes for them to bequeath
215   To the many heires they get;
And when they pay natures debt,
Let their bodies not be found
Dwelling in the sluttish ground,
But translated to those thrones,
220   Only built for blessed ones.
Eccho let these prayers be
Poasted vp to Heauen by thee   **ECCHO**
And if granted let vs know,
Gentle Eccho answere so   *so*
225   So, then 'tis agree'd aboue   *aboue*
That this paire shall liue, and loue: *and loue*
And for euer happie be   *happie be*
In their blest posteritie.   *posteritie*
Eccho, for this newes I'le giue   *giue*
230   Leaue that thou shalt euer liue   *liue*
In this Paradise of theirs,   *theirs*
Theirs Eccho, 'tis no more mine,   *mine*
Theirs, and thine, Eccho euer,   *euer*
Fates decrees alter neuer.   *neuer*

235   A Sonnet sung to the KING and
           QVEENE at Mr Bushells Rock.

          1.

Harke, harke, how the stones in the Rocke
  Strive their tongues to unlock,
240   *And would show,*
  What they know,
Of the Joy here hath beene
Since the King *and the* Queene
  Daigne<d> to say
245   *They would pay*

A visit to this cell:
But all tongues cannot tell;
  Nor language expresse
  Our full thankefullnesse.

250   2.
Harke, harke, how the streames roule along,
    And for want of a tongue
        Vent in teares
        All their feares
255   *Least the* King, *least the* Queene
    Being come, having seene,
        What we have
        In this cave,
    That nothing can delight
260   *That is brought to their sight,*
        Or fully expresse
        Our hearts thankefullnesse.

                            3.

Harke, harke, how the Birds in the groves
265   *Strive to tender their loves,*
        For the spring,
        That the King,
    And the Queene *bring along:*
    Doe but see how they throng
270   *With their notes*
        In their throats,
    On each Banck, in each Bush
    Sits a Larke, and a Thrush,
        That fayne would expresse
275   *Their hearts thankefullnesse.*

                            4.

Harke, harke, we humbly doe intreat
    How your Hosts heart doth beate,
        How it pants,
280   *Cause it wants*
    What he gladly would bring
    To the Queene, *and the* King,
        Daigne to speake,
        Least it breake,
285   *Let him know you are pleas'd*
    That his heart may be eas'd
        Or this Rock or this cave
        Is his Tombe or his grave.

290

The Musick to these songs was compos'd
by SYMON IVE.
FINIS.

III: Collation

In *Mr Bushell's Abridgment,* published by Thomas Newcombe in 1659, the
text of the first two speeches of the entertainment appears to have been set
from a scribal copy of an earlier manuscript of the show. Although Leonard
Lichfield's text of 1636 could have been used, a manuscript seems the likelier
source. It is hard to imagine that a compositor working from the printed version could have misread "gratious" as "glorious" (47), "these" with a long
s for "there" (61), "nature" as "Natures" (70) thereby muddling the sense,
and "Possessor" as "Professor" (80). Nor are these substantive variants, unlike those in the head notes to the two speeches, likely to have been authorial
revisions, all of them being less apt in their immediate contexts than the original readings. The alterations of the notes introducing the songs and speeches
do seem to be authorial; unfortunately, these changes do not establish a consistent pattern of significance. The note setting up the first speech provides
the only evidence of revision per se. In the grammar error in the first line of
the note, there seems to be a trace of the manuscript used by Lichfield in
1636. The use of "ascending," which was correct enough in the 1636 text, is
clearly incorrect in the later, only partially revised, copy of 1659, which
reads, "The Hermits speech whan he ascending out of the ground . . ." (24).
This error, along with the turned *e* in "when" and the incomplete final line
of the second speech, indicates how hastily Newcombe tacked on the ex-
cerpts from the entertainment to the other documents published in *Mr Bushell's Abridgment.*

Printing *An Extract* in 1660, Thomas Leach handled the text of Bushell's
entertainment with more care: the upside-down *e* had been righted, "ascending" replaced by "ascended," and a complete copy of the several speeches
and songs included. Leach may have been working from the same manuscript
used by Newcombe, for *An Extract* incorporates the substantive variants in
lines 46, 61, and 79 and reproduces almost all of the changes in spelling and
punctuation of the 1659 text, even unusual ones such as "inhabite" with a
final *e.* This is unusual because the 1659 text reveals a concerted attempt
to simplify and modernize the spelling. This involves the elimination of the
unnecessary final *e* ("again" for "againe" [55] or "sin" for "sinne" [43])
and the regular substitution of a single consonant for a double one ("lips"
for "lipps" [28]), *v* for medial *u* ("have" for "haue" [28]), *u* for initial *v*
("utterance" for "vtterance" [28]), *i* for *y* ("lies" for "lyes" [116]), *y* for
final—*ie* ("beauty" for "beautie" [115]), *s* for final—*es* ("years" for
"yeares" [121]), *j* for *i* ("enjoy" for "enioy" [82]). The 1660 text proceeds

further in the same direction for the most part, so that "Tonmb-stone in despaire" becomes "Tomb-stone in despair" (66), "Untill" "Until" (69) "Britaines" "Britains" (74), "doteing" "doting" (120), and "wyre" "wire" (134). This version also capitalizes the first letter of more key words that the 1659 text, which capitalized more than that of 1636. In Thomas Leach's shop however, the text of the entertainment seems to have been proofread—hastily and not against copy—but proofread nonetheless, for general comprehensibility. As a result, the printer of *An Extract* corrected the error in 1. 70 of the 1659 text, clarified other lines (105, 137), properly punctuated some questions as such (116–21), and made some verbal exchanges more consistently dramatic (145, 188, 194). Presumably this reading resulted in revisions to the dialogue with Echo: as the introductory note to this speech changes its audience from the king and queen to the queen alone (181–83), so individual lines are adjusted, "her" replacing "his" (199, 210), to eliminate references to the king. However, this pattern of revision is not sustained and from line 215 on, the speech retains the plural terms found in the 1636 version ("they," "their," "this pair," and "theirs") to refer to its audience. Besides introducing this inconsistency, the 1660 text introduced new errors: "defie" for "deifie" (103), "desart a" for "a desart" (124), and "vouchsafe, and taste" for "vouchsafe to" (175). These errors along with variants in punctuation and the incomplete attempt at revision suggest that Leach's shop completed their own independent setting of the entertainment, though perhaps from the same manuscript used by Thomas Newcombe's printing house or from a scribal copy of a common original.

I have collated a scanned reproduction of the Lehigh University copy of *Mr Bushell's Abridgment* (1659) with the British Library copy of *An Extract* (1660) and the text in appendix A, which is based on all the extant copies of the 1636 edition. I have not includeed in the list of variants all the morphological variants mentioned in the preceding paragraph, variants that constitute over 90 percent of the differences. I have recorded all substantive changes as well as changes in punctuation, some of which point toward different (and not necessarily better) rhythms in the performance of the speeches. The 1636 reading appears before the square bracket, those of 1659 and 1660 after it. Because *Mr Bushell's Abridgment* included only the first two speeches, all variants noted in lines 152–290 appear only in *An Extract*.

24–25 The *Hermits* speech ascending out of the ground as the KING entred the Rock] 1659: *The* Hermits *speech when he ascending out of the ground, as the King and some of his Nobility entred Mr.* Bushells *Rock* (in which the *e* in "when" is upside-down); 1660: *The* Hermits *Speech when he ascended out of the ground, as the King and some of his Nobility entred Mr.* Bushels *Rock*

30 Noahs flood,] 1659: Noahs flood; 1660: *Noahs* flood

33 Then . . . this] 1660: Than . . . the

33–35 Holding a serpent in hi<s> hand] 1659, 1660: omitted

36 accoumpt . . . Heauens] 1659: accompt . . . Heavens; 1660: accompt . . . Heaven

43 nought,] 1659, 1660: nought

47 gratious] 1659, 1660: glorious

48 now] 1660: now,

50 sinne] 1660: sin,

52 next . . . conceau'd] 1659, 1660: next, . . . conceiv'd

54 persu'd] 1659: pursu'd; 1660: persu'd

58 he as . . . old, by . . . bound] 1659, 1660: he, as . . . old by . . . bound,

59 Adam] 1659, 1660: *Adam*

61 these] 1659, 1660: there

63 dwell.] 1659: dwell,; 1660: dwell.

66 Toumb-stone] 1659: Tonmb-stone (upside-down *u*); 1660: Tomb-stone

66 dispaire] 1659: despaire; 1660: despair

70 nature] 1659: Natures; 1660: Nature

72 before,] 1660: before;

74 you] 1660: ye

75 Ile,] 1660: Isle

76 may,] 1659: may;; 1660: may

77 mansion from decay.] 1659: mansion from decay,; 1660: mansion, from decay,

79 sinck] 1659, 1660: sink

80 Possessor] 1659: Professor; 1660: Professor

81 devotion-sake this] 1660: devotion sake the

84 health] 1659, 1660: health,

85 men:] 1660: men,

89 inhabit] 1659, 1660: inhabite

96–97 Mr BVSHELL his Contemplation vpon the Rock] 1659: *The Hermites Contemplation upon the Rock;* 1660: The *Hermits Contemplation upon the Rock*

101 sacrifice] 1660: sacrifize

102 memorie,] 1659, 1660: memory:

103 deifie] 1660: defie

105 what's] 1659: whats; 1660: what's

109 well tun'd note] 1660: well-tun'd notes

110 Master-peece . . . now] 1660: Master Piece . . . now,

119 treasurie.] 1659: treasurie,; 1660: Treasury,

120: doting] 1659: doteing; 1660: doting

121 Then . . . thousand . . . before.] 1660: Than . . . thousands . . . before?

122 selves] 1660: self

123 alive,] 1660: alive

124 a desart] 1660: desart a
126 Ile] 1660: I'le
127 treasure,] 1659: treasure.; 1660: Treasure,
128 virgin silence . . . there] 1659: virgin-silence . . . there; 1660: Virgin-silence . . . there,
129 eare] 1659: eare;; 1660: ear;
130 times] 1660: time
132 ayerie] 1660: ayry
135 quire] 1660: quire,
137 their] 1660: they
140 light heel'd streames] 1659: light-heel'd streams,; 1660: light-heel'd streams.
144 sleepe,] 1659, 1660: sleep:
145 sad,] 1660: sad?
151 with thee] 1659: added in long hand except for the initial *w*
154 1.] stanza number omitted
155 *soules*] *Soul,*
156 *poore.*] *poor,*
158 *rude;*] *rude,*
163 2.] stanza number omitted
165 *Eve:*] Eve,
166 *dares*] *dare*
167 *Whilest . . . Majesties stay*] *Whilst . . . Majesty is*
172 3.] stanza number omitted
174 *love.*] *love,*
175 *vouchsafe to taste*] *vouchsafe, and taste*
179 *Italy, and France*] Italy, France
181–83 Mr BVSHELL presenting the *Rock* by an Eccho sung to the KING and QVEENES *Majesty*] *Mr.* Bushel *presenting the Rock by an* Eccho *to the* Queen
184 *The Eccho.*] omitted
185 ECCHO . . . ECCHO] ECCHO, . . . ECCHO.
188 Pleas'd?] Pleas'd!
190 him] him;
191 Eccho, I will . . . not] Eccho I will, . . . not.
192 them] 'em
193 That, like thee, . . . reall] That like thee . . . reall;
194 why all that] Why? All what
198 pretious:] pretious;
199 his] her
200 sure;] sure,
201 both] omitted
204 aire,] air;

210 his] her
211 sea, . . . these Isles] Sea . . . the Isles
212 miles:] miles,
215 get;] get:
221 Eccho let] Eccho, let
222 thee] thee;
222 ECCHO] *Eccho* in the right column on line 222
223 granted] granted,
224 Eccho answere so] Eccho, answer so.
224] Followed by a double space
225 So, then . . . agree'd aboue] So then . . . agreed above,
226 liue, and loue:] live and love
229 newes] news,
231 theirs,] theirs;
232 Theirs Eccho, . . . mine,] Theirs, Eccho, . . . mine;
233 Theirs, and thine, Eccho euer,] Theirs and thine Eccho ever
234 decrees] decreed
236 Mr Bushells] Mr. *Bushels*
237 1.] stanza number omitted
240 *show,*] *show*
241 *know,*] *know*
247 *tell;*] *tell,*
250 2.] stanza number omitted
254 *feares*] *fears.*
258 *this*] *his*
263 3.] stanza number omitted
268 *along:*] *along;*
274 *fayne would*] *strive to*
276 4.] stanza number omitted
277 *intreat*] *intreat,*
278 *Hosts*] *Host's*
279 *pants,*] *pants*
285 *pleas'd*] *pleas'd,*
286 *eas'd*] *eas'd,*
287 *Rock . . . cave*] *Rock, . . . Cave,*
288 *Tombe*] *Tombe,*
289–90] omitted

IV: Commentary

4 presentment] exhibition and presentation, in the sense of an offering or gift
24 *Hermits* speech] preceded by an ornament across the top of the page.
Bushell specifies the philosophical hermits of Bacon's *New Atlantis* as the

source of the character, but Gough, in *The Superlative Prodigal,* observes "that the emphasis and circumstantiality of Bushell's references to Bacon's supposed behests increase proportionately as years go by with his own deepening financial embarassment" (34). The hermit was a common figure in romances and one that reappeared regularly in early modern English entertainments. One that Bushell might well have been aware of is Bacon's device for the Earl of Essex, in which the hermit is the spokesman for the benefits of a life of solitude and contemplation. For Bacon's device, see *The Works of Francis Bacon,* ed. James Spedding, et al., vol. 8 (volume 1 of "The Letters and the Life of Francis Bacon") (London: Longman, Green, Longman, and Roberts, 1862), 374–86, esp. 377–80 for speeches of "the Hermite or Philosopher, in wish of Contemplation or Studies." Given Bushell's mining interests, he may also have conceived of this hermit as a "knocker," one of those inhabitants of the underground who, it was believed, revealed to "some men of Suitable Tempers" rich veins of ore (W. Hooson, ed., *Miners Dictionary* [Wrexham, 1747]).

24 ascending] presumably the hermit interrupted the king's entry by encountering him atop the stairs that led down into the grotto; see figure 1 for a glimpse of the stairs in the right foreground.

26 bended knees] like a properly obeisant recorder of a town on the occasion of a royal visit, the hermit kneels to begin his speech

27 blessed powers] mistaking, for the purpose of compliment, the king and the queen for divine beings. The compliment is elaborated by the effects of their presence, particularly on the hermit's ability to speak. This is a traditional device of praise—the affirmation of the transformative power of the monarch's presence.

30 times Embleme] the emblem of Time is of a serpent with its tail in its mouth; since there is no distance between the serpent's head and tail, the world has no further to go in its journey. Normally the image symbolizes time's passage through daily and seasonal cycles; for a variety of interpretations of it, see George Wither, *A Collection of Emblemes, Ancient and Moderne (1635),* intro. Rosemary Freeman (Columbia: University of South Carolina Press, 1975), 92, 102, 109, and 157. For the hermit, the present moment seems to be an extension of the destruction of the world by "Noah's flood," for he has held Time's symbol since that time.

34 Earths great funerall] the Last Judgment

34 hi<s>] cropped in the BL copy

35 SIR] deliberately mistaking King Charles I for Christ, coming to call the inhabitants to account for their liives

37 daigne] condescend; vouchsafe

39 ought to speak] am duty-bound to admit; posturing as morally upright to justify Bushell's apologia pro vita sua, which follows

40 A Prodigall profuse] Thomas Bushell, resembling the prodigal son of Luke 15

41 nothing studied] applied his mind to acquiring knowledge of; this sets up the contrast between his past "studies" and his new ones in how to "redeeme the yeeres . . . lost in sinne" (49), not to mention his studies of Bacon's mineral theories

42 glorious outside] see above concerning "buttoned Bushell"

45 virtue . . . grace] conjoining classical or commonplace notions of the desirability of virtuous behavior with Protestant teaching concerning the need for grace, which is here explicitly salvific

47 gratious] kind; merciful; picking up as well the theological sense of grace, God's free and unmerited favor

50 redeeme] both to save, or expiate, and to buy back

51 to liue] implying that Bushell's reformation transformed him from a kind of death in sin to life; see, for example, Romans 6:10

53 Confession, contrition, and remorse] penitential ideals that bespeak Bushell's proper acknowledgment of his sins

53 remorse] followed by the signature number, A2, and the catchword, "These"

59 dig'd, and drest] see Genesis 2:15

60 no Riuers such as Eden had] the Garden of Eden was situated by four rivers: the Euphrates, Tigris, Pison, and Gihon (Gen. 2:11–14); here the hermit conveniently overlooks the obvious, the presence of the Glyme River running along the south edge of Bushell's estate.

62 the Owle, not Philomell] the doleful song of the solitary owl contrasts with the beautiful song of the nightingale, i.e., Philomel

65 the great deluge] the Flood; see 1. 30 above

66 Chain'd to this ROCK] alluding to the myth of Prometheus perhaps; the image certainly sets up the hermit's transformation from captivity to freedom, from despair to hope, from darkness to light, specifically the light shot from the "beames" of the king's "Virtues" (67, 68)

70 eyes] enabling him to see; the image of light and enlightenment picks up that used to represent his despair in 11. 67–68

71 grace] beautiful feature; favor

71 owe] have to pay

73 'gainst] for; this observation further aggrandizes the occasion of this occasional entertainment

74 God of Brittaines earth] not only high praise, this style for King Charles suits the subterranean work Bushell has done at Enstone and proposes to do in the mines of Wales

75 as . . . birth] a confirmation of Charles I's inalienable inheritance of kingship; a traditional trope of loyalty

76 Vouchsafe a blessing] grant a request; the religious resonance of the lan-

guage aggrandizes the monarch, since blessings were typically given by God, rulers, religious leaders, and fathers

79 sinck] submerge or bury

79 my owne] that is, this very place, his longtime prison

80 true Possessor] see introduction, n. 21

83 Build Altars] an image continuing the Noah patterns; see Gen. 8:20–21

84 his preseruers] certainly Charles I, but if understood as plural, then the queen and other supportive noblemen, such as the Earl of Danby

86 golden age] specifically characterized in this context as a time when injuries will not be done, injuries such as those perpetrated against Bushell in the development of the property at Enstone. The golden age was part of the creation myth set forth by Ovid and it served as an image of the vision of future idyllic happiness; see *The Metamorphoses* 1:89–112.

88 Such Innocents] an elaboration of the image of the golden world restored and possibly a playful characterization of Bushell, his family, and servants

89 thus] followed by the catchword, "We"

93 please a displeas'd mind] another variation on the theme of salutary transformations

95] A single horizontal line divides the hermit's speech from the one that follows.

96 Contemplation] meditation—a mode consistent with Bushell's representation of himself meditating in the solitude of the Isle of Wight, the Calf of Man, or the rock of Enstone

99 A greater power] God, here seen as a power greater than nature

102 fat of Bullocks] grain-fed, stall-kept young bulls—a special offering; see Gen. 18:7, 1 Samuel 28:24, and Luke 15:23.

103–4 But . . . seene] see Deut. 4:15–18 for evidence of the covenant between Israel and Yahweh, the unseen god, and of the consequent antagonism to idolatry

107 <From>] 1636: For

108 the Muses] as a group, renowned for excellence in singing and for inspiring poets

109 *Parnassus*] the Castalian spring near Mount Parnassus, home of Apollo and a sacred source of inspiration for the Muses

110 Master-peece] the great work of the greatest poets, the poets laureate

111 Lawrell wreath] leaves of the bay or laurel tree, worn as a crown symbolic of poetic excellence

113 painted] artificial, false; contrasting to the naturally beautiful rock

116 on's] on his, given the personification of "the world"

117 obsequies] rites or ceremonies; followed by the signature number, A3, and the catchword, "The"

119 Nature . . . treasurie] an image reinforcing the sense that the end of the

world is imminent; as the dying man opens his treasures to his heirs just before he passes away, so nature has revealed its greatest riches, Bushell's rock

120 doting] old, weak-minded

121 six thousand yeares] an estimate of the age of the world derived from
analysis of biblical texts; Bushell may be relying on Archbishop Ussher who
ultimately calculated that God completed creation on 23 October 4004 B.C.

121 before] 1636: followed by a period; 1660: question mark

124 desart] deserted, isolated, uninhabited, and, given the attractiveness of
the sound of water (125), arid

125 sad] grave, serious

127 The Indies] in this context, Indies East and West. In his published efforts
to win support for his mining projects, Bushell focused on the West Indies,
arguing that King Henry VII had foolishly lost them. King Charles I, however, might find a site similarly rich in natural resources in Welsh and English
mining regions that Bushell proposed to develop; see, for instance, *A Just
and True Remonstrance of His Maiesties Mines Royall in the Principality of
Wales* (London: E. G., 1642), sig. A4.

131 plaine song] the simple melody

132 ayerie Choristers] the artificial birds as singers or choir members; "ayerie" puns on the air occupied by birds in flight, the airs or melodies sung by
the birds, and the air forced through the devices that produce the birdsong

132 division] "a rapid melodic passage, originally conceived as the dividing
of each of a succession of long notes into several short ones" (*OED, sb.* 1.7);
the synchronization of the plainsong of the spring with the songs of the birds
(130–32) alludes nicely to the hydraulic mechanism by which their sounds
are produced.

134 strings] as if the rock itself were a musical instrument, a stringed one

135 consort] to play music with

135 quire] choir

136 raise] build, assemble

137 <they>] as in *An Extract* (1660); 1636: "their"

138 on wing] in flight, in the air (like birds)

139 rais'd . . . whispering] sung out boldly rather than softly and timidly

143 Chymes] perhaps another water-driven device built into the rock, or a
metaphorical reference to the mechanical birds that, like monastic bells, regularly call people to prayer

146 every object] given the pervasive dampness of the place, any object will
provide a lesson in weeping

151 ENSTON] a name varying the theme of rocks/stones

151 three.] followed by the catchword, "A"

152 A Sonnet] preceded by an ornament across the top of the page

152 within the pillar] perhaps with the singer standing in the opening in the

middle of a circular or semicircular table, not in the grotto but in the main
room in the banqueting house above

155 *blest soules*] the king, queen, and attendants

155 *no more*] modifying "Feede"

156 *what is poore*] a conventional trope of humility, for what is called poor
here has been praised as marvelous; see also ll. 163, 170, and 176 for similar
posturing

159 *in a trice*] by one act; in an instant

160 *Chaos paradise*] lofty praise, to liken the impact of the visit of Charles
and Henrietta Maria to the creation of the world; this turn of phrase coheres
with the subseqent portrayal of Enstone as Eden (170)

164 *golden apples*] alluding to the "apple of discord" that Eris threw into
the gathering celebrating the wedding of Thetis and Peleus. Bearing the inscription, "to the fairest," the divisive golden apple led to Paris's judgment
as to which of the goddesses (Juno, Pallas, or Venus) was the most beautiful
and to the Trojan War.

169 *first fruits*] the earliest and the best, hence appropriate ones for sacrifices
or for honored guests. Bushell may have offered fruits grown on the property,
for his planting included various kinds of fruit trees (Hammond, "Short Survey," 82–83).

179 *Italy, and France, and Spaine*] major exporters of fruit to England

180 *vaine.*] followed by the catchword, "Mr"

181 Mr BVSHELL] preceded by an ornament across the top of the page

182 Eccho] John Hollander, *The Figure of Echo: A Mode of Allusion in Milton and After* (Berkeley and Los Angeles: University of California Press,
1981), 8, describes "rocky caves" as the "canonical domain" of the spurned
nymph, Echo. The royal party may have returned to the grotto for this part
of the entertainment, where the space itself could produce the necessary echoes or where, for greater clarity, a performer hidden in one of the rooms behind the rock could deliver Echo's replies.

185 ECCHO] presumably this is part of the speech, the call for Echo
prompting Echo's response, by which she identifies herself and announces
her presence; she remains invisible, like "aire" (193). Here and below (222),
the "ECCHO" in the right column also identifies the speaker of the words in
that column.

187 ought] aught, anything

188 Pleas'd<!>] parallel with other exchanges in this dialogue (189–90,
197–8, 199–200) where a question prompts a statement from Echo; the reading in *An Extract* (1660) is here preferred to that of 1636: "Pleas'd?"

191 that he dispaire not] the transformative powers of the royal couple may
impinge upon Bushell's life; this introduces another little story line, one that
should take him, like the hermit (66 n), from despair to hope; see the final
verse of the concluding song in this regard as well.

203 Then] large capital "T" occupying two lines; "H" in small caps

206 Girles, and Boyes] praise of family life customary in Caroline entertainments

210 wast] waste away, or wane

212 miles:] followed by the catchword, "And"

216 pay natures debt] die

218 sluttish] unclean, dirty

219 translated] carried or conveyed

222 Poasted] carried or conveyed quickly

234 neuer.] followed by an ornament across the page

235 Sonnet] song, a song that calls attention to various aspects of the estate as it personifies them. The first two stanzas would work well if performed in the grotto, "cell" (246), or "cave" (258), but the third stanza offers a wider view of the grounds. Presumably the singer performed at a place from which he could direct attention to the rock, the waters, the groves, and the royal couple's host on this occasion.

239 *their tongues to unlock*] paralleling the hermit's recovery of speech at the outset (28)

241 *know,*] followed by the signature number, B, and the catchword, *"Of"*

244 *Daigne<d>*] 1636: Daigne; graciously agreed

253 *Vent*] express

265 *tender*] offer; communicate

266 *spring*] a metaphor for the joyful season the royal couple has brought

272–73 *On each banck. . Thrush*] perhaps artificial song birds, perhaps real ones, adorned the landscape and chirped airs of gratitude

274 *fayne*] eagerly

275 *thankefullnesse.*] followed by the catchword, *"Harke"*

289–90 The Musick . . . IVE.] set off by horizontal lines above and below the item

291 FINIS.] followed by an ornament filling the white space to the bottom of the page

Appendix B

I: Note on the Text

The British Library copy of *Wit in a Wilderness of Promiscuous Poetry* (11623.aa.17) served as the copy text. I checked for variants a microfilm of the Huntington Library copy, and I am grateful to my colleague, Dr. Sarah Tolmie, for checking the Houghton Library, Harvard University, copy. We found neither variants nor stop-press corrections among the three copies of Jordan's book listed in Wing's *Short-Title Catalogue*. The following tran-

scription preserves the spelling, capitalization, punctuation, typefaces, line
breaks, and format of the original.

II: The Text

A Poem composed, and spoken by the Author to the
late King at the Dedication of Mr. Tho. Bushel's
Rock at Enston in Oxon, 1638. in
the person of Caliope.

5   Loe I *Caliope* chief of the Nine
        And first in order of that triple Trine;
        The Muses *Sisterhood*; (for who is he
        That knows not of our sacred *Hierarchy*)
        Am now at length, through many a weary mile
10   Safely arriv'd upon the *British Isle:*
        The causes of my coming, what they were
        That drew me to this Western *Hemisphere,*
        Are these, the Muses heard (for nothing's done
        Which they discern not in a Vision)
15   Of a strange Rock discover'd under ground,
        That with fresh streams and wonders doth abound,
        Which *Nature* unto such perfection brought,
        It looks like *day* from the old *Chaos* wrought;
        And hath the *Pomp* and pleasures of the place
20   That a great King and Queen have daign'd to grace,
        And with their presence (far transcending ours)
        Oft visit those pure Wells and hallowed Bowers:
        When these glad tydings from our Servant Fame
        Were whisper'd in our eare, I strait way came
25   In person mounted on the fiery wings
        Of our owne *Pegasus,* to view these *Springs,*
        To make a strict survay what waters flow,
        What walks are in it, and what woods doe grow;
        And (as I liked them) they (on my report)
30   Would hither come, and hasten their resort:
        But 'tis known Maids may long, and I would fain,
        (Ere my return) first see that *Soveraigne,*
        That Royall *Charlemaine* whose actions are
        Worthy the Muses and their *Register;*
35   Whose deeds a Patern, and whose life a Law,
        Doth the whole Court to imitation draw
        Of his rare virtues, (without flattery)
        The height of my ambition is to be
        Made happy in the object of his sight
40   And his dear *Spouse* the Consort of his light;

Kiss her faire hand, who is (as Fame doth say)
More bright then is our owne *Urania:*
But stay! what sudden lustre strikes my sence
With some quick, but *Seraphick* influence?
45   Who ever ask'd for *Phoebus* in the Skyes,
Or which was *Iove* amongst the *Deities?*
Foole that I am, 'tis easie to devine,
Where e're the Beames of Majesty doe shine:
Then I address my self great Sir to you,
50   To whom these Titles and these Rites are due:
By me the Muses humbly fall before
Your sacred feet, and prostrate them adore,
Vowing their antient dwellings to forsake,
That they your Princely favours may partake:
55   *Ida, Parnassus,* and the flowry *Plain*
Of *Thessaly* no longer shall detain
Their swift approach, but all the Virgin Pack
In glory seated on the winged back
Of firtil *Zephyrus,* shall hither come,
60   And make these Springs their everlasting home;
Here will they sit, and Carol forth your Fame,
Your nursing Nature, and your noble Name:
Then in exalted numbers tell how great
You are, when mounted in your Mercy seat;
65   And that this pregnant Isle you do inherit,
Not more by right of Bloud, then right of Merit
Could you disclaim the line of your extraction,
And (amongst millions) stand for *Saul's* election,
It would appear conspicuous to beholders,
70   That you excell in soul, as he in shoulders:
This Trinity of Crowns you wear, respect
Your will, your memory, and intellect;
(The number of perfection) for you are
The Muses Evening, and their Morning Star.

III: Commentary

4 Caliope] Muse of epic or heroic poetry
5 chief of the Nine] the preeminence of Calliope in the hierarchy of Muses originates with Hesiod, *Theogony,* ll. 75–80; M. L. West, in his edition of this work (Oxford: Clarendon Press, 1966), 181 (l. 80 note), explains that "Calliope is the most important of the Muses, because she has tutelage of kings." See Hesiod, *Theogony, Works and Days, Shield,* trans. Apostolos N. Athanassakis (Baltimore: Johns Hopkins University Press, 1983), ll. 1–115, esp. 75–80 for the naming of the Muses, with Calliope listed in the climactic final position and described as "preeminent by far" (l. 79). See also Ovid,

Metamorphoses, 5:252-f, for a myth in which Calliope serves as the representative of the other Muses and in which her superiority is acknowledged.

6 triple Trine] triple threesome; the nine Muses

18 *Chaos*] alluding to Genesis 1:1–3

19 *Pomp*] magnificence

23 Fame] messenger of the gods

24 strait way] straitaway; immediately

26 our owne *Pegasus*] mythical winged horse that created Hippocrene, the "Horse's Spring" on Mount Helicon, for the Muses by stamping his hoof on the ground; see Ovid, *Metamorphoses,* 5:252–f.

28 What walks . . . what woods] see Hammond, "Short Survey," 82–83, for observations on these features of Bushell's estate.

30 resort] their move to Enstone

33 *Charlemaine*] Charles I, here likened to one of the Nine Worthies

34 *Register*] record book

40 *Spouse*] Queen Henrietta Maria

42 *Urania*] muse of astronomy, associated with the brilliance of the stars

44 quick] lively

44 *Seraphick*] heavenly

45 *Phoebus*] Apollo as sun-god; the sun obviously being in the sky, the question is rhetorical.

55–56 *Ida, Parnassus . . . Thessaly*] traditional dwelling places and sources of inspiration of the Muses

59 firtil *Zephyrus*] the warm, gentle wind of spring

61 Carol] sing, perhaps with a pun on the Latin form of Charles

64 your Mercy seat] a high compliment; Charles I combines might with mercy and thereby embodies one of the ideals of monarchs.

65 preganant] fruitful; bountiful—an image of Great Britain that coheres with the representation of Charles I as having a "nursing Nature" (62)

67 disclaim] nullify your claim

67 line of your extraction] lineage

68 *Saul's* election] 1 Samuel 10:24

70 shoulders] Saul was literally head and shoulders above all others; see 1 Samuel 9:2 and 10.23.

71 respect] with respect to; symbolizing

73 number of perfection] three, picking up the image of the "Trinity of Crowns" (71), the trinity of qualities with which King Charles is crowned

Notes

I am grateful to Rosalind Hays and Barbara Palmer for the opportunity to present an earlier version of this paper at the International Medieval Congress at the University of Leeds in July 2001. Those who heard the paper there and others who read later drafts of it helped me greatly, in particular Martin Butler, Philip Butterworth, Ken Graham, Lynn Hulse, Janelle Jenstad, David Klausner, Grace and Harry Logan, John Meagher, and Paul Stevens. Librarians at Edinburgh University, Lehigh University, and Yale generously provided information that I would not have been able to obtain otherwise. St. Jerome's University and the Social Sciences and Humanities Research Council of Canada provided indispensable and timely research support.

1. *Calendar of State Papers, Domestic Series, of the Reign of Charles I. 1635,* ed. John Bruce (London: HMSO, 1865), 366 (vol. 297, no. 6): a letter from the King to Henry Danvers, Early of Danby, dated 3 September 1635, ordering Danby to see to it that the highway be rerouted "for better enabling Bushell's endeavours."

2. E. A. J. Honigmann, ed. "The Masque of Flowers," in *A Book of Masques in Honour of Allardyce Nicoll,* ed. T. J. B. Spencer and Stanley Wells (Cambridge: Cambridge University Press, 1967), 156, notes this possibility along with the possibility that Thomas Bushell may have been one of the authors of *The Masque of Flowers,* the "T.B." who signed the dedication of the masque book. "Mr Bvshell his Contemplation" of the 1636 text bears the title "The Hermites Contemplation" when the speech was published again in 1659 and 1660. This may suggest that Bushell wrote the speech that the actor playing the hermit delivered, or, in blurring the distinction between himself and the hermit of Enstone rock, it may be yet another instance of Bushell's ongoing effort to construct himself as a hermit.

3. On Ives, see *The New Grove Dictionary of Music and Musicians,* ed. Stanley Sadie, 2nd ed., 20 vols. (London: Macmillan, 1991), vol. 12; on royal musicians providing music for dramatic entertainments on royal visits, see Julia K. Wood, "Music in Caroline Plays," Ph.D. thesis, University of Edinburgh (1991), especially 1:56–57; concerning Ives, see appendix A.

4. John Aubrey, *Brief Lives,* ed. Richard Barber (London: Folio Society, 1975), 58. Goodall may be the "Goodale" whose instrumental piece survives in Christ Church Manuscript 1022, no. 90. I am grateful to Julia Wood for drawing attention to this information and for suggesting the possibility that arrangements for the music in Bushell's entertainment were made not by Bushell, but by representatives of the court involved in planning the king and queen's trip to Woodstock, Enstone, Aristotle's Wells, and Oxford University. William Lawes was writing some of the music for *The Royal Slave,* performed at Christ Church the week after the royal visit to Bushell's rock, that is, on 29 and 30 August. As a result, he was in a position to know musicians there, such as Goodall and Aubrey's unidentified student, who might help Bushell with his entertainment. Lawes also knew Simon Ives, a friend and a collaborator on *The Triumph of Peace.* What little we know about the performers of Bushell's show suggests that it was a court entertainment in the country, rather than a manor house show or an urban royal entry like those produced for Queen Elizabeth I. Like those shows however, Bushell's entertainment depends upon his peculiar aims and the peculiar geography of the place.

5. See Gerald Eades Bentley, *The Jacobean and Caroline Stage,* 7 vols. (Oxford: Clarendon, 1941–68), 4:487, and, especially, Lynn Hulse, ed. *Cavalier Songs: Thomas Jordan's Collection,* Renaissance Texts from Manuscript, ed. Marie Axton (Cambridge: Cambridge University Press, 2003), forthcoming. Bushell and Jordan

later crossed paths, when the latter wrote "A Song, sung by Mr. Bushell's Miners in Devonshire" (1645), published in *Claraphil and Clarinda: in a Forest of Fancies* (London: R. Wood, [1670?]), D5r–D6r.

6. Lines 1–3; references to other lines from Calliope's speech appear in parentheses. The reason that this speech can only "probably" be assigned to the 1636 entertainment is that Jordan goes on to date the dedication of the site and the delivery of the speech "1638." Although I have found no evidence that the king and queen visited Bushell's rock that year, the king did come to Woodstock, which is only five miles from Enstone, late in the summer. Because people knew that he planned to do so (*Calendar of State Papers, Domestic, 1637–1638,* 604 and 606 [vol. 397, nos. 81, 87, 88]), the opportunity to provide a theatrical device did exist. However, assuming that the "Presentment" and the "Dedication" are the same event, it is likelier that Thomas Jordan erred in noting the year than that he erred in noting the occasion of the performance of the speech. Lynn Hulse, *Cavalier Songs,* has found other instances of Jordan assigning incorrect dates to occasional poems. An error of memory is understandable in this instance: *Wit in a Wilderness of Promiscuous Poetry,* undated, was published at least seventeen years after Bushell's entertainment at Enstone, for it includes an epitaph to a man who died in 1653; indeed the British Library copy (11623.aa.17) gives the date of publication as "1665?".

7. The description of Bushell's rock, banqueting house, and estate is based on the account of Lieutenant Hammond, of Norwich, in "A Relation of a Short Survey of the Western Counties made by a Lieutenant of the Military Company in Norwich in 1635," ed. L. G. Wickham Legg, Camden Third Series, vol. 52, *Camden Miscellany 16* (London: Royal Historical Society, 1936), 81–83. Hammond toured the site in September 1635, shortly after King Charles and a number of noblemen visited and approved of Mr. Bushell's development of it (see n. 1). Hammond's description is of singular importance, since it alone provides details of how Bushell had developed the site by the time of the king and queen's visit. Anthony a Wood, *Athenae Oxoniensis,* 3rd ed. with additions, ed. Philip Bliss (London: T. Davison, 1817), cols. 1007–10, clearly errs in stating that Bushell developed the site within a year following the king's visit in 1635. I have found no evidence to confirm Roy Strong's assertion that "work began on all this [rock, grotto, waterworks, gardens] in 1628" (*The Renaissance Garden in England* [London: Thames and Hudson, 1979], 132). Bushell appears in the Enstone Parish Register in 1626; he and his wife Isabel baptized a son, Francis, on 8 June that year (and buried the baby on 30 October). Given that loss and the death of Sir Francis Bacon, Bushell sought out an isolated cell on the Calf of Man (not on the Isle of Lundy as Strong [130] notes), but he never makes it quite clear when he left his life of solitude there and returned to Oxfordshire.

8. Robert Plot, *The Natural History of Oxford-shire, Being an Essay toward the Natural History of England* (Oxford: The Theatre, 1676), 239.

9. Quoted by Per Palme, *Triumph of Peace: A Study of the Whitehall Banqueting House* (Stockholm: Almquist & Wiksell, 1957), 66.

10. This estimate of the height splits the difference between Hammond's observation that the rock was "some 11. or 12. Foote high" ("Short Survey," 81) and Plot's description of the addition of four feet of lead and stone to a rock that was originally ten feet tall (*Natural History,* 238).

11. In *A Parochial History of Enstone, in the County of Oxford* (London: John Russell Smith; Oxford: Henry Alden, 1857), 19, Rev. John Jordan reports that builders, "digging the foundation of the small house that stands on the left hand side of the road, at the top of the hill going out of Neat Enstone, towards Chipping Norton," uncovered some of the pipes, "made of freestone and carefully cemented together," by which Bushell brought water to his estate. In 1857 that house had "an unfailing well within it, of most excellent water, derived from the very spring, and brought by the very pipes, that originally fed the once celebrated property." That spring along with others to the east and northeast of Bushell's property is shown on the Ordnance Survey Map of 1881. However, the building done by Bushell, both the waterworks and the house, had been demolished by 1857. Some of the stone Bushell had used was probably reused in the construction of "a modest house," still called "Wells Cottage," on the land Bushell had developed (Graham Binns, *The Story of Enstone* [The Enstone Local History Circle, 1999], 19). Renovations to that home in the early 1950s led to the discovery of what appears to be another trace of Bushell's waterworks. The builders unearthed two stones, "circular and about 6 ft. in diameter (?resembling millstones). One had a round hole in its center and a square hole along a radius. Over the square hole was a flat stone which could be inserted in the hole; when this was done water came up in a fountain from the center hole. This would appear to be," R. T. Lattey noted in 1952, "a remnant of Thomas Bushell's Waterworks" (MS. Note, Ref. No. ORCC 46, Local History Section, Oxford Central Library).

12. Hammond, "Short Survey," 81.

13. Hammond, "Short Survey," 81.

14. Hammond, "Short Survey," 82.

15. A facsimile of the 1634 edition has been published in The English Experience series, no. 845 (Amsterdam: Theatrum Orbis Terrarum; Norwood, N.J.: Walter J. Johnson, 1977); see especially 18–23. The new section "Of Voices, Calles, Cryes, and Sounds" occupies pp. 82–86 of John Bate's *The Mysteries of Nature and Art,* 2nd ed. (London, [T. Harper] for R. Mabb, 1635). See also Isaac de Caus, *Wilton Garden: New and Rare Inventions of Water-Works* (New York: Garland, 1982), esp. pp. 20–21 and plates 6 and 7.

16. *An Extract by Mr. Bushell of his late Abridgment of the Lord Chancellor Bacons Philosophical Theory in Mineral Prosecutions* (London: Thomas Leach, 1660), "Postscript," 21, which Rev. Abraham de la Prynne paraphrases in his not altogether trustworthy "Memoir of Thomas Bushell 'The Recluse of the Calf,'" *Manx Miscellanies II,* ed. William Harrison, The Manx Society 30 (1880), 18. Roy Strong, who discusses Bushell's rock in *The Renaissance Garden in England* as an example of "the very real interconnection that existed between the development of garden delights and scientific advance in seventeenth-century England," suggests that the development of Bushell's estate may have been influenced by the *New Atlantis,* which had been published for the first time in 1627. In Bacon's fictional island, as Strong notes, they had houses in which they imitated natural phenomena, such as "snow, hail, rain, . . . thunders, lightenings" (131, 133). Strong may well be correct about Bushell's indebtedness to this particular work of Bacon, for Solomon's House also had deep caves where long-lived hermits lived, artificial wells and fountains, experimental orchards, and "sound-houses" where the sounds of birds and beasts were imi-

tated and "divers strange and artificial echos" produced; see the "New Atlantis," in *The Works of Francis Bacon,* ed. James Spedding, Robert Leslie Ellis, and Douglas Denon Heath, 14 vols. (London: Longman and Co. et al., 1859), 3:156–63. See also n. 22 below.

17. For the mirrors, see Hammond, "Short Survey," 82, and Plot, *Natural History,* 238; for the pool, perhaps a later feature of the waterworks, see Aubrey, *Brief Lives,* 58, Plot, *Natural History,* 242, and figure 3, where the little pool is shown directly in front of the banqueting house.

18. Hammond, "Short Survey," 82.

19. Hammond, "Short Survey," 82; Plot, *Natural History,* 244.

20. "Short Survey," 82, provides these details of the interior of the banqueting house and this interpretation of it.

21. "Short Survey," 83. "Proiecticall" is an apt term to describe Thomas Bushell at this time, for he was a member of the controversial Soapboilers of Westminster monopoly and a farmer of the silk industry attempting to control the dying of silk; see Gough, *The Superlative Prodigal: A Life of Thomas Bushell,* University of Bristol Studies, no. 1 (Bristol: University of Bristol, 1932), 19–22. Probably early in 1637, he and Captain Thomas Whitmore also received a grant from the Crown for their invention of a way of separating silver from lead by using water rather than fire (*Calendar of State Papers, Domestic Series, of the Reign of Charles I. 1637–1638,* ed. John Bruce [London, HMSO, 1869], 58 [vol. 375, no. 52]). The ownership of the property which Bushell developed remains a mystery. While Hammond asserts that it was "another Mans Freeold," the Hermit in the first speech of the entertainment says that Bushell "purchas'd" (56) the land and refers to him as "the humble Owner" (69) and the "true Possessor" (80) of it. Perhaps Bushell purchased the property some time between Hammond's visit and King Charles's. Perhaps the ownership of the property was still at issue in 1636; if so, then the hermit's representation of Bushell may be a form of lobbying aimed at settling the ownership dispute in Bushell's favor. Calling Bushell the "true Possessor" of the estate may have been, under the circumstances, the most accurate, exact, legalistic usage, a possessor being one who, in a legal sense, takes, occupies, or holds something without being its owner.

22. Bushell's image may be an allusion to the story of the hermit of the entertainment, who refers to the cave as his "grave" and his "urn" (64, 94) and the rock as his "Toumb-stone" (65). Robert Graves, taking literally what Bushell presents metaphorically, imagines the hermit arising out of his urn (apparently a coffin, where he sleeps "as a perpetual reminder to himself of our common mortality"), delivering his speech, and then clambering back into it before emphatically closing the lid. For the novelist's fanciful account of the event, see *The Story of Marie Powell, Wife to Mr. Milton* (London: Cassell and Company, 1943), 37–44; the phrase quoted is on p. 40. Because the hermit represents Bushell himself, the character's resurrection may have been understood as a metaphor both for Bushell's delivery of the rock from the underground and for his personal transformation. Bushell certainly thought in these terms; in *Mr. Bushell's Quaeres,* a broadside ostensibly published in Antwerp in 1665, he argues that the recovery of "drowned and deserted mineral works" by "penitent convicted persons" will be seen as "miraculous evidence of Gods Omnipotency to raise the dead," reverse the fall of angels, and convert impudent atheists. See also Bacon's

New Atlantis in his *Works,* ed. Spedding, et al., for the experimental use of animals, including "resuscitating of some that seem dead in appearance' (3.159).

23. For example, see the alternate endings of Sir Philip Sidney's "Lady of May" of 1578 (Robert Kimbrough and Philip Murphy, "The Helmingham Hall Manuscript of Sidney's *The Lady of May:* A Commentary and Transcription," *Renaissance Drama,* n.s. 1 [1968]: 103–19); or the competing appeals of the Soldier and the Scholar at the conclusion of Middleton and Rowley's *The World Tossed at Tennis* (1621), ed. C. E. McGee, in the *The Collected Works of Thomas Middleton,* Gary Taylor, gen. ed. (Oxford University Press, forthcoming); or the entertainment, proposed in a letter to Sir Robert Cecil in 1594 by Arthur Throckmorton, in which he was to prostrate himself before Queen Elizabeth and not arise until she granted him the pardon he sought (R. Kreuger, ed., *The Poems of John Davies* [Oxford: Clarendon Press, 1975], 407).

24. *Calendar of State Papers, Domestic Series, of the Reign of Charles I. 1635,* ed. John Bruce (London: HMSO, 1865), 366 (vol. 297, no. 6).

25. *Calendar of State Papers, Domestic Series, of the Reign of Charles I. 1637,* ed. John Bruce (London: HMSO, 1868), 198 (vol. 361, no. 31). See also *An Extract,* 48–49, for a copy of a letter from Charles I promising Bushell protection and support for his mining projects in Wales, a letter entered in the Signet Book on 23 February 1636/7.

26. F. J. North, *Mining for Metals in Wales* (Cardiff: Amgueddfa Genedlaethol Cymru/National Museum of Wales, 1962), 35. North goes on to suggest that during the civil war Bushell's "profits enabled him to clothe the army and lend the King a considerable sum of money" (42), but in his service to the king, Bushell must have extended his credit where his purse would not stretch, for he admits to being £40,000 in debt when he negotiated the surrender of the Isle of Lundy in 1647 ("Thomas Bushell's Articles for the Surrender of the Isle of Lundy," in *Mr Bushell's Abridgment of the Lord Chancellor Bacons Philosophical Theory in Mineral Prosecutions* [London: Thomas Newcombe, 1659], sig. A4). See also Gough, *Superlative Prodigal,* 55–56.

27. The "new" ideas for draining and ventilating mines, ideas that Bushell in his later writings attributed to Bacon with increasing regularity, had been applied in Germany "since the end of the 13th century" (North, *Mining for Metals,* 39; figures 1 and 2). For the use of such devices in English and Welsh mines, see J. U. Nef, "The Progress of Technology and the Growth of Large-Scale Industry in Great Britain, 1540–1640," *The Economic History Review* 5 (1934–35): 9–11. W. J. Lewis, in "Some Aspects of Lead Mining in Cardiganshire in the Sixteenth and Seventeenth Centuries," *Ceredigion* 1, no. 2 (1957): 177–92 (especially 184–88) provides a fair assessment of Bushell's contributions to the development of mining in Wales. Almost every writer who discusses the relationship between Bushell and Sir Francis Bacon accuses the former of some legerdemain in his use of the name of the latter; a notable exception is Nieves Mathews, *Francis Bacon: The History of a Character Assassination* (New Haven: Yale University Press, 1996).

28. *Calendar of State Papers, Domestic Series, of the Reign of Charles I. 1636–1637,* ed. John Bruce (London: HMSO, 1867), 385 (vol. 344, no. 88).

29. Ibid., 169 (vol. 334, no. 26). In Bushell's petition, dated 22 October 1636, he

argues that he has bought the lease on the silver mines in Cardiganshire from Lady Elizabeth Middleton so that "by way of adit" he "may make it a work *worthy of the royal name*" (my emphasis).

30. *An Extract,* "Postscript," 22; my emphasis.

31. Ibid., 31.

32. Bushell first published Broadway's letter in *A Iust and True Remonstrance of His Maiesties Mines Royall in the Principality of Wales* [London: E. G., 1642], sig. D3v).

33. Henry Ellis, ed., *Original Letters Illustrative of English History,* 2nd series, 4 vols. (London, 1827; New York: AMS, 1970), 3:312–13

34. Aubrey, *Brief Lives,* 56; *The Court and Times of James the First,* comp. Thomas Birch, 2 vols. (1849; New York: AMS, 1973), 2:242: letter from Rev. Joseph Mead to Sir Martin Stuteville, 24 March 1621.

35. Gough, *Superlative Prodigal,* 6.

36. *An Extract,* "Postscript," 20.

37. William Blundell, *A History of the Isle of Man Written by William Blundell, Esq. of Crosby, Co. Lancaster 1648–1656,* ed. William Harrison, Manx Society 25 (1876): 34.

38. *An Extract,* 17; see also pp. 30 and 33 of this work for other versions of this episode of his life.

39. Aubrey, *Brief Lives,* 57.

40. Plot, *Natural History,* 236.

41. "The Impressa of Mr. Bushels Golden Medal" was published on the title page and on a leaf at the end of *Mr Bushell's Abridgment* (1659) and on an unnumbered leaf between Bushell's "Abridgement of Mr. Bacon's *New Atlantis*" and the "Postscript" to *An Extract.* See "Francis Bacon and Thomas Bushell," *The Book-Worm,* n.s. 10 (October 1869): 142–44, for a reproduction of the picture of the medal and the suggestion that Bushell's unprofitable mining projects were a cause of the relative poverty in which Bacon died. Gough, *Superlative Prodigal,* 94–96 also reproduces the design of the medal and discusses the minting of it.

42. *An Extract,* 29.

43. *An Extract,* 33.

44. *Mr Bushell's Abridgment,* sig. A4 of "To the Reader," which is the first of three quires all identified as sig. A.

45. See Gough, *Superlative Prodigal,* 58-f.

46. Petition of Thomas Deacon and Nicholas Corselles (28 May 1646), Historical Manuscripts Commission, *Sixth Report* (London, HMSO, 1878), appendix, p. 118. The document recapitulates the effort of these two merchants of London to obtain the 1250 tons of lead that they purchased from Bushell in 1640.

47. Aubrey, *Brief Lives,* 56.

The Insatiate Countess: Date, Topicality, and Company Appropriation

CHARLES CATHCART

THE Insatiate Countess was published in 1613 with the claim that it had been performed at the Whitefriars theater. The title-page attribution to John Marston of this first quarto is belied by the existence of one copy containing a cancel-leaf stating that the play was written "By *Lewis Machin,* and *William Bacster.*"[1] The alternative attributions are paralleled by the play's most recent editions. Giorgio Melchiori's ascription of the play to "John Marston and others" is balanced by the formula used by Martin Wiggins: "William Barksted and Lewis Machin (from a draft by John Marston)."[2] Legal pressures perhaps forced the alteration to the quarto of 1613.[3] Theoretical perspectives may lie behind the divergent modern title pages.[4] Yet there is little disagreement among scholars as to the broad lines of the play's authorship: Marston composed a draft of the play, and this was expanded and altered by Barksted, by Machin, and perhaps by other writers.[5] But when did the playwriting take place? And for which companies? And could the answers to these questions cast light upon "perhaps the most puzzling play of the Jacobean age"?[6]

This essay will argue that they can. It will contend that the play was first written in or soon after 1601, probably during the time of Marston's connection with the Children of Paul's; that its first published text reflects a version prepared with a view to performance at Whitefriars by the Children of the King's Revels; that the comic underplot alludes to the rivalry between Marston and Jonson known to us as the "War of the Theaters"; and that the homoerotic undertones of this plot are likely to have been exploited by the King's Revels on acquiring the play. Essentially, the two layers of composition reveal the illuminating appropriation by one company of material designed for another.[7]

Marston's work, it is usually thought, took place at the end of his writing career and was interrupted by his imprisonment in June 1608.[8] The Whitefriars performances, for which Barksted and Machin treated the playscript, may have been played by either the Children of the King's Revels or the following tenants, the Queen's Revels. Jean MacIntyre has raised the possibility that the script may have gone from one company to the other "with its principal reviser William Barkstead."[9]

81

Although the text of the play and the circumstances of its composition have received outstanding scholarly attention, there is a danger that we will accept an incorrect date for its first layer of writing, and an inaccurate understanding of the theatrical provenance of the different stages of its inception. In suggesting that *The Insatiate Countess* was first drafted around 1601 and that its adaptation was carried out with a view to performance by the King's Revels, this essay will necessarily challenge the views of Giorgio Melchiori, its Revels Plays editor, who believes *The Insatiate Countess* to have indeed been first conceived at the close of Marston's career, and of Mary Bly, the commentator upon the repertoire and playwriting practices of the King's Revels company, who considers the play to have been revised for that company's successors as tenants of the Whitefriars theater: the Children of the Queen's Revels.[10]

William Ingram has argued that the King's Revels syndicate must have collapsed by the middle of 1608. "At some point during the spring or summer of 1608, the syndicate must have given over the operation. It may well have been in April, shortly after the performance of *Byron* by the Children of Blackfriars that caused the King to close that playhouse and apparently the other playhouses in London as well."[11] Melchiori, believing that the King's Revels operated until 1609, considered that an abandonment by Marston of an unfinished script in 1608 was consistent with signs that associates of the King's Revels treated such a script with a view to performance by that company. Melchiori does not commit himself to the view that the performances mentioned on the play's title pages necessarily refer to a production by that company: "Machin's re-working, if meant for the King's Revels, would have taken place in 1608 and early 1609."[12] Nevertheless, his account is untroubled by any sense of the difficulties involved in reconciling a script abandoned either at the time of an offense (March 1608) or an imprisonment (June 1608) with revising activity undertaken on behalf of a company whose collapse was occurring at the same time. Following Ingram's research, the most sensible account to be made is the following: if it can be shown that *The Insatiate Countess* was left unfinished as Marston was imprisoned, then it must have been completed with a view to performance by the Queen's Revels; or, conversely, if the Whitefriars performances occurred under the aegis of the King's Revels, then Marston's share must have been written well before the summer of 1608.

Bly takes the first view—"given the extremely short acting history of the King's Revels, the play was probably acted by the Queen's Revels"—and indeed, on the usual view of Marston's career, she is correct to link the play with the later Whitefriars tenants.[13] It is a view supported by our knowledge that Barksted acted in plays staged by the Queen's Revels at Whitefriars. Bly offers further evidence to tally with this ascription to the Queen's Revels. Bly's important, persuasive, and thoroughly documented thesis is that King's

Revels playtexts, through their punning emphasis upon homoerotic bawdy, and through the repeated foregrounding of the potential for sodomitical acts which the Whitefriars boys (whether playing boys, men, or women) display, evidence "a marginal theatre celebrating marginal practices, queer puns, and cross-dressed boys."[14] *The Insatiate Countess,* it is suggested, does not conform to this repertory style. Bly draws attention to the way in which the prospect that the husbands of Abigail and Thais will "come in at the back-doors" is countered by the reply: "Nay, and they come not in at the fore-doors, there will no pleasure in't" (2.2.68–70).[15] The bawdy meaning is clear. The preference for vaginal penetration, with its affirmation of female role rather than male actor, contrasts with the celebration of anal penetration manifested by the King's Revels plays, with its concomitant emphasis upon the boy actor playing the (male or female) character on stage. *The Insatiate Countess's* allusions to the Hero and Leander story, moreover, downplay rather than (as with those of *The Turk*) accentuate the homoeroticism to be found in Marlowe's poem. The signs that *The Insatiate Countess* diverges from a disciplined adherence to the company manner of the King's Revels plays dovetail with the external evidence which makes the Queen's Revels the likely sponsors of the play. To be sure, as Melchiori shows, *The Insatiate Countess* is suffused with verbal parallels with almost every King's Revels play, but this may be explained by Barksted's attested scriptwriting role.[16]

The play's bawdy material, however, admits of another interpretation. The erotic wordplay just cited concerns two women whose husbands, Claridiana and Rogero, have failed to consummate their marriages: indeed, they are more concerned with their attempts to cuckold one another. This yearning for sexual gratification by inexperienced women is rare in early modern drama, Bly argues, but profuse within the playtexts of the King's Revels.[17] The eager anticipation of erotic pleasure shown by Abigail and Thais is in itself a detail which would sit neatly with that company's repertoire.[18] On the other hand, as Bly argues, the discarding of the "back-doors" in favor of the "fore-doors" does not. Yet the very raising of the suggestion—an emphatic allusion to anal penetration—may be thought to match the company emphasis. There is also material which seems deliberately to confuse the genders. "Had she been an Hermaphrodite, I would scarce have given credit to you," says Claridiana of Abigail (5.2.152–53). " 'Tis shape makes mankind femalcy," declares Isabella (3.2.45). Melchiori glosses "effeminate" (1.1.58), Isabella's epithet of praise for Roberto, as "gentle or polite, accomplished," yet her description features Juno and Diana as exemplars of his good looks. Suggestive though these comments are, they appear indirect alongside Abigail's statement of her availability to her husband: "I am of as pliant and yielding a body to him, e'en which way he will, he may turn me as he list himself" (2.2.18–20). The same character also makes the observation which most strongly aligns the play's bawdy material with that of the King's Revels repertoire as she tells her neighbor, friend, and fellow intriguer, Thais, that "our back arbours may afford visitation freely" (1.1.227–28). In its invitation to an audience alert for and responsive to homoerotic innuendo, *The Insatiate Countess* fits neatly with the company's attested plays. That *The Insatiate Countess* alludes to the Leander story in similar words to those of *The Turk*, but does so without matching *The Turk*'s responsiveness to Marlowe's description of the encounter between Leander and Neptune, cannot alone deter an ascription to the King's Revels. *The Family of Love,* staged, like *The Turk,* by this company, also alluded neutrally to Leander; indeed, *The Family*'s reference strongly parallels that of *The Insatiate Countess,* for both allusions are placed in the context of an ascent by ladder to a balcony assignation.[19]

If we are not constrained by the external evidence to suggest that *The Insatiate Countess* was started at the point at which the King's Revels was collapsing, then we would have ample grounds, based upon the known role of Machin within the company, the play's profuse verbal overlap with King's Revels plays, and the striking evidence that *The Insatiate Countess* conformed to the distinctive make-up of King's Revels plays, for believing that *The Insatiate Countess* was prepared for playing before the clientele of the first Whitefriars company.

Perhaps, then, we can examine the evidence for *The Insatiate Countess* being a late Marston play: the evidence which would effectively discount the prospect of a King's Revels provenance for the revisions to *The Insatiate Countess.* This assumption rests upon the hypothesis that Marston's contribution to *The Insatiate Countess* was an unfinished one. It also rests upon the neat match between the theory that Marston abandoned the theater in 1608, in the wake of the offense caused by a lost play staged at Blackfriars, and the evidence that additional scriptwriting was undertaken for performance at Whitefriars and by individuals known to have been active at the end of the first decade of the seventeenth century and at the start of the second. Yet this account of *The Insatiate Countess*'s inception is really a rather fragile conjecture. Internal evidence which might connect the play with a date late in Marston's writing career is slight.[20] The connection of the imprisonment of a John Marston in June 1608 with the Blackfriars performance which led to the suspension of playing in March of that year is inviting but unproven. (There is no certain evidence that Marston wrote anything for the professional stage after *The Fawn* and *Sophonisba,* and the composition of both of these may have preceded their March 1606 entries in the Stationers' Register by many months.) That *The Insatiate Countess* was written at that time is a further and quite unattested supposition. We may note that one text which Marston appears to have left incomplete, *Lust's Dominion; or, The Lascivious Queen,* seems to have been a play of 1599–1600.[21]

The case for an early version of *The Insatiate Countess* has been made by Michael Scott, who offers three reasons for his dating: there is no sign of the repeated verbal borrowings from Florio's 1603 translation of Montaigne to appear in Marston's later plays, *The Dutch Courtesan, The Fawn,* and *Sophonisba;* associations are to be found between *The Insatiate Countess* and Marston's earlier, rather than later, work; and the presence of echoes of *Romeo and Juliet,* a feature which suggests a date near to the turn of the century.[22] Although Melchiori has little time for them, Scott's arguments are strong ones.[23] The sequence of articulate and uninhibited women to be found in Marston's later plays—Crispinella, Dulcimel, and Sophonisba—insistently utter sentiments appropriated from "Upon Some Verses of Virgil," and we would have expected to find at least some such borrowings in the speeches of Isabella, the "Insatiate Countess," had the play been composed in 1607 and 1608.[24] As to the connections with Marston's early writings, Melchiori himself notes the relatively high frequency of "verbal analogues" with Marston's early nondramatic poems.[25] And Scott's final point is particularly strong: it is not merely, as he argues, that allusions to *Romeo* appear frequently around 1600, but that several Paul's plays of 1599–1602, among them those of Marston, carefully invoke Shakespeare's tragedy: *Antonio and Mellida, Jack Drum's Entertainment,* and *Blurt, Master Constable.* The citing of *Romeo and Juliet* in *The Insatiate Countess* is explicit, for the factional enmity between Rogero and Claridiana is "Like to the Capulets and Montagues" (1.1.191).

There are supporting arguments to these. The repeated echoes of *Hamlet,* which are profuse during the first act of *The Insatiate Countess,* again show a likeness with those of Marston's plays written for Paul's.[26] Special note may be made of the way in which a repeated recourse to *Hamlet*'s "Hyperion's curls, the front of Jove himself, / An eye like Mars" finds a common shape in Marston's writings.[27] The lines from *The Insatiate Countess,* "Apollo gave him locks, Jove his high front . . . that eye was Juno's" (1.1.61, 64), in their responsiveness to those of *Hamlet,* not only resemble the borrowed phrase in *Antonio's Revenge,* "to the front of Jove," but more closely match a longer passage in *What You Will:* "by the front of Jove methinks her eye / Shoots more spirit in me."[28] Of course, *Hamlet* could have been recalled later, perhaps after the appearance of Q2 during Marston's Blackfriars period (*The Fawn*'s Gonzago was partly drawn from Polonius), though the concentrated recourse to *Jove, front,* and *eye* suggests instead that Marston's work upon *The Insatiate Countess* took place at around the time of *Antonio's Revenge* and *What You Will.* We may note that *Antonio's Revenge* appears to have been written during 1600–1601, and *What You Will* likely to have been drafted within the following year.

So much points toward the strongest evidence for an "early" inception for *The Insatiate Countess.* In 1601 Marston was one of the poets to contribute verses as a coda to Robert Chester's *Love's Martyr,* a volume dedicated to Sir John Salisbury. In Melchiori's edition the textual puzzle posed by the appearance of the line *"Rimatrix, Buglors, Rhimocers"* in all early modern editions of *The Insatiate Countess* is solved by reference to Chester's poem, in which "Rinatrix" and "The *Bugle* or wild *Oxe*" are to be found, together with *"Onocentaure,"* a creature mentioned in *The Insatiate Countess* 1.1.321 and 374 (and where in each case it is coupled with further allusion to "Rimatrix," a word whose first *OED* citation, as Melchiori notes, is to Chester's poem). Melchiori emends the line, which comprises a sequence of insults aimed at Claridiana by Rogero, to read "Rimatrix, Bugle-ox, Rhinoceros" (1.1.160). References to "a crocodile" (1.1.170) and "a dromedary" (1.1.175) may also have their origin in Chester's poem. The debt is clear. It is also narrow: the recourse is to a few stanzas from the bestiary which forms one section of *Love's Martyr* and the debt manifests itself only within the hostile exchanges between the Venetian enemies. This precise indebtedness suggests, however, that when Isabella—alluding to Bacchus—says, "though he be co-supreme with mighty Love" (2.1.190), the expression was fashioned by an awareness of Shakespeare's contribution to the "poetical essaies" appended to *Love Martyr,* in which the Phoenix and the Turtle are dubbed "Co-supremes and stars of Love."[29] Marston certainly knew Shakespeare's verse, for the first of his four signed poems for the volume, which follow those of his fellow poet, alludes to the preceding lines.[30] This forms a further, and quite independent, connection with the *Love's Martyr* volume. The use of "co-supreme" as adjective is unrecorded in the *OED*.[31] In each instance the word is linked with the personification, "Love." Melchiori notes two further parallels between *The Insatiate Countess* and *Love's Martyr*.[32] This multiple responsiveness to the 1601 publication in honor of Sir John Salisbury must be highly significant for assessing the inception of *The Insatiate Countess*.[33] *Hamlet* or *Romeo and Juliet* were like to retain their prominence, and drew many allusions after as well as at the turn of the century, and their valency was periodically affirmed by performance or publication or both. There is little reason to believe that this was the case for *Love's Martyr:* there was a shadowy reissue of the poem in 1611 under a new title, but the likelihood that Marston was writing plays at that time is very small, and nor is there any plausible prospect that other writers were responsible for these borrowings.[34]

This two-part theory, of a first draft in or shortly after 1601, and of a revision undertaken with a view to performance by the King's Revels at Whitefriars, is internally self-reinforcing. An early date for the play's inception makes possible the prospect of a King's Revels performance of the play at Whitefriars; and a King's Revels provenance for the revisions effectively discredits the thesis that *The Insatiate Countess* was abandoned after Marston's disgrace in 1608.

Why, then, might the play have been abandoned, if abandoned it was? Perhaps, as Melchiori suggests, one reason may have been the challenge of attaining the desired "dramatic synthesis" of plot and subplot.[35] In any review of biographical considerations that may have resulted in the play's being laid aside, the most obvious focus for investigation is the possible humiliation involved in the powerful and pointed critique of Marston's writing advanced in *Poetaster.* Commentators have suggested that the absence of known playscripts drafted by Marston in the years immediately following Jonson's attack may have derived from a consequent crisis of self-confidence.[36]

Does the text of *The Insatiate Countess* offer any sign of a concern with the material contested in the "poet's war"? Readers will be aware that the rivalries which involved Dekker, Jonson, and Marston once drew considerable speculation. A past willingness to colonize much peripheral or unconnected work for supposed representations of poets and playwrights onstage has brought attempts to document such rivalries into disrepute.[37] Recent publications by Tom Cain and Matthew Steggle have reaffirmed that representation and counterrepresentation were central to the aims and reception of, in particular, *Poetaster* and *Satiromastix,* and to these may be added the work of James P. Bednarz, who has forcefully argued that allusion and personation extended well beyond these plays.[38] The present discussion rests on the belief that, while Marston's contributions to the "poets' war" are properly to be seen as teasing and suggestive, and critics who believe him to have been advancing provisional or composite portraits best gauge authorial intention, he persistently displayed a strong self-consciousness of the negative depictions of himself by Jonson, and this emerges in a sustained series of glancing self-representations.

In his strangulated six-line commendatory poem to Jonson's *Sejanus* Marston writes that "This worke dispairefull Enuie must euen praise."[39] As *Poetaster* had vividly depicted Envy on stage, and had explicitly associated both Crispinus/Marston and Demetrius/Dekker with envy, this appears to be Marston's fleeting and self-deprecatory appropriation of Jonson's charge against him.[40] One of few known character names to share the root of Crispinus is the Crispinella of Marston's *The Dutch Courtesan,* the play's vehicle for much of its adaptation of Florio's Montaigne.[41] Crispinus, furthermore, was the eponymous "poetaster' of Jonson's play; and Jonson's title itself was to be echoed by that of Marston's *Parasitaster.* And Marston connects himself with the subtitle of this play, *The Fawn,* for the prologue accounts for the author's lavish compliments to his audience by the injunction, "know his play's—*the Fawn.*"[42]

The conflation of author with title is a mark of Marston's choice of titles for his early work. *The Scourge of Villainy* and *Histriomastix* each intimate its writer as well its matter (as Marston's signing himself "Theriomastix" makes clear).[43] The allusion in *Jack Drum's Entertainment* to "the new poet *Mellidus*" appears to refer to *Antonio and Mellida.*[44] *Jack Drum's Entertainment* itself, using the proverbial phrase for a buffeting, emphasizes its title (as "John Drums *entertainment*") exactly as the inductive prologue foregrounds the author.[45] And one of *What You Will*'s pointed allusions to its own title runs "your friend the author, the composer, the *what you will,* seems so fair in his own glass" (75–77). To these projections of himself may be added the explicit and staged discussions of the author in the inductions to *Antonio and Mellida* and *What You Will* and in the inductive prologue to *Jack Drum.*

Many critics note Marston's repeated mention of red hair, a red beard, little legs, or a combination of these.[46] This practice, taken to be a sort of signature, is frequent enough to have been cited by K. Gustav Cross in the course of his case for Marston's authorship of *Lust's Dominion; or, The Lascivious Queen.*[47] One example of this appears in *The Insatiate Countess:* "I ever thought by his red beard he would prove a Judas," says Thais of Rogero her husband (2.2.36). Rogero's very name may, Melchiori suggests, derive from *roggio,* or *red.*[48] Rogero appears in the comic subplot in which he and his long-standing enemy Claridiana pursue their feud. At the play's start, they are newly married, and their wives, Thais and Abigail, have been friends from girlhood. Each man seeks to cuckold his rival, and so intent are they upon this that they fail to consummate their own marriages. Thais and Abigail decide to exploit this situation: each will make an assignation at her own home and with her husband's rival; and each will then take her friend's place and so secure her own husband's sexual attention. For the women, the plan works well: as Thais says, "for the opinion my goodman had of enjoying you, made him do wonders" (3.3.14–15). The husbands, on the other hand, are apprehended as the watch investigates a murder. When they realize that they have been cuckolded, both men prefer to accept guilt for the murder rather than to have their humiliation publicized. They are freed both from punishment and from the shame of cuckoldom by the intervention of their wives at the play's end.

Allusions by Marston to red beards or red hair (which are matched, of course, by those in various plays composed by other writers) certainly do not mark a series of stage self-portraits. They appear at most to constitute a teasing and extradramatic bow to the author. The point at which such a bow might most be supposed to draw attention to Marston himself would be in the wake of *Poetaster* and *Satiromastix,* with their direct personations of Marston in the figure of the ruddy Rufus Laberius Crispinus.[49] If *The Insatiate Countess* was first conceived in 1601, and especially if it should have been intended for playing at Paul's, this would be the time and place in which such a self-allusion would be most resonant. So much offers no more than a weak permissive plausibility for the prospect of a self-staging. Rogero does, however, himself say as he attempts to explain the fiction of his murder of the duke's nephew, "we feared that your kinsman for a mess of sonnets would have given the plot of us and our wives to some needy poet, and for sport and profit brought us in some Venetian comedy upon the stage" (4.1.32–35). The figure of the poet-playwright is summoned up, and the phrase "for sport and profit" may refer not only to the motives of those who stage the rivals but also to the the benefits to be gained by the spectators. There we may see a reflection of Jonson's hope, expressed by *Every Man Out*'s Asper, who looked for "attentiue auditors, / Such as will joyne their profit with their pleasure."[50] A mention of a red beard, a glance at didactic comic drama, and a comment upon the staging of a rivalry are each to be found in the subplot of *The Insatiate Countess*. The figure of Envy which dominates the induction of *Poetaster* may have its match as Thais tells her husband Rogero, "you seem like the issue / The painters limn leaping from Envy's mouth, / That devours all he meets" (1.1.331–33).[51] When Thais says of his rival, "But he's in hope his book will save him" (3.3.38), she alludes to the way in which benefit of clergy could save a man sentenced to hanging. This was the means by which Jonson himself avoided such a penalty. Thais is answering Abigail's own comment about Claridiana, "They say mine has compiled an ungodly volume of Satires against women, and calls his book *The Snarl*" (3.3.36–38). The association of *cynic* (a rough synonym for satirist) with dog (*kunos*) led to many canine references in the vogue for satire, as in Marston's exhortation of his "humble Satyre" to "snarle more dark at secret sin."[52] F. G. Fleay connected Abigail's remark with the *Six Snarling Satires* of T. M., published in 1599,[53] but "snarling" in 1601 seems to have been deployed by Marston for more immediate applications. In the same scene that Quadratus calls Lampatho "you Don Kinsayder" (531), he tells him to "pluck out your snarling fangs" (626), and when Lampatho later begins a satirical tirade, Quadratus again seeks to deflect him: "Come, you'll be snarling now" (1115). It is as Lampatho is most like Marston's Kinsayder and Jonson's Asper that Quadratus characterizes him as "snarling." When Jonson lighted upon the prologue to *Antonio's Revenge* to furnish several items of overwrought vocabulary, one of the phrases he noticed was "*snarling gusts,*" which emerges alongside "*quaking custards*" at the climax of *Poetaster*'s purging of Crispinus.[54] Claridiana applies the term to himself at the close of *The Insatiate Countess* as he faces sentence of execution: "Sir, I am to die a dog's death, and will snarl a little at the old Signior" (5.2.22–23).

What, if anything, may we make of these allusions? The mention of a red beard in itself, though likely enough to be an oblique piece of Marstonian self-promotion, need have no connection with rivalrous stagings. A play staged "for sport and profit" may not allude to Jonson's comic theory, and even if it does, insists upon no extended engagement with Jonson. The reference to benefit of clergy might also, arguably, be innocent of a personal application, though here we should note the way in which Dekker, Jonson, and Shakespeare alike deploy this very allusion in passages considered to refer directly to Jonson's experience.[55] Their appearance in a single play, alongside mentions of "snarl" and "envy," and their situation together within the subplot, render it less likely that they are unrelated to the concerns of the "poets' war": the allusion to verse satire is precise; and the prospect that "the plot of us and our wives" might have been given "to some needy poet" who could have "for sport and profit brought us in some Venetian comedy upon the stage" appears to place these matters firmly in the context of stage personation.

Do we then have a new candidate (however disguised by the accretions and alterations for performance at Whitefriars) of the repertoire of the "War of the Theaters"? Not really. *Poetaster* and *Satiromastix* are plays whose contemporary meaning is simply inaccessible without an awareness that the double staging of Horace intimates not only the attitudes and the values but also the person of Jonson, and of Crispinus and Demetrius, Marston and Dekker. The Hedon and Anaides of *Cynthia's Revels* and the Brabant Senior of *Jack Drum's Entertainment* are less obviously portraits of Marston, Dekker, and Jonson, and strategies of personation are not integral to these plays.[56]

What You Will is less easy to gauge in this respect. Matthew Steggle makes a strong case for retreating from the views of critics, such as Finkelpearl, who believe that situating the play within the stage rivalries of the time is unhelpful. Steggle's view is that Lampatho Doria is a vehicle for presenting aspects of Jonson.[57] In this Steggle is at one with Hoy, Cain, and Bednarz, all of whom share the prevailing interpretation of Roscoe Small, that the figure of Jonson indeed lies behind the stage character of Lampatho. Although such has been the dominant view, it has not been the only interpretation. Amongst others who have analyzed the strategy of personation to be found in *What You Will,* impressions have been more mixed. While J. B. Leishman considers that Lampatho is indeed "a portrait of Jonson" and Quadratus "perhaps to be regarded as an idealised self-portrait of Marston," Josiah Penniman thought that Quadratus represents Jonson and Lampatho Marston. Anne Barton feels that Lampatho "looks very like" a Jonson-figure; M. R. Woodhead, on the other hand, believes that Jonson "is closer to Quadratus." "[I]t is impossible," thinks Alvin Kernan, "that Lampatho was either Marston's spokesman or his image," yet for David Farley-Hills, Lampatho is the character in which Marston "deliberately parodies himself."[58] Crucial to this lack of agreement is the naming of Lampatho by Quadratus as "Don Kinsayder" (531), in which Marston's own pseudonym is applied to a character who in certain aspects resembles Jonson.

Michael Neill and MacD. P. Jackson have put forward another view: Lampatho is "a teasing anamorphic double-portrait of the two rivals," and T. F. Wharton has backed this assessment.[59] So much would at least answer the question of why, when the signs of personal application are so strong as to command the view that decoding the satire is a meaningful aim, there is no firm consensus as to the way it is applied. It would also fit with signs that other allusions made by Marston suggest a conflation of his own persona with that of Jonson. The Chrisoganus of *Histriomastix* may plausibly reflect, as

Bednarz argues, a Jonson viewed by Marston "simultaneously as a mentor and a flawed rival."[60] *Jack Drum's Entertainment* may perhaps be one of those Marstonian titles to project the author; it certainly applies to the Brabant Senior (in some part a Jonson-figure) who receives his comeuppance. Using "dispairefull Enuie" as the construction by which to praise *Sejanus* marks the commandeering of Jonson's opprobrious criticism. When Brabant Senior is asked what he thinks of "the new poet *Mellidus*," Marston's use of his own title character is subject to the put-down of his own fictionalized rival, and the term Brabant Senior uses for his sneer, "slight," is one that Marston uses twice in the prologue to *Antonio and Mellida*, and which he later came to use insistently in the prefatory material of his published play-texts.[61] In sensing that the personal satire of *What You Will* is not apportioned with a care to make clear to the auditor that Lampatho narrowly personates Jonson, and Quadratus Marston, it is important to remember that Marston seems consistently to have represented Jonson as like himself and himself as Jonsonian.

Signs that the subplot of *The Insatiate Countess* deploys allusions to its original composer and his rival of 1601 are altogether of a piece with Marston's practice elsewhere. Rogero is red-bearded (like Marston) and a Catholic (like Jonson). Claridiana wrote snarling satires (like Marston) and may (like Jonson) plead benefit of clergy. They are inveterate rivals and their rivalry is to be brought "for sport and profit" "upon the stage."

How far should this be pushed? Readers will be aware that the present argument requires a double hypothesis: claims that the surviving text of *The Insatiate Countess* reflects the literary and dramatic rivalries of 1601 wholly depend upon the reliability of the dating here proposed. If, however, the case for an "early" Marstonian draft is a just one, then the presence of personal satire should not be unexpected. As this essay has sought to show, signs of self-promotion abound in Marston's writings, and many of these signs betray a consciousness of criticism, and especially of Jonson's criticism. Consequently, if *The Insatiate Countess* is indeed founded upon a draft of 1601 or thereabouts, the concentration of possible allusions to Jonson and to Marston should be deemed significant. The significance is not that the play should stand alongside *Satiromastix* and *Poetaster,* plays for which personation is central to their conception, or even alongside *What You Will,* where the ideological confrontation between rivals is—relative to the feud in *The Insatiate Countess*—more sustained, marked by a greater web of allusion, and broader in its range. The invoking of the playwright's rivalry in the course of developing the sexual competition of the Venetian tradesmen is, on the one hand, like the occasional suggestions that a caricature of Jonson forms part of the conception for Brabant Senior, and on the other, may dovetail with signs that the dedication of *Antonio and Mellida* and the epilogue to *The Malcontent* were shaped by Marston's reflections in the period following *Poetaster*'s staging.[62]

The suggestion above is that the rivalry between competitor playwrights was signaled "in the course of" the comic deflation of sexual competitors. There is likely to have been a closer connection. The juxtaposition in the *Conversations with Drummond* of Jonson's tale of his "many quarrels with Marston" and an account of his own erotic adventures has encouraged critics to see in Brabant Senior's come-uppance (he too confidently encourages Monsieur de la Fo to proposition his wife, only to find that the overtures are welcomed rather than rebuffed) a satire upon such anecdotes, and even to detect an acknowledgment by Jonson of the satire.[63] The significance of Marston's choice of a sexual deflation of his rival's pretensions has not been accentuated. The arrogant self-assurance of Brabant Senior's literary critique (he sneeringly reviews the repertoire of the newly reopened Paul's theater) matches his equally overweening attitude toward his marital security.

There is also an erotic element to the personal satire of *What You Will*. At the start of the play's fourth act, four women characters appear for the first time. The four are to be reunited with a husband, to acquire a partner, or to reject the advances of a lover in an ending which seems to draw from those of *As You Like It* and *Love's Labour's Lost* in equal measure. So minimally sketched are the concluding exchanges that the exact pairings and the outcome of their exchanges are unclear. It seems that Lampatho sues for Meletza, whose response is elliptical: "No sea so boundless vast but hath a shore" (2069). In the earlier appearance, Meletza emerges as the sexually voracious member of the quartet. She is the sister of the play's romantic heroine, Celia, and is, like Crispinella and *Antonio and Mellida*'s Rosaline, one of the characters Marston shaped after Shakespeare's Beatrice. She lists her various "servants" (1467) in a dialogue which features an extensive ruff and a velvet scabbard. They include many of the play's male characters, and most prominently Quadratus, who "holds up the arras, supports the tapestry when I pass into the presence very graciously" (1429–31). Quadratus smooths Meletza's progression through her lovers by recommending Lampatho to her and her to Lampatho. When Lampatho expresses his fascination with Meletza's beauty Quadratus responds, "Why now I could eat thee, thou dost please my appetite" (1597). Clearly, the sharing of a common lover with Lampatho is a source of almost physical satisfaction to Quadratus. Moreover, the name of this lover, "Meletza," once dubbed "Good Mell" by Quadratus (1467), is close to the "Mellida" of Marston's *Antonio* plays. As we have have seen, Marston appears to have adopted the name "*Mellidus*" for himself in *Jack Drum*'s brief exchange about the Children of Paul's. Indications that the gallants' alternating rivalry and alliance were given an erotic twist join further signs that this eroticism involves an odd fusion of identity: signs which receive a specifically homoerotic slant through the remark about Quadratus holding "up the arras" so that Meletza may "pass into the presence." We may further note that there is a third Marston character which shares the basis (*mel:honey*) for her name: *The Fawn*'s Dulcimel. Another of Marston's witty and sexually direct female characters, Dulcimel, like Crispinella, expresses many of the sentiments Marston quarried from Montaigne. *The Fawn*'s editor cites Florio's definition of *dolcemelle:* "Also used for a man's pillicock [penis]."[64] There is a interlinking web of allusiveness—personal, bawdy, and intertextual—to suggest that Marston's rivalry toward and identification with his fellow dramatist was partly expressed through a narrative of sexuality.

It would be easy to term this playful. Yet the comments Drummond recorded—he twice mentions Jonson's claim to have taken Marston's pistols from him—suggest a background of violence.[65] The allusion to benefit of clergy was not only one with direct application to Jonson, but its application involved the killing by Jonson of a fellow professional, for the actor Gabriel Spencer died at Jonson's hands in September 1598, and it was in connection with this offense that Jonson sought benefit of clergy. The incident which lay behind the claim recorded in the *Conversations* is irrecoverable, but the comment stands as a warning to those who see the opposition between playwrights either as manufactured or modest.

What You Will, perhaps, marks the point at which the topical satire of this period comes closest to playfulness. Relative to the painful dilemma of Albano, unable to assert his identity in the web of competing intrigues, the action concerning Quadratus and Lampatho is lighthearted and largely reflects the equable good humor of Quadratus. *The Insatiate Countess,* on the other hand, though it certainly has the potential to allow a highly amusing performance, has never been deemed a sunny play. It may be thought that the signs of personal satire in *The Insatiate Countess* reflect a time after the precisely aimed personations of *Poetaster,* much as Tom Cain detects for *What You Will* an inception prior to Jonson's play,[66] but the evidence for dating either *What You Will* or *The Insatiate Countess* in relation to *Poetaster* does not really allow us to conjecture with any confidence. What we may say is that the fusion of aspects of both Marston and Jonson into both characters in *What You Will* has its echo (or, just conceivably, its anticipation) in *The Insatiate Countess;* and the suggestions in *What You Will* that the rivalry between gallants involves a complex sexual aspect which partly manifests itself in the identification of a common focus for their eroticism have a more fully developed outlet in the highly competitive search for a reciprocal cuckholding, one which suggests the fascination of each with his rival, in *The Insatiate Countess.* The contrast between this comic fancy and the polemical offerings of *Poetaster* and *Satiromastix* (where the well-intentioned and long-suffering authorial proxies high-mindedly reprove their petty and mean-spirited rivals) is a strong one. It suggests an equivalence between the poets, and if it represents their contest as intense, it hardly portrays it as urbane. Maybe we can see a precursor of the awkward peace offerings to be found in the commendation of *Sejanus* and the dedication of *The Malcontent.*

Situating the inception of *The Insatiate Countess* in or soon after 1601 and as a companion piece to *What You Will* on the face of it hardly casts light upon its Whitefriars staging. As has been argued, this dating in turn allows the supposition, itself amply evidenced, that *The Insatiate Countess* was revised with performance by the King's Revels in mind: a supposition untenable if an interrupted first draft of mid–1608 is presumed. So much holds out a solution to a scholarly puzzle but may intensify suspicions that the exceptionally untidy printed text of the play represents the fruit of an unsympathetic adaptation: the extravagant confection probably designed for Paul's was awkwardly forced into the idiosyncratic repertory of the King's Revels.

As we have seen, however, the likeness between *The Insatiate Countess* and *What You Will* involves the collapse of identity, gender, and sexual orientation, and the foregrounding of the kind of bawdy wordplay with a complex resonance that the known playtexts of the King's Revels freely display. Abigail's statement that "I am of as pliant and yielding a body to him, e'en which way he will, he may turn me as he list himself" and her assertion that "our back arbours may afford visitation freely" occur within the underplot of rivalry and attempted cuckoldom. Beyond the punning texture of the dialogue, the comic conceit which features a pair of rivals whose hostility is so charged that each finds his most intense sexual fulfillment in the act (so he thinks) of copulating with his enemy's wife, is one whose attraction to the King's Revels is obvious. So much would see the connection of some six years earlier— the fleeting commentary upon the personations of Paul's and Blackfriars—as coincidental: it was the punning and sexual material of the play, rather than its topical force, which was of interest to the managers of the King's Revels. But such an account neglects the odd concentration upon the debates of the "poets' war" to be found in the repertoire of the Whitefriars company. One of its plays was named *"Humour out of Breath,"* and the dedication signed by John Day is addressed to "Nobody," replicating that of the *Antonio* plays, where the dedicatory epistle appears to be a retrospective upon performances of *Poetaster* and *Satiromastix.*[67] Another play used by the company to furnish its jokes, although by no means necessarily played by the King's Revels, was titled *"Every Woman in Her Humour,"* and the title accurately reflects its absorption with Jonson's *Humour* plays. *What You Will* appears to have shaped the schoolroom scenes of *Cupid's Whirligig.*[68] The prologues of *Cupid's Whirligig* and *Ram Alley* each echo that of *Volpone* with its revisiting of the battle lines of the "War," and the prologue of *The Turk* takes issue with the self-praise of Jonson in the prologue to *Cynthia's Revels.*

Although the presence of topical allusion formed in or close to 1601 appears not to have been a barrier to the Whitefriars appropriation, we must look first to the play's homoerotic bawdy to see its appeal to the King's Revels company and to its audience. Was it, however, the presence of such innuendo as "our back arbours may afford visitation freely" which made Marston's draft attractive to the King's Revels, or merely the suggestive context of the rivalry between husbands? Either is possible. A Marstonian text may have had "queer puns" added to it in the course of adaptation; or it may have come ready-supplied with them; or both may have occurred.[69] Both Melchiori and Bly appear to assume that the wealth of analogies between *The Insatiate Countess* and plays known to have been part of the King's Revels repertory derive from borrowings made in the course of revisions or expansions undertaken by Barkstead, Machin, or others.[70] Yet there is no reason to discount the possibility that expressions found in a preexisting version of *The Insatiate Countess* may not have been used in the composition or adaptation of other plays. Whether an individual term of erotic wordplay took shape in 1601 or some years afterward, however, its designation for a Whitefriars performance marks a creative selection of playing material.

Let us take the adjective "well-shaped." This appears in *The Insatiate Countess* as Isabella speaks to Gnaica: "Such love is mine, believe it, well-shaped youth" (3.2.84). Melchiori notes that Lewis Machin uses the same adjective in his *Eglogs*. As Apollo gazes on Hiacinth we read: "A well shapt face he had, pleasing to view."[71] As the phrase "well-shaped boy" twice appears in Francis Beaumont's erotic poem of 1602, *Salmacis and Hermaphroditus,*[72] it is easy to construct a history in which Machin's reading and composition of homoerotic narrative verse finds its echo in the adaptation of *The Insatiate Countess.* Yet the adjective was also used by Marston. In one of *What You Will*'s catalogs of attractive physical attributes Bidet notes the "well-shap'd leg" of Simplicius (1815–16), and Meletza begins another by praising Lampatho: "A pretty youth, a pretty well-shap'd youth" (1611). The term had been used in Marston's most thorough retreat from stable identity and gender, for in the first part of Marston's double play, Antonio, disguised as an Amazon, reports to Rosaline and Mellida words supposedly received from a dying Antonio. The ladies of the court hear that Antonio addressed the Amazon with "O well-shaped sweet."[73] And so Isabella's adjective may have derived from Marston's draft rather than Machin's revision. Alternatively, we may posit that Marston's writings figured prominently amongst those turned to by the writers of the King's Revels, "a writing community," suggests Bly, "defined by shared reading pleasure."[74]

Clearly we cannot recover the moment—original, secondhand, revising, or redactive—at which Isabella's words were shaped. What may be recovered, this essay suggests, is the way in which a text conceived for playing around the time of *Poetaster* and *Satiromastix* formed the basis for a script revised and expanded some six years later by agents of the King's Revels.

Notes

1. Cited in Giorgio Melchiori, ed., *The Insatiate Countess,* by John Marston and others (Manchester: Manchester University Press, 1984), 2. All references to the play's text will be to this edition. An unattributed quarto was published in 1616, and in 1631 a further appearance again mentioned Marston as the play's writer, yet this ascription also is belied by a single surviving copy with an alternative title page naming "WILLIAM BARKSTEED" as author. See Melchiori, 2–5.

2. Wiggins, ed., *Four Jacobean Sex Tragedies* (Oxford: Oxford University Press, 1997).

3. Melchiori, ed., *The Insatiate Countess,* 3.

4. Wiggins, ed., *Four Jacobean Sex Tragedies,* xxvi. Melchiori amends the confused system of character names to accord with a postulated original intention; Wiggins does the same to fit a supposed revising scheme. See Malchiori's appendix, 189–97, "The names of the characters."

5. Melchiori, ed., *The Insatiate Countess,* 9–16; D. J. Lake, *"The Insatiate Countess:* Linguistic Evidence for Authorship," *Notes and Queries* 226 (1981): 160–70.

6. Melchiori, ed., *The Insatiate Countess,* 1.

7. With respect to date and theatrical provenance, it may be helpful to emphasize which matters this essay seeks to claim strongly, and which it records only as probable. *The Insatiate Countess* was first written in or soon after 1601, it is argued, but the further prospect, that this draft was made with a view to performance at Paul's, is merely deemed likely. Although *What You Will* is almost invariably dated to 1601, the play's quarto of 1607 mentions neither company nor theater. G. K. Hunter, ed., *The Malcontent* (London: Methuen, 1975), xliv, has speculated that *What You Will* may have been played at Blackfriars. The work on *The Insatiate Countess* reflected in the cancel-leaf attribution to Barkstead and Machin, it is claimed, was undertaken on behalf of the King's Revels. This work, however, may not have resulted in performance by that company. The title-page mention of the Whitefriars theater may conceivably, given the late publication of *The Insatiate Countess* and the many closures due to plague in between 1606 and 1608, record a performance by the Children of the Queen's Revels. Consequently, a history which records the presentation by the King's Revels of a play first designed for Paul's, though likely enough, may not be presumed. On the other hand, if this essay is correct in its arguments, we may confidently believe that the text of *The Insatiate Countess* reflects the appropriation by writers for the King's Revels of material drafted some six years previously for another company.

8. See E. K. Chambers, *The Elizabethan Stage,* 4 vols. (Oxford: Clarendon Press, 1923), 2:54, 3:428.

9. "Production Resources at the Whitefriars Playhouse, 1609–1612," *Early Modern Literary Studies* 2:3 (1997). URL: <http://purl.oclc.org/emls/02-3/maciwhi.html>.

10. Melchiori, ed., *The Insatiate Countess,* 16; Bly, *Queer Virgins and Virgin Queans on the Early Modern Stage* (Oxford: Oxford University Press, 2000), 121. In questioning these views I wish to acknowledge my great debt to both scholars: indeed, it is partly a sense of the high achievement of their work which encourages this attempt to clarify the inception and appropriation of the playscript.

11. "The Playhouse as an Investment, 1607–1614: Thomas Woodford and White-friars," *Medieval and Renaissance Drama in England* 2 (1985): 213. See also Bly, *Queer Virgins,* 129–30.

12. Melchiori, ed., *The Insatiate Countess,* 17.

13. Bly, *Queer Virgins,* 121.

14. Bly, *Queer Virgins,* 142.

15. Bly, *Queer Virgins,* 139.

16. Melchiori, 12–13; Bly, *Queer Virgins,* 121–22.

17. Bly, *Queer Virgins,* 39–42. Bly stresses the way in which sexually desiring and sexually direct virgins people the plays of the King's Revels repertory. The uncon-summated marriages of Abigail and Thais seem to place them in this company, al-though a suggestion of previous sexual experience is present at 4.3.32–37.

18. See also the wordplay involving Thais and Abigail at 1.1.234, 2.1.105, 118, 2.2.49.

19. *The Family of Love,* ed. Simon Shepherd (Nottingham: Nottingham Drama Texts, 1979), l. 847. The allusion in *The Family* is noted by Melchiori, ed., *The Insa-tiate Countess,* 115.

20. Melchiori, 29, suggests that *The Insatiate Countess* is indebted to *Measure for Measure:* a connection which, if applicable to a Marstonian layer of composition, would rule out any date before around 1604. The verbal correspondences offered by Melchiori, however, are scanty: a shared deployment of "forbearance" in a sense not noted in the *OED* (59) and the common use of "quits" for "acquits" (139). These are hardly extensive or plentiful enough to show indebtedness in any direction, and con-trast sharply with the number and precision of analogues with *Hamlet* noted by Mel-chiori.

21. K. Gustav Cross, "The Authorship of *Lust's Dominion,*" *Studies in Philology* 55 (1958): 39–61; Charles Cathcart, *Lust's Dominion; or, The Lascivious Queen:* Au-thorship, Date, and Revision," *Review of English Studies* 52 (2001): 360–75.

22. "Marston's Early Contribution to *The Insatiate Countess,*" *Notes and Queries* 221 (1977): 116–17.

23. Melchiori, ed., *The Insatiate Countess,* 46 n. 40.

24. See Martin Wine, ed., *The Dutch Courtesan* (London: Edward Arnold, 1965), 112–20 [appendix 1], David A. Blostein, ed., *Parasitaster, or, The Fawn* (Manchester: Manchester University Press, 1978), 22–23, 41–42, and William Kemp, ed., *John Marston's "The Wonder of Women or The Tragedy of Sophonisba"* (New York: Gar-land, 1979), 11–13, for the fullest accounts of Marston's use of Montaigne.

25. Melchiori, ed., *The Insatiate Countess,* 10.

26. See Melchiori's notes to *The Insatiate Countess,* 1.1.12–13, 37, 40, 60–67, 120–23, 130–34, 159, 458.

27. *Hamlet,* 3.4.55–56, in William Shakespeare, *The Complete Works,* ed. Stanley Wells and Gary Taylor (Oxford: Oxford University Press, 1988).

28. John Marston, *Antonio's Revenge,* ed. W. Reavley Gair (Manchester: Manches-ter University Press, 1978), 5.3.65; *What You Will,* ed. M. R. Woodhouse (Notting-ham: Nottingham Drama Texts, 1979), ll. 1593–94. Citations of *What You Will,* by line number, are made to this edition. For Marston and *Hamlet,* see Harold Jenkins, ed., *Hamlet* (London: Methuen, 1982), 7–13, and Charles Cathcart, "*Hamlet:* Date and Early Afterlife," *Review of English Studies* 52 (2001): 341–59.

29. "The Phoenix and the Turtle," line 51, in Shakespeare, *The Complete Works,* 782.

30. Marston's first poem begins: "O Twas a moving *Epicideum!*" *The Poems of John Marston,* ed. Arnold Davenport (Liverpool: Liverpool University Press, 1961), 177.

31. Suggestive, given the play's other correspondences to the volume of 1601, is the line, "Thou hast wronged the Phoenix, of all women rarest" (4.2.58), which yokes the phoenix and "rarest," in praising Isabella. The epithet is an obvious one for its subject, yet it is worth noting that Marston deploys *rare,* or one of its derivatives, to characterize the issue of the phoenix and the turtledove no less than four times within the span of his contributions to *Love's Martyr:* see *The Poems of John Marston,* 177–79. Melchiori glosses the "turtle" of the lines which lie at the odd and gripping opening of *The Insatiate Countess,* "What should we do in this Countess's dark hole? / She's sullenly retired, as the turtle" (1.1.1–2), as "tortoise, rather than dove," but we may look to more than the quickly following appearance of "dove-like spleen" (1.1.26) to question this reading.

32. *The Insatiate Countess,* 165, 181.

33. We may note contemporary references in other plays to the "poeticall essaies" of the *Love's Martyr* volume. In Jonson, *Poetaster,* ed. Tom Cain (Manchester: Manchester University Press, 1995), 4.3.62–63, Crispinus mentions "an essay of my poetry." In *What You Will,* Lampatho is called "an essayist" (1600). In each case the play's editor notes a verbal usage antedating other recorded instances. The relationship between the Horace of *Satiromastix* and the Welsh knight, Sir Vaughan ap Rees, seems to allude to a patronage connection between Jonson and Sir John Salisbury, dedicatee of both Chester's poem and the "poeticall essaies." On this last point, see Tom Cain, ed., *Poetaster,* 283–84.

34. See John Roe, ed., Shakespeare, *The Poems* (Cambridge: Cambridge University Press, 1992), 42 n. 1.

35. *The Insatiate Countess,* 37.

36. Keith Sturgess, ed., *"The Malcontent" and Other Plays* (Oxford: Oxford University Press, 1997), xviii.

37. The views of F. G. Fleay in *The Biographical Chronicle of the English Drama, 1599–1640,* 2 vols. (London: Reeves and Turner, 1891), are often cited and castigated. R. A. Small, in *The Stage-Quarrel Between Ben Jonson and the So-Called Poetasters* (Breslau: M. & H. Marcus, 1899), repeatedly seeks to challenge and to correct Fleay's conjectures. John J. Enck, "The Peace of the Poetomachia," *PMLA* 77 (1962): 386–96, offers a strong assertion that the plays are best viewed from other perspectives than those of literary and dramatic rivalry.

38. Tom Cain, ed., *Poetaster;* Matthew Steggle, *Wars of the Theatres: The Poetics of Personation in the Age of Jonson,* English Literary Studies, vol. 75 (University of Victoria, 1998); and James P. Bednarz, *Shakespeare and the Poets' War* (New York: Columbia University Press, 2001).

39. *The Poems of John Marston,* 181.

40. See *Poetaster,* 5.2.610, 617, and Cain's note to 3.1.248.

41. See Thomas L. Berger, William Bradford, and Sidney L. Sondergard, *An Index of Characters in Early Modern English Drama: Printed Plays, 1500–1660,* rev. ed.

(Cambridge: Cambridge University Press, 1998). No instance of any character name beginning "Crispin . . ." is recorded prior to *Poetaster* and *Satiromastix.*

42. *Parasitaster, or, The Fawn,* Prologus, 35.

43. On *The Scourge* and *Histriomastix,* see James P. Bednarz, "Marston's Subversion of Shakespeare and Jonson: *Histriomastix* and the War of the Theaters," *Medieval and Renaissance Drama in England* 6 (1993): 103. As Bednarz points out, Marston's use of "Theriomastix" as signature at the conclusion of *The Scourge* evidences the conflation of agent and action. Roslyn L. Knutson, "*Histrio-Mastix:* Not by John Marston," *Studies in Philology* 98 (2001): 359–77, seeks to categorize *Histriomastix* as an anonymous play.

44. *The Plays of John Marston,* ed. H. H. Wood, 3 vols. (Edinburgh: Oliver and Boyd, 1934–39), 3:221.

45. *The Plays of John Marston,* 3:179.

46. For a discussion which cites several such references, see W. Reavley Gair, ed., *Antonio and Mellida* (Manchester: Manchester University Press, 1991), 9.

47. "The Authorship of *Lust's Dominion,*" 58.

48. *The Insatiate Countess,* 53.

49. See Cain, ed., *Poetaster,* 9, 65.

50. *Every Man Out of his Humour,* Induction, 201–2, in *Ben Jonson,* ed. C. H. Herford and Percy Simpson, vol. 3 (Oxford: Clarendon Press, 1927). The difference of emphasis between Jonson's Horatian ideal and Marston's narrower goal was to be pointedly summarized in the prologue to *The Dutch Courtesan,* ed. David Crane (London: A & C Black, 1997), prologue, 8, "We strive not to instruct but to delight."

51. *Satiromastix,* "To the World," 51–53, in *The Dramatic Works of Thomas Dekker,* ed. Fredson Bowers, 4 vols. (Cambridge: Cambridge University Press, 1953–61), I, certainly alludes to *Poetaster*'s staging of Envy.

52. *Certain Satires,* III, 93, 95, in *The Poems of John Marston.*

53. Fleay, *The Biographical Chronicle,* 2:81.

54. *Poetaster,* 5.3.513; *Antonio's Revenge,* prologue, 4.

55. See Bednarz, *Shakespeare and the Poets' War,* 48. Most insistent are Dekker's repeated allusions to the benefit of clergy, to be found in *Satiromastix,* 1.2.114–17, 4.1.136, 4.2.61–62, and 4.3.105–06.

56. For stronger claims, see Bednarz, *Shakespeare and the Poets' War,* 133–74.

57. *Wars of the Theatres,* 40–48.

58. Leishman, ed., *The Three Parnassus Plays (1598–1601)* (London: Ivor Nicholson & Watson, 1949), 87; Penniman, *The War of the Theatres* (Boston: Ginn, 1897), 138–43; Barton, *Ben Jonson, Dramatist* (Cambridge: Cambridge University Press, 1984), 63; Woodhead, ed. *What You Will,* iii; Kernan, *The Cankered Muse* (New Haven: Yale University Press, 1959), 154; Farley-Hills, *Shakespeare and the Rival Playwrights, 1600–1606* (London: Routledge, 1990), 54.

59. Neill and Jackson, eds., *The Plays of John Marston* (Cambridge: Cambridge University Press, 1986), xiv; Wharton, *The Critical Fall and Rise of John Marston,* (Columbia, S.C.: Camden House, 1994), 15. Steggle, *Wars of the Theatres,* 131 n. 4, also notes this reading, without accepting it, observing that Quadratus and Lampatho "are similar in their social milieu and intellectual interests."

60. Bednarz, *Shakespeare and the Poets' War,* 91.

61. There are three uses of "slight" in the eighteen lines of the prologue to *The Dutch Courtesan,* for instance, and three in the induction to *What You Will.*

62. See Charles Cathcart, "Ben Jonson and the Dedication of *Antonio and Mellida,*" *Notes and Queries* 245 (2000): 100–103.

63. *Conversations with William Drummond,* line 280, Ben Jonson, *The Complete Poems,* ed. George Parfitt, rev. ed. (Harmondsworth: Penguin, 1988). See Bednarz, *Shakespeare and the Poets' War,* 138, for a summary of such approaches.

64. Blostein, ed., *The Fawn,* 75.

65. See Cain, ed., *Poetaster,* 30.

66. See Cain, ed., *Poetaster,* 35–38.

67. Cathcart, "Ben Jonson," 101.

68. Hunold Nibbe, ed., *The Fleire* (Louvain: A. Uystpruyst, 1912), 39–40; Christopher Gordon Petter, ed., *A Critical Old Spelling Edition of The Works of Edward Sharpham* (New York and London: Garland, 1986), 349.

69. On gender, sexuality, and punning in Marston's plays, see the trio of consecutive essays in T. F. Wharton's collection, *The Drama of John Marston: Critical Revisions* (Cambridge: Cambridge University Press, 2000): Richard Scarr, "Insatiate Punning in Marston's Courtesan Plays," 82–99, William W. E. Slights, "Touching the Self: Masturbatory Marston," 100–123, and Sukanya B. Senapati, "'Two Parts in One': Marston and Masculinity," 124–44.

70. Melchiori, ed., *The Insatiate Countess,* 13; Bly, *Queer Virgins,* 121–22.

71. *Mirrha, The Mother of Adonis: or, Lustes Prodegies.* By William Barksted. . . . *Whereunto are added certaine Eglogs.* By L.M. (London, 1607), sig. F. Machin also writes of a "well shap't paire," sig. E3ᵛ.

72. *Salmacis and Hermaphroditus,* 79, 618, in Sandra Clark, ed., *Amorous Rites: Elizabethan Erotic Verse* (London: Everyman, 1994).

73. *Antonio and Mellida,* ed. Gair, 1.1.25.

74. Bly, *Queer Virgins,* 97.

"All his intents are contrary to man": Softened Masculinity and Staging in Middleton's *The Lady's Tragedy*

KEVIN CRAWFORD

THE Jacobean tragedy invoked in this paper's title introduces much more than the allegorical, hagiographic morality detailed in Anne Lancashire's influential 1978 introduction to the play, then commonly called *The Second Maiden's Tragedy*.[1] Middleton develops and scrutinizes the early modern ideal of masculinity in his play's major male characters, whose respective moral, sexual, and political failures (even the victors do not "win") are inextricably linked to what I will call their "softened masculinity."

This fascinating play has long been neglected, prompting only a small number of in-depth studies beyond the usual nod in larger discussions of Jacobean tragedy, courtly love, sexual deviance, and tyranny. Its stage history might optimistically be described as dismal, realistically as nonexistent: Lancashire was unaware of any productions from the Restoration to the publication of her edition, and I have been able to locate only four since then, two not even titled or attributed properly—one of which I directed in addition to playing the Tyrant.[2] The tragedy's authorship issues have, no doubt, been the major cause of this neglect and the play's subsequent identity crisis. With the inclusion of the play in the forthcoming *Collected Works of Thomas Middleton,* attributed solely to him, we may hopefully expect more attention, scholarly and theatrical, paid to this macabre work.[3]

My study is twofold. Firstly, I will examine *The Lady's Tragedy*'s major male characters in light of recent studies of the early modern period's notions of maleness, a reading that necessarily must look beyond the mere binary oppositions of good and evil, sexual purity and deviance, earthbound idolatry and spiritual grace; in particular, and with a glance at Shakespeare's young Veronese lover, I will address that "softened maleness." The play's men are continually shown as unmasculine, repeatedly failing in their efforts to maintain masculine control of their country, their homes, and their sexual interests. Bruce Smith's recent study of Shakespearean masculinity argues that, for the stage, demonstrative masculinity is often "a matter of contingency, of circumstances, of performance," suggesting that "early modern writers seem to have responded to the situation, emotionally at least, in ways remarkably similar to one another."[4] Middleton is not mentioned in Smith—there are precious few early modern writers besides Shakespeare addressed, in fact— but must be here. As in Burton and Shakespeare, the dominant males of *The Lady's Tragedy* (all of whom *unsuccessfully* try to dominate) "attempt to maintain masculine rationality" and control "in the face of effeminating passion," an "ultimately hopeless situation."[5] They also, moreover, "keep talking about anxiety in order to *contain* anxiety. In particular, they must keep talking about their anxieties about women."[6] My argument will apply Smith's paradigm to Middleton's men, placing the Tyrant, Govianus, Anselmus, and Votarius under the most intense spotlight of masculine investigation; Anselmus's wife and Govianus's lady, the necessary catalysts to the respective romantic triangles they mold and instigate, are appropriately present throughout, and prompt portions of this study much like they prompt their suitors into action (though with hopefully less disastrous results). Secondly, I will discuss the play as it was realized in my production, and will address both the problems involved in producing Middleton in a Shakespeare-dominated theatrical paradigm and the potential utility in such productions of a reading informed by theories of early modern masculinity.[7]

The Tyrant's power—his political and social sense of masculinity—is defined through the feminine. This is not uncommon in tyrannical characters of the period. Bushnell's study of tyranny on the Elizabethan and Jacobean stages observes, "The tyrant's lust conventionally marks both his vulnerability and his essence of power. Even though it drives him to rape and oppress others, lust unmans the tyrant when the object of desire comes to control him."[8] Indeed, like Richard III, the Tyrant "fashions power through strategies of seduction, making himself a powerful object of desire"[9]—or rather, in the Tyrant's case, trying to do so, with the result of getting caught "in a web of dependency." Middleton's Tyrant is totally possessed by a "woman's longing," similar to other stage tyrants, such as Herod and Sejanus: "in the end they need to be desired themselves as much as they want the crown."[10] This feminine-dependent masculinity is apparent even in the Tyrant's handling of Govianus's overthrow.

The Tyrant's rise to power is not based on any significant military campaign; there was, as I discuss below, little warlike—masculine—conflict. It is marked from the play's opening as a rise precipitated by romantic yearning. Proudly announcing, "We're now the kingdom's love" (1.1.4), as if he were the darling of the court, he explains that statecraft and lust for power had nothing to do with prompting his ascension: "There was but one / In whom my heart took pleasure (amongst women), / One in the whole kingdom, and in her / You dared to be my rival!" (10–13). Sexual rivalry, then, is introduced in the tragedy's first ten lines—a conflict potentially heightened through strategic casting[11]—with the Tyrant foolishly believing that the mere presence of the crown on Govianus's head illicited the Lady's affection for the former king (perhaps not so foolishly; Govianus is not exactly a model king, and weak in many ways).

In the play's earlier moments, the Tyrant is almost pitiable when we observe how much his desire for the Lady has unmanned him. He simply cannot understand why a woman would not want him as king, and when she defiantly enters in black to greet him after his usurpation, he desperately tries to bestow gifts on her:

> Why mourns the kingdom's mistress? Does she come
> To meet advancement in a funeral garment?
> Back! She forgot herself. 'Twas too much joy
> That bred this error, and we heartily pardon't.
> Go, bring me her hither like an illustrious bride
> With her best beams about her; let her jewels
> Be worth ten cities.
>
> (115–21)

When the Lady stands with Govianus, and does not bow to her father's wishes, the Tyrant's position as king brings no solace to him; he realizes, perhaps for the first time, how much she controls him, Govianus, and their respective places of power and control. The Tyrant must now define his political and social existence in relation to her:

> There's the kingdom
> Within yon valley fixed, while I stand here
> Kissing false hopes upon a frozen mountain,
> Without the confines. I am he that's banished;
> The king walks yonder, chose by her affection,
> Which is the surer side, for where she goes
> Her eye removes the court.
>
> (142–48)

If, as Foyster suggests, male dominance of the household depends on male sexual control and female sexual satisfaction, we see the Tyrant completely stripped of any opportunity to wield that power.[12] Govianus, for all of his masculine shortcomings, is still lord of the manor by virtue of his role of sexual dominator—which, tellingly, the Lady chooses to offer him after we have watched him resignedly accept her probable defection to the Tyrant's embraces. When the Lady kisses Govianus at 1.1.165, against her father's wishes and in the presence of the Tyrant, a usurper is essentially cuckolded in his own house/kingdom and a father striped of his sexual authority over his daughter. Nothing is but what is not, and the Lady, shunning one phallic

symbol of power offered by one man not long before she usurps a phallic
weapon from another, will not "change that misery for [the Tyrant's] sceptre" (171).[13]

This rapid unmanning of the Tyrant continues apace, and by the time we
see Govianus and the Lady together again, the guards have taken pity on them
and allow the couple to spend as much time together as they want; the Tyrant,
sexually and increasingly socially impotent, is hardly able to control his desires and all but a few of his nobles. Waiting for the Lady's response to his
romantic demands, he complains, "My joys have all false hearts; there's
nothing true to me / That's either kind or pleasant. I'm hardly dealt withal. /
I must not miss her. I want her sight too long" (2.3.1–3). Soon, in this very
scene, Helvetius will abandon his sycophantic pandering of his daughter—
which is not only politically motivated but also a desperate attempt to reestablish a father's control—forcing the Tyrant to employ his idiotic hanger-
on, Sophonirus, as pander, and finally, when that fails, to order her kidnap by
his soldiers. This marks a major blow to The Tyrant's sexual power, for in
act 1, force was not a possibility. When Helvetius had reminded the usurper
that he might force the Lady into submission and "pluck her from [Govia-
nus's] arms" (1.1.189), the Tyrant scoffed,

> Thou talk'st unkindly.
> That had been done before thy thought begot it
> If my affection could be so hard-hearted
> To stand upon such payment. It must come
> Gently and kindly, like a debt of love,
> Or 'tis not worth receiving.
>
> (189–94)

Now, in desperation, soldiers will "with violence break in themselves / And
seize on her for [the Tyrant's] use" (2.3.119–30). This despair reaches its
extreme ends when the Lady's suicide prompts the Tyrant to plunder her
grave.

The Tyrant's necrophilia is the play's most sensational element, and the
one for which most people marginally familiar with the plot remember it at
all. It is, as far as we know, the only example of active, criminal necrophilia
in early modern drama.[14] Discussions of it are usually brief, and often address
other peripheral themes. Lancashire reduces it almost entirely to an idolatry
issue, and Bamford interestingly presents it alongside other "rapes that are
not rapes" of the period. I have not been able to locate a thorough discussion
of its sexual deviance, however, a fact I find odd given recent media attention
to the atrocities of Jeffrey Dahmer and Dennis Nilsen.[15] I am not claiming
that Middleton was being eerily prophetic or is "timely" now, as he had more
than enough historical inspiration for his stage necrophiliac. Middleton

points to the legend of Herod and Mariamne directly in 4.3, and Europe had already seen a notorious necrophiliac and sexual sadist in Gilles de Rais, *maréchal* of France and a nobleman who fought with Joan of Arc.[16] His crimes were more cruel and violent than the Tyrant's, however, and in those differences we might see Middleton going after something less sensational, but ultimately more disturbing. A psychopathic lust murder committed by an inhuman and sadistic monster, followed by some necrophilic sex (elements that go hand in hand in modern studies of sexual deviancy), wasn't going to be enough.

That "something more disturbing" Middleton seems to work toward is evoking a sense of pity for the Tyrant, even though the text suggests that he at least intends—if not commits—sexual relations with the Lady's corpse. I will discuss below my own position with regard to this point of interpretation. Whether active or intentional, though, the Tyrant's necrophilia does not involve the breaking of any other taboo often associated, in the period, with this particular crime: murder, cannibalism, or witchcraft. It might be difficult and uncomfortable to defend the actions of the Tyrant, but we're also dealing with a playwright who—more than Shakespeare—toys dramatically with a variety of sexual deviances for a variety of theatrical effects.[17] The Tyrant's necrophilia warrants a specific classification, necrostuprum, "in which the necrophiliac steal the corpse."[18] Initially, this is textually and emotionally prompted by what Ernest Jones distinguished as "inherent necrophilia," which is an extension of love in mourning.[19] It's important to remember, though, that these were not his original intentions, and that his repeated unmanning by his desire for the Lady has essentially forced him to this. He's shocked by the idea himself, "ashamed" in spite of the prospective "joy" he anticipates (4.2.33, 35). In fact, it's interesting to recall as well how often the Tyrant *doesn't* use force. While his ordering of the soldiers to seize her body in 2.3 is physically threatening, he does her no physical harm when she's alive; as we know, he scorns the idea of raping her and doesn't even harm his sexual and political rival, Govianus. If Middleton is at pains to reflect early modern masculinity in these authorial decisions, we may look to Foyster: "men judged each other's sexual prowess by their ability to be so sexually attractive and skillful that force becomes wholly unnecessary."[20] The Tyrant's tomb visit is not just grotesque, cruel, disgusting, or whatever we individually see it as. It is part of the self-conscious undermining and public destruction of a man's sexual reputation. I don't think I'm entirely out of line in saying that, in the circumstances, he's not a complete tyrannical and monstrous freak. This does not excuse his necrostuptic venture, but it should serve to render our response to the motivation and extremity of it—not just the sex itself—problematically ambiguous, perhaps laced with some pity. Her suicide enrages and crushes him emotionally and psychologically, mostly for the one reason might not want to believe: he truly loves her.[21] We

have already seen that his political ambitions were prompted only by desire
for her. Wiggins correctly compares the Tyrant's initial onstage behavior
with that of "a lovesick Orsino," not a "potential rapist."[22] With her death,
he has "lost the comfort of her sight for ever" (4.2.30), his life is an "everlasting torment" (32), and the kingdom he obtained for her meaningless to
him. These lines contain "a potential for tragedy which is missing in the
overwhelming assurance of a lover's paradise which is so often expressed in
the drama."[23] The answer to his own question—"Did she choose / Destruction before me? Was I no better?" (4.2.15–16)—is brutally clear. Propheti-
cally, strangely, and almost touchingly in light of his responses to it, her self-
destruction reveals the nature of sycophancy to him (17–26), and drives the
point home, finally, that she has chosen another man. What the Tyrant does,
then, to the Lady's dead body presents a double climax—pun shamelessly
intended—for the contest of masculinity between him and Govianus: it marks
the ultimate softening of *his* sexual power over the Lady (unsuccessful as
conventional masculine wooer, he can have her only in death), while paradoxically signaling a complete triumph over *Govianus*'s sexual control over
her (the Tyrant does possess her, even if she's dead, while Govianus's actions
essentially relinquish her to the Tyrant, nullifying whatever sexual relations
the former may have shared with her).

Readers could very well argue about what the text indicates should occur
to the Lady's body through staging—my performance account below will
make clear what certain audiences *saw* happen to it. Some take comfort in
the ambiguity of his "serious pains" and the "sinful kiss" that the ghost describes (4.4.68, 72). Bamford, for example, thinks that those serious pains
"suggest corporeal penetration, but do not specify it: The precise extent of
the Tyrant's crime remains vague" (98). Let's address it textually here, and
at least cover what we might imagine while *reading* the play. We know that
he at least touches her, holds her, and kisses her. He "clasps[s] the body for
the spirit that dwelt in't" (4.3.113), orders his "slaves" to "receive her humbly from our arms" (125), and after announcing "I'll prove a kiss" (91),
cries, "By th' mass, thou'rt cold indeed!" (94). The latter is most important
for my discussion, for kisses in *The Lady's Tragedy* most often extend metaphorically to sexual congress. All couples who kiss are or have been sexually
active with one another. The Lady, with all of her lord's talk of virtue and
purity, might seem an exception, but the extent of her relations with Govianus is ambiguous. Daileader notes that she is never referred to as a virgin or
maiden—a particularly refreshing and stimulating observation for a play that
finds its critics bent on beatifying its titular heroine—and without threatening
her sexual "purity" the Lady nevertheless demonstrates her sexual allegiance
to Govianus by kissing him.[24] If we think of the duke's illicit encounter with
Gloriana's skull in *The Revenger's Tragedy,* and recall that the duke's kisses
were those of a "slobbering Dutchman" (3.5.165), it is quite easy to imag-

ine—and stage—most lascivious (live) kissing in *The Lady's Tragedy* as open-mouthed, with the phallic tongue penetrating the vaginal mouth: the Tyrant's contact with the body must be similarly if not actually sexual in nature.[25] Firstly, Govianus's vengeful, murderous poison applied to the Lady's dead lips in act 5 is not going to be effective with a mere peck, because it's apparently not acidic, like Vindice's preferred brand (an issue of dramatic realism, admittedly, but a crucial one).[26] Secondly, and more telling, is Govianus's railing against the Tyrant's sexual drive after the poisoning:

> Does all things end with death, and not thy lust?
> Hast thou devised a new way to damnation,
> More dreadful than the soul of any sin
> Did ever pass yet between earth and hell?

> (5.2.132–35)

The "new way to damnation" must be the Tyrant's sexual handing of the Lady, and no amount of idolatry references or footnotes (which Lancashire dutifully and necessarily doles out repeatedly) can make us forget, especially in performance, that a man is fondling and kissing a dead body that he had constantly marked as a sexual conquest.[27] Indeed, modern psychological opinion points to a likely if obvious drive behind the Tyrant's decision to ravish her dead body: "the idea of intercourse with a dead body may fulfill wishes for complete domination and a partner unable to reject any demand."[28] There is, at last for the Tyrant, "no resistance or opposition, no chance of rejection or retaliation."[29]

Poisoned by kissing copulation, we see in the Tyrant's final moments a man reduced to his present state in the presence of the feminine, stripped of crown and sexual object of desire. But I should make clear that the feminine cannot be *blamed* for his actions; it more often than not affects as catalyst what seems to be the Tyrant's—and, as we'll see, Govianus's—*inherent* softened maleness. Such a distinction is important here, for it's quite easy to rely on the many discourses of early modern masculinity that project the blame of emasculation onto women; Eaton, coming uncomfortably close to a "let's-blame-the-victim" argument, notes accusingly that "alive and dead, [the Lady] has been the source of violent dramatic reactions," and "has been responsible for creating the deadly chaos that results in the Tyrant's death and in Govianus's restoration as king."[30] The two men are not accorded the appropriate accountability in such an assertion. If the Tyrant's single state of man has been more than shaken, his own weaknesses must be acknowledged.[31]

Much of what I have argued until this point hinges on one scene, the one that was, not surprisingly, the most difficult to stage: the disinterment of the Lady in 4.3. My production followed the text's directions for this scene less than those for any other's, preferring to emphasize the sexual unmanning in the scene's necrophilia rather than retard its pace with all of its comic asides and elaborate set design issues. Textually, a tomb, "richly set forth," is discovered at scene's opening, and the Tyrant is called upon to hack his way through the tomb's stone lid before three terrified and silly soldiers remove the pieces and the Lady's body for him. The first to go were the soldiers. As I have discussed elsewhere,[32] grotesque moments of horror rely on the presence of the comical, but I think Middleton's early seventeenth-century theatrical reality leaves us with mixed purposes; the necrophilia of the scene is so terrifying, so theatrically unprecedented, that the comedy of the soldiers reads as a forced and strained audience defense mechanism designed to "soften the blow," so to speak, of the scene's action. Modern presentations of necrophilia—the films *Nightwatch* and *Kissed* in particular[33]—present the necrophiliac alone. This is not surprising: the few documented and convicted necrophiliacs of this century, especially Nilsen, Peter Kürsten, and the Rev. Emyr Owen, rarely shared their activities with anyone (if they did it was usually with an accomplice) until they were arrested.[34] As such, we felt that the Tyrant should visit the tomb alone, sneak the Lady's body back to his chambers as secretly as possible, and not leave the three stooges to run freely around the kingdom telling everyone they'd been graverobbing with the king the night before. We were grappling, again, with problems of dramatic realism, not just the emotional mechanics of the scene. Arguments could be made that the soldiers' presence and dialogue provide human responses to the Tyrant's ever-increasing madness: people *are* talking about his strange behavior, as Memphonius's speech at B4.2.a makes clear.[35] But we wanted audiences to respond to a man holding and fondling a dead body, protesting his love for it, and detailing his plans for it without being influenced by other voices, especially the voices of comic idiots. The comedy here keeps the play from moving forward and strangely comforts the audience, two things we didn't want. We wanted the audience to squirm; when people are onstage squirming for them, they've ben too easily let off the hook.

The Lady's tomb, after many experiments in blocking and scenic design, was cut and placed offstage. The violence done to her tomb mirrors the violence done to her body, but building a realistic stone tomb and chopping one's way into it is bound to appear farcical even with some inventive staging. The textually specified moonlight that reflects off the tomb can shine from offstage onto the Tyrant's face and body (which it did in my production), and strange, unidentifiable sounds suggesting the sliding of a sarcophagus lid unseen by the audience produce a far more eerie, disturbing moment than knock-kneed servants fighting over who must do the breaking and entering. (I have read of *The Winter's Tale*'s statue scene being produced this way, with Hermione's statue placed offstage, to considerable success.)[36] Lines must necessarily be cut, but we felt more than justified. I entered alone, to the neo-Medieval chanting of our soundtrack. The stage was bare now, with a small amount of fog drifting throughout the playing space. The soldiers had provided keys as indicated in 4.2 (we used no "lanthorns and a pickaxe"), which I held. I began speaking at 4.3.9, at which "The monument woos" the Tyrant, and continued to lines 22–23: "All thy still strength, / Thou grey-eyed monument, shall not keep her from us." I then left the stage, walking into the light offstage left that shone from the Lady's tomb. While the sounds of sliding stone echoed, Memphonius appeared in a special light far down-stage right, as if speaking at a private meeting, and announced what is textu-ally placed at B4.2a.4–11:

> All his intents
> Are contrary to man, in spirit or blood.
> He waxes heavy in his noble minds;
> His moods are such, they cannot bear the weight,
> Nor will not long, if there be truth in whispers!
> The honorable father of the state,
> Noble Helvetius, all the lords agree
> By some close policy shortly to set free.[37]

The transposition and inclusion allowed for what we deemed two important necessities. It provided time for me to get the Lady's body while still offering more than *empty* time; it also emphasized the Tyrant's lords' deteriorating loyalty and his increasing dementia without what I believe is the weakening comic effects of the soldiers' banter. After Memphonius's light special went out, I entered carrying the Lady's body, which was draped in a diaphanous burial gown.

What to do with the Lady's body became the subject of much discussion. Action too violently sexual, or a melodramatic line delivery, would have im-mediately thrown the scene back into a comically grotesque mode, which we didn't want. These were, however, the first moments of the Tyrant's complete defeat, sexually, of Govianus. *Something* had to happen, especially if we were going to dramatize the play's "necrophile excitements."[38] Textually and dramatically, without the soldiers, the scene plays very well. I spoke lines 61–68, 82–86, and 94–124; that's a fair amount of verse to be speaking to a dead body all by one's lonesome, but it created a mood which many audience members described as "uncomfortably voyeuristic."[39] This is certainly what we hoped for, and another justification for cutting the soldiers from the scene: if the soldiers are there, in an odd transferring of what I like to call "dramatic permission," it's "ok" for the audience to be there. With nobody present, it's as if we're watching something we're not supposed to see.[40] While speaking, I placed the Lady's body on the stage and kneeled beside her. Very gently, especially where the text indicated physical contact (and only after carefully

obtaining my wife's permission), I caressed her body. When I proclaimed
"Thou art mine now, spite of destruction / And Govianus, and I will possess
thee" (115–16), I took her hand and stroked my face with it, mimicking the
way in which she had bid Govianus farewell in 1.1. Invoking the legend of
Herod immediately after, I slowly mounted the Lady, and while I didn't explicitly mime the act of copulation, as the speech rounded out and the lights
began to fade I trailed my lips down the Lady's body, over her breasts, until
my head rested between her legs just as the lights went completely out. The
cyclorama remained a deep blue, and I picked her up and carried her off in
silhouette, confirming exactly her earlier prediction that she would be forc-
ibly seized and ravished. The blocking here was in part developed to emphasize the different sexualities and masculinities of the Tyrant and Govianus,
for immediately following the disinterment of 4.3 is Govianus's visit to the
Lady's tomb in 4.4. Her ghost appears to inform him of current events regarding her corpse, of course, but rather than placing him in a heroic, saviorlike
role, our staging, complemented by the ghost's lines, only reminded audiences of his earlier weaknesses (which are discussed below). When the
Lady's ghost referred to her "cold breast" (4.4.70), audiences remembered,
just moments ago, the Tyrant actually kissing it. They *saw* his "sinful kiss
upon [her] senseless lip" (72).[44] By this point in the unfolding of the drama,
the Lady's defiant kissing of Govianus in 1.1 is a far distant memory, and
though the ghost is understandably not pleased about it, here the Tyrant
clearly holds the title of sexual conqueror.

Govianus, the play's "rightful" king, has for most critics been the force of
"good" set opposite the "evil" of the Tyrant. Lancashire casts him as the
ultimate savior:

> Govianus himself—the righteous man and true king—becomes (like the Lady)
> Christ-like, descending into "prison," undergoing a mock death in his swoon in act
> III, and eventually, in the killing of the Tyrant, harrowing the hell which the king-
> dom, political and moral, has become under usurpation.[42]

Perhaps. But hardly likely, especially to the modern reader and audience. Nor
necessarily true for the play's original audience, or all of it, at least. Lancashire is responding more to the *written* text in these assertions, it seems to
me, and in a *performance* text Govianus's failure to take action is accentuated
and impossible to overlook.[43] His behavior is extremely questionable, weak,
and at times self-destructive; his lady is demonstrably more masculine in confidence and action, and plays a major role in Govianus's vengeance (which
she, as a ghost, must prompt). The deposed king's name may recall Jove or
Jupiter, but an audience would find it difficult to remember that fact based on
what we see.

The Tyrant's revolution is still in its final stages as the play begins. He is the "new usurping Tyrant" (1.1.0) and has not yet decided what to do with his rival. We hear of no great struggle in the overthrow, however, and all of the nobles have taken the change in power very well; their "powers and constant loves," according to the Tyrant, have given him the hollow crown, and they not only mock Govianus but advise the Tyrant as to what to do with the deposed king. Some violence seems to have supported the *coup d'état,* for the Tyrant refers in frustration to the "bodies . . . hewn down" (179) on his path to "greatness," but it has not been an entirely ruthless campaign without Machiavellian prudence—Govianus will live for the Tyrant's fear "that the world would call our way to dignity / A path of blood" (73–74). Even Govianus's brother Anselmus is strangely at peace with his brother's overthrow, assuaging Votarius's voiced concerns repeatedly, rationalizing, "Sorrow for him? Weak ignorance talks ont like thee. / Why, he was never happier" (1.2.4–5). It's sweet that Anselmus thinks that all Govianus needs is the sight of the Lady to be happy, but why doesn't a brother care about the deposition of a rightful king? Or his own safety as a member of the royal family after the *coup?* Was Govianus a weak, ineffectual ruler who practically asked to be toppled? He blames his fall on "the adulterate friendship of mankind, / False fortune's sister" (1.1.7–8) rather than on any poor statecraft. Why? And why is he so submissive in defeat? He assumes that the Lady will, in fact, follow the crown whither it goes, dejectedly noting,

> O, she's a woman, and her eye will stand
> Upon advancement, never weary yonder;
> But when she turns her head by chance and sees
> The fortunes that are my companions,
> She'll snatch her eyes off, and repent the looking.
>
> (63–67)

He later concludes, "She's lost forever" (76). The Lady proves him wrong, and in retrospect these lines call his character into question. Here, he doesn't have faith in that constancy, purity, and chastity that he keeps invoking throughout the play. Ironically, he's most comfortable carrying on about the Lady as a "fair spring / Of honest and religious desires" (3.1.248–49) only after she's dead; and, while she's not a willing participant (but clearly aware of it, as her ghost tells us), even then her body is used by the Tyrant in a highly unchaste fashion, grimly rendering Govianus's assessments of her various states of sexual allegiance null and void. Govianus doesn't even have the strategic wherewithal to accept his sentence of banishment as a boon by which he might return and supplant his recent deposer, whining in a disturbingly Romeo-like fashion, "What could be worse to one whose heart is locked / Up in another's bosom? Banishment! / And why not death? Is that too easy for me?" (1.1.70–72). No wonder he lost the throne.

Similarly softened, if more profound, is his response to the Tyrant's sending of force to abduct the Lady. This is a tricky point: ordinarily, we couldn't
really consider a man spineless or wrongheaded when he can't bring himself
to kill his beloved at her command. But we can in a Middleton play, for some
of the same reasons that we can feel—for a fleeting moment at least—
sympathy for a necrophile. Once again, we need to resist looking at this court
and these characters through the Shakespearean lens we're more accustomed
to using.[44] Middleton's great thrust here in light of the play's masculine ideal
is that he *should* kill her, and we—like the Lady—should *want* him to. Unsettling as it is, in the context of the play we know the Tyrant will stop at nothing
to possess the Lady, and we know that Govianus has not the strength to do
anything about it. She is superhumanly resolute and will not be taken and
ravished. Her protesting, though, is to some readers excessive, even tiresome,
and extremely "remote from ordinary human standards."[45] Why should we,
then, hold Govianus to those "ordinary" standards and say in his defense,
"Gosh, I couldn't do it either . . ."? And why would Middleton put all those
attacks on Govianus's masculinity in the Lady's mouth if we were meant to
see it otherwise? She is perfectly clear: "Away with me; / Let me no more be
seen. I'm like the treasure / Dangerous to him that keeps it. Rid thy hands
on't" (3.1.74–76). When Govianus pauses—a pause which this play's action
and his required role in it will not tolerate—she cries,

> Sir, you do nothing; there's no valour in you.
> Y'are the worst friend to a lady in affliction
> That ever love made his companion.
> For honour's sake, dispatch me! Thy own thoughts
> Should stir thee to this act more than my weakness.
> The sufferer should not do't. I speak thy part,
> Dull and forgetful man, and all to help thee!
> Is it thy mind to have me seized upon
> And borne with violence unto the Tyrant's bed,
> There forced unto the lust of all his days?
>
> (88–97)

She is forced, at the moment of death which she alone will have the strength
to cause, to paint the picture of her rape for the man who should be doing
everything to prevent it. When Govianus finally attempts to kill her, he faints.
He is, as the Lady understatedly notes, a "poor-spirited" and a "fearful" man
(150, 158). I find it very difficult to see this swoon as a metaphorical decent
into hell, as Lancashire does, especially when the Lady knows she's been
cheated: "hast thou served me so?" (152). I agree with Bramford that "the
playwright takes a risk in emasculating his hero at this critical moment," but
I don't believe, as she suggests, he "gains a great deal by it."[46] I reject the
notion that "the Lady's suicide relieves Govianus of any blood guilt,"[47] be-

cause there's blood enough elsewhere for him to be too concerned about guilt any more; he's already killed one man and will use the Lady's lifeless body to kill another. I think it is much more unmasculine and cowardly than honorable that Govianus "has no part" in his lady's death, a suicide that "is her idea, her desire, and, finally, her deed."[48] Accentuating his failure to do her command, Govianus wakes up after her death only to marvel, "hast thou, valiant woman, overcome / Thy honour's enemies with thine own white hands, / . . . all without help?" (3.1.175–77). Even the Tyrant, quite unmanned himself as he speaks later to her dead body, is amazed that the Lady could commit the deed:

> And where got'st thou such boldness from the rest
> Of all thy timorous sex, to do a deed here
> Upon thyself, would plunge the world's best soldier
> And make him twice bethink him, and again,
> And yet give over?
>
> (4.3.108–12)

When we hear or read these lines, Govianus is invoked as we remember him present for the deed, and by extension he is placed in comparative juxtaposition opposite that "world's best soldier," reminding us that he certainly doesn't warrant that superlative title: his Lady, ironically, does.[49] After the Lady's death, Govianus cowardly props up the one dead body he's miraculously managed to produce, Sophonirus's, against the door in hopes that the soldiers breaking it down will believe that they've accidentally killed the man themselves.[50] Think of Othello's discovered crime scene, and remember that any distortion of it—particularly the cause of Desdemona's death—is ultimately damnable; "she's like a liar gone to burning hell. / 'Twas I that killed her," he admits after his wife has falsely exonerated him. (*Oth.* 5.2.138–39). For Othello, a factor of masculinity is confessing even to horrible crimes. Govianus, on the other hand, lies his way out of his situation, after not killing the lover who begs him to, and after blaming his murderous deed on other parties.

He does not shift comfortably into the role of revenger, either, and when he does it is in a conspicuously unmasculine way. He is far too emotional for the early modern masculine ideal. Firstly, he cries too easily. Upon entering the Lady's tomb, he weeps, "Already mine eye melts. The monument / No sooner stood before it but a tear / Ran swiftly from me, to express her duty" (4.4.1–3). When he kneels while his page boy sings, he will keep musical time with his tears: "At every rest mine eye lets fall a bead / To keep the number perfect" (12–13). Men on the early modern stage are often *fighting back* tears: Lear will not let "women's weapons, water drops, / Stain [his] man's cheeks"; "Tear falling pity dwells not" in Richard III's eye; and Hal's uncle Exeter "had not so much of man" as "mother" in himself to keep tears from falling for York and Suffolk's death.[51] In this stage world, men are not supposed to cry, and are given to the feminine when they do. 'Tis unmanly grief. Govianus is so emotionally weakened and unmasculine in this scene that rather than be prompted to revenge by heaven and hell, he wants to die and "walk together / Like loving spirits" with the Lady's ghost (82–83). Hearing this, and given his behavior until now, we are hardly confident in his later resolve: "Her body I will place in her first rest, / Or in th' attempt lock death into my breast" (89–90). Bowers reminds us that in 5.2 he *still* wants to delay his vengeance, even to his own shame.[52]

For me, though, the most startling moment in Govianus's displayed softened masculinity comes precisely when many suppose him to be finally doing what a "real man'" should be, killing the Tyrant and avenging the Lady's death and his own overthrow all at once. The "poisoned lips trick" had worked for Middleton before, but here I find it an extreme attack on Govianus's ability to sexually protect and control the Lady. In *The Revenger's Tragedy,* briefly alluded to above, Vindice uses Gloriana's skull (dolled up, of course, with poison where lips had been) to kill the evil duke, who had poisoned her nine years earlier. The scene is much more violent and physically disturbing than the climax of *The Lady's Tragedy*—the duke's teeth are eaten away, he is forced to watch his bastard son in an incestuous interlude with his duchess, and he has his tongue nailed to the stage with a dagger before being stabbed to death. Not a good day by any means, but strangely acceptable and logical in that play and in that court. Vindice had been fondling the skull onstage from the drama's outset, one instance among many in the play that serves "at once to parody and to interrogate contemporary, increasingly scientist notions of the body,"[53] a play that links death, putrefaction, and sex together throughout. Vindice also has no problem repeatedly prostituting the women in his life, dead or alive, for whatever ends he deems necessary. This is not so in *The Lady's Tragedy.* We see, for the first half of the play, various members of the *dramatis personae* trying to keep the Lady out of the Tyrant's grasp, something that we learn death itself cannot prevent. The Lady, we recall, is demonstrably allied sexually with Govianus through her kisses; the Tyrant attempts to rob Govianus of that allegiance when he takes her body to his court and, by the ghost's account, kisses her (among other caresses). Why, then, would Govianus give the Tyrant another opportunity to do exactly what the Lady's ghost complained about in the first place? Pat, obvious answers don't completely satisfy here. Of course there is the "destroyed by lust" theme prevalent throughout the play; of course Govianus is admitted as an "artist" to restore the body of his (and now the Tyrant's) beloved, and therefore has to "paint" something; of course it's a shocking and wonderfully grotesque design. But I find it highly problematic that Govianus *chooses* to extract his revenge in a method that places the body of his lover in a metaphorical sexual embrace with another man, and in front of him as well. The two men are alone, the Tyrant having ordered his soldier away. Govianus could attack the Tyrant easily, and we know from Memphonius that the court has already swung its political favor away from the Tyrant. At least Vindice knows that Gloriana's flesh is long gone and that her skull requires an entire costume to trick the duke. Indeed, Coddon reminds us that Gloriana's skull is gendered "only because we are told so."[54] It's not a person. The Lady, extremely gendered and very much physically present, is only recently dead, slightly pale, and in the Tyrant's probable madness still feels "warm." What Govianus devises and watches is much more voyeuristic and realistic than anything in *The Revenger's Tragedy,* precisely because the Lady's body is, comparably, so "real."

Govianus's restoration onstage is almost as troubling as the Tyrant's violent demise. The nobles have no idea that their former king has finished killing their present one; they are happy to switch allegiances yet again. Memphonius complains that the "tyranny of [the Tyrant's] actions grew so weighty, / His life so vicious" that he "became as hateful to our minds" as death itself (5.2.188–89, 192). So everything was fine at first? Govianus's next usurper should remember that as far as the nobles are concerned, overthrowing the king is fine, but a bad temper mixed with necrophilic exploits is just too much. Furthermore, Govianus's first act as king is to make the Lady his queen and crown her, placing her body on the throne, which in light of moral readings of the play is more idolatrous than anything the Tyrant does with her body.

The regal members of the main plot are hardly more masculine than their counterparts in the play's subplot. Drawn from Cervantes's "Tale of the Curious Impertinent" in *Don Quixote,* it serves, as many have observed, to homilectically reveal the dangers of unchecked lust.[55] The similarities and anologous relationships between the main and minor plots are too numerous to address here, and, considering my focus, better served elsewhere. What I should like to investigate in the subplot is the softened maleness complementary to the main one: as the Lady undermines the Tyrant's and Govianus's masculinity, Anselmus and Votarius both reveal and increase their softened maleness in responses to the Wife.[56] Many discussion of the subplot echo Lancashire's moralistic reading; Anselmus is ruined by his suspicions, and Votarius is "killed' by his uncontrolled lust. I find the sources of their destruction elsewhere: both men fail to be men according to early modern strictures, most notably in their inability to control their jealousy. Anselmus's fears of being cuckolded ironically lead him to sexually neglect the Wife and send her into the arms of his best friend, marking his loss of both social and sexual control of his household. Votarius, only briefly reluctant to test the Wife's faithfulness and fidelity, tries it too successfully and descends into a fit of pathological jealousy that, when checked and countermanded, kills him.

Foyster argues that early modern literature "reveals a profound uneasiness and discomfort about how manliness could be affected by emotional experience and expression."[57] Jealousy was often interpreted as an indication of sexual ineptitude—why would a man doubt his wife's fidelity unless he wasn't keeping her satisfied? This rather simple logic was so prevalent that "men were unlikely to admit to [jealousy] in any public forum."[58] With this in mind, Anselmus's employment of Votarius points not only to an overly suspicious mind, but an unmasculine one at that. The origins of Anselmus's unease are difficult to place. Brodwin feels that "Having witnessed the Lady's noble defense of her chaste love against temptation, Anselmus desires to put his own wife to a like proof."[59] He does compare his brother's and his own romantic situation almost immediately upon entering:

> My brother's well attended; peace and pleasure
> Are never from his sight! He has his mistress;
> She brought these servants and bestowed them on him.
> But who brings mine?
>
> (1.2.18–21)

He seems to suggest here that he's never had "peace and pleasure," or hasn't in a while; however long ago he'd begun to worry about his wife's powers to resist temptation, he's unmanned by his fears now, ignoring her socially and sexually and admitting it to his friend. Even worse, the Wife complains to Votarius about her husband's remissness:

> I want his company.
> He walks at midnight in thick shady woods
> Where scarce the moon is starlight. I have
>
> . . . .
> Stood in my window, cold and thinly clad,
> T'observe him through the bounty of the moon
>
> . . . .
> And when the morning dew began to fall,
> Then was my time to weep. 'Has lost his kindness,
> Forgot the ways of wedlock, and become
> A stranger to the joys and rites of love.
> He's not so good as a lord ought to be.
>
> (98–100, 103–4, 106–10)

To the early modern mind, this speech marks Anselmus as a weak lover and a failure as husband/head-of-household, not a man justifiably suspicious of his soon-to-be adulterous wife: "If a wife committed adultery contemporaries believed that this provided a clear sign that a man had failed in his duty to maintain household control. A woman was not seen to be an adulteress without some fault of her husband."[60] Moreover, his obsessive drive to test her faithfulness displays an extremity of emotion that bespeaks his already unmanned state, and his begging Votarius to "set to her" essentially admits to his friend that there are sexual shortcomings enough already. This is why Votarius succeeds so well and so quickly: he knows, by virtue of Anselmus's initial doubts, that the Wife is "easy prey" (she knows it too, and says as much at 1.2.222–24). The fact that Leonella knows immediately that something has developed between her employer's wife and his houseguest strongly suggests that the entire household is aware of Anselmus's sexual ineptitude, which could, and does, lead to "catastrophic and widespread" disaster.[61] The moment the Wife inquires nervously about Votarius's whereabouts after his departure, Leonella quips in an aside, "Yea, madam, are you prattling in your sleep? / 'Tis well my lord and you lie in two beds' (1.2.283–84). She has, as she puts it, her "ladyship in the wind!" (277). Leonella is the embodiment of the early modern belief that a wife's infidelity "destroyed all claims that her husband had to household authority."[62] It is Leonella's knowledge of her master's unmasculine behavior, not his moralistic struggles, that leads to her ever-increasing boldness and the deaths of everyone involved in the subplot.

Anselmus's greatest mistake—he could, after all, change his behavior toward her—is exacerbating the already dangerously competitive situation inherent in Votarius's living with the couple. Considering the early modern practice of a married man taking a friend in under his roof and the often disastrous results, Votarius's and Anselmus's ultimate masculine failures are not surprising. The two men are, or were, obviously close, as many exchanges make clear. Anselmus is suitably shocked and offended when Votarius's hesitates at the proposed fidelity testing plan:

> Have I a friend?
> And has my love so little interest in him
> That I must trust some stranger with my heart
> And go to seek him out?
>
> (1.2.63–65)

and the two mens' "friendship" has reached whatever level we might imagine for Anselmus to believe Votarius's protestations in 5.1:

> Your friendship, sir,
> Is the sweet mistress that I only serve.
> I prize the roughness of a man's embrace
> Before the soft lips of a hundred ladies.
>
> (4–7)

As the early modern period reintroduced many ancient texts that praised homosocial friendship, this passionate proclamation (even if partially dissembled here) is not surprising: "in the Elizabethan period there were circumstances in which men as friends could openly express love for each other . . . and share close physical intimacy by becoming 'bedfellows'."[63] This intimacy, however, blinds Anselmus to the threat of male competition, and keeps him from turning his attentions from his male friend to his wife as he tries to entertain them both, as host and husband respectively. Foyster suggests that a recurring motif in the drama of the early seventeenth century "was that male guests who enter the home of a married couple could be disruptive both to the husband/friend relationship and the husband/wife bond" (127–28).[64] Even in this period that "extolled the virtues of same-sex friendship," marriage introduced a social realm in which men established a reputation through "sexual prowess and control" (126–27).[65] The unmarried man/friend, then, views his married friends as better established and reputed sexual rivals. The equality inherent in a younger stage of friendship (Foyster points to Leontes' and Polixenes' exchange of "innocence for innocence") transforms into the more adult world of "competitors and sexual rivals," a world of "sexual politics" in which "it is men who betray and cuckold other men."[66]

Votarius, initially opposed to the testing of Anselmus's wife, quickly turns competitor, even violently so. It takes little time (one scene) for devotion to his host and friend to turn to hatred, and praise for his host's "kind, worthy lady [and] chaste wife" (1.2.22) to turn to lust. Acknowledging that he has "played away my soul at one short game" (2.2.2), Votarius is not, despite his grief-laden soliloquy, entirely penitent: "Her very sight strikes my repentance backward" (22). His successful seduction is demonstrably masculine in its sexual prowess, but before Votarius can revel in his role of sexual usurper his achievements are undermined. After lying to Anselmus repeatedly while recounting his first, half-hearted attempts to seduce the Wife, Votarius begins to establish his position as new head-of-household, but his presumptions are laced with jealous fear:

> I do not like his company now; 'tis irksome.
> His eye offends me. Methinks 'tis not kindly
> We two should live together in one house;
> And 'tis impossible to remove me hence.
> I must not give way first. She is my mistress,
> And that's a degree kinder than a wife.
> . . . .
> I do not like his overboldness with her;
> He's too familiar with the face I love.

(84–89, 94–95)

The abrupt end to their friendship had been heralded moments earlier upon Anselmus's return, as Votarius verbally demonstrates the sexual fears that have been ironically transferred from host to friend:

His very name shoots like a fever through me,
Now hot, now cold.
. . . .
I would he would keep from home like a wise man;
'Tis no place for him now. I would not see him
Of any friend alive! It is not fit
We two should come together. . . .

(37–38, 40–43)

Votarius's new-found jealousy—amidst masculine usurping desires that Anselmus simply leave the house to his guest's care—is not directed to one man only. When Votarius spies Bellarius sneaking through Anselmus's house soon after his host's return, and immediately suspects the Wife of carrying on a sexual affair with the "bawdy-house ferret" as well, he descends into a rash fit of jealousy that reveals his own fear of losing sexual control over the Wife. The passion of it is so strong that he virtually relinquishes his sexual interest in the Wife, insinuating to Anselmus that she has been unfaithful with Bellarius, a ridiculous petard-hoisting move that he immediately regrets:

But how has my rashness and jealousy used me!
Out of my vengeance to mine enemy
Confessed her yielding, I have locked myself
From mine own liberty with that key.

(2.2.144–47)

The Wife berates him soundly for his weakness, wondering if his "wit was fetched out about other business" or if the "way" to her body was "too free" to not be content with their arrangement and throw her into suspicion with her husband (4.1.7, 20).

The noblemen's deaths are particularly unmasculine. Anselmus is slain by a low-class villain who slinks around his house between dalliances with Leonella—a relationship that flourishes precisely because Anselmus has lost all control over what goes on in his house, a loss that is directly linked to his sexual failures as a man and husband. His wife's final words, which he hears, announce her wishes to join her lover in death. He dies ignorant of his own fault in her adultery, railing on her whorishness and not his own sexual inadequacies. Votarius is killed partly through the wicked machinations of Leonella (with Bellarius's encouragement), who doesn't tell him to don "some privy armour" so that the Wife "may feing a fury without fear" (4.1.112–13), and who supplies "some empoisoned weapon" for the deed. When the Wife pretends to ward off Votarius's staged advances, she wounds him mortally. A moralistic lesson may surely be had here, but I believe in light of recent studies that it's more important to note that Votarius is killed not in battle, or even in a duel, but by the independent work of two women who have no "masculine" skills at weaponry—just as the Lady takes control from her man to expedite her own death. Votarius's softened manhood is momentarily usurped by the steely resolve of the Wife, who thrusts a phallic sword into him: "you prick me madam" indeed (5.1.103).

As for the play's discussion of masculinity, we have seen that, for the character's discussed here, not only do "women threaten to undermine masculine self-possession from within,"[67] but they find themselves in the company of the softened maleness their men constantly display. This male-perceived undermining threat becomes a twofold reality embodied in the Lady and the Wife, who in their respective roles and plots see their men fail to be men: a weak, overemotional king is deposed; a would-be suitor goes mad and plunders a tomb to obtain a lover; a nobleman's wife and household are afforded the opportunity to engage in and are driven to sexual and social insubordination and revolt; and a lord's guest is infected with both a desire to cuckold his host and a resulting jealousy that ultimately ends the affair and five lives. The Lady's, and the play's, actual tragedy is that there are no real men to prevent it.

*   *   *

I hope that the performance accounts in this discussion encourage more investigation into an increasingly necessary academic and theatrical issue: how can smaller regional companies produce the work of Middleton and other early modern playwrights?[68] My production's sometimes shameless use of Shakespeare's name was not entirely exploitive, and in a strange way— then—necessary. For now, all Middletonian performance and study is informed by Shakespeare. My production's design and marketing were responses not only to the many issues that Middleton's drama raises, but also to reactions from a company named after, and devoted to performing the works written by . . . The Other Guy. The undeniable fact that Shakespearean productions far outnumber the presentations of his contemporaries' work, and therefore set the governing standards of what should or should not be done when offering up Renaissance fare to modern audiences, is not likely to alter drastically or rapidly in the immediate future. But that doesn't mean it won't ever, and it certainly doesn't mean we shouldn't start anticipating some considerably new courses to be charted by companies producing early modern drama. What did or didn't "work" for us was determined by usual variables in the theater: a cast, a director, a budget, an audience, a venue. But the Palm Beach Shakespeare Festival was able to successfully produce a non-Shakespearean drama and bring it to New York only by promoting it as Shakespearean, a literary conspiracy theory brought to dramatic life. Universities and colleges can perform Marlowe, Middleton, Jonson, even Lyly, by virtue of educational missions that often encourage experimentation.[69] The Royal Shakespeare Company can pull out *Women Beware Women* or *Tamb-*

urlaine in between every-other-season productions of *A Midsummer Night's Dream* because, well, they're the Royal Shakespeare Company; even so, if critics lambast their halfhearted Shakespearean efforts—which they often do—audiences still demand their hero.[70] When I sat down in production meetings to hammer out budgets for *Cardenio* I couldn't sell it just by relying on the enthusiastically choice words of my producer and PBSF co-founder Kermit Christman: "This play's about killing, fucking, and spooks. It's brilliant!" Backers and donors busied themselves at fund-raisers by helping Hamilton bring his brave, bold assertions to light, doting on a play that could only be brought to the stage by a lie (which might be the real instance of grave-robbing in all of this). Meanwhile, we were in the rehearsal hall saying, "We don't care who wrote this damn thing, it's *good*."

And it is good. And entertaining (when did that become a literary fault?). And not Shakespeare. Jensen reports on an experiment, performed a few years after my production, that attempted to prove Hamilton's *Cardenio* thesis through a staged reading.[71] No audience members thought it was by Shakespeare. Jensen does not record, however, whether anyone thought it was an enjoyable piece of drama. During a postperformance discussion in which the director and actors talked about lines "not fit[ting] in the actor's mouth" like in Shakespeare,[72] the audience was less concerned about just having had an enjoyable night out at the theater than with a different verdict that hinged on a myopic bit of logic: if it's not by Shakespeare, it's not good. Too many of us conveniently forget that the most popular play of the English Renaissance was not written by the Stratford lad.[73] We still produce our efforts in a climate that drives critics to praise a wildly successful production of *The Maid's Tragedy* at the recently reopened Globe in London, only to later moan, "But how one wishes Shakespeare could have breathed down Beaumont's and Fletcher's necks to nudge their pens in the direction of genius."[74] I don't. I adore Shakespeare, and have pretty much built my thinking and artistic lives around him, but I don't want him breathing down anyone's neck; his windy suspiration is fine kept to itself and his voluntary—not twenty-first century wished-for—collaborations. Along these lines, I hope that Middleton finds for himself an increasingly important place on all of our stages so that he can begin to cast off the looming dramatic shadow of his elder contemporary. That way, I can dream of winning, like the fictional actor Nicholas Craig, "Best Actor In A Hitherto Unperformed Late Jacobean Tragedy."[75]

Notes

1. Lancashire defines the play as "an orthodox Jacobean tragedy in that it functions as a dramatic moral exemplum—or set of exempla—showing the rewards of

virtue and the evil consequences of vice." Anne Lancashire, ed. *The Second Maiden's Tragedy*. Baltimore: Johns Hopkins University Press, 1978, 38; hereafter *SMT*. In light of all of the play's Christian themes, however, she admits that as a "theatrical tour de force," its effects have "been lost for modem readers because of our unfamiliarity with the conventions and motifs—for example, of the saint's life—upon which it depends" (33), a problem discussed throughout this paper.

2. I first came to produce the play by way of Shakespeare, when in 1994 handwriting expert Charles Hamilton tried to pass off *The Second Maiden's Tragedy* as *Cardenio,* the now-lost play attributed in the Stationers' Register to Fletcher and Shakespeare. Hamilton's book was a laughably argued conspiracy theory, casting naysayers as blind defenders of Shakespeare's canon, unenlightened by truth. But for the Palm Beach Shakespeare Festival, which I helped found as a young actor in 1990 and for which I was serving as co-Artistic Director at the time, it shone light on a play that was more than likely never going to get produced without the kind of attendant publicity Hamilton's argument brought. We found enough interest and money to mount *Cardenio* in south Florida and then move the show to a month long off-Broadway run that generated mostly favorable reviews in both the New York and national presses: pre-show flutter was stirred up enough that Donna Karan designed the costumes. I will call that production *Cardenio* throughout this discussion, for at the time and for all associated with it, that's what it was (a rationalization dealt with in my conclusion).

3. I am grateful to Gary Taylor for providing galley proofs of *The Lady's Tragedy* from the forthcoming Oxford Middleton, for which he serves as general editor. The Oxford edition of the play, edited and with critical commentary by Julia Briggs, includes two complete texts, printed in parallel. These are the "Original" and "Playhouse" texts, respectively, designated by the obvious original material and the additions and cuts marked by George Buc and the King's Men in the sole surviving manuscript (it certainly served as a prompt book for the troupe). Throughout my discussion, unless otherwise noted, I cite the "A" text. See Briggs's introduction for the text's history; Julia Briggs, ed., *The Lady's Tragedy,* by Thomas Middleton, in *The Collected Works of Thomas Middleton,* gen. ed. Gary Taylor, (Oxford: Oxford University Press, forthcoming).

For authorship arguments, see Lancashire, *SMT,* 19–23; Julia Briggs, "'The Lady Vanishes': Problems of Authorship and Editing in the Middleton Canon," in *New Ways of Looking at Old Texts, II,* ed. W. Speed Hill (Tempe: Renaissance English Text Society, 1998), 109–20; Eric Rasmussen, "Shakespeare's Hand in *The Second Maiden's Tragedy,*" *Shakespeare Quarterly* 40 (1989): 1–26, and "Reply to MacD. P. Jackson," *Shakespeare Quarterly* 41 (1990): 406–7; MacD. P. Jackson, "The Additions to *The Second Maiden's Tragedy:* Shakespeare or Middleton?" *Shakespeare Quarterly* 41 (1990): 402–5.

4. Bruce R. Smith, *Shakespeare and Masculinity* (London: Oxford University Press, 2000), 4.

5. Smith, *Shakespeare and Masculinity,* 5.

6. Ibid.

7. I have been asked more than once by colleagues and mentors whether I'm speaking as an actor/director or a scholar in these assertions, especially in a paper that

discusses both the academic and theatrical. My choices as the former are often informed by my studies as the latter, and vice versa: my production wouldn't have gone up without my academic work, and this academic work is very much inspired by that production. I hope, then, that I am speaking as both, though it seems not everyone would accept that claim. See Worthen for a worthy, indepth exploration of the "anxiety about the location of a legitimate Shakespeare—in the words on the page or in their embodiment on the stage" in which he also addresses the very type of work I'm introducing here. See W. B. Worthen, *Shakespeare and the Authority of Performance* (New York: Cambridge University Press, 1997), 97, esp. 135–33. I trust he will be pleased to learn that I not only know who Stephen Orgel is—Worthen laments that Orgel and other scholars "representative of the state of contemporary critical thinking about Shakespeare . . . are absent" in the *Players of Shakespeare* series (126)—but have benefitted from his comments on my previous work and cite him below as well.

8. Rebecca W. Bushnell, *Tragedies of Tyrants: Political Thought and Theater in the English Renaissance*. (Ithaca: Cornell University Press, 1990), 121.

9. Bushnell, *Tragedies of Tyrants*, 120.

10. Bushnell, *Tragedies of Tyrants*, 118.

11. For *Cardenio*, male actors were practically cast in pairs as carefully as they were put opposite their female counterparts, and I relied on a few obvious, if stereotypical, male and unmanly attributes for costuming and vocal performance. Govianus (E. Patrick Murphy) was clean-shaven, crop-haired, somewhat boyish in appearance, described by one critic as "a fugitive from *West Side Story*" (Hap Erstein, "Cardenio' fast-paced, full of sex, violence." Rev. of *Cardenio*, by William Shakespeare, Palm Beach Shakespeare Festival, Old School Square Theater, Delray Beach FL, *Palm Beach Post*, 19 Feb. 1995, 10B), which says a great deal about how easy it is in performance to see Govianus as more of a boyish Romeo than heroic revenger. As the Tyrant, I was fully bearded, had longer, unruly hair, and was much different vocally: while Murphy's Govianus was a soft-spoken, emotional poet king, my Tyrant grew increasingly manic in speech as he repeatedly failed to win the Lady's affections, a choice that led to my performance being critiqued as "verbally nimble and forceful" (10B). I'm afraid I tore a passion to tatters in the final scene, though, which on some nights produced an unlooked for *grand guignol* finale that produced various degrees of laughter.

12. An explanation for my use of "household" here. The Tyrant has gained political control of a kingdom, but has not achieved domestic control over his seat of power: the castle that is his home. A single-set design, which we employed in the form of a mostly bare stage, produces interesting effects. With virtually no scene changes—only two or three chair/throne placements and removals; the Lady's tomb I address below—and scenes running rapidly one into the other, it seemed as if the play's action took place in one castle: a Poe-like "castellated abbey," as it were. All of the nobles could live "at court." References to various "houses" work, as the word can signify more of an apartment than a single structure. Ultimately, Anselmus's suggestion of the "unbounded kingdom of the mind" (1.2.13) leads to images of an autonomous corrupt court and castle representing the ills of an entire country. Wickham, Doebler, and Lancashire have all addressed Shakespeare's dialogue-established castles merging thematically and metaphorically into one, and Middleton employs the

device, if it can be called that, to great success in *The Changeling.* The most powerful visual effect this single emblematic castle/household setting achieved for our production occurred between 5.1 and 5.2. After 5.1, which leaves five dead bodies onstage, the stage went dark with a red cyclorama behind, producing a silhouette effect. The dead actors slowly rose to dirgelike music, went upstage, and replicated their earlier, dead, positions. During this, the Tyrant, the Lady's corpse, and her chair were brought on and as the lights came up 5.2 began. For the remainder of the play, all five dead bodies could be seen in the shadows upstage, and the Tyrant's chamber, and by extension his castle and kingdom, became a "circumscribed hell." Wickham and Doebler are cited in Lancashire. (See Anne Lancashire, 'The Emblematic Castle in Shakespeare and Middleton," in *Mirror up to Shakespeare,* ed. J. C. Gray (Toronto: University of Toronto Press, 1984), 224–27. See also Neill for a discussion of *The Changeling,* its castle, and "The Castellated Body." Michael Neill, *Issues of Death: Mortality and Identity in English Renaissance Tragedy* (New York: Oxford University Press, 1997), 168–97.

13. I may have been way out of order, but when I played Macbeth for PBSF in 1996, I sometimes grabbed my crotch in anger and frustration at 3.1.62–63: "Upon my head they placed a fruitless crown, / And put a barren sceptre in my grip." All references to Shakespeare in this paper are to the modern-spelling edition of the Oxford *Complete Works.*

14. There are many innocent variants of this theme on the early modern stage, most obviously Romeo's kissing of Juliet's "dead" body. As Bamford notes, the subject of active and actual sexual necrophilia is addressed only in dialogue (not staging) in *Periander,* presented in February 1608 at St. John's college, Oxford. Karen Bamford, *Sexual Violence on the Jacobean Stage* (New York: St. Martin's Press, 2000), 194.

15. Dahmer's crimes are more familiar to American readers than Nilsen's. Nilsen, bizarrely described (like it's a contest) as "one of the more accomplished of recent necrophiliacs," was a British civil servant who admitted to killing as many as sixteen young gay men in London and using their corpses in ways identical to Dahmer's: for intercrural sex and as masturbation objects, followed by dismemberment. Roy D. Eskapa, *Bizarre Sex* (New York: Quartet Books, 1987), 244.

16. See Bataille for the most detailed account of the Frenchman's crimes (George Bataille, *The Trial of Gilles de Rais,* trans. Richard Robinson. [Los Angeles: Amok, 1991]). He murdered and mutilated scores of young children, often masturbating while killing them and sometimes over their dead bodies. His sensational trial, documented in painful detail, sent him to the rope and then the stake in October 1440. Most documented cases of necrophilia involve saddism and murder, with the necrophilia serving as an extension of violence. See Eskapa, *Bizarre Sex,* 244–48; D. J. West, *Sexual Crimes and Confrontations: A Study of Victims and Offenders* (Brookfield: Gower, 1987), 186–93; and Richard D. Laws and William O'Donohue, *Sexual Deviance: Theory, Assessment, and Treatment* (New York: Guilford, 1997), 198–200.

17. This is an issue my performance account continues to discuss throughout, particularly as it pertains to staging Middleton. Middleton is hardly a vague playwright when it comes to sex. Shakespeare, of course, can be pretty creative with the issues of sexuality, violence, and death, but Middleton out-Herods Herod in this department, presenting incest, parental pimping, spouse selling, marital rape, voyeurism, castra-

tion, masturbation, transvestitism, pedophilia, and sexual cannibalism in his work. Gary Taylor, *Castration: An Abbreviated History of Western Manhood* (New York: Routledge, 2000), 26–27. The Lady foreshadows the sexual reality of the Tyrant's necrophilia when she envisions in act 3 being dragged to his bed and raped. In act 4, we see the dragging and can hardly be doubtful about what follows.

18. Laws and O'Donohue, *Sexual Deviance,* 198.

19. Laws and O'Donohue, *Sexual Deviance,* 406.

20. Elizabeth Foyster, *Manhood in Early Modern England: Honour, Sex and Marriage* (New York: Longman, 199), 10.

21. Inhuman monsters can be dramatically sympathetic, even necrophilic ones. Francis Ford Coppola's 1993 film *Bram Stoker's Dracula* betrayed its title's proclamation of authorial authenticity by introducing a huge background subplot for the origins of Gary Oldman's Dracula. In the film, Dracula is "forced" to become a vampire after attacking the church for refusing to give his suicidal wife a Christian burial (she had killed herself in despair, thinking that he'd been slain in battle). Centuries later, though his wife is "dead," he finds her reincarnated in Mina Harker. Pursuing her "beyond the grave," the film's marketing slogan was demonstrably necrophilic: "Love Never Dies."

22. Martin Wiggins, ed., *Four Jacobean Sex Tragedies* (New York: Oxford University Press, 1998), xvi.

23. Rowland Wymer, *Suicide and Despair in the Jacobean Drama* (Brighton: The Harvester Press, 1986), 125.

24. Celia Daileader, *Eroticism on the Renaissance Stage: Transcendence, Desire, and the Limits of the Visible* (New York: Cambridge, 1998), 94.

25. See Stallybrass for a fascinating study of Bakhtinian grotesqueness and bodily consumption in *The Revenger's Tragedy,* in which the tongue not only "stands in for the arts of rhetoric, which are conceptualized both in terms of female seduction and excess," but "in terms of phallic domination" as well. Peter Stallybrass, "Reading the Body and the Jacobean Theater of Consumption," in *Staging the Renaissance,* ed. David Scott Kastan and Peter Stallybrass (New York: Routledge, 191), 215. I imagine, though Stallybrass does not explicitly suggest it, that the domination of the phallus is made possible by the tongue metaphorically replacing it, be it in a man's or a woman's mouth.

26. I had the wicked pleasure of playing Vindice in a staged reading of *The Revenger's Tragedy,* directed by Andrew Hartley, for the Georgia Shakespeare Festival's Middleton Symposium, held in Atlanta 30 March–1 April 2001. My wife remarked how strange it was to hear the Tyrant's voice faintly echoed in Vindice's speeches to the skull.

27. Daileader recalls the "powerful eroticism" inherent in watching two performers engaged in postinterment stage action in a production in Bristol in 1994 (100–101). I am much indebted to Professor Daileader for her guidance and encouragement throughout the development of my argument.

28. West, *Sexual Crimes,* 79.

29. Laws and O'Donohue, *Sexual Deviance,* 407.

30. Sara Eaton, "'Content with Art'?: Seeing the Emblematic Woman in *The Second Maiden's Tragedy* and *The Winter's Tale,*" in *Shakespearean Power and Punish-*

ment: A Volume of Essays, ed. Kendall et al. (Madison N.J.: Fairleigh Dickinson University Press, 1998), 72.

31. Romeo, of course, is quick to blame Juliet for his own masculine shortcomings: "O sweet Juliet, / Thy beauty hath made me effeminate, / And in my temper softened valour's steel" (3.1.113–15).

32. See Kevin Crawford, "'He was torn to pieces with a bear': Grotesque Unity in *The Winter's Tale,*" *Journal of the Fantastic in the Arts* 10.3 (1999): 206–30.

33. *Nightwatch* belongs to the horror/suspense genre, and features a sadistic killer who has sex with his victims' corpses (his motive for killing, we are led to believe); it features Nick Nolte trying very hard to be Boris Karloff, to amusing success. *Kissed* is much more interesting and unique, and presents a younger, female protagonist who works in a funeral parlor and believes that an energy, sometimes sexual, emanates from a life-form changing states. The extent of her activities becomes obsessive for her, and leads her boyfriend to commit suicide: so he can "be with her."

34. Kürsten earned the moniker "Monster of Düsseldorf" for the attempted or actual murder of over forty people (often involving sexual torture, rape, and necrophilia) and was executed in 1931 (West, *Sexual Crimes,* 190); Englishman Owen was convicted of molesting corpses in 1985, some of which were prepared for burial in his own village church graveyard (Eskapa, *Bizarre Sex,* 247).

35. This brief speech, quoted at full below, is in the "Playhouse," or "B" text. In 1995, my company was using Lancashire's edition, which is a conflated text, and we found the speech necessary for staging reasons, discussed below. We were justifiably engaged, I like to think, in same kind of dramatic rearranging and cutting that resulted in a "B" text in the first place.

36. See Alexander Leggatt, *"The Winter's Tale* Retold," *Shakespeare Quarterly* 44 (1993): 483–87, and Crawford, 223–24.

37. I have always admired, and tried to emulate here, Derek Jarman's handling of Marlowe's *Edward II* 4.239–73 in his 1992 film adaptation of the play. Though textually heavily cut, Nigel Mortimer here handles the planning of Gaveston's murder over a boardroom table surrounded by the lords, discussing it as if he were organizing a social function.

38. Neill, *Issues of Death,* 357.

39. Daileader notes that the 1994 Bristol production left "the audience with a disturbing sense of their voyeuristic participation" (102), debating as well the directorial options of using a live actress or a doll figure to "play" the Lady's corpse. While both my production and the Bristol effort had the actress playing the Lady stand in as her corpse, it is equally disturbing to note for the opposing option of a mannequin that "men who purchase, and use, inflatable plastic or vinyl life-size dolls . . . which are equipped with the necessary orifices for sexual intercourse, are manifesting a form of latent necrophilia" (Eskapa, *Bizarre Sex,* 247).

40. Soliloquies are quite different, obviously. What is at work in this scene, particularly as we cut it, is similar to *Cymbeline* 2.2, in which Giacomo emerges from a trunk and observes Innogen's partially revealed nude body (at least her breast is visible to him, as he sees its "mole, cinque-spotted" (38). He behaves the way he does precisely because he is unobserved. We are vicariously made part of that ocular and sometimes physical ravishment, as we are to a certain degree in our cut scene of *The*

Lady's Tragedy. Bamford also discusses similarities between these two scenes (81–97).

41. This play, like *The Revenger's Tragedy,* has an obsession with "lips." Discussing the latter drama, Coddon notes that "while [Glorianna's] sexual organs have presumably long turned to dust, the fact that the skull kills with its 'lips' suggests the *vagina dentata,* even without an actual vagina." Karin S. Coddon, " 'For Show or Useless Property': Necrophilia and *The Revenger's Tragedy," ELH* 61 (1994): 76. The audience could make what they might out of the "senseless lip" reference in *The Lady's Tragedy,* though the placement of my head at the end of 4.3 left little doubt as to which lips the Tyrant had most recently been kissing on stage.

42. Lancashire, *SMT,* 45.

43. As a director who often wields a line-, speech-, and sometimes scene-slashing pen, I am fond of pointing to Stephen Orgel's essay regarding "authentic" Shakespearean text, which suggests that Elizabethan and Jacobean playwrights knew full well the authorial control they would lose through performance rearrangement and cuts. The *acting* text supplanted the *written* text, which was invariably too long for the accepted playing time of the era, "a situation [those playwrights] understood, expected, and helped to perpetuate." Stephen Orgel, "The Authentic Shakespeare," *Representations* 21.4 (1988): 7. This usurpation goes beyond mere cutting, of course, into the realm of performance: our responses to a character on the page can alter with the slightest vocal or physical attributes of the actor delivering those lines. This does not—or, I should say, *should* not—threaten the "authority" of the text, just as the work of academic scholars should not seek to undermine the work of actors and directors.

44. We might look at this scene, in which true lovers are forced apart by political or parental forces, as one steeped in a tradition of courtly love, as Brodwin does; she calls the play "the most important Courtly Love tragedy after *Romeo and Juliet."* Leonora Leet Brodwin, *Elizabethan Love Tragedy 1587–1625* (New York: New York University Press, 1971), 194. But what we'd "normally consider," as I phrase it above, doesn't really work here, nor do simple genre classifications completely satisfy me as audience or reader. This scene anticipates a rape, and a necrophilic one at that. We are brought into a completely different, peculiarly Middletonian, sexual dimension, and as the sexual world of this play changes, so must our conventional view of the lovers in it. For discussions more thoroughly devoted to the issues of reading and performing Middleton in Shakespearean-dominated theatrical and academic scenes, see Gary Taylor, "The Incredible Shrinking Bard," *Shakespeare and Appropriation,* ed. Christy Desmet and Robert Sawyer. (New York: Routledge, 1999), 197–205, and "Bardicide," *Shakespeare and Cultural Traditions: Proceedings of the Fifth World Shakespeare Congress.* ed. Tetsuo Kishi, Roger Pringle, and Stanley Wells. (Newark: University of Delaware Press, 1994), 333–49. Taylor also delivered a comparison of the playwrights' addressing of matters sexual entitled "Middleton in Bed" for GSF's Middleton Symposium keynote lecture.

45. Wiggins, *Sex Tragedies,* xvii.

46. Bamford, *Sexual Violence,* 96.

47. Ibid.

48. Ibid.

49. See Daileader for a discussion of the Lady as Christ (92–106). In this reading, Govianus might be seen metaphorically as the church, and, accordingly, more weak and more feminized than the Lady herself.

50. I strongly disagree with Bamford's assertion here as well, that this "resurrects Govianus in our eyes as the clever hero of the revenge tradition and signals his commitment to some form of struggle in this world" (96–97). Outwitting moronic soldiers after napping through his girlfriend's suicide is not clever. Moreover, he's not committed enough to earthly struggles to beat down suicidal urges at 4.4.81–83.

51. *Lr.* 2.2.451–62; *R3* 4.2.67; *H5* 4.6.30–31.

52. Fredson Bowers, *Elizabethan Revenge Tragedy 1587–1642* (Princeton: Princeton University Press, 1966), 179–83.

53. Coddon, "For Show or Useless Property," 71.

54. Coddon, 'For Show or Useless Property," 76.

55. Lancashire, *SMT,* 33–34, 45–47.

56. In our production, Votarius and Anselmus—like Govianus and the Tyrant—were cast for sexual contrast. Votarius (square-jawed, chiseled, handsome Chris Shaw) was constantly eyeing women during his opening scene, as we had young female servants busying themselves upstage as Anselmus tried to keep his friend's attention, especially as the maids giggled and flirted. Later, Votarius became physically aggressive with the Wife very quickly, coupling "The roses on your cheeks are but new blown" (1.2.187) with a stroke of her face, and attempting an embrace while announcing "I'd be the man myself should serve your pleasure" (214). Once the Wife had been seduced, the two could hardly keep their hands off one another (the Wife was conveniently and sensually played by Shaw's then wife, Heidi Harris). Anselmus (more pretty than handsome, a soft-featured Paul Cameron), had no interest in any feminine presence and doted on his houseguest to the obvious neglect of his wife, with strong homoerotic undertones. He often touched Votarius's shoulders as they spoke, shrunk from the Wife's physical entreaties, and, while very much concerned about her fidelity, seemed to be more worried about his reputation than the actual sexual betrayal. When the Wife remarked "You parted strangely from me" (2.2.52), he borrowed her compact mirror and checked his face for blemishes with a blasé "That's forgotten," and then moved quickly to other interests: "Votarius! I make speed to be in thine arms" (53). It was quite apparent that "the sweet mistress" of their friendship, and "the roughness of a man's embrace" that Volarius invokes, was what Anselmus preferred as well.

57. Foyster, *Manhood,* 139.

58. Foyster, *Manhood,* 130.

59. Brodwin, *Elizabethan Love Tragedy,* 95.

60. Foyster, *Manhood,* 66–67.

61. Foyster, *Manhood,* 66.

62. Ibid.

63. Foyster, *Manhood,* 126.

64. Foyster, *Manhood,* 127–28.

65. Foyster, *Manhood,* 126–27.

66. Foyster, *Manhood,* 127.

67. Smith, *Shakespeare and Masculinity,* 108.

68. This question was addressed at the eighth meeting of the Group for Early Modern Culture Studies, November 2000, during a panel that included Kate Levin wrestling with staging *A Chaste Maid in Cheapside* (accompanied by a video of her production for CUNY); Ralph Cohen discussing Middletonian comedy for predominantly Shakespearean audiences (his delightful conclusion: "Do the dick jokes!"); Andrew Hartley's take on metatheatrical cruelty in *The Revenger's Tragedy;* Paul Yachnin's hopes for a "Big-Time Middleton"; and my delivery of the performance account in this paper.

69. For a rare and interesting discussion on directing Jonson, see Kate D. Levin, "Unmasquing *Epicoene:* Jonson's Dramaturgy for the Commercial Theater and Court," *New Perspectives on Ben Jonson,* ed. James Hirsh (Madison: Fairleigh Dickinson University Press, 1997), 128–53.

70. Taylor, "Shrinking Bard," 200.

71. Michael P. Jensen, "Testing *The Second Maiden's Tragedy* in Performance," *Shakespeare Bulletin* 15.2 (1997): 29.

72. In the past ten years for PBSF, I have played Macbeth, Hamlet, Benedick, Prospero, both Dromios, Sir Andrew Aguecheek, and Leontes, among others. All of those parts have lines, even entire speeches, that do not easily "fit in one's mouth" and roll trippingly off the tongue. Leontes alone can induce slurring and lisping on a grand scale. This is hardly a reasonable litmus test for authorship.

73. Taylor, "Bardicide," 344.

74. Kate Kellaway, Rev. of *The Maid's Tragedy,* by Francis Beaumont and John Fletcher. Shakespeare's Globe. Globe Theater, London, *Theatre Record* 17 (1997): 1084.

75. The RSC's 2002 ensemble season of Jacobean plays mounted incredibly successful productions of Shakespeare's *Edward III;* Marston's *The Malcontent;* Johnson, Marston, and Chapman's *Eastward Ho!;* Massinger's *The Roman Actor;* and Fletcher's *The Island Princess.*

The Career of Andrew Cane, Citizen, Goldsmith, and Player

JOHN H. ASTINGTON

IN *The Jacobean and Caroline Stage* G. E. Bentley indexes Dudley Carleton and Viscount Dorchester as two distinct persons, whereas they were, from 1628 onward, one. Sir Dudley Carleton's habitual role in theater history is largely a passive one, as the expatriate recipient of letters on current affairs from John Chamberlain and other correspondents, but in 1631 he stepped, however briefly, into the spotlight as an agent of theater business and management of men. As a secretary of state he arranged the issue of a royal license "vnto Andrew Kayne And others by the name of Seruants to the Prince" to operate as a playing company at the Salisbury Court playhouse in London, and in cities and boroughs throughout the kingdom. Cane and his fellow actors were sworn as royal servants—grooms of the chamber in ordinary, the traditional rank of players in royal service[1]—in the following May, 1632.[2] In late 1631 the future King Charles II was eighteen months old, and hardly required a troupe of players to entertain him. There was undoubtedly some royal initiative behind the foundation of the company, however, since Edward Sackville, Earl of Dorset, who was lord chamberlain to the household of Queen Henrietta Maria, appears to have been involved in choosing Cane and his fellows; his wife, Mary, Countess of Dorset, was the first official guardian of the infant prince.[3] She was succeeded by William Cavendish, Earl of Newcastle, a figure who will concern us later in this essay. So, although Bentley characterized Prince Charles's Company as "an inferior troupe"[4] they actually went on to enjoy consistent royal patronage during the remaining decade before the wars. They also seem to have been successful in their commercial life in the popular north London theaters, the Red Bull and the Fortune, for which larger buildings they abandoned the Salisbury Court playhouse soon after their foundation, although we know virtually nothing of what they played there; a number of the actors from the troupe went on to playing in continental Europe during the Commonwealth. Their leading comic actor, Andrew Cane, was one of the legendary performers of the 1630s, remembered for many years afterward. He seems to have taken seriously the oath he swore in 1632 as a royal servant, leaving London for Oxford after 1642, although he probably did not live to see the restoration as king of the prince he had served as a player.

Cane's biography can now be considerably expanded beyond the limits described by Bentley, chiefly on the basis of records in the Apprentice Books and Court Books of the Worshipful Company of Goldsmiths. They make clear that however eminent he became as a performer and leader of an acting troupe, he was in the first instance a goldsmith, serving an apprenticeship, running a shop, apparently throughout his years as a player, and returning to his trade in London in the 1650s. His son Edward became a goldsmith, and his grandson Andrew continued the family tradition into the eighteenth century. Throughout his working life as a freeman the first Andrew Cane took on apprentices, at least some of whom were also apprentice players. Although Cane was not the only leading actor to be a freeman of the company—Robert Armin was first apprenticed as a goldsmith in 1581, and took up his freedom in 1604, while John Lowin was a "brother" of the company[5]—the conduct of his concurrent careers, one in his shop, manufacturing and selling silverware, and the other in the playhouses and royal palaces, creating a quite different and less tangible product, seems to be unique, and is of great cultural interest. The milieux in which he operated in the two decades before the wars included those of the court, the rich city culture of one of the great companies, the day-to-day London life of making and selling goods in an increasingly "consumerist" market, and the rather raffish circles of popular entertainment. He must have known a great range of people from these divided and distinguished worlds, as we tend to think of them now, and his own view of the political events of his lifetime was no doubt informed by his particular and unusual breadth of experience. His width of observation is also likely to have influenced his playing; if we cannot now calculate how we can at least say something of the raw material on which he had to draw.

Cane belonged to the first generation of his family to become members of one of the great companies and citizens of London, unless he had some relationship to a rather older practicing goldsmith, a matter I will return to below. Andrew was preceded by his older brother Richard Cane, who was apprenticed to the goldsmith Christopher Ledane for ten years beginning at Christmas 1593, but who was granted his freedom on 16 January 1600. A little more than two and a half years later his brother became Richard Cane's apprentice, which Andrew witnessed in the company's apprentice book in his own hand:

Memorandum that I Andrew Kene the sonne of Robert Kene of Windesor bucher have put my selfe prentes to Richard Kene for tenn yeres begeneng at Bartholmutide in anno domine 1602

By me Andrew Kene.[6]

He in turn was granted his freedom in January 1611. That the two Canes, or Kenes, as they both signed their names as young men, were indeed brothers is confirmed by Richard's own apprenticeship bond, which described him as "the Soone of Robart Kene of Eaton in the countey of Buck Bucher."[7] Robert Cane evidently moved across the river in pursuit of his own trade.

Cane (and its variants) was a common name in the Windsor area in the later sixteenth and early seventeenth centuries. A tailor named Thomas Keyne was active in Eton in 1605, and in the same year one Anthony Keyne was admitted as a singing man of St. George's Chapel, becoming one of the clerks of the chapel in 1618, and a stipendiary of St. Anthony's in 1635.[8] Andrew Cane was not the only man of his surname in royal service. Many Canes are recorded in the parish books of both Windsor and Eton. A Robert Kayne married Ester Reddinge at the parish church of St. John, New Windsor in February 1566, and possibly the same man, now a widower, married "Lucresia Androes" on 14 June 1573.[9] This latter pair may have been the parents of Richard and Andrew Cane: the date and one of the names are right. (The Windsor entries do not record occupations, and the baptismal entries do not give parental names.) No baptismal record for a Richard Cane appears in the Windsor book—one might expect it between 1570 and 1580—and the Eton books do not survive before 1594. Nor do any Andrews appear in the Windsor book when one might expect an entry, roughly ten years after Richard, but on 2 March 1589 an unnamed "Keane" is recorded as having been baptized, the space for a Christian name left a blank, like several other entries in the book. If the name the clerk forgot was Andrew, then he was thirteen and a half when he became an apprentice. If this seems rather young, it was not unusually so in the Goldsmiths' Company: Cane's own apprentice Arthur Saville was just a year older when he bound himself for an eight-year term in 1631;[10] John Wright, apprenticed to Cane in 1629, was between thirteen and fourteen when he began.

Cane became a freeman of the Goldsmiths' Company and a citizen of London, then, at the company's court of 25 January 1611, when with two other graduating apprentices, Isaac Woodcock and Stephen Wren, "Andrewe Kene app[r] wth Richard Kene were sworne and made free by service": each paid his fee of three shillings.[11] Cane was, possibly, just a few weeks short of his twenty-second birthday. Freedom allowed one to open a shop and practice one's trade; it also allowed one to think of getting married. One sign of his immediate entry into business is that a little less than a year later Cane engaged the first of the nine apprentices he is known to have trained during his career:

John Hilton the sone of Henry Hilton of ffulham In the Countey of Midelsex yeoman have put my selfe A prentice to Andrew Cene Citizen and Gould Smith of

London for the tearme of Ten yeares at the bearth of o^r Saviour Christ last past being the 25th of December 1611.[12]

If Cane was setting himself up in London, however, there are also indications that he kept in touch with his native district, and may have married there. On 1 June 1612 in the parish church of St. John the Evangelist, Eton one Andrew Keine married a woman the latinized register records as "Maria Homses": Mary Holmes, perhaps, in a modern transcription. In the following year, practically nine months to the day later, the baptismal entries include, on 28 February 1613, "Richardus Keine filius Androe Keine." To name one's firstborn after one's elder brother and master would have been quite appropriate; if the father of this child was Andrew Cane the goldsmith, however, his wife was not living in London at this date. The name Mary, at least, corresponds with the record of seven years later, printed by Bentley, from 24 January 1620 in the parish book of St. Leonard Shoreditch: the baptism of "Thomas Cane s of Andrew Cane and Mary his wife."[13] If this family was Cane the goldsmith's neither Mary nor any of her recorded children appear to have survived Andrew Cane's lifetime. At his death his widow was named Anne, née Spencer, and his only surviving child was his son Edward, who must have been born no later than 1628, and hence was not Anne's natural son (see below).

Cane did not engage another apprentice until July 1621, just before John Hilton's stipulated term of service would have been complete, although there is no record of Hilton's having taken his freedom. From the following year, 1622, comes the first surviving notice of Cane as a player, from Sir Henry Herbert, who called him one of "the chiefe of them at the Phoenix," that is with the Lady Elizabeth's company at the Cockpit in Drury Lane.[14] The confusion in Herbert's records—Cane is listed as also being a member of the Palsgrave's company at the Fortune—has been interpreted to mean that he had just moved to the latter troupe; certainly he was with them for the following three years, until they disbanded in 1625.

So if Cane was a "chief" actor by July 1622 his stage career presumably began some years earlier, during the first decade of his career as a goldsmith. As we shall see, his activities as player and goldsmith were simultaneous: he did not stop working as one and become solely the other until political circumstances forced him to do so, and when Richard Kendall told Thomas Crosfield in July 1634 that "Mr Cane a goldsmith" was a chief player with Prince Charles's company at the Red Bull he did not mean that Cane *had been* a goldsmith—he still was, and one might buy goods from his shop.[15] In 1641 that shop was in the parish of St. Giles Cripplegate—somewhere near the Fortune playhouse, perhaps—and the parish book entry of July 1623 printed by Bentley, recording the christening of a foundling "taken up at Andrew Keines stall" seems to indicate that he had been long established there.[16]

It is impossible to say what may have led Cane, a provincial boy from a relatively prosperous background, like a famous predecessor, but unlike him set to make good in a profitable city career, to the stage. Cane's biography perhaps offers further evidence that the successful exploitation of theater business was regarded as well worthwhile, and possibly was more profitable than traditional trades, even those with a high status. Commercial calculation, at any rate, is as likely to have influenced Cane's enterprises as some romantic itch to act. It is pleasant to consider that the latter motive may have been encouraged by his loyalty to his company: he may have been initiated in the excitements of theatrical production in the very year he became a freeman. In October 1611 Sir James Pemberton, a goldsmith, became Lord Mayor, and the costs of mounting the annual show devolved upon the Goldsmiths' Company. Anthony Munday was hired to write the speeches and to plan the devices—the result was *Chrusothriambos*—and John Lowin was enlisted as the chief performer, in the part of Lepstone. Members of the company took part in the traditional processions, but also as whifflers and as the crew and costumed combatants in the water shows. On 9 August "50 of the young men of the company" were assembled at a session of the court to have their duties, in purse and in person, urged upon them. Later, in the middle of October, it became clear that the queen was intending to watch the water shows, and they were suitably expanded, with the help of foreign-born goldsmiths, to include more firepower: "in all betweene three & foure score shott wth theire moores & pages."[17] It seems entirely likely that Cane would have been involved in all this activity; if he had no direct contact with John Lowin he may have reflected on the famous actor's example.

Since two of Cane's apprentices, John Wright and Arthur Saville, bound respectively in September 1629 and June 1631, were certainly apprentice players as well as apprentice goldsmiths, it is possible that all the apprentices he took on during his theatrically active years were engaged with an eye to their usefulness in Cane's parallel career.[18] Assuming Cane began acting at least two or three years before he became a "chief" player, his other apprentices between 1620 and 1642 were Thomas Stayne (from July 1621 for eight years), Hugh Pusey (from Christmas 1626 for eight years), and Thomas Gibbins (from Christmas 1633 for nine years). We may here have the names of three more boy actors who played female roles in the various troupes with which Cane was associated; that their names have not been recorded in any surviving theatrical documentation is not strongly counterindicative, given the marginal status of most boy players in adult companies. Of the above five apprentices, three are known to have take their freedom as goldsmiths: Pusey in 1635, Saville in 1639, and Wright, finally, in 1646, under interesting circumstances, to which I will return. One more man may have trained under Cane solely as a player: there is no indication that he was ever connected with the Goldsmiths. This was William Hall, who in a suit against the King's

Company in 1660 explained the beginning of his career: he had "served an Apprenticeship in the Art of Stage playinge" and joined what he called Cane's company at Salisbury Court; his name appears among those sworn as "The Prince's Players" in 1632.[19]

During the first half of the 1620s Cane was a leading figure in the two companies named by Herbert. He appears to have joined the Palsgrave's company in the interim between the burning down of the first Fortune in December 1621 and the opening of the second (the spring of 1623?), perhaps recruited to add attractive new blood to a troupe in a difficult position, and certainly indicating that they were performing in some other theater while they waited for their new one. Cane may also have taken some leading role in the management of the company, although there is no direct evidence that he held shares: in early 1624 he was entrusted by the dying Francis Grace to administer payments to Grace's creditors, and in April of the same year he signed a bond with six other leading actors to keep together and play at the Fortune, on pain of forfeiture of a fine.[20] What happened to Cane's career after the bad plague closure of 1625 until 1631 remains unclear. When in the 1640s and 1650s he was sued by the heirs of Richard Gunnell, Cane's one-time colleague and the instigator of the 1624 bond, for an £80 debt to the estate, his written reply declared that money was payable only if the signatories left the company and the theater, and none of them did so. Bentley reads this statement to suggest that the entire group of actors, including Cane, continued to play at the Fortune until the later 1620s within a reconstituted troupe, the King and Queen of Bohemia's company.[21] The bond itself, however, had a term of only six months, and certainly one way of reading it, given what Cane says in his deposition, thirty years later, about its having been a "customary" and understood practice within the company, is that it was no longer binding after 1 October 1624. One of the original series of such documents, in other words, happened to survive in Gunnell's papers, and his daughter and her husband, the actor William Wintersel, attempted to capitalize on it after theatrical property had become worth very little, choosing as their target a suitably surviving, and perhaps suitably prosperous, signatory. What happened to Cane's career as a player after March 1625, then, beyond the term of the bond of agreement, when all playhouses closed for nine months, is far from clear.

At the least we know that he remained in London and continued goldsmithing, taking on the apprentices Pusey and Wright in late 1626 and September 1629. That Wright was clearly involved in the theater two years after his term began may suggest that if Cane had ceased playing in the mid twenties he had resumed by the end of the decade: his reappearance as the leader of a troupe in late 1631 is unlikely to have been directly from retirement, and he may indeed never have retired. In the 1630s, however, his various enterprises can be tracked more fully. Whether he himself looked back on the ten years before the wars—when he was in his forties and early fifties, if we accept the baptismal entry cited above—as the most intense and active of his life they certainly appear so from a modern perspective.

Bentley tends to write down to Prince Charles's company, reading the remaining evidence of its activities as signs of struggle and marginality. The title of his 1978 article, "The Troubles of a Caroline Acting Troupe," is indicative, as if other companies did not experience similar internal squabbling and litigation, in the 1630s or previous decades.[22] His view of playing at the Red Bull is that it was common, low, and rough, and hence that the move from Salisbury Court, which seems to have taken place at some point during 1633, was a step on the path to ruin. He expresses some surprise at the account from Norwich in 1636 that the company were "well clad and act by candlelight,"[23] as if such finesse were rather above them—forgetting that the same standards would have been demanded at court, where they performed numerous times during the six years from 1633 to 1639. As I read the evidence it seems that the company depended on the enterprise and management of two men: Cane and his partner Ellis Worth, who was a near contemporary, born in 1587 and dying at the age of seventy-two in 1659. Worth was also a neighbor, a resident in White Cross Street in 1654.[24] This pair apparently engaged the difficult actor William Bankes in 1632 or 1633, who subsequently took them to law, and they were also consistently named as leading players in other documentation to do with the troupe. In the course of their depositions in the Bankes affair Cane and Worth state that the move to the Red Bull was a company decision, jointly taken, and not the result of a crisis.[25] That is to say that some professional and commercial calculation governed it. They also give an estimate of the income Bankes had received as a player during the two years before he sued them as £40 per annum.[26] As Bentley points out, this was not comparable to the very rich income of sharers in the King's Men, but nor was it negligible. In early 1635, the date of the litigation, Prince Charles's Men were doing quite well playing at the Red Bull. The "odd transfer," as Bentley calls it,[27] to the northern playhouse is likely to have been undertaken as an informed move rather than a *pis aller*. The Red Bull may not have been as fashionable as Salisbury Court, but it was considerably larger and consistently popular, and perhaps could be rented more cheaply; Worth, who had long experience of playing there as a member of Queen Anne's Men, was in a good position to judge its relative advantages.

Three years after moving theaters the company survived the long plague closing of 1636–37 apparently without adverse effect, as other troupes did not, a testimony to their cohesion and resilience, and perhaps to the skill of their leadership. Bentley appears to think, given the company's title, that they should have done better for themselves in the social hierarchy of audiences, whereas I would read their career as commercially successful in choosing a certain share of the market. The social life and the tastes of the northwestern side of London, outside the walls, were intimately known by the two leaders of the troupe, who lived there.

At precisely the same time as he was establishing his new acting company Cane continued his parallel commerce, running his shop as a goldsmith. Perhaps his busy life led him to relax his standards a little, since in the annual search and inspection of goods undertaken by the company wardens in September 1633 Cane was fined for various items which were short in weight when assayed. The goods were all domestic and decorative silverware, perhaps Cane's specialty as a craftsman: two trencher salts (small bowls to contain salt on a dining table), a platter, a tobacco box, three pairs of hooks, and two buckles.[28] This is Cane's only appearance in such documents, but his son Edward had his goods examined and fined on three occasions, in 1656, 1658, and 1661. Edward made jewelry and other small items in gold and silver: rings of various kinds (including seal rings) as well as decorative buttons.[29] Since he had been trained by his father, we may take it that Andrew Cane made and sold such items also.

In the third summer of their existence, 1634, Prince Charles's company was chosen to accompany the king and queen on progress, an event which may not have been unique, but is so in having been recorded. Apart for the famous provision of a tent for the players, and the fee of £100, which Cane and Worth subsequently called "progress money," quite what their responsibilities may have been—how often they performed, where, and for whom—is not clear, but they evidently were retained to entertain the court and its various hosts as the traveling party moved from place to place.[30] As I shall suggest, perhaps one host in particular had some special interest in their skills. The progress lasted six weeks, and moved north as far as Nottinghamshire and southern Derbyshire, where the royal guests were entertained by William Cavendish, Earl of Newcastle, with whom they stayed at Welbeck and who feasted them at his second house on 30 July with the accompaniment of Ben Jonson's show, *Love's Welcome at Bolsover.* Bentley thinks that "the company did not stay with the court throughout the King's journeyings,"[31] but they were certainly in Nottingham in August, when they played for the town,[32] and then at Leicester and Coventry, parallel with the royal return journey southward, with its stays near Derby and Northampton. Perhaps the players, legitimately enough, represented themselves as a branch of the royal visit; they certainly rejoined the court in September, when they played at Hampton Court.

My interest is in their possible involvement with Newcastle's entertainment at Bolsover, which could have been produced with local talent from the earl's own household, as perhaps the show of the previous year, *The King's Entertainment at Welbeck,* had been.[33] Newcastle's wooing of the king over the course of two years was not entirely disinterested generosity: he was seeking to improve his profile at court and to gain some important post there;

some years later, in 1638, he became the governor of Prince Charles.[34] If this was being considered in 1634, then it would have been entirely appropriate to engage the prince's own players in an entertainment, in a mutual conferral of honor, and if both host and guests were aware of this in advance we may have some explanation of why this particular company was chosen to go on progress in the first place. *Love's Welcome at Bolsover* is not beyond the powers of amateurs, but the satirical portrait of Jones, Colonel Vitruvius, would have been considerably enlivened if played by a talented comic actor such as Andrew Cane, who probably knew something of its original. There are also parts for two boys, cast as Eros and Anteros, and a final speech by Philalethes that would have been more assured of its intended effect in the mouth of an experienced professional. Since the whole thing is short and dramatically simple it would not have required much rehearsal: it "could for need" have been learnt at short notice. The later account in his wife Margaret's *Life* of Newcastle speaks of his preparing the occasion "with all possible care and industry, sparing nothing that might add splendour" and spending "between fourteen and fifteen thousand pounds."[35] It seems to me likely that having commissioned Jonson as writer Newcastle availed himself of the professional players who arrived on his estates, and who perhaps had been specifically requested. We know the name of only one of Cane's stage roles—Trimalchio in *Holland's Leaguer*—but Jonson's Colonel Vitruvius, I propose, was a second, a part in key with Cane's general reputation for sprightly and lively acting.

Topical and satirical material seems to have been in Cane's line as a performer. He was known for performing jigs, in the tradition of Tarlton, and in September 1639 he was performing in a "scandalous and libellous" play which mocked contemporary taxation, the city government, and the law, acted at the Red Bull "for many days together."[36] As with other such infractions, however, an official inquiry seems to have been followed by no particularly harsh consequences for the actors, even at a time of deepening crisis. Cane was assessed and presumably paid his share of one contemporary tax in August 1641, the poll money administered by the Goldsmiths' Company as a contribution to the costs of the Scottish wars. As one of the "poore Freemen of the Company"—his standing from the Goldsmiths' point of view—he contributed one shilling.[37] By this time in his other career he was "Cane of the Fortune," as he is titled in the pamphlet *The Stage-Players' Complaint* (1641). A year earlier Prince Charles's company and that playing at the Fortune had exchanged theaters, for unknown reasons, and Cane ended his prewar playing on the stage of a playhouse where he had first appeared twenty years earlier, in the late Jacobean years.

His affiliation throughout most of the 1630s, however, ensured that he was known as "Cain the Clown at the Bull" when he featured in a demonstration at the Guildhall at the end of 1642.[38] Cane went to Oxford, the center of royalist administration, at some time after this, and stayed there for several years, until after the fall of the town to parliamentary forces in June 1646. According to Margaret Gunnell and William Wintersel, who attempted to sue him for debt on the 1624 players' bond in 1644, he was in the king's army, while according to the news pamphlet *Mercurius Britannicus* he was working as an engraver in the royalist mint, a task perhaps more suited to his age and experience—although he may well have been involved in both.[39] There is no official record of his work for the mint, the activities of which were in any case sporadic, with unreliable and intermittent supplies of bullion.[40] The leading royalist engraver, however, was another theatrical figure, the dramatist Thomas Rawlins, whom Cane may have known in London; it seems not unlikely that the two men worked together on the royal coinage.

During Cane's absence from London his apprentice John Wright, the boy player of Millicent in *Holland's Leaguer* of 1631, whose term should have been completed in September 1637, determined to take his freedom as a goldsmith. He had not done so before, evidently, because he had become principally involved in playing, independently of Prince Charles's company by 1639, when he was with Beeston's Boys at the Cockpit; he had perhaps joined them in 1637, at the end of his formal connection with Cane. After 1642 it became plain that goldsmithing paid more than playing, though it apparently took some years for Wright to be convinced of this, unless he too had enlisted in the army. After Naseby, but before the fall of Oxford, in March 1646, when he was thirty-two or thirty-three years old, Wright finally presented himself at Goldsmiths' Hall to pay his fee and take his oath as a freeman.[41] His sponsor was, unusually, not either his master or another goldsmith, but someone who knew both master and apprentice well.

> At this Courte John Wright app[r] to Andrew Keyne & his service certified by Ellis Worth was sworne & made free by service 2s 3d.[42]

Cane, Worth, and Wright had not only been colleagues as players, but belonged to the same parish and neighborhood: Wright's apprenticeship entry of 28 November 1629 describes him as "the sonn of John Wright of St Giles Criplegate Baker."[43]

As Wright returned to his first trade, so did Cane, possibly soon after Wright took his freedom. By October 1649 he had taken a new apprentice, Nathaniel Cooper, whom Cane subsequently presented for his freedom in January 1656. In the following month of November of 1649 Cane presented his son Edward to the court as freeman "by patrimony & vpon the testimony of John Hastings and Leonard ffletcher goldsmithes."[44] Two further apprentices, George Barrett and John Winnall, were taken on in 1653 and 1654, both with terms that extended beyond Cane's death: there is no indication that they ever took their freedom. The last personal appearance of Cane at

Goldsmiths' Hall, then, is likely to have been the occasion of Cooper's freedom in 1656.

While resuming the activity of his London shop Cane evidently did not
abandon the stage entirely. It is now clear that after the major battles of the
war had been fought many actors expected to be able to reestablish their careers and reopen the playhouses, particularly in the years between 1647 and
1649.[45] Surreptitious playing continued throughout the Commonwealth period, and we know about it now only through records of its having been
stopped. According to *Mercurius Pragmaticus* there was a raid on the Red
Bull playhouse on 21 January 1650, when Cane and other actors were arrested and imprisoned.[46] He was then about sixty, and may have decided that
enough was enough as far as the theater was concerned, although his participation in other protests against authority suggests a character given to asserting himself.

One further manifestation of his tendency to resistance occurred in December 1652 when both Andrew and Edward Cane signed a petition of certain
goldsmiths to Parliament "against the present Government of the Company,"[47] but they both did so using the surname "Decayne," which, in various forms, seems to have become the favored family name from the 1650s
onward. As he changed his name, so he appears to have moved his shop. In
1653 he was a parishioner of Holy Trinity, Minories, on the east side of the
city, just outside the walls, north of the Tower. With his son launched in life
Andrew Cane remarried in 1653, under his new surname, to a fellow parishioner named Anne Williams, probably a widow. The ceremony took place at
St. Nicholas Cole Abbey on 19 May.[48] Andrew's widow signed her will,
made in May 1661, as "Anne Decane," and referred to other members of her
family with that spelling of the surname;[49] her stepson's will, made in January 1688, refers to its principal subject as "I Edward de Cayne," his wife as
"Sarah D^e cayne," and his children (Sarah, Edward, Ann, and Andrew) with
the form "Decayne."[50] Such a change might smack of social pretension, or
might suggest that Cane the Clown of the Bull was attempting to put his past
behind him by taking on a new identity, with an extra syllable, as a respect-
ably established senior tradesman and citizen. It may, however, have been a
genuine resumption of an older form of the name, directly connected with
the city of London rather than Cane's native district of Berkshire and Buck-
inghamshire. On 30 August 1566 the Goldsmiths' Company granted freedom
by oath to one Lucas De Cayne: this probably meant that he was an alien
seeking to work in London, and no doubt French (De Caen?).[51] Even in 1611
there was a considerable cohort of foreign goldsmiths in the city, and the
company was glad to receive the assistance, for the Lord Mayor's Show, of
"dyuers french and other aliens workmen of this misterye."[52] How Lucas De
Cayne or other members of his family may have been related to his contemporary Robert Cane, butcher of Eton and Windsor, is impossible to know,

but there was perhaps some link that Andrew Cane himself discovered, or chose to recognize, only later in life. Certainly kinship connections were important in securing apprenticeships, particularly in the great companies, and it may be that Lucas De Cayne's contacts were significant in arranging Richard Cane's initial apprenticeship with Christopher Ledane (another Gallic surname) in 1593.

There is an intriguing clause in Anne Decane's will that suggests her husband was still discovering family connections at the time of his death; we might even read some exasperation into it.

> And lastly I doo give and bequeath unto all the Rest of the Kindred of my said Husband Andrew Decane that can any wayes make out unto my Executo[rs] hereafter named themselves to have any alliance or affinity of blood in the law the sume of Twelve pence apeece.[53]

Otherwise the will gives no clue of any residual connections with theater folk by 1661. Anne was then living in the parish of St. Botolph Aldgate, well away from Andrew Cane's old district, and her executors were respectable city people, two merchant tailors and a barber-surgeon. We learn of a godson of Andrew Cane, "Mr Horne a Barber liveing neer the Stocks London," who was willed five pounds,[54] but generally the will is of interest in indicating the Canes' relative wealth. Anne Decane left cash bequests of at least two hundred pounds to family and friends, and the phrasing of the will makes it clear that Edward Cane had already received his share of his father's estate (probably as least as much as Andrew Cane left to his wife): his stepmother bequeaths Edward a token ten pounds. So if Andrew Cane had been a "poor freeman" of the Goldsmiths he was so only by the very rich standards of that company: it appears that he left his family quite comfortably off. He no doubt died and was buried in the parish of Holy Trinity, Minories in the late 1650s. The burial records of the surviving parish book for that period peter out in early 1644, and do not resume in systematic detail until fifteen years later.

One other item of interest lies in the material evidence of Anne Decane's will as a physical object: it is both signed and sealed, the wax on the final sheet of five sheets of paper bearing the imprint of Anne's seal ring. The ring itself, worn on the finger of the living woman in 1661, is very likely to have been made by her husband, so that in the indented wax we have one remaining testimony to Andrew Cane's workmanship.

Had he lived to see the Red Bull reopen in 1660 Cane would have been in his early seventies, relatively no older than the indefatigable Richard Baxter, born in 1593 and still acting in 1664, but unlike Baxter without a network of colleagues with whom he had retained contact throughout the interregnum. The new profession was dominated by the exiles, and by former associates of the King's Men. The continuum in Cane's life was his work as a goldsmith, at which he appears to have labored steadily and consistently as apprentice and master for fifty-five years or so. Making and selling the kinds of goods we read about in the 1633 inspection record was his constant business; his hours upon the stage fluctuated with the fortunes of the companies in which he played and with the political and social upheaval of his lifetime. For twenty years he was far more famous as both a popular and a court performer than Baxter ever was, and he is surely the only leading actor of the pre-Restoration period to have maintained, for as long as he could, a double career. Other actors were freemen of various London trade companies, and yet other actors retired from the stage to take up other professions; no one else we know of combined the player's calling with the active business of a city tradesman in quite the manner of Andrew Cane.

Notes

1. E. K. Chambers, *The Elizabethan Stage,* 4 vols. (Oxford: The Clarendon Press, 1923), 2:104–5.

2. G. E. Bentley, *The Jacobean and Caroline Stage,* 7 vols. (Oxford: The Clarendon Press, 1941–68) [hereafter cited as *JCS*], 1:302–3.

3. Ibid., 303–4.

4. G. E. Bentley, "The Troubles of a Caroline Acting Troupe: Prince Charles's Company," *Huntington Library Quarterly* 41 (1978): 217–49, 243.

5. Armin was apprenticed for a term of eleven years in September 1581, and Lowin for eight years in December 1593. See Malone Society *Collections III* (Oxford: Malone Society, 1954), 141, 167. Armin's first master, John Lonyson, died in 1582, and he was reapprenticed to John Kettlewood for nine years. See Chris Sutcliffe, "Robert Armin: Apprentice Goldsmith," *Notes and Queries* (1994): 503–4, and Jane Belfield, "Robert Armin, Citizen and Goldsmith of London," *Notes and Queries* (1980): 158–59. That Lowin at least was granted his freedom is indicated by the terms by which he is referred to in the documents to do with his involvement in the 1611 Lord Mayor's Show (*Collections III,* 80–82).

6. Worshipful Company of Goldsmiths, Apprentice Book 1, f. 142 r. I am grateful to the company for granting access to their library, and for permission to quote their manuscript records. I would particularly like to thank the librarian, Mr. David Beasley, for his courteous assistance and advice.

7. Goldsmiths' Apprentice Book 1, f. 100 r.

8. Shelagh Bond, ed., *The Chapter Acts of the Dean and Canons of Windsor, 1430, 1523–1672* (Windsor: Oxley, 1966), 53, 55, 102, 168.

9. All quotations from the Windsor books are from transcriptions in the Library of the Society of Genealogists, London, checked against microform reproductions in the Berkshire Record Office, Reading. The Eton records are quoted from microfilm provided by the Mormon Family History Center, Toronto.

10. See William Ingram, "Arthur Savill, Stage Player," *Theatre Notebook* 37 (1983): 21–22.

11. Goldsmiths' Court Book for 1610/11, f. 702 r.

12. Goldsmiths' Apprentice Book 1, f. 201 r. Entry dated 7 January 1612.

13. *JCS,* 2:399.

14. Ibid., 398–99.

15. *JCS,* 1:309.

16. *JCS,* 2:399. That an infant might be left at his door after he had become a relatively young leading player could suggest further biographical speculation in two directions, not necessarily unrelated: paternity and prosperity.

17. *Collections III:* 80–84.

18. Cane, Wright, and Saville all appear in the cast list of the published version of Shakerly Marmion's *Holland's Leaguer* (acted in 1631 and printed the following year): Cane played *"Trimalchio, a humorous gallant,"* Wright and Saville respectively the female roles of *"Milliscent, daughter to Agurtes"* and *"Quartilla, Gentlewoman to Triphoena."* See *JCS,* 1:302–8, 321.

19. Judith Milhous and Robert D. Hume, "New Light on English Acting Companies in 1646, 1648, and 1660," *The Review of English Studies,* 42 (1991): 487–509, 489. See also *JCS,* 2:303.

20. Susan Cerasano suggests that Cane may have "served as the business manager." See S. P. Cerasano, "The 'Business' of Shareholding, the Fortune Playhouses, and Francis Grace's Will," *Medieval & Renaissance Drama in England* 2 (1985): 231–51; also E. A. J. Honigman and S. Brock, ed., *Playhouse Wills 1558–1642* (Manchester: Manchester University Press, 1993), 130–31.

21. *JCS,* 1:148–49, 263–64.

22. See note 4.

23. *JCS,* 1:312–13.

24. See C. J. Sisson, "The Red Bull Company and the Importunate Widow," *Shakespeare Survey* 7 (1954): 57–68.

25. Bentley, "Troubles," 237–38.

26. Ibid., 241–43.

27. Ibid., 238.

28. Goldsmiths' Court Books, 6 September 1633.

29. Ibid., 23 August 1656, 17 March 1658, 23 August 1661.

30. *JCS,* 1:310; Bentley, "Troubles," 241–42.

31. *JCS,* 1:311.

32. Unpublished transcript of Nottingham civic records, Records of Early English Drama, Toronto. I am grateful to Professor Alexandra Johnston, Director of REED, and to Professor John Coldewey, editor of the forthcoming Notthinghamshire volume, for permission to consult and refer to this material.

33. *JCS,* 4:648–49, 653–54.

34. See G. Trease, *Portrait of a Cavalier* (London: Macmillan, 1979), 67–76. Newcastle had a London house in Clerkenwell, in the district of the Red Bull, from about 1632. It was built on, and from, the ruins of St. Mary's Nunnery, and directly abutted the parish church. Its plan may be seen on Ogilby and Morgan's map of 1676, and a rather sketchy representation of it appears in the top left part of Hollar's *A Map or Groundplott of the Citty of London* (1666); the building survived until the 1790s. Newcastle's London residence stood roughly two hundred yards southwest of Red

Bull Yard, and it seems hard to imagine that the theater-loving earl did not visit such a conveniently local playhouse. His direct contact with the players who worked there may have increased after the early part of 1638.

35. *JCS,* 4:653.

36. Ibid., 1:314.

37. W. S. Prideaux, *Memorials of the Goldsmiths' Company,* 2 vols. (London: Eyre and Spottiswoode, 1896), 1:342.

38. *JCS,* 1:400.

39. Ibid., 400–401.

40. C. E. Challis, ed., *A New History of the Royal Mint* (Cambridge: Cambridge University Press, 1992), 281–83.

41. Wright's testimony about his age is given in a legal deposition cited by Sisson, op. cit., 67, n. 8.

42. Goldsmiths' Court Books, 13 March 1646.

43. Goldsmiths' Apprentice Book 1, f. 295 v.

44. Goldsmiths' Court Books, 23 November 1649.

45. See Milhous and Hume, 487–509.

46. *JCS,* 1:401.

47. Goldsmiths' Court Books, December 1652. See Prideaux, 2:21–25.

48. Parish book for 1650–1695, Guildhall Library Ms. 5686. I am grateful to Professor William Ingram for checking this entry for me.

49. Guildhall Library, Ms 9052/14.

50. Guildhall Library, Ms 9171/41.

51. Goldsmiths' Court Books, 30 August 1566.

52. *Collections III:* 83.

53. Guildhall Ms 9052/14, sheet 4.

54. Ibid., sheet 3.

"As proper a woman as any in Cheap": Women in Shops on the Early Modern Stage

LESLIE THOMSON

THEATER audiences of early modern London consisted of those who worked in shops and those who patronized them. As part of everyday life and shared experience the shop world seems a fitting context for the plots of plays these Londoners went to see. Perhaps, though, the commonplace was thought insufficiently exciting and exotic to be of interest; for whatever reasons, shop scenes are in fact relatively uncommon in late sixteenth- and early seventeenth-century drama. In the period from 1580 to 1642, only about thirty-two extant plays have stage directions that mention a shop or include dialogue, action, and props that define the location as a place where goods are sold. In some, shop scenes are substantial and central, but in others the shop element is merely incidental. Ten plays with significant shop scenes appeared between 1602 and 1613,[1] which doubtless reflects the growing importance of the shopkeeping class in the world of early Jacobean London. What all these scenes most obviously have in common is variety—of plot function, merchandise, setting, and action. But closer consideration reveals that about twenty of them share not only a shopkeeper but also a shopkeeper's wife (or sometimes a daughter)—a female character whose role increases significantly over the forty-five-year period from 1594 to 1639, during which it is possible to see the evolution of a minor dramatic and theatrical convention with a topical subtext. In particular, the wife who shares the running of a shop with her husband is depicted as not only an object of desire—put on display like a commodity for sale—but also a figure whose role in running the shop gives her a significant degree of freedom and authority. The paradoxes inherent in this duality are reflected in the erratic but nonetheless telling and increasingly ironic treatment of the shop women in these domestic-mercantile plays.

Women were of course important participants in the running of shops long before the sixteenth century. Writing of medieval London, Derek Keene observes that

> Retail trading in shops and selds offered a means of earning a livelihood to a very wide range of individuals. In particular, it provided an opportunity for women, who

145

might organise the distributive side of the family economy while their husbands manufactured items in the workshop or travelled in search of goods. Women might also look after a shop or a stall at the same time as supervising a household or children.[2]

It is difficult to know how such women were perceived in the early modern period because those few contemporary historians who comment on shops have little or nothing to say about the shopkeepers. John Stow, for example, mentions the kinds of shops on a given street and their history, and sometimes provides lists of the tempting goods they sold, but his focus is primarily on wealthy merchants who spent money on buildings and other good works.

Such silence can be contrasted to the frequent allusions to shopkeepers' wives as either comic or dangerous figures of temptation and disruption in satirical writings and the dialogue of plays. But these offer an ambiguous if not completely contradictory range of views. Among the most overt in implying that women in shops were literally for sale is a Ben Jonson epigram: "Hornet, thou hast thy wife dressed, for the stall / To draw thee custom: but herself gets all."[3] Similarly, in *The Family of Love,* Purge, an apothecary, seems to comment on how things are:

> The grey-eyed morning braves me to my face, and calls me sluggard: 'tis time for tradesmen to be in their shops; for he that tends well his shop, and hath an alluring wife with a graceful *what d'ye lack?* shall be sure to have good doings, and good doings is that that crowns so many citizens with the horns of abundance.[4]

Pasquils Palinodia similarly refers to "euery *Cuckold,* that cries *What de'e lack.*"[5] The speaker in this satiric poem offers advice for shopkeeping success:

> And therefore let a Tradesman that would thriue,
> First get a shop in some faire streete of taking,
> My next aduice is, that he fairley wiue,
> For such a toye is many a yong-mans making.
>
> ([B4v])

Other writers, while using the idea that a woman in a shop is a come-on, seem less ready to imply that their husbands are necessarily cuckolds. In *The Dutch Courtesan,* a shop wife's commercial importance is conveyed when Mistress Burnish, a goldsmith's wife, is said to be "as proper a woman as any in Cheap" because "she paints now, and yet she keeps her husband's old customers to him still. In troth, a fine-faced wife in a wainscot carved seat is a worthy ornament to a tradesman's shop, and an attractive, I warrant; her husband shall find it in the custom of his ware."[6] In *Tell-Trothes New-yeares Gift,* the author actually seems to blame the shopkeeper for the wife's seductive behavior; he offers an "Inuectiue against Jelosy," describing different kinds of jealous husbands:

> But these of the first kinde, are knaues in graine, that hauing lauisht their stockes leaudly by badd meanes, and seeing their estates to grow weake, will seeke out wiues not of the common sorte for properness, but suche matchlesse paragons, as are for neatnesse not to be mated in a countrey. These must bee sett in their shoppes to tole in customers, unto whome if they show not themselues good-fellowes by gentle speeches, their houses will proue to hoat for them. They must not sticke to promise fairley and to kisse, so they do it closely, onely this proviso must be had, that they keep them out of their money boxes and closecubberds. Which practice proouinge profitable, and thereby their estates being amended, straight false measure is suspected, and thereby on this their owne inuention misliked off.[7]

Some twenty years later, Thomas Gainsford expresses his criticism in a way that indicates the potential power available to a shopkeeper's wife:

> A citizen is more troubled with his wife then his wares; for they are sorted, locked vp and neuer brought out, but by constraint for the profit of their master; but his wife is decked, adorned, neatly apparelled, sits for the gaze, goes at her pleasure, and will not be restrained from any sights or delights, or merry-meetings; where they may shew their beauties, or riches, or recreate themselues.[8]

Recent studies have cited criticisms such as Gainsford's to argue that the primary focus of contemporary attacks on women was their insatiable desire for goods. Citing Stow, Karen Newman describes how

> The proliferation of goods described in the *Survey* and their availability for sale in the London exchanges and growing West End represent an early episode in the process of commodification under capitalism. Goods from the continent and from more exotic lands were for the first time available in numbers in England. . . . In the early seventeenth century, woman became the target for contemporary ambivalence toward that process. She is represented in the discourses of Jacobean London as at once consumer and consumed—her supposed desire for goods is linked to her sexual availability.[9]

And Ian Archer notes that "Consumption was a moral problem because the desire for goods was linked with sexual desire. The Christian tradition had conflated luxuria and lust: luxury was equated with desire, and desire with disobedience." He quotes moralists who "drove home the parallels between prostitution and trade" and observes how "The drama suggests that shopping expeditions by court gallants were as much occasions for sexual aggression against citizens' wives as for the purchasing of goods." He concludes:

Thus shopping became a locus for anxieties about the gender order: the apparent availability of women in the shops and the desire of city women for consumer goods threatened the patriarchal order on which the authority of citizen husbands rested.[10]

Certainly there is evidence to support this view, but while dramatists do sometimes present women as ravenous consumers, the plays with actual shop scenes are in fact more interested in the behavior of shopkeepers' wives and daughters when they are perceived as objects of desire—tokens in a commercial exchange with a customer or husband-to-be. Earlier in his essay Archer makes the important point that "Women probably enjoyed more independence in the capital because of the nature of their work, participating at the front of the shop, running an alehouse, buying provisions in the market" (p. 184). This idea—that women in shops enjoyed freedoms and acquired responsibilities analogous if not equal to those of men, and that these women were therefore perceived as a threat to social boundaries, which in turn exacerbated sexual and class tensions—is, I would argue, a view that goes a long way in explaining how female figures in stage shops are treated by both the other characters and the playwrights.

As the seventeenth century began, the growth of trade and the concomitant expansion of commercial London helped create a real-world context for plays set in the streets frequented daily by their audiences. Furthermore, the way this mercantile world was often created onstage, by discovering a woman in a recognizable "shop"—with table or shop board, merchandise, and apprentices—was itself an overtly theatrical event: the manner of presentation invited spectators to look at the figure onstage much as they might a real woman in a real shop. When the shop women in these plays complain of their vulnerability to the male "gaze" there is almost certainly more than one level of significance operating. Indeed, Stephen Gosson's criticisms of women in theater audiences suggests an attitude that might easily have included women in shops: "For this is general, that they which show themselues openly, desire to bee seene. . . . Thought is free: you can forbidde no man, that vieweth you, to noate you, and that noateth you, to iudge you."[11] He later warns, "You neede not goe abroade to bee tempted, you shall be intised at your owne windowes[.] The best counsel that I can giue you, is to keepe home, & shun all occasion of ill speech" (F4r). Women who sat in shops calling out "what d' ye lack?" would seem to have been acting contrary to this advice, thus posing a threat to male authority of the sort represented by Gosson.

The relationship between what is depicted in plays with shop scenes and what actually happened in the real world of the audience is of course virtually impossible to ascertain after four hundred years. Certainly it is dangerous to assume that the events and characters were, or were intended as, an accurate rendition of reality. But given the exaggeration typical of mildly satiric comedy, it is nevertheless possible that we are getting a response to (if not a reflection of) everyday experiences and attitudes. If the evident power and authority of women in the real shops were seen as threatening the established hierarchies of society and commerce, it would not be surprising if dramatists found ways to appeal to audiences by reflecting their ambivalence or resistance to such women. In fact, however, rather than encouraging or confirming spectators' reactionary prejudices, the women in shop scenes are never simply victims of successful patriarchal dominance. While the idea that a woman in a shop is "for sale" is certainly present, it is repeatedly used as a context for characters and events that call the fantasy stereotype into question. Furthermore, in the short-lived vogue for shop scenes in the plays of the early seventeenth century it is possible to see the convention developing in such a way that the women in them acquire more freedom over time rather than less.

The increase in the number of shops, and therefore of women in them, probably helps to explain why these women began to be seen in an increasing number of plays. In Robert Wilson's *The Cobler's Prophecy* (c. 1590, pr. 1594), Ralph Cobbler enters *"with his stoole, his implements and shooes, and sitting on his stoole, falls to sing."* [12] His wife Zelota calls to him from within, "year best leaue singing and fall to work by & by while I to buy meat for our dinner to market doo hie." Ralph replies, "And you were best leaue your scolding to, & get you away," threatening to "knock [her] on the head" if she comes out. When she does so, however, *"He creepes vnder the stoole"* (ll. 67–69, 71, 75), a stereotypical browbeaten husband. But then the play's supernatural element takes over, with Zelota being charmed by Mercury as punishment. She reappears again later, still "mad," and when she stabs and kills "a traitor" (l. 1358), she and Ralph are arrested. The play ends happily with Ralph deciding to give up his prophetic powers and become a cobbler again, to which Zelota agrees. There is no indication that she plays a role in the shop. This can be contrasted with the episodic *Locrine* (1591, pr. 1595), in which the clown Strumbo first appears as a cobbler. The scene opens with Strumbo, his wife Dorothy, and Trompart mending shoes and singing "we Coblers lead a merie life." [13] It seems clear that husband and wife are equals when Dorothy sings, "Most happie men we Coblers bee" and Strumbo refers to "our shop" (ll. 585, 589). Trompart urges Dorothy to "Drinke to thy husband" (l. 599) and she does so, after which she is silent for the rest of the scene and appears no more in the play. Her function here seems to be to establish that Strumbo's domestic life is carefree before he is conscripted into the army, but in doing this the playwright presents Dorothy as both a shop wife and fellow cobbler. In a third early play, Robert Yarington's *Two Lamentable Tragedies* (1594, pr. 1601), Merry is a tavernkeeper and Rachel is his sister who helps him in the tavern but also keeps house for him. One of the play's "tragedies" is the historical event of Merry's murder of a competitor and its consequences. Rachel is eventually executed with her brother for helping him to hide the evidence of his guilt. She appears in the shop, but as Merry's accomplice rather than his business partner.[14] In all of these early plays, although the shop world context is an important element of the plot and characterization, the shop women are not noteworthy as such.[15]

The particular theatrical convention I am tracing seems to have originated with Thomas Heywood's *1 King Edward IV* (1599, pr. 1600), which is partly a dramatization of that king's real-life conquest of Jane Shore, a goldsmith's wife. Significantly, many of the elements introduced in this play reappear in later treatments of similar material, but without the limitations imposed by historical events. That is, while the Jane Shore character might well be the basis for later shop wife figures, they can and do resist following in her footsteps. This play's first shop scene begins, "*Enter two prentizes preparing the Goldsmiths Shop with plate*"; and soon after, "*Enter Mistris Shoare with her worke in her hand.*" She commands the apprentice: "Sir boy, while I attend the shop myself, / See if the workmen haue dispatcht the cup" whereupon "*The boy departs, and she sits sowing in her shop. Enter the king disguised.*"[16] Noteworthy is how Heywood creates a commercial setting for Jane and establishes that she is in charge of the shop. At the same time, however, she is specifically described as having "work in her hand" and "sewing," a domestic task practiced by women both offstage and on.[17] The visual thus emblematizes the duality and potential conflict embodied in the role of a "shop wife." King Edward enters disguised because, having already seen Jane at a dinner party hosted by her husband, he intends to seduce her. As he enters looking for the shop his words help to generate a vivid impression of the London location and setting: "Soft; here must I turn; / Heres *Lombard Streete,* and heres the *Pelican;* / And there's the phoenix in the pelicans nest." He then describes Jane as if she were a piece of jewelry displayed for sale—her eyes are diamonds, for instance. Jane, both a good wife and attentive shopkeeper, addresses him as a potential customer: "What would you buy, sir, that you look on here?" (p. 64). The ensuing exchange between them consists of her trying to sell a ring and him wanting her "hand," to the point where the dialogue becomes seductive wordplay on buying and selling. Later in the scene, King Edward leaves after being recognized by the returning Shore, whose jealous question is voiced in language similar to the king's, but from a husband-shopkeeper's point of view: "Keep we our treasure secret, yet so fond / As set so rich a beauty as this is / In the wide view of euery gazers eye?" (p. 68). After much resistance, Mistress Shore eventually agrees to become the king's mistress, as the audience doubtless knew she must. But Heywood seems particularly to stress how Jane's changed circumstances serve to increase not only her status but also her role as a figure of commerce. At the end of the play she is shown being approached by supplicants who try to "buy" her with bribes to intervene for them with the king; the language of her insulted response betrays her shopkeeper origins, but it also conveys her power: "What think ye that I buie and sell for bribes / His highness fauour, or his subiects blood?" (p. 82). Many of the elements in *Edward IV* reappear in later plays, especially a female in charge of a shop and a customer whose purpose is seduction. When history is not a determinant, however, the woman is usually far less compliant. Nevertheless, it is worth keeping the story of Jane Shore in mind, since it remains as a referent just below the surface of many of the subsequent treatments of women in shops.

Thomas Dekker's *The Shoemaker's Holiday* (1599, pr. 1600), probably written soon after Heywood's play, has a similar scene with a wife minding the shop and sewing as a man approaches: "*Enter* Iane *in a Semsters shop working, and* Hamond *muffled at another doore, he stands aloofe.*"[18] Hammond echoes King Edward: "Yonders the shop and there my faire loue sits." During this admiring speech he observes, "How prettily she workes, oh prettie hand! / Oh happie worke, it doth me good to stand / Vnseen to see her." He describes how he admires her in the shop from "afar": "Muffeled Ile passe along, and by that trie / Whether she know me" (ll. 1, 13–15, 20–21). Like Jane Shore, her namesake here gives the recognizable call of a real London shopkeeper: "Sir, what ist you buy? / What ist you lacke sir? callico, or lawne, / Fine cambricke shirts, or bands, what will you buy?" An aside from Hammond establishes his interest in her sexual goods: "That which thou wilt not sell, faith, yet Ile trie" (ll. 21–24). Again like Edward, he soon asks, "how sell you then this hand?" (l. 27). During the long wooing scene between them, Jane repeatedly refuses Hammond's advances, protesting (surely with Jane Shore in mind) that her husband, Rafe, is away at war but still alive and "Whilst he liues, his I liue, be it nere so poore, / And rather be his wife then a kings whore" (l. 78–79). Later, believing her husband to be dead, Jane agrees to marry Hammond, but Rafe returns and intervenes before the wedding. The contrast between these two early treatments of a shop wife is telling: in one, historical events dictated the socially superior seducer's success; in the other, fantasy dictates his failure. Dekker's Jane is a wife who remains true, even to an absent husband.

Having begun with two plays in quick succession, the brief and minor fad for theatrical shop scenes flourishes from about 1602 to 1613 with a group that seems to be aware of what might be called the Jane Shore paradigm, while repeatedly reworking and complicating it in such a way as to counter expectations associated with it. The first of these is another play from Thomas Heywood, *The Fair Maid of the Exchange* (1602, pr. 1607), a title that encapsulates the idea at the heart of the shop scenes surveyed here. The maid, Phillis (possibly the daughter of the "mistress" to whom she refers), is presented as being in charge of a shop in the Royal Exchange, a London microcosm of buying and selling. She scolds her apprentice for wasting time and threatens to beat him with the yard. As they "*Sit and worke in the shop,*" two men enter and approach it; Phillis calls out "What lacke you Gentle-

men?" to which Gardiner replies, "Faith nothing, had I thee. / For in thine
eye all my desires I see." She tries to interest him in the merchandise, but he
wants her: "let me weare / This shape of thine, although I buy it deere." [19] In
the exchange that follows, Phillis matches wits with Gardiner, calling him a
"stall-troubler" (l. 1262—perhaps a type familiar to the audience), until he
angrily departs. Interestingly, one reason for Phillis's refusal of Gardiner's
advances is that she is in love with Cripple, who is himself a shopkeeper and
whose shop Phillis has already visited, in a reversal of the usual formula of a
man "shopping" for a woman. In a later scene, Phillis again takes the initiative and goes to Cripple's shop where, unknown to her, she sees Frank, another of her suitors, in Cripple's clothes (at the latter's behest). Sounding
very much like the conventional male shop customer, Phillis says, "yonder
sits the wonder of mine eye" (l. 1991), after which she approaches and tells
him she loves him. Still later, after many complications and by a circuitous
route, Frank is offered Phillis by her mother—whose language certainly suggests a shopkeeper's mind: "Disdaine her not because I proffer her, / I tell
you sir, Merchants of great account / Haue sought her loue, and Gentlemen of
worth, / Haue humbly sude to me in that behalfe" (ll. 2360–63). A bargaining
session ensues between parents and suitor that indicates how completely Phillis is a "maid of the Exchange," an impression which her about-face rejection
of Cripple and acceptance of Frank only confirms.

In *Wise Woman of Hogsdon* (1604, pr. 1638), Heywood returns to the visual formula of a woman sewing in a shop: "*Enter* Luce *in a [Goldsmith's]*[20]
shop, at worke vpon a lac'd Handkercher, and Joseph *a Prentice*"; again the
woman is a daughter. When she asks Joseph her father's whereabouts, he
replies, "Mistresse, above, / And prayes you to attend below a little." She
voices her reluctance to do so in terms that emphasize both the idea that such
shop women are "on display" and the potential danger this creates:

> I doe not love to *sit thus publikely:*
> And yet upon the traffique of our Wares,
> Our provident Eyes and presence must still wayte.
> Doe you attend the shop, Ile ply my worke.
> I see my father is not jelous of me,
> That trusts mee to *the open view of all.*
> The reason is, hee knowes my thoughts are chast,
> And my care such, as that it needes the awe
> Of no strict Overseer.
>
>   (p. 285; my emphasis)

When Boyster comes to the shop Luce tells Joseph to serve him, but Boyster
addresses her: "Tis heere that I would buy." She innocently replies, "What
doe you meane sir, speak, what ist you lack? / I pray you wherefore doe you
fixe your eyes / So firmely in my face? what would you have?" (p. 285). Of

course he wants her: he woos, she refuses, he leaves. Then another suitor, Chartely, enters with gifts, hoping to seduce Luce into becoming his mistress; she, however, successfully bargains for a proposal of marriage, to which she responds in the language of trade: "in exchange / Of this your hand, you shall receive my heart" (p. 288). This sequence of customer-suitors effectively conveys how women in shops were perceived to be vulnerable to seduction; at the same time, though, it suggests that such women had not only the "business sense" but also the freedom to strike a deal to their advantage.

1 The Honest Whore (1604, pr. 1604), by Dekker and Thomas Middleton, has one of the few shop scenes not set in London. But perhaps the Milan location is ironic, since Viola, the shopkeeper Candido's wife, complains because her husband will not get angry or jealous (singularly un-Italian!). She asks her brother, Fustigo, who is unknown to Candido, to visit their shop and pretend to seduce her. The audience gets a shop scene—"*Enter* Candido, *his* Wife, George, *and two Prentices in the shop:* Fustigo *enters, walking by*"[21]— but the convention of the vulnerable shop wife is rather explicitly subverted when this one organizes her own apparent seduction. The playwrights further undermine expectations when the avowedly "patient" Candido is either too dim or too phlegmatic to be gulled. Indeed, the ironies increase because he seems to be more concerned with making a sale at any cost than with losing his wife. Dekker's sequel, *2 The Honest Whore* (1605, pr. 1630), is also set in Milan, but Viola is dead and Candido has a new wife. The shop scene begins: "*Enter at one doore* Lodouico *and* Carolo; *at another* Bots, *and Mistris* Horsleach; Candido *and his wife appear in the Shop.*"[22] The first four talk amongst themselves, then Lodovico says, "Stay, is not that my patient Linen Draper yonder, and my fine yong smug Mistris, his wife?" (3.3.19–20). When Carolo voices an interest in the wife, Mistress Horseleach, a bawd, offers to distract Candido while the men approach the wife. So this time it is the husband who calls "What is't you lacke, Gentlewoman? Cambricke or Lawnes, or fine Hollands? Pray draw neere, I can sell you a penny-worth" (ll. 33–34). But when the wife is approached by Bots, she immediately refuses his overtures and exits. In fact, then, although these two plays use the idea of the vulnerable shop wife, the effect is ironic: in the first the wife is not seduced and in the second, not seduceable. It seems worth asking whether the playwrights, by capitalizing on audience expectations, are questioning their validity; that is, does the treatment of the shop women in these plays implicitly acknowledge that in the real shops of Jacobean London women were also often more powerful than victimized?

Michaelmas Term (1604–06, pr. 1607) is Middleton's first uncollaborative play set in the London shop-world—although Quomodo is as much a trickster-usurer as a shopkeeper. While there are no stage directions for his shop, the dialogue places the action there and merchandise is shown, so probably this is an instance of Middleton's typically minimalist directions. In the first of the scenes almost certainly set in the shop (2.3),[23] Quomodo—who has observed of the gentry, "They're busy 'bout our wives, we 'bout their lands" (1.1.107)—enters to find his wife in conversation with another woman. He seems to establish his authority, sexual and otherwise: "How now, what prating have we here? Whispers? Dumb shows? Why, Thomasine, go to; my shop is not altogether so dark as some of my neighbors', where a man may be made cuckold at one end, while he's measuring with his yard at tother" (2.3.31–35). Soon after, as Quomodo begins his gulling of Easy, he tells his wife to leave; Thomasine replies, "Why, I hope I may sit i'th' shop, may I not?" (l. 75). When he insists, she exits with an aside, "Well, since I'm so expressly forbidden, I'll watch above i'th' gallery, but I'll see your knavery" (ll. 78–79). Thomasine's subsequent presence above both visually establishes her as a figure of power and gives her knowledge that she later uses to trick her husband and seduce Easy. Indeed, rather than being staged or perceived as a commodity, this shop wife actively offers herself to one of her husband's customer-victims. Her forced return to Quomodo at the end is presented as a victory for neither.

What is probably the best known shop scene is also unique: Middleton and Dekker's *Roaring Girl* (1611, pr. 1611) is the only play with anything like the direction *"Three shops open in a rank: the first a pothecary's shop, the next a feather-shop, the third a sempster's shop:* Mistresse Gallipot *in the first,* Mistresse Tiltyard *in the next,* Master Openwork *and his* Wife *in the third. To them enters* Laxton, Goshawk *and* Greenwit."[24] Worth noting is the multiplication of everything, including shop wives, all of whose names have bawdy connotations. In addition, with its "rank" of three shops displaying merchandise, it is emphatically a place where goods are bought and sold. This commercial setting is the visual and thematic context for all that happens in this long scene, which begins with Mistress Openwork calling "Gentlemen, what is't you lack?" (l. 1).[25] But the three men approach Mistress Gallipot's shop and the ensuing exchange between Mistress Gallipot and Laxton establishes a secret relationship that amounts to Laxton pretending he loves her, her giving him money, and him spending it on other women. Here as in other plays the husband is a victim, but now so too is the wife. Multiplicity allows for a contrast between the Gallipots and Openworks: in the latter partnership Mistress Openwork clearly has the upper hand in both the marriage and the business. When Moll Cutpurse enters and moves from shop to shop, it is worth noting that, on the one hand, she is a rare female shop customer, while on the other, she is seen as a sexual threat. When Moll is greeted by Openwork, his wife exclaims, "How now, greetings, love-terms with a pox between you, have I found out one of your haunts? I send you for hollands, and you're i'th' low countries with a mischief. I'm served with good ware by th' shift, that makes it lie dead so long upon my hands, I were as good shut up shop, for when I open it, I take nothing" (ll. 204–9). Of course this is double entendre, but it has a literal meaning too, which again suggests that this is a shop wife with considerable authority, who responds very differently to Moll than to the male customers. Moll replies that she "come[s] to buy" but Mistress Openwork is adamant: "I'll sell ye nothing; I warn ye my house and shop" (ll. 213–14). Since one of the explicit concerns of this play is the perception and treatment of women in contemporary London, it is noteworthy that Moll, whose sexual ambiguity affords her an unusual degree of independence, first appears with two wives whose positions in a shop also give them a certain power over their husbands.

Moll (or *Mall*) Cutpurse is again a character in Nathan Field's *Amends for Ladies* (1610–11, pr. 1617). This time unthreateningly androgynous, Mall comes to Seldom and his wife Grace *"working as in their shop,"*[26] and having engineered Seldom's departure by asking for "hangers" she has ordered, then gives Grace a letter from a knight. Grace rejects the implication that she would stray, but then Lord Proudlie enters, asking permission to "take a pipe of tobacco" (l. 66) in the shop. Seldom is only too accommodating: "Seldome *hauing fetch a candle, walk's off at th' other end of the Shop,* Provd. *sits by his wife*" (ll. 71–72). When Proudlie *"whispers to Grace,"* Seldom observes complacently, "This custome in vs Cittizens is good, / Thus walking off when men talk with our wiues, / It shew's vs curteous, and mannerly" (ll. 84–86). Grace rebuffs Proudlie's attempts at seduction and when she and Seldom are again alone, says "I wonder Sir you will walke so and let anie bodie sit prating to your wife! were I a man Id'e thrust 'em out ot'h shop by the head and shoulders" (ll. 159–61). This husband-shopkeeper's response is that he knows his wife is virtuous so there is no danger, and if he did as she suggests, he would "loose their custome" (l. 163). Given the title of this play, one wonders if Field was deliberately going against the view quoted earlier that a shopkeeper who put his wife on display to attract customers virtually ensured his being cuckolded. That it is a virtuous wife and not a jealous husband who prevents this, tellingly counters two popular stereotypes. Contemporaneously with *Roaring Girl* and *Amends for Ladies,* John Cooke's *Greene's Tu Quoque* (1611, pr. 1614) reworks the conventions yet again. It begins with "A Mercers Shop discovered, *Gartred* working in it, *Spendall* walking by the Shop: Master *Ballance* walking over the Stage: after him *Longfield* and *Geraldine*."[27] Spendall is not the husband but an apprentice, who has been left with his mistress Gartred to run the shop because his master is off being knighted. Spendall is in front of the shop to drum up business; indeed he, like Candido, Seldom, and even Quomodo, is so eager to make a sale that he is easily gulled into leaving the woman alone and vulnerable—like a piece of merchandise to be shoplifted. But although Gerald tries to seduce Gartred, she resists, once more suggesting that being in charge of a shop and therefore having a certain independence could give a woman power to hold her own against such advances.

Middleton's *A Chaste Maid in Cheapside* (1613, pr. 1630) comes at the end of the sequence of plays from the early years of James I's reign that feature shops and those who run them. As often with Middleton, his treatment of a convention implies both an awareness of it and a desire to use it for his own, usually ironic, purposes of social commentary. Here there is only one shop scene, but it starts the play—"*Enter* Maudline *and* Moll, *a shop being discovered*"[28]—firmly establishing the concern with buying and selling that dominates the action. Yellowhammer, whose wife and daughter these are, is, like Jane Shore's husband, a goldsmith in Goldsmiths' Row in Cheapside, probably the most exclusive street of shops in the real London of the audience. A contemporary verse by Henry Parrot captures an attitude to young women in these shops to which Middleton's punning title also alludes:

> A scoffing mate, passing along Cheapside,
> Incontinent a gallant lass espied;
> Whose tempting breasts (as to the sale laid out)
> Incites this youngster thus to 'gin to flout.
> "Lady," quoth he, 'is this flesh to be sold?'
> "No Lord," quoth she, "for silver nor for gold
> But wherefore ask you?" (and there made a stop).
> "To buy," quoth he, "if not, shut up your shop."[29]

In the play it immediately becomes clear that mother and daughter are at odds because, as the title suggests, the daughter will not market herself for an upwardly mobile marriage. Simply by locating this exchange in the shop, Middleton highlights how Moll is seen by her parents as a commodity to be polished for sale—an idea emphasized by Maudline's remark to her: "You dance like a plumber's daughter and deserve / Two thousand pound in lead to your marriage, / And not in goldsmith's ware" (1.1.21–23). When Sir Walter Whorehound enters with a whore he plans to market as a Welsh gentlewoman, he echoes this view: "I bring thee up to turn thee into gold, wench, / And make thy fortune shine like your bright trade; / A goldsmith's shop sets out a city maid" (ll. 100–102). The allusions to Jane Shore are apparent, but Moll successfully resists the overtures of Whorehound, the knight her parents want her to marry. Ironically, however, although she marries Touchwood Junior for love, she gets money and social position too. The play ends with Yellowhammer happily inviting all present to Goldsmiths' Hall to celebrate the marriage. As often in Middleton, the sinners are rewarded; here he also manages to create a sympathetic goldsmith's daughter who will not be sold like a piece of jewelry.

The next shop scene appears in Dekker's *Match Me in London* (1611–13,[30] pr. 1631). Despite a gap of some years, it includes what seems yet another direct echo of *Edward IV*. In this case Lady Dildoman, a pandress, interests

the king in Tormiella, the new wife of a shopkeeper, and the king decides to
go in disguise to see her. When they come to where Tormiella sits silently,
minding the shop with two apprentices in her husband's absence, the king
asks to try a glove on her hand. Throughout the scene, Tormiella is demurely
reticent, leaving most of the bargaining to an apprentice, although it is clear
that the king's interest is in her, not the merchandise. To continue the king's
seduction away from the shop, Lady Dildoman tries to tempt Tormiella with
"rich embroidered stuff" they have elsewhere, but she resists: "My Husband
is from home, and I want skill / To trade in such Commodities, but my man /
Shall wait upon your Ladiship."[31] Only after she is tricked into going alone
with them does she leave the shop and put herself in jeopardy. In the next
scene the ironic contrast between Tormiella's innocent resistance to temptation and the behavior of other shop wives, notably Jane Shore, makes for
some very titillating and effective theater. Once she realizes the king's intentions, Tormiella cries "Ile kill ten Monarches ere Ile bee one whore" (2.2.59).
In a plot too complicated even to summarize, Tormiella, forced to live in the
palace, is confronted by the jealous queen with an accusation that surely reflects attitudes to the growing presence and prosperity of shopkeepers in Dekker's London. The queen says that the court has gone

> to th' shop of a *Millaner,*
> The gests are so set downe, because you ride
> Like vs, and steale our fashions and our tyres,
> You'l haue our Courtiers to turne shopkeepers,
> And fall to trading with you, ha!
>
> (3.3.20–24)

Interestingly, like both of Dekker's *Honest Whore* plays this is set in Spain
(despite the title). Whether deliberate or not, the implicit ironic contrast between English and Spanish shop wives adds to the impression that London
women have freedoms others do not and take advantage of them. In this play,
although Tormiella is forced into the king's bed, she never goes willingly. As
a result, the king finally repents: his concluding words express his amazement
and invite the audience to share it: "well were that City blest, / that with but,
Two such women should excell, / But there's so few good, th'ast no Parallel"
(5.5.86–88).

Middleton provides yet another ironic take on the shop scene in *Anything
for a Quiet Life* (1621, pr. 1662), his only collaboration with John Webster.
The first stage direction for the shop is *"Enter (a Shop being discover'd)
Walter Chamlet, his Wife Rachel, two Prentices, George and Ralph,"* although Rachel does not actually enter until a few lines later, thus marking a
break from the convention of the woman being first seen sitting in the shop.
Indeed, her entering words are in response to George's call of "What ist you

lack?" Coming to the shop like a customer, she replies, "I do lack Content
Sir, Content I lack: have you or your worshipful Master here, any Content to
sell?" Her surprised husband asks, "How didst thou get forth? thou wer't
here sweet Rac. / Within this hour, even in my very heart."[32] Rachel is angry
because she believes (wrongly) that Chamlet has fathered two "bastards";
her insistence that "though your shop-wares you vent / With your deceiving
lights, yet your Chamber Stuff / Shall not pass so with me" ([C3v]) makes
clear the equation of "shop wares" and "chamber stuff." Through much of
the play, Chamlet tries to make Rachel see reason, which he finally manages
to do with the help of his apprentice, George, whom Rachel has earlier
fired—in a significant demonstration of her power and authority. A shop wife
who suspects her husband of adultery rather than being tempted or committing it herself is clearly a danger to business in this twisted version of an
established, even tired, convention.

The last play incorporating the formula is Richard Brome's much later *A
Mad Couple, Well Matched* (1639, pr. 1653), with some complex and extended shop scenes that could well be ironic responses to a dated dramatic
cliché. Although there is no stage direction, the dialogue and use of props
indicate that 2.1 takes place in the shop of Saleware, yet again a goldsmith.
The scene begins with the wife, Alicia, in charge and making a sale to Lady
Thrivewell. When a suitor, Bellamy, attempts seduction, a willing Alicia observes about her absent husband and other shop owners: "They pretend onely
that wee should overlooke our servants, when they but set us there for shew
to draw in custome: but in making us such overseers they are overseene themselves; Shopkeepers-wives will be meddling and dealing in their kinde, and
as they are able, as wel as their husbands."[33] To her eavesdropping apprentice
Alicia says, "Pray attend you the tother end o' th' Shop. If I cannot handle a
Customer, why dos your Master trust mee?" (p. 25). Soon Alicia is making
overtures to Bellamy, telling him that if he is afraid of being overheard, he
can whisper: "But that is a right shop-whisper indeed with Trades-women
that are handsome" (p. 26). Later, she tells her husband, "*Thomas,* your
hopes are vaine, *Thomas* in seating mee here to overreach, or underreach any
body," then departs saying, "let your shop be your own care for the rest of
this day. I have some busines abroad" (pp. 29–30). Having become the mistress of Sir Oliver Thrivewell, Alicia begins to dress like a lady; blissfully
unaware of the reasons for her changed appearance, Saleware imagines to his
wife how some will "prate while others shall admire thee, sitting in thy shop
more glorious, then the Maiden-head in the Mercers armes, and say there is
the Nonparrell, the Paragon of the Citie, the Flower-de-Luce of Cheapside,
the Shop Court-ladie, or the Courtshop Mistris" (p. 59). Alicia, however, is
a shop wife who leaves to live in a house provided by Thrivewell; Saleware,
wrongly assuming he is being invited to join her, worries "Must I then give
up Shop, or lie so far remote?" But she responds, "No, you must keepe your

Shop Friend, and lie here if you please," assuring him that "my Lord will bring and send you such custome, that your Neighbours shall envy your wealth, and not your Wife; you shall have such commings in abroad and at home, that you shall be the first head nominated i' the next Sheriffe season, but I with my Lord will keepe you from pricking. Bee you a Cittizen still Friend, 'tis enough I am Courtly" (pp. 59–60). Although perhaps not intentional, this is an ironically distorted replay of Jane Shore's upward mobility in *1 Edward IV,* forty years earlier.

In a series of Characters published in 1631, Francis Lenton describes "A Sempster Shopkeeper":

> She is very neatly spruced up and placed in the frontispiece of her shop, of purpose (by her curious habit) to allure some custom, which still increaseth and decreaseth as her beauty is in the full, or the wane. She hath a pretty faculty in presenting herself to the view of passengers by her rolling eyes, glancing through the hangings of tiffany and cobweb-lawn, that the travellers are suddenly surprised and cannot but look back, . . . and, in affection to her comeliness, must needs cheapen her commodity, where they are rapt into a bargain by her beauty. . . . In her trade, she is much troubled with stitches, amongst which, back-stitch is the most ordinary, easy, and pleasant to her; and if you cannot bargain for her ruffs in her shop, she will fit you with choice at your chamber, so you will pay her well for her pains.[34]

The sexual and—or therefore—commercial power of such a woman is readily apparent, and while the tone of this description does not overtly convey resentment, the innuendo at the end suggests that not only her sewing but also her body are available for money. In the dramatic shop scenes surveyed here, this attitude is repeatedly countered by showing shop women who are either aware of being used as lures for customers and resist, or who simply behave in such a way as to demonstrate the freedom from masculine control their position evidently gives them. While doubtless there were women in the shops of early modern London who sold themselves along with their merchandise, it is unlikely that they were in the majority. Rather more probable is that women in shops, who were the wives or daughters of shopkeepers or shop owners themselves, spent their days sitting in the shop doing what male shopkeepers did: selling goods to customers, buying the materials and making those goods, and delivering purchases to customers, as well as managing the family household. Rather than being denied or distorted in theatrical shop scenes, this reality is the basis for the depiction of women who demonstrate its implications for better and for worse.[35]

Notes

1. The dates of plays are those of *The Annals of English Drama 975–1700,* by Alfred Harbage, revised by S. Schoenbaum, third edition revised by Sylvia Stoler Wagonheim (London and New York: Routledge, 1989).

2. "Shops and Shopping in Medieval London," in *Medieval Art, Architecture and Archaeology in London,* ed. Lindy Grant (London: The British Archaeological Association, 1990), 41.

3. Ben Jonson, *The Poems of Ben Jonson,* ed. Ian Donaldson (London, New York: Oxford University Press, 1975), epigram 78.

4. *The Family of Love,* in *The Works of Thomas Middleton,* 8 vols., ed. A. H. Bullen (London: Bullen, 185–86; rpt. New York, 1964), 3:2.1.1–5.

5. Anon., *Pasquils Palinodia* (London, 1619), [A3v].

6. John Marston, *The Dutch Courtesan,* ed. David Crane (London: A. C. Black; New York: W. W. Norton, 1997), 3.3.8–14.

7. Anon., *Tell-Trothes New-yeares Gift* (London, 1593), C2r.

8. Thomas Gainsford, *The Rich Cabinet* (London, 1616), 28.

9. "City Talk: Women and Commodification," in *Staging the Renaissance,* ed. David Scott Kastan and Peter Stallybrass (New York and London: Routledge, 1991), 183–84.

10. "Material Londoners?" in *Material London, ca. 1600,* ed. Lena Cowen Orlin (Philadelphia: University of Pennsylvania Press, 2000), 186.

11. "To the Gentlewomen Citizens of London, Flourishing dayes with regarde of Credite," in *The Schoole of Abuse* (London, 1597), F2r.

12. Robert Wilson, *The Cobler's Prophecy,* ed. W. W. Greg (London: The Malone Society, 1914), ll. 52–53; long *s* has been regularized in this and subsequent quotations.

13. Anon., *The Tragedy of Locrine,* ed. Ronald B. McKerrow (London: The Malone Society, 1908), ll. 569–71.

14. Lena Cowen Orlin notes that "As an unmarried woman living in Merry's establishment, [Rachel] characteristically owes her brother the obedience that a married woman would owe her husband—and in fact enjoys less independence than the mistress of a household." *Private Matters and Public Culture in Post-Reformation England* (Ithaca and London: Cornell University Press, 1994), 114.

15. Interestingly, besides the two "cobbler" plays mentioned here, William Rowley's later *A Shoemaker, a Gentleman* (1607–09, pr. 1638) also has a wife who although clearly part of the family business is also not perceived or treated as a sexual object. Perhaps shoemakers' wives were another kind of stereotype?

16. Thomas Heywood, *The first part of King Edward the fourth,* in *The Dramatic Works of Thomas Heywood,* ed. R. H. Shepherd, 6 vols. (London, 1874), 1:63–64.

17. On the association of women with sewing see Ann Rosalind Jones and Peter Stallybrass, *Renaissance Clothing and the Materials of Memory* (Cambridge: Cambridge University Press, 2000), chapter 6. Stage directions for female characters to be so occupied occur in a number of plays. See the entries for *sewing* and *work* in Alan C. Dessen and Leslie Thomson, *A Dictionary of Stage Directions in English Drama, 1580–1642* (Cambridge: Cambridge University Press, 1999), 193, 254.

18. Thomas Dekker, *The Shoemaker's Holiday* in *The Dramatic Works of Thomas Dekker,* ed. Fredson Bowers, 4 vols. (Cambridge: Cambridge University Press, 1953–61), 1:3.4.0.

19. Thomas Heywood, *The Fair Maid of the Exchange,* ed. Peter H. Davison and Arthur Brown (London: The Malone Society, 1963), ll. 1196, 1222–24, 1235–36.

20. Thomas Heywood, *The Wise-woman of Hogsdon*, in *Dramatic Works*, 5:284. The quarto direction is for a "sempster's" shop, but in both the dramatis personae and dialogue Luce is described as a goldsmith's daughter.

21. Thomas Dekker and Thomas Middleton, *1 The Honest Whore*, in *Dramatic Works*, 2:3.1.0.

22. Thomas Dekker, *2 The Honest Whore*, in *Dramatic Works*, 2:3.3.0.

23. Thomas Middleton, *Michaelmas Term*, ed. Richard Levin (Lincoln: University of Nebraska Press, 1966).

24. Thomas Middleton and Thomas Dekker, *The Roaring Girl*, ed. Andor Gomme (London: Ernest Benn, New York: W. W. Norton, 1967), 2.1.0.

25. It is easy to imagine that men in the audience would have offered suggestive responses to this question, helping to emphasize the topicality and "realism" of the scene.

26. Nathan Field, *Amends for Ladies*, in *The Plays of Nathan Field*, ed. William Peery (Austin: University of Texas Press, 1950), 2.1.1.

27. J. Cooke, *Greene's Tu Quoque or, The Cittie Gallant*, ed. Alan J. Berman (New York and London: Garland, 1984), 1.1.0.

28. Thomas Middleton, *A Chaste Maid in Cheapside*, ed. R. B. Parker (London: Methuen, 1969), 1.1.0.1.

29. *Epigrams* (London, 1608), G1v; qtd. in Lawrence Manley, ed., *London in the Age of Shakespeare* (London and Sydney: Croom Helm, 1986), 244–45.

30. This is the usually accepted date, as given in the *Annals*, but Cyrus Hoy argues persuasively for a later date, 1620–21; see *Introductions, Notes, and Commentaries to Texts in "The Dramatic Works of Thomas Dekker,"* 4 vols. (Cambridge: Cambridge University Press, 1980), 3:143–48.

31. Thomas Dekker, *Match Me in London* in *Dramatic Works*, 3:2.1.224–26.

32. Thomas Middleton and John Webster, *Anything for a Quiet Life* (London, 1662), [C3r].

33. Richard Brome, *A Mad Couple, Well Matched*, in *The Dramatic Works of Richard Brome*, 3 vols. (London, 1873), 1:23.

34. Francis Lenton, *Characterismi: Or, Lentons Leasures;* qtd. in *London in the Age of Shakespeare*, 327.

35. I would like to thank the Folger Shakespeare Library for the Short-Term Fellowship that enabled me to do the research for this study.

Pent-Up Emotions: Pity and the Imprisonment of Women in Renaissance Drama

PHILIP D. COLLINGTON

> The world's a Theater, the earth a Stage,
> Which God, and nature doth with Actors fill,
> Kings haue their entrance in due equipage,
> And some there parts play well and others ill.
> The best no better are (in this Theater,)
> Where euery humor's fitted in his kinde,
> This a true subiect acts, and that a Traytor,
> The first applauded, and the last confin'd.[1]

IN these lines prefixed to *An Apology for Actors,* Thomas Heywood juxtaposes the treatment of true and false subjects in order to defend stage plays on the grounds that they discourage sedition. Traitors, at the very least, should be imprisoned for their crimes. Heywood echoes Sir Philip Sidney's earlier observation that in tragedies, "if evil men come to the stage, they ever go out . . . so manacled as they little animate folks to follow them."[2] But Sidney goes on to acknowledge that drama based on historical events can also present rather mixed messages, "For see we not valiant Miltiades rot in his fetters; the just Phocion and the accomplished Socrates put to death like traitors?" (35). The central problem is this: How should audiences respond to characters accused of treason and imprisoned while awaiting trial? To Sidney it is neither morally nor emotionally healthy to watch bad things happen to good characters, yet as Shakespeare's Hermione points out at her own trial for treason, the reverse is also true. She admonishes supporters to reserve their tears for when good things happen to bad people:

> Do not weep, good fools,
> There is no cause. When you shall know your mistress
> Has deserv'd prison, then abound in tears
> As I come out.[3]

Just about the only point upon which commentators agreed was the capacity of performances to "animate" playgoers using powerful sensory stimuli, especially the ease with which the English could be moved to tears. Thomas

Nashe describes the "tears of ten thousand spectators" who witnessed the death of Talbot in *1 Henry VI*,[4] a decades-old phenomenon that earlier prompted Stephen Gosson to complain that "The beholding of troubles and miserable slaughters that are in Tragedies, driue vs to immoderate sorrow, heauines, womanish weeping and mourning, whereby we become louers of dumpes, and lamentatio[n], both enemies to fortitude."[5] Yet Nashe does not mention widespread listlessness or effeminacy afflicting those departing Shakespeare's play, possibly because they were rather more energized by the performance. Heywood observes (again clearly echoing Sidney) that representations of powerful emotions onstage can *inspire* audiences, "animating men to noble attempts" (17).

Due to the bewildering variety of prisoners and carcereal situations in the drama, it is impossible to generalize about audience reactions to stage prisoners. Such variables as gender, social class, marital status, age, and the legal and moral status of confined individuals intersect with the manner in which they are treated by captors and the environment in which they are kept in order to narrow considerably (although never to limit completely) the range of appropriate cognitive and affective reactions to their plight. In his recent study of punishment and sensibility, David Garland points out that in any given society feelings of fear and hostility compete with ones of compassion and pity "to define the proper response to the law-breaker."[6] Renaissance dramatists worked to elicit audience responses along a similar spectrum, attempting to "animate" playgoers but also to direct the resulting affect in certain directions.

For example, in the finale of Thomas Dekker's *2 The Honest Whore* (c. 1605) the Duke of Milan and his guests gather at Bridewell Prison to watch a kind of "variety" show where inmates are paraded before the onstage audience which hurls lewd comments like "Fie, punk" and "ye bitch"; meanwhile the women's requests for bail and respite from the whip are greeted with gales of laughter: "OMNES. Ha, ha, ha!"[7] Even though the women are presented using such symbolic trappings of woe as tattered clothes, shackles, chains, and the workhouse spinning wheel, their suffering does not elicit much sympathy. Why not? First, by their own admission Dekker's Duke and his guests come to their city's "hell" predisposed to gawk and laugh at its low-class "she-devils" (and are soundly rebuked for this by one guard). Second, once the women prisoners arrive—impudent, unrepentant, and spouting obscenities—the audience appears to feel justified to express hostility.[8] According to Jean Howard, these prisoners present an "exemplary spectacle" designed to warn onlookers about the fate awaiting wrongdoers. Rather than present pathetic prisoners to evoke audience pity and tears, Dekker juxtaposes their merited suffering with the wondrous reformation of such main-plot characters as Bellafront, the titular "honest whore."[9] The fact that the inmates are not thanked for entertaining the Duke's guests but subjected to hard labor ("give her the blue gown, set her to her chare" [5.2.398–400]) supports the implication in my epigraph, that audiences withheld applause from actors portraying characters adjudged guilty of fictional crimes. As John Webster's Ferdinand observes, "we observe in tragedies / That a good actor many times is cursed / For playing a villain's part."[10]

As I shall demonstrate, the derision generated onstage by Dekker's unrepentant inmates contrasts sharply with the powerful ambivalence surrounding Marlowe's Turkish empress Zabina in the two-part *Tamburlaine the Great* (c. 1587) and Webster's Duchess in *The Duchess of Malfi* (c. 1614)—two women notoriously mistreated while incarcerated for traducing the state. The derision also contrasts with the unanimous pity elicited by three royal characters confined on trumped-up charges of treason or familial treachery: In *Cymbeline* (c. 1610), Imogen is called a "disloyal thing" by her father and locked in a dungeon for secretly marrying Posthumus (1.2.131); in *The Winter's Tale* (c. 1609), Hermione is called "a traitor" by Leontes and forced to deliver her baby in a prison cell because the king mistakenly suspects she is an adulteress (2.1.89); and in Heywood's *1 If You Know Not Me, You Know Nobody* (c. 1604), Princess Elizabeth is accused by her Catholic half-sister Mary of complicity in the 1554 Wyatt Rebellion and confined in a variety of locations including London's "tower[,] that fatall place" (v. 460).[11] Each victim maintains her innocence, and through her suffering generates pity, tears, and support from other characters—largely because of their dramatists' use of didactic exposition and heavy-handed emotional prompting.

By providing playgoers with incontrovertible evidence that these last three female prisoners are being wrongfully accused and cruelly confined, Shakespeare and Heywood join in two contemporary debates—one concerning the purportedly negative role of affect in the theater, and the other concerning the real-life mistreatment of accused traitors in carcereal settings. England's princesses Imogen and Elizabeth and Sicily's queen Hermione demonstrate how the purportedly debilitating effects of Aristotelian *katharsis* can inspire courageous acts of political advocacy leading to social renewal instead. Although Gosson derides pity and tears as involuntary, irrational, and emasculating, these three plays demonstrate that the reverse may have been the case. Rather than merely encourage the release of pent-up emotions (pun intended), Shakespeare and Heywood dramatize positive *kathartic* functions of affect and contribute to the refinement of cultural sensibilities regarding incarceration that penal observers argue originated in the sixteenth century.[12]

*   *   *

Pity is defined as "a feeling or emotion of tenderness aroused by the suffering, distress, or misfortune of another, and prompting a desire for relief, compassion, sympathy," as in Hobbes's formula: "Griefe, for the Calamity of another, is Pitty."[13] Martha Craven Nussbaum points out that, according to

Aristotle, far from stemming from "mindless surges of affect," emotions have "a rich cognitive structure"; and that even powerfully felt ones do not hamper reason (as was subsequently asserted in the Renaissance), but rather stem from the exercise *of* reason.[14] In order to experience grief at the calamity of another, the subject must determine whether several cognitive conditions are being met: first, that the other is undeserving of misfortune; second, that the subject could be vulnerable to a similar misfortune; third, that the suffering is significant (Nussbaum, 308–9). The first criterion entails the exercise of moral judgment, the second imaginative empathy, and the third socially ingrained evaluations which will determine the intensity of response. If pity is over loss, then what is lost must have been esteemed; as Nussbaum points out, one doesn't pity another for losing a nail (312). Moreover, what is esteemed varies with historical and cultural differences, and the appropriateness of a response to the loss thereof is transmitted to individuals through processes of acculturation. In other words, emotions are not innately present but acquired through social interactions in early life; affects are then refined by presentations of stimulae prompting inward empathetic evaluations and outward physiological manifestations which are either sanctioned or rejected by others.[15] The stage is one of myriad cultural forms which contribute to this ongoing process of affective refinement.

But what happens when what is presented onstage appears rather unrefined, such as in melodramatic scenes which evoke inordinate weeping? Does the pity generated represent a passive and debilitating or an active and enlivening response? If we distinguish the concept of *sympathy* ("being affected by the condition of another, with a feeling similar or corresponding to that of the other," particularly his or her suffering or sorrow [*OED* s.v.]) from that of *empathy* ("a mode of perceiving by vicariously experiencing . . . the psychological state of another person"),[16] we can better see how Shakespeare and Heywood work to generate the latter response. Sympathy stops at fellow feeling, whereas empathy extends to perception, motivation, and response—a distinction made by modern psychoanalysis but already present in the early seventeenth century. In his *Anatomy of Melancholy* (c. 1621–51), Robert Burton repeats the charge made by opponents of the stage that sorrow debilitates—"he that so faints or fears, and yields to his passion, flings away his own weapons, makes a cord to bind himself, and pulls a beam upon his own head"—only to counter that, far from weakening playgoers, witnessing *represented sorrows* can actually toughen them up: "accustom thyself, and harden beforehand by seeing other men's calamities, and applying them to thy present estate."[17] This empathetic application to one's own life of lessons learned by observing stage characters is a peculiarly English trait: "The Italians most part sleep away care and grief . . . Danes, Dutchmen, Polanders, and Bohemians drink it down; our countrymen go to plays. *Do something or other,* let it not transpose thee" (Burton, 2:185, emphasis added).

Both Shakespeare and Heywood generate audience empathy by specifying which characters are being wronged by circumstances through exposition and demonstration. The technique may be observed in the opening scenes of *Cymbeline* in which Imogen is being held under house arrest for refusing to wed her half-brother, Cloten. The play's opening quickly establishes the unjustness of the princess's confinement, and suggests an appropriate emotional response:

> *1. Gentlemen.*   [She] hath referr'd herself
> Unto a poor but worthy gentleman. She's wedded,
> Her husband banish'd, she imprison'd: all
> Is outward sorrow.
>
>   (1.1.6–9)

Her plight is clearly pathetic, but before we can reach for our handkerchiefs Shakespeare complicates the emotional situation. It all hinges on the "outwardness" of the sorrow at court. Officially, they must support the king's confinement of his daughter, but the British courtiers secretly empathize with Imogen and are "glad at the thing they scowl at" (i.e., her evasion of Cloten [1.15]). As Cymbeline grows increasingly frustrated by her resolve, he orders the further curtailment of her movement—"pen her up"—and declares, that, unless she agrees to wed Cloten, hers will be an indefinite sentence: "let her languish / A drop of blood a day, and being aged / Die of this folly!" (1.1.153–58).

By banishing Posthumus and isolating his daughter, the king subjects her to insidious forms of physiological and psychological torture. In a passage in the *Anatomy* that may serve as commentary on much of *Cymbeline,* Burton expresses sympathy for those

> that are mewed up like hawks, and locked up by their jealous husbands! How tedious is it to them that live in stones and caves half a year together . . . Nay what misery and discontent do they endure, that are in prison! They want all those six non-natural things at once, good air, good diet, exercise, company, sleep, rest, ease, etc., . . . If it be irksome to miss our ordinary companions and repast for once a day, or an hour, what shall it be to lose them for ever? (1:345)

Confinement thus affects both one's physical and emotional well-being. Cymbeline's decree that Imogen "languish / A drop of blood a day" recalls a form of gendered melancholy that Burton attributes to maids, nuns and widows. Separated from men and hence prevented from childbearing, such women are "offended with those vicious vapours which come from menstruous blood." This blood may be regularly discharged, but meantime women's insides become clogged with vapors emanating from "that fulginous exhalation of corrupt seed" which rise to trouble the heart and brain with devastating results: "the whole malady proceeds from the inflammation, putridity, black smoky vapours, etc.; from thence comes care, sorrow, and anxiety, obfuscation of spirits, agony, desperation, and the like" (1:414–15). In the context of humoral psychology, Imogen risks *literally* rotting in her cell—more reason for onlookers to pity her and inveigh against her cruel parents.[18]

Thus confined and with her father's complaint that she "tookst a beggar" ringing in her ears, Imogen laments the fact that noble birth has separated her from Posthumus (1.1.141). Imogen longs for the freedom of choice that she attributes to her social inferiors: "Blessed be those, / How mean soe'er, that have their honest wills, / Which seasons comfort" (1.6.7–9). Her lines recall the famous "milkmaid" lament of Elizabeth I. In his account of "The Miraculous Preservation of the Lady Elizabeth" from Marian persecution, John Foxe reports that during the princess's confinement at Woodstock Castle, "[she] whished herself to be a milk-maid . . . saying that her case was better, and life more merry than was hers, in that state as she was."[19] Heywood's dramatization of this report further suggests the ability of a virtuous stage princess's "weeping and wishing" to generate unanimous pity in onlookers: "It would haue moou'd a flinty hart to melt" (*1 If You Know* xvi.1184–94).

When Imogen is visited in her chamber by the would-be seducer Jachimo, their dialogue further prompts audiences' emotional response:

> *Imogen.*   You look on me; what wrack discern you in me
> Deserves your pity?
>
> *Jachimo.*   Lamentable! What,
> To hide me from the radiant sun, and solace
> I' th' dungeon by a snuff!
>
>   (*Cym* 1.6.84–87)

Hiding a princess from the "radiant sun" by placing her in a dungeon exposes her to many potential dangers; however, as Jachimo's subsequent inventory of Imogen's decorated chamber reveals (2.2.11–51), her surroundings are rather more hospitable than a cold cell in the Tower. His comment about her "dungeon" serves less to reflect a verisimilar stage setting than to foment a vivid *symbolic* setting in audience imaginations. Imogen is virtuous; her confinement is cruel; and her accusers are mistaken (Cymbeline, Cloten, and Posthumus variously call her disobedient, sinful, and adulterous). As Pisanio observes upon receiving instructions from Posthumus to murder her:

> Disloyal? No.
> She's punish'd for her truth, and undergoes,
> More goddess-like than wife-like, such assaults
> As would take in some virtue.
>
>   (3.2.6–9)

Like the sorrowful courtiers mentioned at the play's outset, Pisanio is out-
wardly affected by her plight and secretly inspired by her resilience, transforming pity into action by helping to engineer her escape. Ironically, the one
person in *Cymbeline* who could most justifiably display Gosson's pejora-
tively termed "womanish weeping and mourning" is the princess herself who
neither weeps nor succumbs to Burton's putrid menstrual vapors. Instead, Imogen takes a more proactive "masculine" approach, racing to Wales in search
of her lost husband, and spurring on her traveling companion, Pisanio: "Why,
one that rode to 's execution, man, / Could never go so slow" (3.2.70–71).
Her courage seems to have made an impression on at least one playgoer;
Simon Forman's diary entry detailing in part how she "turned her self into
mans apparrell & fled to mete her loue at milford hauen" remains the earliest
extant account of the play in performance.[20]

*   *   *

Dramatists seeking to elicit certain emotional responses in playgoers had to
counter persistent social ambivalence toward those confined in early modern
England. The period's well-documented anxieties concerning neighborhood
crimes, household disorder, and religious and political sedition led many
Londoner's to hold little sympathy for the city's growing prison population.[21]
In a nation that favored corporeal punishment over the institutional reformation of character, "the administration and supervision of prisons was casual,
often ramshackle, and low in everyone's list of priorities."[22] Heywood's *The
Rape of Lucrece* (c. 1607) featured a street cry suggesting the extent of the
problem:

> Here lies a company of very poore
> Women, in the darke dungeon,
> Hungry cold and comfortlesse night and day,
> Pity the poore women in the darke dungeon.
>   Thus go the cries where they do house them,
>   First they come to the grate, and then they go lowse them.[23]

Despite their cries to be "lowsed" (i.e., set free), many of London's disad-
vantaged prisoners met with spectacular exploitation, not charitable release.
For example, in early 1602 the administration of Bridewell was farmed out
to private contractors who transformed the building into a brothel, forcing
female inmates to prostitute themselves while dressed in sumptuous gowns
and serving exotic dishes to patrons.[24] Women inmates were sexually exploited by guards and inmates elsewhere too; writing from the King's Bench
prison in 1617–18, debtor Geffray Mynshul observed that "A whore entering
into a prison is a hony-pot, about which all the flyes come buzzing, as crowes
to a carrion."[25] The "entertainments" such women provided London gallants

likely informed Dekker's depiction of Milan's "swaggering whores." But if art occasionally imitated life, so too did life imitate art, such as when prisoners (including women and children) were marched out of Bridewell to scour ditches and clear night soil from the streets:

> (yoakt in Carts) they now must purge the street
> Of noysome Garbage, carry Dirt and Dung;
> The Beadles following with a mighty throng;
> Whilst as they passe the people scoffing say,
> Holla, ye pampred Iades of Asia.[26]

Seventeenth-century Londoners who quoted Marlowe to mock real-life chain gangs and who "enthusiastically" tormented "victims of the scaffold, the stocks, and the whipping post" too were evidently not predisposed to pity low-ranking convicts when these appeared onstage.[27]

Marlowe's two-part *Tamburlaine the Great* made a lasting impression on the popular imagination, while confronting audiences with precisely the kind of moral ambiguities that Sidney wrote of in his complaint about the mixed messages sent by plays. In the first part, audiences are invited to share vicariously in Tamburlaine's sadistic glee as he demeans the Turkish emperor Bajazeth and his wife Zabina. In one scene the emperor is released from his cage to serve as Tamburlaine's footstool, while his wife is "chided" by a handmaid (4.2.71). Soon after, Tamburlaine entertains guests at a banquet by forcing the caged emperor to eat from his sword point and by threatening to serve Zabina as an entree: "Here is my dagger. Dispatch her while she is fat" (4.4.48). This "goodly show" appears to please the guests; one exclaims, "Methinks 'tis a great deal better than a consort of music" (l. 59). As Richard Levin has convincingly documented, educated and unrefined playgoers alike delighted in the scarlet-robed infidel, Tamburlaine, as he lorded it over the Turkish royal family.[28] In fact, playgoers may have been indirectly chided for their vicarious cruelty a few scenes later. When Tamburlaine's queen Zenocrate discovers that the two captives have "brained" themselves in despair, she makes a speech that seems partly designed to shame those onlookers who applauded their torture:

> Pardon my love! O, pardon his contempt
> Of earthly fortune and respect of pity,
> And let not conquest, ruthlessly pursu'd,
> Be equally against his life incens'd
> In this great Turk and hapless emperess!
> And *pardon me that was not mov'd with ruth*
> *To see them live so long in misery.*

> (5.1.364–70, emphasis added)

To a certain extent, jeering and cruelty were to be expected from un-Christian captors, but not from purportedly civilized Christian audiences; as Mynshul observed, "To bee a slaue to a Turke is not so much, because hee is a Turke, a monster whose teeth are sharpned of purpose, (by diuine sufferance) to bite and draw blood . . . but for a Christian to bee slaue to a Christian, as a prisoner is to an insulting jailor, is as repugnant to nature, as for an elder brother to eat scraps from a younger brother's trencher" (75). Just as Tamburlaine toys with prisoners, Marlowe toys with audience affect—encouraging vicarious cruelty in one scene, pity and remorse in the next.[29] In the process, he evokes Garland's broad spectrum of "proper" responses to punishment, though ultimately without committing morally to either extreme.

In *The Duchess of Malfi*, Webster likewise toys with audience affect, alternately presenting the disconcerting specter of an assertive widow who defies her male kinsmen, and the sad spectacle of a young duchess imprisoned and tortured for marrying a steward beneath her station.[30] The Duchess's house arrest in act 4 is a remarkably ambivalent theatrical experience, in that as her plight becomes increasingly pathetic, she becomes more adamant that witnesses *not* pity her. Webster primes playgoers for their first glimpse of her demise in an exchange between her captor and chief tormentor:

> *Ferdinand.*   How doth our sister Duchess bear herself
> In her imprisonment?
>
> *Bosola.*   Nobly; I'll describe her.
> She's sad, as one long used to't: and she seems
> Rather to welcome the end of misery
> Than shun it: a behavior so noble
> As gives a majesty to adversity:
> You may discern the shape of loveliness
> More perfect in her tears, than in her smiles.
>
> (4.1.1–8)

In the scenes that follow, her behavior shifts from "sorrow" and "despair" to courage and defiance as she considers forms of suicide as a way to escape her brother's torments. Initially comparing herself to one broken upon the wheel and healed only to be broken anew (4.1.80–84), by the time of her last appearance she has become hardened by suffering:

> I am acquainted with sad misery,
> As the tanned galley-slave is with his oar.
> Necessity makes me suffer constantly,
> And custom makes it easy.
>
> (4.2.27–30)

This image suggests that rather than succumb to Gosson's "womanish weeping," the Duchess has become tougher, increasingly masculine, even *muscular* in her ability to withstand pain and sorrow. While her stoic resistance increases, Bosola's malice dissipates and he comes to pity her—pleading with Ferdinand to "go no farther in [his] cruelty" (4.1.118). Playgoers taking emotional cues from Bosola (if *he* weeps for the Duchess, then surely they should too!) are rebuffed by her admonition not "to waste . . . pity on a thing so wretched / As cannot pity itself" (4.1.90–91); but then are encouraged to indulge in proto-Dickensian weeping when, moments before her murder, she bids Cariola not to forget to give her son medicine and help her daughter say her prayers after their mother is gone (4.2.202–4).

The Duchess's image of the tanned slave is particularly significant in a play replete with class-conscious and aspiring characters. She has been reduced to a galley slave, but eschews another trait generally attributed to the lower classes: immoderation. The contrast between duchess and slave is made quite striking when Ferdinand arranges to send her "masques of *common* courtesans" and have "mad folk" from the "*common* hospital" "practice together, sing, and dance, / And act their gambols to the full o' th' moon" (4.1.124–30, emphasis added). Despite their intrusions into her privacy, their "noise and folly" fail to madden the Duchess, in part because she is just that, *a duchess;* through her noble self-control, she can transcend the immoderation of the "wild consort" (4.2.6, 2). Their tumult only makes her more introspective and their common abandon makes her uncommonly noble, such that her outward displays of grief are limited to more subtle physical changes; as Bosola observes, "*Thou art some great woman sure;* for riot begins to sit on they forehead (clad in gray hairs) twenty years sooner than on a merry mild-maid's" (4.2.135–37, emphasis added).[31]

As was the case with most noble prisoners during the period, the Duchess is kept under house arrest and initially spared the overcrowding and other indignities of the common prison cell; but Ferdinand's machinations soon ensure that she is exposed to many of its perils including extreme darkness and death in 4.1, and noise, filth, and overcrowding in the form of the visiting lunatics of 4.2.[32] During their masque, the Duchess is also "chained," whether metaphorically or literally, by her jailers (4.2.60). In her farewell to Cariola following the mad interlude, the Duchess compares her lot to that of new arrivals in London prisons who were compelled to pay fees to guards for lodgings and lighter shackles, and "garnishes" to other inmates in the form of rounds of drinks purchased at greatly inflated prices: "In my last will I have not much to give. / A many hungry guests have fed upon me" (4.2.200–201). For example, according to Mynshul a new prison arrival was referred to as "Woodcocke" and preyed upon by other inmates who "neuer leaue feeding vpon him vntill they haue pickt him to the bare bones" (83).[33] Soon after, Webster's Duchess is visited by the city's "common belman" and strangled by executioners (4.2.175). Her stoic acceptance of death also contrasts with the frenetic brutality of Cariola's murder shortly thereafter, as the latter bites and scratches her attackers, even pleads her belly ("I am quick with child") in a desperate attempt to stay her execution (ll. 250–56). Thus Webster's Duchess is exposed to but remains untainted by some of the harsh realities of life in such notorious places as the King's Bench, Newgate, Ludgate, Bridewell, or the Counters.[34] After all this horror, Bosola admonishes Ferdinand (and by extension, playgoers) who failed to pity the pathetic madmen, pregnant lady-in-waiting, and stoic Duchess *at the very least* to pity her murdered children: "Fix you eyes here . . . Do you not weep?" (4.2.259). Ferdinand's riddling response, "Mine eyes dazzle" (l. 263), underscores the fact that despite the scene's powerful emotional impact, Webster gives playgoers little direction on whether they should weep or wonder at the Duchess's final moments. Audiences have long been "animated" by *The Duchess of Malfi,* but to what sort of "noble attempt" remains something of a puzzle.

The Duchess's incarceration recalls the protracted ordeal of Scotland's own remarrying widow, Mary Queen of Scots, who following the death of her first husband Lord Darnley, married his accused killer and was forced to abdicate. She fled to England where from 1568 until her death in 1587 she was shuffled from stronghold to stronghold by a suspicious Queen Elizabeth. In the voluminous correspondence which she once calls "the sad and pathetic complaint[s] of an afflicted queen prisoner," Mary describes her life in the unsanitary conditions at Carlisle, Tutbury, and later at Sheffield where for more than a decade she was regularly denied baths, fresh air, and outdoor exercise.[35] In a letter from Carlisle Castle, she complained: "I have endured injuries, calumnies, imprisonment, famine, cold, heat, flight, not knowing whither . . . I have had to sleep upon the ground, and drink sour milk, and eat oatmeal without bread . . . [and] to crown all, I am little else than a prisoner" (21 June 1568, pp. 163–64). Like Webster's Duchess, Mary was gradually, stripped of her servants and train, and while at Tutbury Castle she complained to Elizabeth that her trunks had been rifled and her chamber invaded by men armed with pistols, "putting [her] in bodily fear"; she went on to beg her cousin "to put a ransom upon me, and not leave me to waste away here in tears and complaints" (1 October 1569, pp . 173–74). She was never ransomed, though, and things were little better as Sheffield where Mary wrote of the roughness of her captors, "there is not a single rudeness nor indignity which I have not already experienced at their hands" (7 January 1571, pp. 179–80), and complained of being repeatedly threatened with "menaces of poison and other violent deaths" (March 1571, p. 191). Through it all Mary remained defiant toward her captors and unwavering in her Catholic faith: "I am resolved to die steadfast" (18 September 1571, pp. 221–22). She was Queen of Scots still, in spite of years spent "languish[ing] unmercifully" in a kind of proto-Websterian cell: "I am confined to my chamber, of which they wish again to wall up the windows, and make a false door by which they may enter when I am asleep" (7 November 1571, pp. 227–28). To pass the time, Mary became an "inveterate plotter," engineering unsuccessful rebellions including a plot against Elizabeth's life for which Mary was convicted of high treason and beheaded on 8 February 1587.[36] Her confinement and execution elicited both grief and defiance among English recusants and other European supporters, some of whom contributed epitaphs such as the following fictional account of Mary's final words: "Waile not my death, rejoice at my repose; / It was no death to me, but to my woe."[37]

Elizabeth I was also anxious to establish her innocence of charges of treason and to avoid such demeaning spectacles at the hands of a relative. While confined at Woodstock Castle in 1554–55, Elizabeth marked the window and wall of her chamber with exculpatory graffiti such as, "Much suspected by me, / Nothing proved can be, / Quoth Elizabeth prisoner," as well as verses expressing defiance at her "guiltless" confinement, self-pity at her "troubled wit," and anger at her political opponents including "wavering" Fortune itself: "God send to my foes all they have thought."[38] Denying that she ever received notes from "the traitor Wyatt" in a letter to Queen Mary dated 16 March 1554, Elizabeth was anxious that she "be not condemned without answer and due proof," and not be transferred to the Tower; but above all, she voiced concern for her reputation, "that thus shamefully I may not be cried out on."[39] Decades later, when as queen she was forced to decide the fate of her cousin Mary Stuart, Elizabeth answered Parliament's petition for an execution order with characteristically measured words: "we Princes, I tell you, are set on stages, in the sight and view of all the world duly observed. The eyes of many behold our actions; *a spot is soon spied in our garments, a blemish quickly noted in our doings.* It behoveth us, therefore, to be careful that our proceedings be just and honorable."[40] Although adopting a kind of masculine persona ("we Princes . . ."), Elizabeth's concerns regarding specifically feminine purity emerge in metaphors of clothing and complexion (one simply can't picture her father Henry VIII worrying before Parliament about a spot on his doublet). Yet women were held up to greater moral scrutiny than men, such that the moral denigration caused by imputations of wrongdoing and the literal degradations caused by the material conditions of incarceration would be that much more difficult to erase after the fact.[41]

Countless English prisoners faced conditions like those artfully engineered by Ferdinand or imposed on the exiled Scottish queen, yet to the abuses inflicted on accused traitors and common criminals society generally turned a blind eye. Caught in a catch-22, the only prisoners deserving of pity were the wrongfully accused, yet these had to survive the perils of confinement to get to the trial that would effect their release. Guilty or innocent, they were in effect punished either way—in part because of the harsh conditions that antedated the prison advocacy inaugurated by John Howard or Elizabeth Fry, but in larger part because *the loss of liberty itself* was a punishing ordeal for early modern men and women: "To a free borne generous spirit no jewels are halfe so precious as his natiue liberty . . . the nobility of his mind indures such wounds, as a woman in labor doth her throwes, the stroakes of death are easie to her passions" (Mynshul, 76). Mynshul's comments contradict modern accounts of early modern imprisonment as simply an ad hoc and temporary form of pretrial custody.[42] Whatever the (un)systematic intentions were, the effect was almost invariably to impose hardships on captives through the deprivation of liberty—in other words, a de facto form of punitive confinement.[43] This is certainly the case elsewhere when Heywood's Frankford pronounces "judgement" on his wife taken in adultery:

> I'll not martyr thee,
> Nor mark thee for a strumpet, but with usage
> Of more humility torment thy soul,
> And kill thee, even with kindness.

More so than physical torture or public humiliation, Anne Frankford's perpetual house arrest will be her husband's form of extralegal revenge—highlighting the degree to which even "kind" captivity could be a punishing ordeal.[44]

Mynshul repeatedly lamented the loss of friends and reputation that resulted from his protracted confinement in much less discrete surroundings; he felt like "a subject of nine day's wonder in euery barber's shop" as well as among "midwiues and talkatiue gossips" and those passers-by who gawked at debtors through prison grates.[45] Women were additionally vulnerable because of the social stigma that could accompany incarceration; even in cases where they were accused of nonsexual offenses, for many, confinement became synonymous with whoredom.[46] And though nobles were also confined more discretely than Dekker's Bridewell whores, they were especially sensitive to threats of public humiliation, such as when Mary Stuart's jailer Shrewsbury warned her not to impugn Elizabeth's honor or she would risk having her own exposed "to the world."[47] As we have seen, common prisoners were often transformed into derisive spectacles, and even the privately confined Duchess of Malfi acknowledges that although she is primarily a witness to her brothers' spectacle of horrors, she too is being thrust onto a kind of stage: "I account this world a tedious theater, / For I do play a part in't 'gainst my will" (4.1.83–8.4).

*   *   *

The Winter's Tale demonstrates how a dramatist presents a character's confinement as unambiguously immoral and therefore worthy of unanimous pity. Early on and at her husband's behest, Hermione importunes Polixenes to delay his return to Bohemia by issuing the following playful ultimatum: "My prisoner? Or my guest?"(1.2.55). As has been extensively documented in criticism of the play, Leontes interprets her success as evidence that the two are secretly lovers; though if she were being flirtatious, Polixenes hadn't noticed. He begs Camillo to explain why Leontes is so angry: "[let me] be inform'd, imprison't not / In ignorant concealment" (1.2.396–97).[48] When Camillo reveals Leontes' jealousy and engineers Polixenes' escape from Sicily by bribing the city's posterns, it is therefore executed like a kind of moonlit jailbreak. Unfortunately, this escape is taken by Leontes as proof of wrongdoing—recalling long-standing statutes that "one accused of treason who escaped should be treated as convicted of that offence." The escape also inculpates Hermione, who as Polixenes' symbolic jailer, is liable for the loss of her prisoner according to early modern practice.[49]

Leontes responds to the apparent discovery that his wife is an "adulteress" and a "traitor" by committing her to prison (2.1.88–89, 103). Initially, she appears to be sentenced to an indefinite stay in jail without hope of trial; and those who witness her arrest are sworn to silence on pain of imprisonment as accomplices. Nevertheless, Antigonus, Paulina, and several unnamed lords speak up in defense of Hermione, reminding audiences that the queen is "spotless," and risking their lives in the process (1. 131). In fact, in the scenes following her arrest Hermione's innocence is reiterated *ad nauseam* as part of a concerted public relations campaign to restore her reputation and counter Leontes' slanders.[50] The groundswell of pity they generate forces Leontes to try her in a public court: "Let us be clear'd / Of being tyrannous, since we so openly / Proceed in justice" (3.2.4–6).

At the center of the controversy is Hermione, unambiguously innocent yet demonstrably uneasy with her new role as victim in the tear-jerking spectacle that ensues. She addresses her supporters:

> Good my lords,
> I am not prone to weeping, as our sex
> Commonly are; *the want of which vain dew*
> *Perchance shall dry your pities;* But I have
> That honourable grief lodg'd here which burns
> Worse than tears drown.
>
> (2.1.107–12, emphasis added)

Hermione recognizes the very real danger that her stoicism may be interpreted as defiance. Such was the case for Anne Askew, interrogated by Mary's Catholic officers in 1546. As Foxe recounts, the intensity of Askew's torture stemmed from her refusal to incriminate other nonconformists: "Then they did put me on the rack . . . and theron they kept me a long time; and *because I lay still, and did not cry,* my lord chancellor and Master Rich took pains to rack me with their own hands, till I was nigh dead" (5:547, emphasis added). Hermione needs men's tears, for these may mitigate the harshness of her

treatment in custody and generate outside support for her cause; but she eschews *self-pity,* lest this be taken as an admission of guilt. And as we have
already seen in lines cited in my introduction, she admonishes her female
supporters to reserve their tears for the liberation of the guilty, not the confinement of the innocent (2.1.118–21). While Hermione subtly manipulates
affect to her own advantage, in the process she implicates women in Gosson's
claim that immoderate tears can flood the seat of reason itself:

> the Poetes that write playes, and they that present them vpon the Stage, studie to
> make our affections ouerflow, whereby they draw the bridle from that parte of the
> mind, that should euer [b]e curbed, from runninge on heade: which is manifest trea-
> son to our soules, and deliuereth them captiue to the deuill. (201)

Hermione encourages the men to cry because, unlike her women, she can
trust them *not to cry too much:* "Beseech you all, my lords, / With thoughts
so qualified as your charities / Shall best instruct you, measure me" (2.1.112–
14). According to the *Oxford English Dictionary,* "charity" in the singular
variously denoted love, benevolence, or the legal disposition to judge others
leniently; but the rare plural form (not cited before 1667, but clearly in usage
here) was defined more broadly as "feelings" or "affections."[51]
Thus Hermione indissolubly links reason and affect, justice and mercy—
strengthening her case precisely by not debilitating her weaker female supporters through the generation of unbridled tears.

During the twenty-three-day interim between her arrest and her appearance
at trial, Leontes' tyranny becomes more pronounced, as he variously ponders
burning alive his son, his wife, Paulina, and his infant daughter. Meanwhile,
Paulina attempts to visit Hermione in prison, only to be told that the queen
has been denied all "gentle visitors" (2.2.10) with the exception of Emilia
who has aided her during childbirth. Emilia's report of the queen's condition
seems guaranteed to intensify the pathos of her plight, saying that she in "her
frights and griefs" gave birth prematurely to an infant girl whom she addressed, "My poor prisoner, / I am innocent as you" (11.21–27). These
scenes show Shakespeare at his most heavy-handed, as he stacks the deck
emotionally in favor of Hermione and against her increasingly irrational husband *cum* judge. Every time she is thrust derisively into the public eye, her
stoic demeanor and rational speech (see especially her lines beginning
"Spare your threats . . ." [3.2.91–106]) bear witness to the routine mistreatment of criminals awaiting trial, and to the spectacular abuses inflicted on
religious dissenters and prisoners of conscience.

That Hermione could be considered in these latter categories, and not simply as a woman wrongfully accused of cuckolding her husband, is suggested
by her appeal to the oracle as a higher arbiter of justice than the king. During
her trial, she exclaims:

> if I shall be condemn'd
> Upon surmises (all proofs sleeping else
> But what your jealousies awake), I tell you
> *'Tis rigor and not law.* Your honors all,
> I do refer me to the oracle:
> Apollo be my judge!
>
> (3.2.111–16, emphasis added)

Her invocation of "rigor" echoes documents left behind by two of England's most famous prisoners of conscience, Askew and Sir Thomas More. From his cell in the Tower, More wrote rational letters in his own defense (often using only a piece of coal), including a subtle appeal in which he wrote that "the Kyngis Hyghnes was a prynce not of rygour but of mercy and pytty."[53] More was beheaded shortly thereafter. Likewise, Askew wrote in vain hope from her cell in Newgate that she had been assured "that I [would be] handled with no rigour." She was racked and burnt the following year.[54] Hermione's use of the term "rigor" cuts to the heart of the debate about whether prisoners deserve pity by simultaneously invoking contradictory connotations of extreme (even illegal?) harshness, but also of the meticulous application of the law. In Robert Green's prose version of Hermione's tale, *Pandosto, The Triumph of Time* (1588), the shipmen charged with abandoning Bellaria's infant daughter "began to accuse the King of rigour, and to pity the child's hard fortune."[55] In fact, when a subject is wrongfully accused, confined or otherwise punished, the presiding ruler is frequently described using this multivalent word, in part because *rigor*'s ambiguities protect the utterer. More exercised such caution in the wording of his letter: the death sentence was, strictly speaking, in accordance with newly passed legislation. More therefore cushioned his complaint about legalistic precision by clearing Henry VIII of acting out of spite.

In Shakespeare's plays and sources, however, those presiding over the fate of wrongfully confined prisoners *are* acting out of a kind of irrational malice bordering on cruelty. In many cases, as Valerie Traub has suggested, male anxieties about female agency (expressed in terms of sexual intemperance and characterized in terms of excessive heat) prompt men such as Othello, Leontes, and Hamlet to adopt three "strategies of containment" that transform the women who threaten them into "jewels, statues and corpses" respectively. In effect, the anxious male's response to the perceived chaos of female sexuality is to objectify, cool, and above all immobilize his sexual partner.[56] This desired "stasis" can be attained through responses ranging from silencing their voices to murdering them outright (27). Traub does not examine imprisonment as a method of imposing "stasis" on women, in part because it does not represent a long-term solution: "confining Hermione to prison is not sufficient; only the fantasy of her death brings Leontes psychic calm" (44).

Traub's investigation highlights the demonstrably irrational psyche of certain Shakespearean men. Particularly in the case of Leontes, his ability to rule effectively is hampered by psychological anxieties that border on physiological affliction. The *OED* furnishes additional senses of *rigor* as both a sudden chill accompanied by fits of shivering that often precede high fevers, and the onset of stiffness that in a corpse is now known as *rigor mortis* (s.v.). In *Measure for Measure,* rigorous Angelo's blood is "very snow-broth" (1.4.58) until a meeting with Isabella leaves him "corrupted" with lust, like "carrion" in the hot sun (2.2162–67). His source-play counterpart experiences even more extreme symptoms:

> *Promos.*   [Love] makes us haunt that which our harmes doth move,
> A sicknesse lyke the Fever Etticke fittes:
> Which shakes with colde when we do burne like fire.
> Even so in Love, we freese through chilling feare,
> When as our hartes doth frye with hote desire.[57]

The corrupt ruler thus tries to contain in others what he most fears in himself. Confronted with what appears to be the intemperate heat of his spouse— "Too hot, too hot!" (1.2.108)—Leontes likewise succumbs to rigors, confining Hermione to a cold cell while his court grows "so hot" (2.3.32). Leontes becomes, in contrast to Antigonus, hottest of all: "You smell this business with a sense as cold / As is a dead man's nose; but I do see't, and feel't" (2.1.151–52). His ensuing sleeplessness and "heavings" (as Paulina terms them) represent an affliction in need of her "medicinal" cure that will "purge him of that humor" (2.3.35–39). In Greene's version, Bellaria also languishes in "cold prison," while her husband's rigors include disordered bouts of "fury . . . frenzy . . . rage . . . [and] choler" (165). The inability to pity others and the onset of rigors are thus presented as readily identifiable symptoms of political tyranny. Despotism becomes a kind of affective disorder— but one which can be treated.[58]

Whereas rendering women jewels, statues, and corpses can result in permanent damage, Traub's unexamined fourth strategy of containment enables the incarcerating ruler to reconsider, to recover from rigors, and to acquire (however slowly) the formerly absent ability to experience vicarious pity and fear. In his much-discussed definition of tragedy as an action which, "through pity and fear [effects] the proper purgation [*katharsis*] of these emotions," Aristotle seemingly implies that witnessing misfortunes purges or eradicates these emotions (*Poetics* 57). The spectator "thrill[s] with horror and melt[s] to pity at what takes place" (63) but leaves the scene depleted rather than energized. Meanwhile, the kind of empathy that I have located in the plays of Heywood and Shakespeare transforms pity and fear into advocacy and action. Heywood describes the process in his *Apology for Actors:*

[the playgoer,] beeing wrapt in contemplation, offers to him [the actor] in his hart
all prosperous performance, as if the Personator were the man Personated, so bewitching a thing is liuely and well spirited action, that it hath power to new mold
the harts of the spectators and fashion them to the shape of any noble and notable
attempt. (12)

As Marvin Carlson has pointed out, *katharsis* only appears in one passage in
Aristotle and is not adequately defined in *The Poetics*. Translations that render the concept *purgation* imply a kind of "homeopathic medicine, treating
a disorder by the administration of milder does of similar agents; in this case,
the emotions pity and fear." By the seventeenth century, however, commentators increasingly viewed the concept as entailing a *purification* or *refinement* of emotion, rather than an outright discharge.[59] The goals are not to
render spectators insensitive, but to heighten their responsiveness and to
channel their emotions in productive directions.

O. B. Hardison identified three forms of "catharsis" in Renaissance drama:
moral catharsis in which drama induces confession in audience members
(such as in Heywood's oft-cited anecdote about the Dutch husband-mur-
derer); religious catharsis in which poetic justice reassures playgoers that
wickedness is punished; and literal catharsis in which emotional involvement
leads to a deeper understanding of events depicted onstage.[60] This last definition, with its emphasis on "clarification," complements Sidney's and Heywood's emphasis on "animation" cited above. Playwrights thus used a kind
of two-pronged approach to inducing *katharsis* in playgoers, first instructing
them on how to interpret the scene, and then prompting them on what to feel
and do. Animation becomes a form of intellectual and affective manipulation
that may have stemmed from condescension toward the same playgoers
whom, as Stephen S. Hilliard points out, antitheatricalists considered "unsure
of [their] values" and "made up of unlicked bear cubs."[61] The suffering
Leontes inflicts on his family, court, and country is eventually transformed
via diffusion of pity and fear into a profound change of heart. The Sicilian
queen's sixteen-year isolation in Paulina's "poor house" (5.3.6) symbolizes
a kind of prison sentence which mirrors Leontes' own affective quarantine in
which he follows a strict penitential regimen of prayer and atonement—also
directed by Paulina. In the end, Leontes is invited to examine the mysterious
statue of Hermione, and his reaction is to beg the "stone" to chide him for
his pitiless behavior: "I am asham'd; does not the stone rebuke me / For
being more stone than it?" (5.3.37–38). Hermione's descent from the pedes-
tal symbolizes the release of wrongfully convicted prisoners leading to social
renewal; her magic *reanimation* serves to animate all those who "look upon
[her] with marvel" (5.3.99–100).[62]

*   *   *

Shakespeare's Hermione, Foxe's Askew, and Heywood's Elizabeth share
a number of points in common, including being prisoners of conscience, sur-

viving myriad abuses while awaiting trial, and enduring harsh interrogations by men who abuse their authority. The latter two women also shared a common tormentor in the figure of the Bishop of Winchester. In *1 If You Know Not Me, You Know Nobody,* Winchester is the chief villain in a court full of zealous Catholics intent on eradicating Protestantism from the land. In our first glimpse of the newly crowned Queen Mary, we see the bearer (Dodds) of a petition for religious freedom from her Suffolk supporters being sentenced by Winchester to the pillory for his "insolence"; then Elizabeth's messenger (Sentlow) committed to the Tower for daring to ask for a face-to-face meeting that might "cleare her selfe of all supposed treasons" (ii.55132). Heywood deftly compresses materials from Foxe in order to establish an atmosphere of dread in which justice is arbitrary, punishment is cruel, and Mary's nascent tyranny is exacerbated by malevolent counselors.[63] This situation lends considerable forward energy to the basic action of the play: will the princess survive carcereal abuses long enough to get a hearing with Mary? As such, the narrative both mirrors a dilemma faced daily by the commonest prisoners in the land (will they survive the dangers of captivity and get to the trial that may exonerate them?) and replicates a stock situation in the Jacobean public theater: "Poverty and injustice exist, and the king may be surrounded by evil counselors, but if you can get at him directly all will be well."[64]

Elizabeth undergoes a physical and emotional ordeal as she is shuffled from Ashridge to Westminster (where she is first interrogated) to the Tower (where she languishes in a stifling cell) to Woodstock castle (where she narrowly escapes an assassination attempt) and finally to Hampton Court (where she gets an audience with her half-sister). Wherever Elizabeth is taken, she impresses onlookers with her stoicism, faith, and virtue. In her first scene she is rudely awakened by soldiers sent by the queen and ordered to travel to Westminster—in spite of her high fever and Gage's protests that they "pity . . . her weaknes, and lowe state" (iii.180). Soon after, in an emotional scene juxtaposed with the nuptial celebrations of Mary and Prince Phillip of Spain (scene 4). Elizabeth is subjected to her first interrogation by Winchester and his henchmen (scene 5). Heywood engages in especially heavy-handed prompting when, shortly before the bishop's arrival, his terrified "prisoner" speaks to her household servants:

> *Elizabeth.* Why weepe you, gentlemen?
> *Cook.* Not for our selues, men are not made to weepe
>   At there owne fortunes, our eies are made of fire,
>   And to extract water from fire is hard,
>   Nothing but such a Princesse griefe as yours,
>   So good a Ladie & so beautifull, so absolute a mistris,

And perfect as you haue deliuered been,
Haue power to doo't, your sorrow makes vs sad.

(v. 324–31)

If her suffering generates tears in the eyes of men accustomed to the heat of a smoky kitchen, then we may infer that Heywood's playgoers were likewise moved to pity her. In fact, the play's Earl of Sussex declares that it would be unpatriotic *not* to pity the princess: "my Lords, if it were held fowle treason / To grieue for her hard vsage, by my Soule / My eyes would hardly prooue me a true Subiect" (vii.553–56).

In this manner Heywood's plot features key elements of what Alexander Leggatt defines as public theater "taste": patriotism bordering on xenophobia, pro-Protestant and virulent anti-Catholic sentiments, and a "love of fixed patterns" such as type characters and stock situations (28–39). Heywood's scenes are also suited for the public theater acting style in which emotions were declaimed more than they were impersonated, with a view to focusing the affective energies of "voluble and responsive" audiences (Leggatt, 40–44, 77–85). The cook's last line encapsulates this principle of vicarious involvement in declaimed affect: "your sorrow makes vs sad." Just as audiences enjoined to participate in Elizabeth's grief were more apt to revile the play's Catholic villains, so too are the princess's household servants moved to pity their lady and risk their lives in her defense.

The play's sorrowful apogee occurs when an exhausted Elizabeth, drenched with Thames water following a mishap in her barge, is refused a chair by the Constable of the Tower and collapses onstage before its infamous Traitor's Gate: "See gentle men, / The pittious heauens weepes teares into my bosome, / On this cold stone I sit, raine in my face" (vii.602–4). Yet Heywood makes a point of showing that in spite of such pathetic outbursts, Elizabeth is incapacitated by physical infirmity, not merely wallowing in self-pity. Elsewhere she is courageous and clear-headed, such as during her interrogation when she defiantly rejects the charges leveled against her ("I Spit at treason," she says to Winchester) and cleverly unravels the case against her by exposing the absence of incriminating evidence (v. 411–12).

Just as Hermione refuses to confess to her husband but refers herself to the oracle, Elizabeth refuses to "submit" to Mary unless incontrovertible evidence can be found: "My Lords, let pale offenders pardon craue, / if we offend, Lawes *rigor* let vs haue" (v. 421–22, emphasis added). Rigorously examined, the legal cause against her melts into air, prompting Winchester to launch increasingly desperate "plots" and "polices" against her (xviii.1332–36). In his last scene the bishop exhibits those disordered physiological symptoms that we have already seen in the stock tyranny of Angelo and Promos, Leontes and Pandosto. "I grow faynt," Winchester complains as he plots Elizabeth's downfall; "the feauer steales on me, / Death like a vulture tyres vpon my hart" (xviii. 1337–38). As long as she is subjected to his rigors, rather than to the rigorous application of England's law, her life is in danger. The constable of the Tower is even worse, indulging in sadistic fantasies about "torture," about placing snakes in Elizabeth's bed, and about depriving her of light so she can't read her prayer book (ix. 714–23). Finally in lines reminiscent of Cymbeline's threats to Imogen, the constable envisions draining her blood: "Oh that I could but draine her harts deare blood, / Oh it would feede me" (ix 755–56).

As many commentators have pointed out, Heywood exaggerated the dangers faced by Elizabeth in order to propagate the myth of "good Queen Bess" as virgin/martyr/defender of the faith during the years immediately following her death in 1603. The number of pirated quarto editions (eight printed between 1605 and 1639) certainly attests to the play's broad appeal.[65] In spite of Irving Ribner's dismissive observation that the play is "of little significance, either as history or biography" (221), for contemporary audiences it had great significance as both—particularly among individuals unable to afford Foxe's massive *Acts and Monuments* or to read the copy on display at their local church.[66] Heywood's historico-biographical melodrama disseminated such legendary incidents as Elizabeth's enigmatic message *Tanquam Ouis* to supporters when she feared for her life (xi.887–97); the couplet she engraved on her window in Woodstock Castle (xiv.1037–38); and the boy beaten for smuggling in nosegays to sweeten her chamber in the Tower (x.775–804).[67] Heywood's Elizabeth displays exemplary stoicism, courage and largesse; even when confined to stifling rooms with shuttered windows, she endeavors to help other inmates: "This tower hath made me fall to huswiffry, / I spend my labors to releeue the poore" (x.808–9).[68]

In moments such as this, Heywood reassures audiences that the queen who frequently called herself their prince was no virago. Elizabeth's femininity is further emphasized when observers describe her "wondrous crazey" fevers ("Her sleepes are all vnquiet, and her head / Beats and growes giddy with continuall griefe" [iii.150–52]), and when she articulates her grief in gendered terms during her much-anticipated meeting with Mary:

> *Queen.*   Wherefore do you cry?
>   To see your selfe so low, or vs so hye.
>
> *Elizabeth.*   Neither dread Queene, mine is a womanish teare,
>   In part compeld by ioy, and part by feare:
>   Ioy of your sight, these brinish teares haue bread,
>   For feare of my Queenes frowne, to strike me dead.
>
>   (xviii.1253–58)

As with Hermione who enlists a synthesis of men's "thoughts" and "charities" before and during her trial, here Elizabeth deftly combines admissions of disordered feminine weakness, reasoned appeals for justice, and shrewdly timed flattery. Although her performance is dismissed by Mary as spitefull "teares of spleene," Phillip is convinced and emerges from hiding behind an arras to broker a peace between the queen and her prisoner: "Myrror of vertue and bright natures pride, / Pitty it had been, such beauty should haue dy'd" (1259, 1282–83). In part onstage intervention to save the princess, his declaration also invokes audience nostalgia for their recently deceased queen.

Time and again, Heywood's play demonstrates how powerful affect can have profound political consequences. Pity garners support for the princess, and rather than siphoning off the energies of new followers, the very act of weeping invigorates and emboldens them. Taking his cue from Foxe's description of how, when Elizabeth was carried through the streets to Court for interrogation, "a great multitude of people there were standing by the way, who then flocking about her litter lamented and bewailed greatly her estate" (8:607), Heywood repeatedly dramatizes groundswells of support for the princess. Thames bargemen attempt to delay her transport to the Tower after witnessing the "piteous eie she cast" back at her half-sister hoping for a reprieve (vii.517). Later her cook attacks one of the queen's soldiers for handling her food (ix.760-72), and some common townsmen are set in the stocks as "Traytors" for ringing bells as she passes by (xi.870–73). Above all, her Gentleman Usher, Gage (who in Foxe's account frequently bursts into tears [e.g., 8:609, 614]) is moved to defy her jailer Beningfield and promises to deliver her conciliatory letter to the queen, "Were I to bear it through a field of pikes, / And in my way ten thousand arm'd men ambusht" (xiv.1023–24). Elizabeth's popular support is such that when her half-sister finally dies, the Lord of Tame must admonish boys spending their pennies on wood for accession-day bonfires to save a few sticks and "funerall teares" for Mary's hearse (xxii. 1484).

* * *

In his discussion of Heywood's *Apology for Actors,* Steven Mullaney observes that the "affective powers of the stage" troubled its opponents as much as the theater's potential for generating political unrest. The raucous processes of "vicarious participation and identification" encouraged by stage plays blurred the boundary between actor and playgoer.[69] Affect became a potential powderkeg, as playgoers who empathized with suffering depicted onstage experienced, not a *kathartic* purgation of pity and fear, but an empowering sense of social agency. Thus the theater did not merely reflect but could actively "reshape" the self of playgoers, and by extension society too (Mullaney, 101). However, Phyllis Rackin points out that Heywood's *Apology* is a conservative, not radical, document which defends plays on the grounds that they encourage deference to authority by depicting the horrible fates of those who cause trouble. Since (*pace* Sidney) historical drama could provide an ideal means for the continued "ideological indoctrination" of politicized audiences, dramatists had an extra burden of responsibility not only to entertain the masses, but to channel their energies in socially constructive directions.[70] In *1 If You Know Not Me* Heywood practiced what he preached: while the Catholics in the play are demonized, at no point do Elizabeth or her followers encourage sedition or religious persecution.[71] Instead, the weeping generated by the play recommends such virtues as tolerance, patriotism, obedience and passive endurance to those who vicariously experience what the play's subtitle refers to as *The Troubles of Queene Elizabeth*.[72] An England characterized by temperance and justice is the hope expressed in Foxe's contrast of the reigns of Mary and Elizabeth: "then, moderation had no place, but all was ruled by rigour, contrary now, clemency hath all the operation" (8:601).

Although Heywood and Shakespeare presented their incarcerated royals in a sympathetic light, they do not appear to have been advocates of prisoners' rights *per se*. In other plays, prisoners are blithely neglected (e.g., the hungry women in *The Rape of Lucrece*), killed (e.g., the French POWs in *Henry V*), tortured (e.g., Iago's promised fate at the end of *Othello*), even mutilated (e.g., Ragozine's substituted head in *Measure for Measure*) without anyone onstage batting an eyelid. However, when it came to the wrongfully accused, both dramatists encouraged playgoers to empathize with the suffering of characters; as Elizabeth requests of her supporters, "Pray for me in your harts, not with your tongues" (xi.859). Pendry's survey of early modern prison legislation reveals that despite ongoing concerns with prevention of escapes, the upkeep of buildings, and the extortions of jailers, to such concerns "the well-being of the prisoners took second place." Not surprisingly, the penal issue most hotly debated in Parliament was the *Act for the Better Securing of the Subjects from Wrongful Imprisonment,* first introduced in 1621 and enacted into law with the *Petition of Right* of 1628.[73] Perhaps what playgoers saw onstage gave them food for thought as they returned home south from Heywood's Red Bull Theater past the stench of Newgate Prison, or north from Shakespeare's Globe across London Bridge past the gloom of Tower Hill.[74] If these dramatists contributed to the "ideological indoctrination" of playgoers, then part of this process entailed the refinement of English sensibilities regarding the wrongfully confined.

The dramatists' two-pronged approach of generating emotion tempered by reason seems designed to ensure that audiences captivated by a performance not succumb to the kind of captivity envisioned by Gosson in which playgoers become "prisoners to the Deuill"—a captivity from which, Gosson hastens to add, "hee craueth no ransome for our release" (211, 172). Their plays seem designed to appeal to thinking *and* feeling spectators, ones mindful of the law but also able to empathize with innocent victims and resist abuses of power. English audiences seem to have been remarkably free of preconceptions regarding prisoners, recognizing (as did Mynshul, writing from the King's Bench) that "Some there bee . . . [who] deserue no pity or compassion," but that others there be who did (22). When it came to affective manipulation, playgoers were open to suggestion—but no more than *suggestion*—regarding whether or not to pity or scorn prisoners onstage. For playgoers, weeping needed not be "womanish" (as Gosson contends) nor needed internal vapors be noxious (as Burton contends) so long as *katharsis* could serve to enliven the spirit: "As this Earthy Body is washed by Water, so is that Spirituous Body Cleansed by Cathartick Vapours."[75] Also, as long as these cleansing tears were patriotic (as Heywood's Sussex contends), the physiology of affect could benefit society. And finally, as long as the mistreatment of particular prisoners could be adjudged to be inappropriate (such as Marlowe's Zenocrate observes of Bajazeth's and Zabina's suffering), then receptive audiences could be enjoined to pity event he sharp-toothed Turk: "Earth, cast up fountains from thy entrails. / And wet thy cheeks for their untimely deaths" (*1 Tamburlaine* 5.1.347–48).

Pity is only debilitating when it becomes an end in itself, rather than the means to an end. Imprisoned in the Counter, Askew elicited sorrowful speeches from London's Lord Mayor's interrogator, who said that "it was great pity that I should be there without cause," and the Bishop who stated that "he was very sorry for my trouble" (Foxe, 5:538–39). Yet neither man lifted a finger to prevent the suffering of one of the period's most outspoken religious dissenters. However, Askew's suffering did generate tangible popular support. While in prison, she describes how one maid courageously "went abroad in the streets, [and] made moan to the prentices, and they, by her did send me money" (5:547). And when Askew was burnt at Smithfield, railings had to be erected "to keep out the press" in which, as suggested by the woodcut accompanying Foxe's text, there may have been as many weeping for the prisoner as there were egging on her Marian executioners (5:550–51). Whereas Marlowe and Webster replicated such divisive social spectacles by sending mixed messages to audiences, Shakespeare and Heywood clearly established the guilt or innocence of their royal female prisoners, directing playgoers' vicarious affective participation in the pity and release of those unjustly confined on the stage. In so doing, they liberated empathy from the clutches of the antitheatricalists' devil and elevated it to a social virtue of the highest order: "Pitty is a Godlike property, but hardnes of heart . . . and imperious domineering ouer men dejected, argue base, ignoble, cowardly and diuellish dispositions" (Mynshul, 70).

Notes

1. Thomas Heywood, "The Author to his Booke," prefaced to *An Apology for Actors,* 1612, in *The Seventeenth-Century Stage: A Collection of Critical Essays,* ed. Gerald Eades Bently (Chicago: University of Chicago Press, 1968), p. 11, ll. 1–8.

2. Sidney, *An Apology for Poetry,* 1585, ed. Forrest G. Robinson (Indianapolis: Bobbs-Merrill, 1970), 34–35.

3. *The Winter's Tale* 2.1.118–21. Quotations from Shakespeare's plays are taken from *The Riverside Shakespeare,* ed. G. Blakemore Evans, 2nd ed. (Boston: Houghton Mifflin, 1997).

4. Nashe, *Pierce Penilesse his supplication to the Devil,* 1592, excerpted in *Eyewitnesses of Shakespeare: First Hand Accounts of Performances 1590–1890,* ed. Gāmini Salgādo (Sussex: Sussex University Press, 1975), 16. For a discussion of attacks on the sensory stimulations and other dangers of "Sathans Synagogue," see Jean E. Howard, *The Stage and Social Struggle in Early Modern England* (London: Routledge, 1994), 22–46.

5. Gosson, *Plays Confuted in Fiue Actions* (1582); reprinted in *The English Drama and Stage Under the Tudor and Stuart Princes 1543–1664, Illustrated by a Series of Documents, Treatises and Poems,* ed. W. C. Hazlitt (1832; reprint, New York: Burt Franklin, 1969), 157–218, quotations on pp. 180–81.

6. See Garland's chapter on the refinement of "punitive manners" in *Punishment and Modern Society: A Study in Social Theory* (Chicago: University of Chicago Press, 1993), 213–47; quotations on pp. 213-14, 224.

7. Dekker, *The Second Part of the Honest Whore,* in *Elizabethan Plays* ed. Hazelton Spencer (Boston: D. C. Heath, 1933), 5.2.293–527. Approximate dates of first performances are taken from the chronological table in A. R. Braunmuller and Michael Hattaway, ed., *The Cambridge Companion to English Renaissance Drama* (Cambridge: University Press, 1995), 419–46.

8. That those offstage may have echoed such harshness is suggested by Isabella Whitney's poem "The Manner of her Will" (1573), in which even a woman who expresses sympathy for the plight of prisoners admits that she too would "oft" visit Bedlam and Bridewell in order to gawk at inmates who talked "out of tune" and performed such menial tasks as the "turning of the mill." See her poem in *Women Writers in Renaissance England,* ed. Randall Martin (London: Longman, 1997), 290–302, ll. 225–32.

9. Jean E. Howard, "Civic Institutions and Precarious Masculinity in Dekker's *The Honest Whore* (draft version)," *Early Modern Culture* 1 (2000): 21–25; http://eserver.org/emc/l-l/howard.html. Philip Shaw argues that, if anything, Dekker understated the real-life suffering of Bridewell inmates in his play; see "The Position of Thomas Dekker in Jacobean Prison Literature," *Publications of the Modern Language Association* 62 (1947), 366–91, pp. 368–70. On the varieties of institutional confinement of women during the period, see E. J. Burford and Sandra Shulman, *Of Bridles and Burnings: The Punishment of Women* (New York: St. Martin's Press, 1992), 138–62.

10. Webster, *The Duchess of Malfi* in *Drama of the English Renaissance II: The Stuart Period,* ed. Russell A. Fraser and Norman Rabkin (New York: MacMillan, 1976), 4.2.286–88.

11. Quotations from Heywood's play are taken from *If You Know Not Me You Know Nobody Part 1,* ed. Madeleine Doran, Malone Society Reprints (Oxford: Oxford University Press, 1935).

12. Garland, *Punishment and Modern Society,* 231–47 and sources cited there.

13. See *The Compact Edition of the Oxford English Dictionary,* 3 vols. (Oxford: Oxford University Press, 1987), s.v., "pity" (sb I.2.) for this definition and the citation from *Leviathan* (1651).

14. Nussbaum, "Aristotle on Emotions and Rational Persuasion," in *Essays on Aristotle's Rhetoric,* ed. Amélie Oksenberg Rorty (Berkeley: University of California Press, 1996), 303–23, quotations on p. 309. Quotations from Aristotle's other relevant work, *The Poetics,* are taken from *Literary Criticism: An Introductory Reader,* ed. Lionel Trilling (New York: Holt, Rinehart and Winston, 1970), 53–77, discussed below.

15. Nussbaum, "Aristotle on Emotions and Rational Persuasion," 318–19; see also Garland, *Punishment and Modern Society,* 213–15, 219–22.

16. Burness E. Moore and Bernard D. Fine, ed., *Psychoanalytic Terms and Concepts* (New Haven: Yale University Press, 1990), 67.

17. Burton, *The Anatomy of Melancholy,* ed. Holbrook Jackson, Everyman Edition, 3 vols. (London: J. M. Dent; New York: E. P. Dutton, 1932), 2:185.

18. Burton is especially critical of "tyrannizing pseudo-politicians" and "hard-hearted parents" who impose this unnatural state of "enforced temperance" on their charges (1:418). On the gendering of "womanly blood" as superfluous bodily waste see Gail Kern Paster, *The Body Embarrassed: Drama and the Disciplines of Shame in Early Modern England* (Ithaca: Cornell University Press, 1993), 64–84.

19. *The Acts and Monuments of John Foxe,* 1563, 1570, ed. George Townsend, 8 vols. (London, [1837–41]; reprint, New York: AMS Press, 1965), 8:619.

20. Forman's once-disputed account describes a performance in the spring or summer 1611, possibly at the Globe theater, and is reproduced in J. M. Nosworthy's introduction to *Cymbeline,* Arden Shakespeare (1955; reprint, London and New York: Routledge, 1991), xiv–xv.

21. On the deplorable conditions confronting England's poor prisoners, see J. E. Thomas, *House of Care: Prisons and Prisoners in England 1500–1800* (Nottingham: University of Nottingham Department of Adult Education, 1988) esp. 6–48; Clifford Dobb, "London's Prisons," *Shakespeare Survey* 17 (1964): 87–100; Christopher Harding, Bill Hines, Richard Ireland and Philip Rawlings, *Imprisonment in England and Wales: A Concise History* (London: Croom Helm, 1985), 59–60, 66–73; and E. D. Pendry, *Elizabethan Prisons and Prison Scenes,* 2 vols. (Salzburg: Universität Salzburg, 1974).

22. Thomas, *House of Care,* 37.

23. In *The Dramatic Works of Thomas Heywood* 6 vols. (1874; reprint, New York: Russell and Russell, 1964), 5:256, italics omitted. Also cited in Pendry, *Elizabethan Prisons and Prison Scenes,* 9.

24. This cash-grab lasted until October 1602 when authorities closed the operation down. See Pendry, *Elizabethan Prisons and Prison Scenes,* 48–49; and Russell P. Dobash, R. Emerson Dobash, and Sue Gutteridge, *The Imprisonment of Women* (Oxford: Basil Blackwell, 1986), 25–26.

25. Mynshul, *Essayes and Characters of a Prison and Prisoners* (1618; reprint, Edinburgh, 1821), 89. Subsequent references will be incorporated in my text. On Dekker's hand in ghost-writing the collection, see Shaw, "The Position of Thomas Dekker in Jacobean Prison Literature," 386–88. On prison rape, see Harding et al., *Imprisonment in England and Wales,* 40.

26. R. M., *Micrologia. Characters, Or Essayes, Of Persons, Trades, and Places,* 1629; cited in Pendry, *Elizabethan Prisons and Prison Scenes,* 41–42, italics omitted. Cf. Christopher Marlowe, *Tamburlaine the Great, Parts I and II,* ed. John D. Jump, Regents Renaissance Drama Series (Lincoln: University of Nebraska Press, 1967), pt. 2:4.3.1 ff.

27. Meredith Anne Skura, *Shakespeare the Actor and the Purposes of Playing* (Chicago: University of Chicago Press, 1993), p. 203 and note.

28. Levin, "The Contemporary Perception of Marlowe's Tamburlaine," *Medieval and Renaissance Drama in England* 1 (1984): 51–70.

29. Zenocrate's shaming may have had only a fleeting effect, as many extant allusions to these scenes' spectacular cruelty are celebratory, not critical; see Levin, "The Contemporary Perception of Marlowe's Tamburlaine," 58–62.

30. There is much commentary about the moral ambivalence of the Duchess; see for example, Sara Jayne Steen, "The Crime of Marriage: Arbella Stuart and *The Duchess of Malfi,*" *Sixteenth Century Journal* 22 (1991): 61–76; and more recently, Elizabeth Oakes, "The Duchess of Malfi as a Tragedy of Identity," *Studies in Philology* (1999): 51–67.

31. For a discussion of the much-ignored *sovereignty* of the Duchess, and of the "mixed messages" sent by Webster in making his protagonist variously a hapless victim, a political prisoner, a martyr, and a Patient Griselda, see Theodora A. Jankowski, "Defining/Confining the Duchess; Negotiating the Female Body in John Webster's *The Duchess of Malfi,*" *Studies in Philology* 87 (1990): 221–45.

32. On the special treatment accorded state prisoners in England, see Pendry, *Elizabethan Prisons and Prison Scenes,* 86.

33. On the exploitative system of fees and garnishes, see Dobb, "London's Prisons," 94–96; and Pendry, *Elizabethan Prisons and Prison Scenes,* 78–80.

34. Women at the Counters were segregated from the men and forced to sleep like animals on straw on the floor in an unsanitary chamber called the "Sty" (likely because of the foul smell); see Pendry, *Elizabethan Prisons and Prison Scenes,* 78–80.

35. All quotations from Mary's letters are from the collection, *Letters of Mary Stuart, Queen of Scotland,* ed. Prince Alexander Labanoff, trans. William Turnbull (London, 1845), here from the letter dated 29 October 1571 (p. 225). On the locations of her prolonged captivity, see Gordon Donaldson, *Mary, Queen of Scots* (London: English Universities Press, 1974), 156–77.

36. Donaldson, *Mary, Queen of Scots,* 159, 177.

37. Anon. [Robert Southwell?], *An Epitaph vpon the Death of the Most Gratious and Vertuous Ladie Marie,* transcribed in *The Last Years of Mary Queen of Scots: Documents from the Cecil Papers at Hatfield House,* ed. Alan G. R. Smith (London: The Roxburghe Club, 1990), 88–91, stanza 8.

38. Elizabeth I, "Written with a Diamond on Her Window at Woodstock" and "Written on a Wall at Woodstock," in *The Longman Anthology of British Literature,* volume 1, gen. ed., David Damrosch (New York: Longman, 1999), 1023–24.

39. Elizabeth I, "Letter XVII. To Queen Mary," in *The Letters of Queen Elizabeth* ed. G. B. Harrison (London: Cassell, 1935), 19–21.

40. Elizabeth I, "On Mary, Queen of Scots" (1586), in Damrosch, ed. *The Longman Anthology of British Literature,* 1028–31, p. 1030, emphasis added.

41. On the exacting standards of female beauty and controversial remedies for concealing spots and blemishes, see Frances E. Dolan, "Taking the Pencil out of God's Hand: Art, Nature, and the Face-Painting Debate in Early Modern England," *Publications of the Modern Language Association* 108 (1993): 224–39.

42. E.g., see Burford and Shulman, *Of Bridles and Burnings,* 139–42; and Harding et al., *Imprisonment in England and Wales,* 6–7. On English prison reform in subsequent centuries, see Randall McGowen, "The Well-Ordered Prison: England, 1780–1865," in *The Oxford History of the Prison: The Practice of Punishment in Western Society,* ed. Norval Morris and David J. Rothman (New York: Oxford University Press, 1998), 71–99.

43. *Pace* Burford and Shulman, who assert misleadingly that "It is a stark fact that not until habeas corpus was promulgated in 1679 . . . did the ordinary man and woman have any concept of personal liberty"; *Of Bridles and Burnings,* 142.

44. Heywood, *A Woman Killed with Kindness,* 1603, in *Three Elizabethan Domestic Tragedies,* ed. Keith Sturgess (London: Penguin, 1985), 4.4.156, 151–54; for a discussion of how this charitable life sentence becomes in effect an uncharitable death sentence, see Jennifer Panek, "Punishing Adultery in *A Woman Killed with Kindness,*" *Studies in English Literature. 1500–1900* 34 (1994): 357–78.

45. Mynshul, *Essayes and Characters of a Prison and Prisoners,* 6, 18, 44–46, quotation on p. 24.

46. See Pendry, *Elizabethan Prisons and Prison Scenes,* 44–45.

47. Donaldson, *Mary, Queen of Scots,* 161.

48. On the psychology of Leontes' jealousy, see Janet Adelman, *Suffocating Mothers: Fantasies of Maternal Origin in Shakespeare's Plays* Hamlet *to* The Tempest (New York: Routledge, 1992), 220–38; Derek Cohen, "Patriarchy and Jealousy in *Othello* and *The Winter's Tale,*" *Modern Language Quarterly* 48 (1987): 207–23; and Peter B. Erickson, "Patriarchal Structures in *The Winter's Tale,*" *Publications of the Modern Language Association* 97 (1982): 819–29. Paster argues that forcing Hermione to give birth in prison represents a desperate bid by Leontes to reassert patriarchy by wresting control of his family from female influences in court; *The Body Embarrassed,* 260–80.

49. See Harding et al., *Imprisonment in England and Wales,* 21–26, quotations on p. 24.

50. Courtiers and ladies alike agree that both Mamillius and the newborn girl are a "copy of the father" Leontes (1.2.208, 2.3.100–08); Camillo diagnoses that king's opinion as being "disease'd" and "dangerous" (1.2.296–98) and calls the Bohemian king "good Polixenes" (1.353); Hermione and other lords "dare [their] life lay down" to protest her innocence (2.1.130, 95); Antigonus and Paulina go so far as to call the charges laughable: "Here's such ado to make no stain a stain / As passes colouring" (2.1.199, 2.2.18–19).

51. *OED* s.v., definitions 2–4, especially 2b. This is the only occurrence of "charities" (pl.) in Shakespeare's plays.

52. Leontes' subsequent treatment of his wife and children may have appeared particularly egregious to early modern consumers of those popular accounts of infanticide and child abandonment discussed in Frances E. Dolan, *Dangerous Familiars: Representations of Domestic Crime in England 1550–1700* (Ithaca: Cornell University Press, 1994), 159–70.

53. See More's letter to Margaret Roper dated 2 or 3 May 1535, transcribed in *The Correspondence of Sir Thomas More,* ed. Elizabeth Frances Rogers (Princeton: Princeton University Press, 1947), 550–54, quotation on p. 552. More carefully worded his letters to Margaret, knowing full well that they would be intercepted, read, and possibly even copied by court officials.

54. Askew, *The Examinations,* 1546, 1547, reprinted in Martin, ed. *Women Writers in Renaissance England* 58–79, quotation on p. 65.

55. Greene's novel is reproduced in *An Anthology of Elizabethan Prose Fiction,* ed. Paul Salzman (Oxford: Oxford University Press, 1991), 151–204, quotations on p. 167. Definitions are taken from the *OED,* s.v. "rigour."

56. Traub, *Desire and Anxiety: Circulations of Sexuality in Shakespearean Drama* (London and New York: Routledge, 1992), 25–49.

57. George Whetstone, *1 The Historie, of Promos and Cassandra;* rpt. In *Narrative and Dramatic Sources of Shakespeare: Volume II The Comedies, 1597–1603,* ed. Geoffrey Bullough (London: Routledge and Kegan Paul; New York: Columbia University Press, 1963), 3.1. p. 458.

58. When sexually propositioned by Promos, Whetstone's Cassandra begs for her brother's life by saying that "none but lustfull leachers should with rygrous law be payd" (*1 Promos and Cassandra* 2.3.p. 452).

59. Carlson, *Theories of the Theatre: A Historical and Critical Survey, from the Greeks to the Present* (Ithaca: Cornell University Press, 1984), 16–19. Cf. the definition in the supplement to the *OED* (vol. 3, ed. R. W. Buchfield), Catharsis, b. "the purification of the emotions by vicarious experience."

60. Hardison, "Three Types of Renaissance Catharsis," *Renaissance Drama* n.s. 2 (1969), 3–22. For a more recent discussion, see David Konstan, "the Tragic Emotions," *Comparative Drama* 33 (1999): 1–21.

61. Hilliard, "Stephen Gosson and the Elizabethan Distrust of the Effects of Drama," *English Literary Renaissance* 9 (1979): 225–40 (cited from p. 238).

62. Again, subtle departures from his source materials emphasize the point made in Shakespeare's play. In Greene's *Pandosto, The Triumph of Time,* it is not a female attendant outraged because she is barred access to the imprisoned queen, but a jailer pitying Bellaria's "bitter tears" and overhearing the "heavy passions" in her cell who finally confronts Pandosto and exposes to the other courtiers "the King's cruel sentence." Transforming pity into advocacy on behalf of a stranger is rare event, one which Shakespeare perhaps cynically omits from his version of events. Salzman, ed. *An Anthology of Elizabethan Prose Fiction,* 164–65.

63. On Heywood's indebtedness to Foxe, see Barbara J. Baines's discussion of the play in *Thomas Heywood* (Boston: Twayne, G. K. Hall, 1984), 26–32.

64. Alexander Leggatt, *Jacobean Public Theatre* (London and New York: Routledge, 1992), pp. 35–36. See also his chapter-length discussion of the stagecraft of Heywood's play (164–80). Baines plots a similar narrative as one which follows Foxe's archetypal pattern of ordeal leading to triumph and "virtual sainthood"; *Thomas Heywood,* 32.

65. Baines, *Thomas Heywood,* 26–28; Kathleen E. McLuskie, *Dekker and Heywood: Professional Dramatists* (New York: St. Martin's Press, 1994), 41–46; Irving Ribner, *The English History Play in the Age of Shakespeare* (London: Methuen, 1965), 219–21.

66. On the literacy of public theater audiences, see Leggatt, *Jacobean Public Theatre,* 32–33 and sources cited there.

67. Heywood transposes the Woodstock couplet from a window to the princess's prayer book. These and other incidents recorded by Foxe and dramatized by Heywood have become standard features in modern biographies of Elizabeth; e.g., Christopher Hibbert, *The Virgin Queen: A Personal History of Elizabeth I* (London: Viking, 1990), 39–61; and Paul Johnson *Elizabeth I: A Study in Power and Intellect* (London: Omega/Futura, 1976), 38–61. See also Georgianna Ziegler, "England's Savior: Elizabeth I in the Writings of Thomas Heywood," *Renaissance Papers,* Southeastern Renaissance Conference (1980): 29–39.

68. The performance of this sixth corporal work of mercy (ministering to prisoners) was a favored method of Heywood's to generate sympathy for his wronged heroines. Cf. Jane Shore's distribution of benevolences in the Marshalsea, and later the widespread pity her confinement in the Tower generates, in *2 Edward IV* (c. 1599); in *The Dramatic Works of Thomas Heywood,* 1:120–23, 158–83 *passim.*

69. Mullaney, *The Place of the Stage: License, Play, and Power in Renaissance England* (Chicago: University of Chicago Press, 1988), 98–103.

70. Rackin, *Stages of History: Shakespeare's English Chronicles* (Ithaca: Cornell University Press, 1993), 111–14.

71. No such actions are taken, in part because none are needed: in the final scenes of the play, Elizabeth's chief enemies (Mary, Winchester, and Poole) each die of natural causes, paving the way for a peaceful transition back to the Reformation practices begun by her father and brother before her.

72. Historiographical research suggests that many Elizabethans shared their queen's general tolerance of nondisruptive (i.e., not Continental, Jesuitical, or recusant) forms of Catholicism in the realm; see M. C. Questier, "What Happened to English Catholicism after the English Reformation?" *History: The Journal of the Historical Association* 85 (2000): 28–47. For a more partisan view of the play as Puritan "propaganda," see Gerald M. Pinciss, *Forbidden Matter: Religion in the Drama of Shakespeare and his Contemporaries* (Newark: University of Delaware Press, 2000), 67–75.

73. Pendry, *Elizabethan Prisons and Prison Scenes,* 15–24, quotations on p.23.

74. For the locations of London's prisons, see Mullaney, *The Place of the Stage,* figure 2, pp. 28–29; and John D'Auby Briscoe, Robert Lathrop Sharp, and Murray Eugene Borish, *A Mapbook of English Literature* (New York: Henry Holt, 1936), map 3, pp. 10–11.

75. Ralph Cudsworth, *The True Intellectual System on the Universe,* 1678, p. 787; cited in the *OED* s.v. "Cathartic" A.2.

Genus Cygnus: Three Species of the Swan

JUNE SCHLUETER

I. Karl Theodor Gaedertz's Swan

MORE than a century ago, Karl Theodor Gaedertz, a librarian at the König-liche Bibliothek in Berlin, introduced the drawing of the Swan theater to the scholarly world. In print for the first time was a facsimile of this uniquely important document, which remains the only known contemporary drawing of the interior of a Bankside theater in Shakespeare's time. Given the questions surrounding the reliability of the Swan drawing, which is available only in Aernout van Buchell's redrawing of Johannes de Witt's original, it is ironic that Gaedertz's 1888 presentation of the document introduced difficulties that rendered the facsimile suspect. Indeed, although Henry B. Wheatley corrected Gaedertz's presentation within months of its publication,[1] reproductions of Gaedertz's Swan persist to this day, mostly in drama textbooks, but even in the multivolume *Encyclopedia of the Renaissance* and the print version of the magisterial *Encyclopædia Britannica.*[2] Hence, it may be useful to begin this trio of essays with a discussion of the inaccuracies of Gaedertz's Swan and a cautionary word about archival research.

The news of the Swan drawing appears in Gaedertz's *Zur Kenntnis der altenglischen Bühne,*[3] a seventy-nine-page book (or "pamphlet") that collects information on three topics: the Swan drawing at the Rijksuniversiteit Utrecht,[4] a Pyramus and Thisbe play at the British Library, and Washington Irving's sketchbook at Stratford-upon-Avon. Gaedertz's Swan purported to be a facsimile of the drawing and a transcript of the text, yet two features of his presentation were peculiar. First, despite his considerable skill as a researcher, Gaedertz seemed not to have noticed the full text of the description of London accompanying the drawing; apparently, an Utrecht librarian later sent it to him, and, just before going to press, he added as end matter, entitled "Nachrichten von Johannes de Witt" [News of Johannes de Witt], the twenty-seven lines of the description that he had omitted from the body of his essay.[5] (He also included as end matter several letters from de Witt to van Buchell and to Lambert van der Burch, a deacon at St. Mary's Church, Utrecht, where de Witt was a canon, letters that were sent him by P. A. Tiele, head of the Utrecht library.)[6] Second, the facsimile that he published appears to have been from a pen and black-ink copy; Gaedertz described his reproduction as being "after" an existing hand-drawn one in Utrecht from 1596 ("Nach einer in Utrecht befindlichen Handzeichnung vom Jahre 1596"). A careful look at the Gaedertz copy (fig. 6) in comparison with the version published by Wheatley in *Transactions of the New Shakspere Society* (fig. 7) reveals subtle variations as well as one obvious, distinctive feature: "Ex Observationibus Londinensibus Johannis De Witt," which is situated as a title atop the description on the facing page in the van Buchell layout, appears *beneath* the drawing in Gaedertz, in place of the three lines of text.

Wheatley's reproduction, in contrast to Gaedertz's, is made from a photograph, secured when van Buchell's *Adversaria* was on loan to the British Museum. Except for size, and with allowances for imperfect technology, his is an exact facsimile of the van Buchell drawing, showing the three lines of text beneath it and offering an intact (though mislined) typescript of the full forty-three-line description. The physical layout of the drawing described by Wheatley accurately reflects the document as it appears in van Buchell's notebook, altering any false impression one might have derived from the Gaedertz arrangement. However important the news of the Swan drawing was and however illuminating Gaedertz's analysis, the presentation was not careful, and Wheatley's corrective was essential.

Graciously, Wheatley made no effort to account for the disparities between Gaedertz's presentation and the text and drawing as they appear in van Buchell's notebook. Undoubtedly, however, he understood how these differences had materialized, for Wheatley communicated with Tiele, the Utrecht librarian whom he credits with having discovered the drawing at least a year before Gaedertz's book appeared.[7] Left with no explanation, scholars studying the Gaedertz Swan today must, on their own, puzzle out its problems, the most notable of which is the placement of the title "Ex Observationibus Londinensibus Johannis De Witt" atop the page opposite the drawing in van Buchell but *beneath* the drawing in Gaedertz. It is a problem exacerbated by Gaedertz's verification of the layout: "Unter dieser merkwürdigen Abbildung, von welcher ich ein Facsimile biete, steht zu lessen: Ex observationibus Londinensibus Johannis De Witt"[8] [Under this remarkable drawing, of which I offer a facsimile, is written: Ex Observationibus Londinensibus Johannis De Witt].

Equally puzzling was Gaedertz's news that while he was preparing his essay, a second excerpt by van Buchell was found in the Utrecht library and sent to him by Tiele.[9] That "excerpt," which he published in his end matter, consists of the first twenty lines of the twenty-seven lines of the description that appears on fol 131v of van Buchell's notebook, opposite the drawing. The transcript that Gaedertz was to publish in the body of his essay began with line twenty of fol 131v, continued with the three lines that appear at the bottom of fol 132, and concluded with the thirteen lines on fol 132v. That he was initially unaware of the first twenty lines of the description is underscored

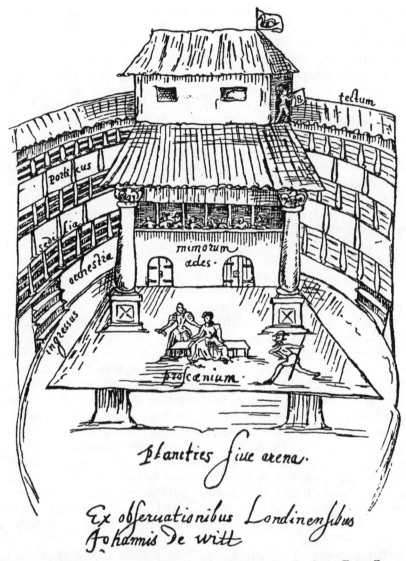

Figure 6. The Swan drawing as presented by Karl Theodor Gaedertz. From *Zur Kenntnis der altenglischen Bühne* **(Bremen: C. Ed. Muller, 1888).**

by his surprise and excitement over receiving the "second excerpt,"[10] which mentions a date—1596, in connection with the memorial to Joannis Bourgh in Westminster Abbey—that sets a *terminus ad quem* for de Witt's visit to London. But that date appears on line twenty of fol 131v immediately before the passage describing the theaters, which Gaedertz clearly knew. One could

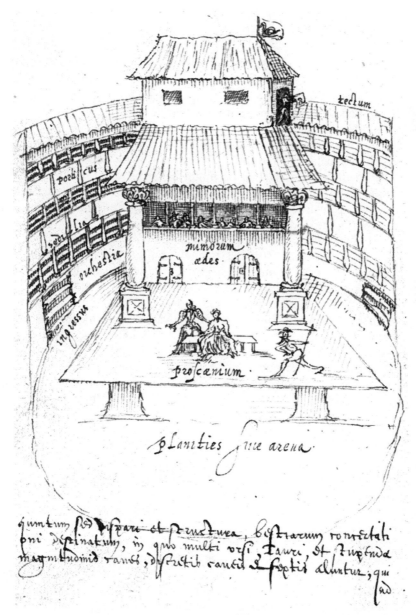

Figure 7. The Swan drawing as presented by Henry B. Wheatley. From "On a Contemporary Drawing of the Interior of the Swan Theatre, 1596," *Transactions of the New Shakspere Society, 1887–92,* **series 1, part 2 (1888), 215–25. Courtesy of Bibliotheek der Rijksuniversiteit Utrecht.**

only wonder at how he missed seeing the date and, even more incredibly, how he failed to notice the first twenty lines of the description on the same page that contains the seven lines he transcribed. And, finally, one had to ask how he could have referred to the opening lines of the description as a "second excerpt," subsequently discovered. Readers may readily see how curious the situation was by referring to figure 8, which shows a typescript of the forty-three-line description in relation to the drawing, as it appears in van Buchell's *Adversaria*.

Finding it inconceivable that anyone who had just examined the van Buchell notebook could be offering the observations that Gaedertz was making, I entertained the possibility that he might be describing not van Buchell's copy of the Swan but de Witt's lost original. Two points in Gaedertz's narrative, however, foreclosed the idea. First, Gaedertz offers the judgment that the final item in the description of London, concerning de Witt's visit to the shop of Abraham der Kinderen, where he saw a complete set of Dürer's engravings, was an abstract (by van Buchell) rather than a transcript of de Witt's report, an observation consistent with the way in which van Buchell typically recorded his correspondence. (Indeed, other parts of the description may also be abstracts, though it would appear that the commentary on the London theaters was of sufficient interest to van Buchell for him to copy it all.) Whatever the substantive value of Gaedertz's judgment, it is important as an indication that he was working with the van Buchell entry and not with an original de Witt description. Moreover, his publication of the title of the description confirms this conclusion, for the title, whether a transcript or van Buchell's addition, is in van Buchell's hand: to determine this, one need only compare the word "Observations" in van Buchell's account of Italian theaters[11] with the word as it appears in the notebook and in Gaedertz's publication. (The occasionally discussed possibility that de Witt himself made the entry in his friend's notebook is not supported by the handwriting, which, as Johan Gerritsen notes, is consistent with van Buchell's early hand.[12]

My second observation came in the form of a recognition: Gaedertz, in fact, never says that he actually examined the Swan drawing in its physical setting—or even that he was in Utrecht. The opening line of the foreword to his three-part book refers to his having found the material he discussed on his "Reise im Ausland," but it may be that his foreign travels took him only to London (for the Pyramus and Thisbe play) and Stratford (for the Irving sketchbook). (He does say that he spent half a year in England in 1886.)[13]

Dismissing the idea that Gaedertz was describing not van Buchell's Swan but de Witt's, I realized that the explanation for the disparity between his presentation and van Buchell's lay in the fact that Gaedertz, however sedulous in his acknowledgment of colleagues in Utrecht, including Tiele, was not working with the primary document but with a copy, a copy that was, at least initially, incomplete. When he received the "second excerpt" from the

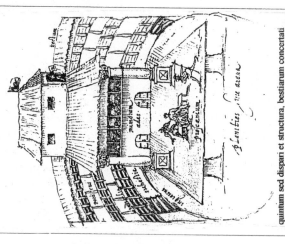

Figure 8. Diagram showing layout of "Ex Observationibus Londinensibus Johannis de Witt" and the Swan drawing in Aernout van Buchell's *Adversaria* (fol 131v, 132, 132v). Transcript by Johan Gerritsen, "de Witt, van Buchell, the Swan and the Globe: Some Notes," in *Essays in Honour of Kristian Smidt*, ed. Peter Bilton, Lars Hartveit, Stig Johannson, Arthur O. Sandved, and Bjørn Tysdahl (Oslo: University of Oslo Institute of English Studies, 1986), 44–46 n. 17. From a reprint with extra plates and a "corrected," i.e., properly aligned, text in note 17. Copyrighted by Gerritsen in 1988, the enhanced reprint is available at the Folger Shakespeare Library and the University of Utrecht.

Utrecht library, representing for first part of the description and not, as he thought, another, newly discovered document, he saw the handscripted title "Ex Observationibus Londinensibus Johannis De Witt" for the first time. Wanting it to be part of his primary presentation, he pasted it beneath the drawing, in place of the typed or modern hand caption that was apparently put there in Utrecht to identify the manuscript from which the drawing derives.

The lesson is a familiar one attending all historical research: if one is to speak with authority, one must examine the primary material. It is ironic that the man to whom the scholarly community owes an immeasurable debt went to press with his announcement and analysis without having seen the original of the van Buchell Swan.

II. Aernout van Buchell's Swan

Implicitly questioning the reliability of the drawing of the Swan, J. Dover Wilson, in a 1948 essay, dismissively referred to the document as "one Dutchman's copy of another Dutchman's sketch of what he remembered about the interior of the Swan Theatre after a single visit."[14] Though some may not accept Dover Wilson's assumption that de Witt's drawing was a memorial reconstruction, the august Shakespearean is not alone in asking the underlying question: just how capable were de Witt and van Buchell as draftsmen? Were they admirably accomplished, as Martin Holmes contends in a 1956 essay? "The artist," Holmes observes (without saying if he is speaking of de Witt or van Buchell), "whether or not he knew anything about theatres, certainly knew about drawing. A man who could give the necessary effect of emphasis or recession by the precision of his line and the intensity of his ink is not likely to have been guilty of muddled thinking or inaccurate memory when sketching something that had impressed him."[15] Or were they woefully inept, as J. Le Gay Brereton contends in a 1916 essay? De Witt, Brereton proposed, was "a curious foreigner, who was not a skilled draughtsman," and the efforts of a second unskilled draftsman, van Buchell, compounded the problem: "One supposes that Van Buchell, puzzled by inconsistency in the original rough sketch, and trying to give definiteness to the lines and to make them fit his ideas of propriety, introduced further confusion."[16] In truth, the range of opinion on the abilities of de Witt and van Buchell is considerable, and the question, after a century of assessment, remains unresolved.

In this second essay, by way of lending credibility to the Swan drawing, I first want to report on the extent and intensity of de Witt's and van Buchell's interest in art and then, through a comparison that has not previously been made, to nuance the assessment of van Buchell's competence as a draftsman, even at the risk of discrediting a skill that the evidence suggests exceeded the ordinary.

The first project is assisted by an important 1981 essay published in *Shakespeare Quarterly,* in which John B. Gleason documents de Witt's and van Buchell's fascination with art.[17] Gleason references A. Hulshof and P. S. Breuning's edition of the correspondence between the friends,[18] which indexes some forty artists whose names appear in de Witt's letters; van Buchell's notes on painters, published in 1928 as *Res Pictoriae;*[19] de Witt's now lost *Coelum Pictorium,* a catalog of artists, in preparation for years, modeled on Carel van Mander's 1604 *Schilder-Boek;*[20] and the hundreds of surviving sketches of antiquities, monuments, and coats of arms that de Witt and van Buchell, lifelong antiquarians, drew.[21]

Gleason also records the Dutchmen's interest in Roman architecture, particularly the amphitheater, and persuasively argues that the conventions of drawing employed by their former University of Leiden professor and mentor Justus Lipsius, in his own volume on the amphitheater, guided de Witt's drawing practices as well. Presenting ample evidence of the wide circulation of Lipsius's *De amphitheatro,*[22] in its several editions, each containing a large folding plate of the Roman Colosseum (fig. 9) and certain evidence of both de Witt's and van Buchell's familiarity with the work, Gleason discusses the depiction of the Roman theater not as an attempt at photographic accuracy but as an effort to convey information pictorially. Such a drawing includes all the elements "essential to its full apprehension, whether or not these elements were strictly simultaneous" and eliminates elements "that either were present but immaterial, or could safely be taken for granted."[23] Hence Lipsius's Colosseum bears the superscripted caption "Amphitheatri interior facies qualem eam fuisse cum omnibus membris suspicamur" [The inner façade of the Amphitheater, such as we surmise it to have been with all its constituent parts]. The structure is rendered in vertical half-section, its parts labeled in the legend. As with the Swan drawing, there is action on the stage, but the theater is not filled with the thousands who, presumably, would have been in the audience during a performance; instead, the Roman emperor, implausibly but suggestively, sits as the lone spectator. In the Swan drawing, audience members (if they are such) sit only in the gallery above the stage. Including the thousands of bodies, Gleason notes, would not increase the pictures' informational value. Gleason's analysis places Lipsius's drawing of the Colosseum and de Witt's drawing of the Swan within a well documented early modern artistic tradition.

Indeed, de Witt's own observations suggest that he considered himself an artist of more than modest talent. Commenting on a painting by Abraham Bloemaert in a 1611 letter to van Buchell, de Witt writes: "I believe I too have a real flair in this matter of painting and, to use Cicero's expression, a not untutored eye."[24] In a 1614 letter, he registers the interest engravers have taken in his collection of drawings, noting that some "are quite skillfully delineated by me, the Graces not withholding their favor."[25] An engraving of

AMPHITHEATRI INTERIOR FACIE QVALEM EAM
FVIISE CVM OMNIBVS MEMBRIS SVPICAMVR.

C

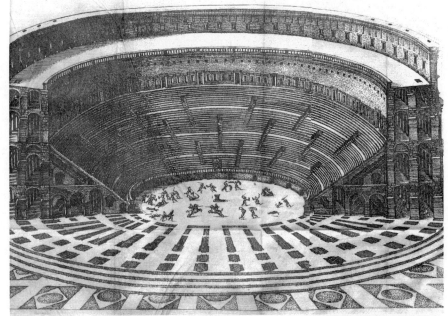

Figure 9. Justus Lipsius's drawing of the Roman Colosseum. From *De amphitheatro liber* (Antwerp: Christoffel Plantijn, 1585). Courtesy of Special Collections, Lafayette College, Easton, Pennsylvania.

Jacob Foeck, de Witt's uncle, flanked by the figures of Prudence and Piety and angels bearing the family arms (fig. 10), made from a de Witt drawing, documents an artistic intelligence and subtlety that suggest that de Witt's opinion of his skill was not misplaced. Indeed, Gleason concludes, "There is abundant evidence that both men were unusually capable in drawing and preened themselves on being connoisseurs of painting."[26]

Notwithstanding Gleason's judgment, Gerritsen offers a more discriminating assessment. After studying hundreds of drawings in de Witt's and van Buchell's hands, Gerritsen concludes that de Witt was an excellent draftsman but van Buchell was not: "As long as small-scale impressionism is enough, his work can be quite attractive; as soon as he has to be precise he fails, particularly in architecture."[27]

It was Gerritsen who first pointed to the presence in the Utrecht collection of two drawings, one by de Witt and one by van Buchell, of the de Vriendt monument in Antwerp (figs. 11 and 12).[28] Unfortunately, although each is suggestive of the respective artist's abilities—de Witt's would appear finer than van Buchell's—the potential for comparison is twice compromised: first by the dissimilarity of the drawings (the figure of Fame in de Witt's has upright wings and a single trumpet; van Buchell's figure has horizontal wings and two trumpets) and second by the fact that this family funeral monument no longer exists.

We know of no other structures that de Witt and van Buchell both drew. But we do know the work of a Dutch Golden Age artist who, like van Buchell, left several renderings of St. Mary's Church in Utrecht. That artist is Pieter Saenredam, who frequently painted exterior and interior views of Dutch churches. One of these is a view of the west façade of the Utrecht church, the same view that van Buchell drew in his *Diarium.* A comparison of Saenredam's rendering and van Buchell's effectively juries the question of van Buchell's draftsmanship, confirming Gerritsen's assessment. For although van Buchell's drawing (fig. 13) appears more than competent, a look at it alongside Saenredam's (fig. 14) reveals its limitations. Saenredam's view is the work of a master of proportion and perspective, a fact readily confirmed by his most striking view of St. Mary's and Mariaplaats from the west, dated 1662 (fig. 15), and by numerous renderings of other churches, many of which (unlike St. Mary's) still stand.[29] Van Buchell's drawing, by comparison, is crude: it succeeds in capturing an impression but not in presenting accurate detail.

If van Buchell was indeed a practiced draftsman but deficient with detail, how much trust should Shakespeareans invest in this second Dutchman's drawing? Does the comparison of van Buchell's work with Saenredam's confirm Dover Wilson's inference that the van Buchell Swan is an untrustworthy copy of an original sketch that was itself suspect? Or might the favorable

Figure 10. Engraving of Jacob Foeck based on a 1614 drawing by Johannes de Witt. Courtesy of Rijksmuseum, Amsterdam.

Figures 11 and 12. Drawings of the de Vriendt monument by Johannes de Witt, MS 1647 (left), and Aernout van Buchell, MS 1648 (right). Courtesy of Bibliotheek der Rijksuniversiteit Utrecht.

assessment of de Witt's abilities as an artist override van Buchell's apparent limitations?

It is here that Gerritsen's work in the Utrecht archive proves especially germane. For after studying the size and the characteristic folds of the paper bound in MS 1647, the bibliographic scholar determined that it would have been consistent with de Witt's practice for the traveler to have made *two* drawings of the Swan, the original on his visit to the Southbank of the Thames and a copy, some time later, for a booklet he prepared for his friend.

MS 1647, a forty-two-page octavo-size manuscript that binds several disparate items, includes two eight-page booklets in de Witt's hand, one containing drawings, from 1604–6, of provincial Dutch monuments and the other containing drawings, from 1611, of monuments in Antwerp. Bound with the booklets are five disjunct leaves, one clearly a cover letter for the provincial monuments: dated 1609, it refers to the monuments depicted in the first booklet, as well as to the copy of Lipsius's *Epistolae* that de Witt was returning to van Buchell, apparently having borrowed it from him. A second cover letter, dated 25 August 1610, announcing de Witt's departure for Rome, is apparently unrelated, in content or its material features, to this booklet or to the second, on Antwerp monuments, dated April 1611.

Gerritsen extrapolates from this evidence the existence of a third booklet,

Figure 13. Aernout van Buchell's drawing of the west façade of St. Mary's Church, Utrecht. Courtesy of Bibliotheek der Rijksuniversiteit Utrecht. van Buchell's drawing (MS 798, fol 19) is color washed; primarily beige, the church is shown with a green central door, a blue rose window, pink columns, and a blue canopy jutting out from the tower. Entries in van Buchell's *Diarium* date from 1588 to 1599.

on the classical monuments to which de Witt's 1610 letter refers, which do not appear in the volume—or elsewhere in the Utrecht holdings. Moreover, with characteristic astuteness, he observes that the inscription for the first booklet—"INSCRIPTIONES. Variaque tam PRISCJ æuj, quam MEDIJ | et MODERNJ sæculj Monumenta. | Diuresis in locis et Regionibus obseruata | Ea quæ in GALLIJS et ANGLIA adnotata, pecul. | et designat. Libello conscripsimus. | In hac vero schæda sunt quæ apud | PHRISIOS. GROEN-NINGENSES. | GELROS et BATAVOS vidimus.||"—references not only the provincial monuments of Frisia, Groningen, Guelders, and Holland that the booklet contains but also monuments in France and England, suggesting that a fourth—and possibly a fifth—booklet also exists (or existed). Of special interest to Shakespeare scholars, of course, is the booklet on England, which may well hold the record of de Witt's visit to London during or after 1596.

The analysis is provocative, allowing as it does for yet another lost Swan drawing. But so also is it comforting, for it restores confidence in the de Witt

Figure 14. Pieter Saenredam's 1636 drawing of the west façade of St. Mary's Church, Utrecht. Courtesy of Gemeentearchief Utrecht.

drawing that van Buchell saw: twice-drawn, by an accomplished draftsman intent on conveying the features of this "Roman" theater to his friend. Equally important, it positions van Buchell as a copyist, whose project was to scale up, perhaps mechanically, this intriguing drawing—the only one he included in *Adversaria.* If Gerritsen's meticulous examination has yielded a responsible conclusion, as I believe it has, then the second Dutchman had only to reproduce, in quarto size, the first Dutchman's octavo-size drawing.

Figure 15. Pieter Saenredam's 1662 painting of St. Mary's Church and Mariaplaats, Utrecht. Courtesy of Museum Boijmans van Beuningen, Rotterdam.

Hence, judgments about proportion and perspective—not van Buchell's strengths—would already have been made.

III. Johannes de Witt's Swan(s)

There is, of course, only one way to determine with certainty just how closely van Buchell's Swan matches the drawing that his friend sent him, and that is to find de Witt's Swan. Yet there can be little thought of discovering the drawing among the van Buchell papers in the Utrecht university library, where materials are scrupulously cataloged and librarians well aware of their treasures. Although the recent discovery of documents of importance to Shakespeareans is inspiriting—MS 1647, for example, containing the two booklets previously described, only showed up in 1906, at auction, and a second copy of "The View of the Cittye of London from the North Towards the Sowth" (c. 1597), with unique side panels, just turned up in 1996, tucked into a book by John Speed[30]—scholars in search of the drawings from England that de Witt sent to van Buchell have little more than serendipity to fortify them.

Those in search of de Witt's *original* drawing of the Swan, however, have brighter prospects, for they have access to a trove of letters and abstracts associated with de Witt's final itinerary, via France to Rome.[31] Few Shakespeareans know that de Witt regularly spoke of his drawings in his letters from France, when he considered selling them to an engraver. Nor do they realize that when de Witt died in Rome in 1622, he left behind more than a thousand manuscript pages and a substantial collection of drawings. In the last and most intriguing of this triptych of essays, I shall explore clues to the whereabouts of de Witt's papers, which may well have among them the original Swan.

Letters from France

The French part of de Witt's final itinerary involved an extended stay in Paris and Lyon, where he lived for at least six years, possibly as many as eight and a half.[32] De Witt's letters from Paris record political events in France during the regency of Marie de Médicis (1601–14) and the monarchy of Louis XIII (whose majority was declared by Parliament in 1614). They also record de Witt's interest in art. In the early years, the traveler speaks of being happily occupied with his study of antiquities, registering pleasure at the many examples he has collected. In 1612, he writes of the magnificent royal works, the hall of antiquities, and the Parisian antiquarian Jacques de Breul, who accompanied him on a tour of the de Breul collection, praised the sharp eyes of "Flemish" observers, and admitted de Witt into the society of antiquarians. (The French, de Witt notes in a later letter, refer to all Dutch people as "Flemish.") Also in 1612, he sends Gilles van Ledenbergh, secretary of the state of Utrecht, a copperplate engraving of the "exchange of princesses" ceremony in Paris, with notes in the margins of the brochure. In letters to van Buchell and van Ledenbergh, he describes the fireworks displays in 1613 at the Louvre and near the Arsenal; to both van Buchell and van Ledenbergh, he sends a printed brochure of the event. He does the same with the program for the erection at Pont Neuf of a bronze equestrian statue of Henry IV sculpted by Giovanni da Bologna. In 1615, he offers comfort to van Buchell, who has sent him his own portraits of the Princes of Brandenburg, which van Buchell could not get published. Even Dürer sustained rejections, de Witt reminds his friend, and, though he does not understand why, it would appear that the art of portrait painting is declining.

However interesting the commentary on politics and on art, the primary importance of de Witt's letters from France, at least to Shakespeareans in search of the Swan drawing, rests in their references to printers and engravers. For de Witt, now in his late forties, was intending to sell his drawings. In a letter to van Buchell of 5 February 1614, de Witt names Hendryck de Coninck of Dordrecht, whose offer, he says, would assure a good source of income. In a letter dated 21 May 1615, he asks van Buchell to seek the professional opinions of an art dealer named Wolffswinckel and metalworkers Johanni Croeck and Adam van Vianen. Van Buchell's abstract of a letter of 17 June 1616 notes de Witt's praise for the French engraver Claude Frémy, who forged the faces of the nobility of France. De Witt frequently sends his regards to their friend Bloemaert, himself an engraver. In 1612, he expresses admiration for Bloemaert's painting of the Nativity and pleasure in van Buchell's report that the famous engraver Crispijn van de Passe[33] had moved from Cologne to Utrecht and that van Buchell, Bloemaert, and other artists had been meeting regularly with him and were planning to found an "academy" in Utrecht, which de Witt hoped he could join upon his return.[34]

Determining which engraver, if any, acquired de Witt's collection, or a part of it, may be the key to finding the Swan. de Witt reports that when de Coninck learned that he had assembled the collection for his uncle and his friends, the engraver ended his inquiries; and he says little more about Croeck and van Vianen. But he does mention Frémy several times. In a letter to van Buchell of 21 May 1618, for example, his last from Lyon, de Witt encloses a coin engraved with the profile of his father, Steven de Witt, explaining that he had shown the Burgundian metalworker a portrait of the elder de Witt painted by Joachim Wttewael and that Frémy had used that painting to engrave the coin.[35] de Witt willingly gave him the commission, for he knew that Frémy would create a worthy piece. So pleased was he with the result that he compares Frémy to the ancient Lysippus, offering the judgment that his work far surpasses that of other modern engravers. Also in that letter, he encloses an engraving of the Queen of France, Anna of Austria, as a gift for his aunt, Gauborga Foeck; he entreats van Buchell to give it to her but also invites his friend to judge the work, adding that he himself considers it perfect. Clearly, de Witt admired Frémy's abilities, and clearly he had contact with him. Might he have entrusted the Burgundian engraver with his collection of drawings? Where, one might ask, are Frémy's papers now?

De Witt's connection to the van de Passes who joined the Utrecht academy is also intriguing. The catalog of engravings by three generations of the van de Passe family reveals that de Witt's friend, van Buchell, had another occupation, as a writer of epigrams and verse. His name or initials are on numerous drawings in the catalog, including at least two of interest to Shakespeareans: Jacobus [John] Caius, physician to England's Edward VI, Mary, and Elizabeth; and Elizabeth, daughter of James I and wife of the Elector Palantine, Frederick V.[36] Although de Witt is not referenced among the artists, one of the drawings invites attention. Entitled "Vanitas," by Simon van de Passe, with verse by van Buchell (fig. 16), the piece may be a *memento mori* to van Buchell's seventeen-year-old son, Aernt. If it is, then it would not be unreasonable to attribute the drawing to one of van Buchell's inner circle of artist friends, possibly Bloemaert. But neither would it be unreasonable to recall the condolences, the poem, and the epitaph that de Witt sent to his friend on 21 June 1612, after learning of the death, and to ask whether the drawing might be de Witt's. (Although Aernt died in 1611, both the drawing and de Witt's letter are dated 1612.)

The one known engraving of a drawing done by de Witt and signed by him is that of his uncle, mintmaster general of the United Provinces (fig. 10). Indeed, the Paris letters are filled with comments on the drawing, which de Witt made, from memory, after his uncle's death. In letters to van der Burch dated 13 August 1614 and 26 November 1614, he speaks of having drawn a portrait of Foeck and decorated it with emblemata and inscriptions. By November, he reports that the engraver has completed much of his work and that he will soon be able to send a copy to his Lordship. On 19 May 1615, he keeps his promise, sending van Ledenbergh several copies. Two days later, he sends

Figure 16. "Vanitas": Memento Mori, 1612, engraved by Simon van de Passe, with verse by Aernout van Buchell. Courtesy of Museum Boijmans van Beuningen, Rotterdam. Included in Daniel Franken, *L'Oeuvre Gravé des van de Passe* (Amsterdam: G. W. Hissink, 1975), 220, #1241; reproduced in *TLC: The Low Countries: Arts and Society in Flanders and The Netherlands* (Rekkemi Flemish-Netherlands Foundation "Stichting Ons Erfdeel," 2000), 10.

van Buchell a copy printed on satin and several on paper, suggesting that he distribute these to his friends and specifically asking that Bloemaert, Wolffs-winckel, Croeck, and van Vianen be given copies.

As proud as de Witt was of his own accomplishment, however, he was not happy with the engraving. For it did not, in his opinion, sufficiently capture the likeness of his uncle. The engraver, he reports, has defended his work, chiding de Witt for his harsh judgment when he himself was not accomplished in the art. Nonetheless, de Witt expected more: though he had not seen his uncle for some years, his memory was clear and his drawing accurately reflects the man; he is astonished that the engraver has not been able to reproduce the shadings he has drawn. De Witt invites van Buchell to criticize the work and to distribute it to his friends so that they might judge it. The copperplate itself, he says, he gave to his mother's sister, Gauborga Foeck, as a gesture of respect.

An undated letter from van Buchell to de Witt provides the criticism de Witt invited. In it, van Buchell admires de Witt's ability to draw from memory but notes the judgment of some that the head is bigger than it should be. Indeed, the prefect of the mint has even tried to correct certain things, justifying the changes on the basis of his daily contact with his former colleague and on his fresher memories. Van Buchell tells de Witt that he will try his best to get van de Passe to improve the engraving. In a letter dated 31 July 1615, de Witt speaks to the proposal: with the caution that he would not like to see dramatic changes or a more aged likeness that would prevent him from remembering his uncle as he knew—and drew—him, he gives reluctant approval. Did van de Passe—or anyone in Utrecht—follow through?

For all the provocative leads that the letters from France provide, they also deliver dreadful news. For de Witt responded to his uncle's death with more than an engraving. Deeply depressed over the loss of the man who had been a father to him, de Witt writes, on 5 February 1614, of how his heavy heart has stopped his studies. Without his "Maecenas," patron of—or at least audience for—his work, his enthusiasm and motivation are gone. In a gesture that only the grieving mind could think appropriate, de Witt *tore up*—or said he tore up—his entire set of drawings, saving only a few gatherings to show his friend as examples of how much effort he had put into them and how exacting they were. His grief, he explains, prompted him to do so, for he had made the drawings for his uncle and now he could not look at them without feeling sick. He reasoned that because the man had been taken so suddenly from him, it would be fitting that he sacrifice the drawings. The letter ends with a prayer that his uncle's spirit accept his humble offering, proffered from a foreign country far from his fatherland.

Which drawings did de Witt destroy, which save? Which did he have with him in the first place? Which others, in earlier years, had he given to his uncle? And where are his uncle's papers now?

De Witt recovered from his depression and began drawing monuments again. In 1615, he writes of his plan to resume his journey to Rome, via Avignon and Lyon. Before leaving Paris, he responds to van den Burch's question as to why he had tarried so long there. In a letter dated 21 May 1615, he speaks of having been commissioned to reconstruct the chronicle of Charles VI,[37] which had been recorded earlier by a monk at St. Denis but which was in deteriorating condition. The commission entailed considerable work, the chronicle consisting of twenty-one codexes: he speaks of having spent much labor over many nights on the project. In the end, he basks in the praise of his achievement offered by the famous Godefroy, who, he reports, had not expected such perfection from a "Flemish" person but who now conceded that any Frenchman or scholar would have had much difficulty matching de Witt's work. Following this accomplishment, de Witt was asked to work with other manuscripts as well, namely, the work of Pascham, who lived during the time of Charles the Bold, another time-consuming project that he first refused but then decided to undertake. By his own report, he also corrected mistakes in manuscripts by or about Fulgentius, Nicholas de Bray, and the history of Albigenzer. The recognition that de Witt enjoyed for his work with the pen—reportedly from princes and noblemen—undoubtedly encouraged him to remain.

When de Witt finally resumed his journey, his letters once again speak of the book of artists, from Gyges's time to the present, that he hoped would supersede van Mander's. Clearly, *Coelum Pictorium* was an ongoing project for de Witt, begun at least as early as 1610, during his stay in Antwerp, where, he observes, he found some sixty artists worthy of inclusion (far more than he found in France). Just as clearly, *Coelum Pictorium* was not among the materials he destroyed. Anticipating his journey to Lyon and Northern Italy, de Witt looks forward to discovering art and artists that he might include in his catalog. Later letters secure the fact that he remained engaged in this project, as well as in the work of the artists at the Utrecht academy.

De Witt's first letter from Lyon, dated 12 December 1617, and van Buchell's abstract of his second letter, dated 18 March 1618, confirm de Witt's renewed occupation with antiquities. He was once again transmitting effigies and drawings to van Buchell, of monuments he had observed in the provinces of France. And he was once again speaking of engravers' interest in his work. Flattered and amused at their urgings that he make more drawings, de Witt nonetheless gave priority to Italy's allure: he was, he tells van Buchell, longing to continue his much delayed journey.

Letters from Rome

Once de Witt arrived in Rome, he remained there for at least two and a half years: on 7 January 1620, he wrote to van Buchell confirming his arrival, and on 30 June 1622, he sent his last communication to his friend. In all, de Witt's correspondence from Rome is represented by seven abstracts, written by van Buchell, and two letters, to which the abstracts are companions. De Witt's correspondence, along with two letters from van Buchell after de Witt's death, set yèt another course, distinct from the engravers, for sleuthing the Swan. For they speak of the many pages of drawings in de Witt's possession when he died and of the disposition of his belongings.

We learn from the correspondence that de Witt was not well in Rome. In 1620, he twice complained to van Buchell of the troublesome Roman air, and on 27 June 1621, he wrote that he was considering a return, via Venice and Germany. Ill health apparently intervened, however, and, after a year's silence, he wrote his friend again, to say he had not gone to Venice after all. Once he was rested and the hot, dry weather was over, he would go there for the winter, see Padua, Mantua, and Milan, then return to Utrecht via either Germany or France. Despite his intentions, there is no evidence that de Witt left Rome and good reasons to believe that he did not. In the margin of de Witt's letter of 30 June 1622, van Buchell wrote that de Witt died in Rome: "At Romae mori debuit, sic Deo placuit." Elsewhere, in his biographical sketch of his friend in *Vitae eruditorum Belgicorum,* he gives the death date, at age fifty-six, as 30 September 1622, three months after de Witt wrote of his plans.

Despite ill health, de Witt proved an active observer of Roman religio-political affairs and Italian antiquities. It is not surprising that the letters of this lifelong Roman Catholic speak of the death of Pope Paul V, the inauguration of Pope Gregory XV, the deaths and elections of cardinals, and the arrival of the Hohenzoller cardinal in Italy, as well as of marriages and funerals and Utrecht artists living in Rome. Nor is it surprising that even in the closing years of his life, de Witt was still collecting antiquities. The abstract of his first letter from Rome refers to illustrations from provincial France; others document various excursions in 1620 and 1621 to places of interest to an antiquarian. De Witt's final letter reports that he has been keeping notes, sufficient to form a whole book, on ceremonies celebrating the canonization of saints: Isidore Matritius, Ignatius of Loyola, Francisco de Yasur of Xavier, Filippo Neri, and Teresa of Avila. De Witt also refers to his other foreign observations, a collection so extensive that it comprises some thousand pages. With obvious pride, he tells his friend that the fatherland would see his work as evidence that it has a citizen who is neither slothful nor ungrateful.

But three months after writing about his collection, de Witt was dead. And the letter he sent to his friend was embellished with a marginal note. Alongside the sentence about their fatherland, which was underlined, van Buchell wrote: "Indien ze niet in vreemde handen verloren zijn gegaan" [Unless they (de Witt's papers) have fallen into the hands of strangers]. Yet when he wrote his biographic entry for de Witt in *Vitae eruditorum Belgicorum,* after de

Witt's death, van Buchell noted that his friend had left his collections with Johannes Honorius Axel de Seny, a countryman and lawyer.[38] Equally important, in 1635, some thirteen years after de Witt's death, van Buchell wrote to Axel to inquire after de Witt's papers.[39] In that letter, he refers to de Witt's having spent the last days of his life with Axel and explains that he had heard from de Witt's relative "D. Foco" (probably Bruno Foeck, also a canon of St. Mary's) that de Witt's papers were in Axel's possession.[40] Though Axel's reply, if there was one, is not among van Buchell's letters, the inquiry suggests that a search for Axel's papers could yield not only the book-length manuscript on the canonization of saints but also de Witt's thousand pages of foreign observations. (Axel, who had made Rome his permanent home after earning a Juris Doctor degree in Bologna in 1580, died in 1636, bequeathing his library and manuscripts, his household goods and furniture, his gold and silver to the College of St. Norbert's in Rome.)

*   *   *

"*Genus Cygnus*: Three Species of the Swan" has had three purposes: first, through the essay on Gaedertz's Swan, to caution scholars about the 1888 presentation of the de Witt drawing and to reinforce the necessity of examining manuscripts in their material context; second, through the essay on van Buchell's Swan, to revisit the question of the second Dutchman's competence as a draftsman, particularly when compared with Saenredam, and to suggest that the judgments about proportion and perspective reflected in van Buchell's copy may have been de Witt's rather than his; and third, through the essay on de Witt's Swan(s), to renew Gerritsen's proposal for a second de Witt drawing, to record clues to the whereabouts of the original, and to interest others in sleuthing the Swan. Unfortunately, the essay has not ended with the announcement that de Witt's original drawing has been found. But in ferreting out information from seldom examined materials, in German, Dutch, and Latin, it has provided fresh perspectives on three, and possibly four, views of the Swan.

Notes

1. Henry B. Wheatley, "On a Contemporary Drawing of the Interior of the Swan Theatre, 1596," *Transactions of the New Shakspere Society,* 1887–92, series 1, part 2 (1888): 215–25.

2. See, for example, Martha Berthold, *The History of World Theatre from the Beginnings to the Baroque* [1972] (New York: Continuum, 1991), 398; Sam Smiley, *Theatre: The Human Art* (New York: Harper and Row, 1987), 209; and Theodore W. Hatlen, *Orientation to the Theater,* 5th ed. (Englewood Cliffs: Prentice Hall, 1992), 350. The encyclopedia references are to "Shakespeare, William," *Encyclopedia of the Renaissance* (1999), 6:5, and "Elizabethan Theatres," *The New Encyclopædia Britannica,* 15th ed (1989), 28:572.

3. Karl Theodor Gaedertz, *Zur Kenntnis der altenglischen Bühne nebst andern Beiträgen zur Shakespeare-Litteratur. Mit der ersten authentischen innern Ansicht des Schwan-Theaters in London un Nachbildung von Lucas Cranachs Pyramus und Thisbe* (Bremen: C. Ed. Müller, 1888), 3–18. For *The Times'* announcement of Gaedertz's book, see [Berlin correspondent], "London Theatres in the Sixteenth Century," *The [London] Times,* 11 May 1888, p. 5.

4. MS 842, fol 131v–132v. Van Buchell's drawing is in his *Adversaria,* a quarto notebook of poems, comments, quotations, and observations in use from 1592 to 1628.

5. Gaedertz, *Zur Kenntnis,* 51–65.

6. Gaedertz, "Briefe von Johannes de Witt," 65–75. The section reprints portions of letters to van Buchell dated 23 February 1604 and 27 October 1605, from Amsterdam; 17 June 1611, from Antwerp; and 5 February 1614 and 31 July 1615, from Paris, as well as portions of letters to van der Burch dated 21 June 1612, 13 August 1614, 26 November 1614, and 21 [May] 1615, from Paris (65–75). All of the letters subsequently appeared in A. Hulshof and P. S. Breuning, eds., "Brieven van Johannes de Wit aan Arend van Buchel en Anderen," *Bijdragen en Mededeelingen van het Historisch Genootschapp* 60 (1939): 87–208f, and "Zes brieven van John. De. Wit aan Arend van Buchel," *Bijdragen en Mededeelingen van het Historisch Genootschapp* 61 (1940): 60–99. (For ease of reference, I have cited the dates as they appear in Hulshof and Breuning.)

7. Volume 1 of the catalog of holdings of the Utrecht library, published in 1887, lists van Buchell's *Adversaria* and summarizes its contents, including fols 131b–132b, described as "Ex Observationibus Londinensibus Joh. De Witt (cum effigie theatri Londinensis *the Swan*)." As *Bibliothecae praefectus,* Tiele oversaw the compilation of *Catalogus Codicum Manu Scriptorum Bibliothecae Universitatis Rheno-Trajectinae* (The Hague: Martinus Nijhoff, 1887). Hence, Wheatley is undoubtedly correct in stating that it was Tiele who discovered the manuscript and recognized its importance to the history of the English stage. Wheatley indicates that, following *The Times'* announcement of the publication of Gaedertz's book, Tiele facilitated the loan of the van Buchell notebook to the British Museum (p. 217n). Unfortunately, Tiele died before the Wheatley essay was published, only months after Gaedertz's book appeared.

8. Gaedertz, *Zur Kenntnis,* 5.

9. Gaedertz, *Zur Kenntnis,* 51: "Nachträglich fand sich in der Universitätsbibliothek zu Utrecht ein zweites, von Dr. Tiele mir gütigst mitgetheiltes und gleichfalls von Arend van Buchell herrührendes Excerpt: Ex Observationibus Londinensibus Johannes de Wit." [Subsequently a second excerpt by Arend van Buchell, 'Ex Observationibus Londinensibus Johannis De Witt,' was found in the university library at Utrecht; Dr. Tiele graciously informed me of it].

10. Gaedertz, *Zur Kenntnis,* 51: "Meine Bemühungen, einen historischen Beleg für die Richtigkeit meiner Zeitbestimmung zur geschilderten Darstellung des Schwan-Theaters sowie biographische Daten über Johannes de Witt zu erhalten, sind mit schönem, ja unerwartet glänzendem Erfolge gekrönt worden" [My efforts to obtain historic proof of the accuracy of my time frames for the described drawing of the Swan Theater as well as biographical data on Johannes de Witt were crowned with a wondrous, though unexpected, glorious success].

11. MS 843, fol 29–34v (Rijksuniversiteit Utrecht).

12. Johan Gerritsen, "De Witt, van Buchell, the Swan and the Globe: Some Notes," in *Essays in Honour of Kristian Smidt,* Peter Bilton, Lars Hartveit, Stig Johansson, Arthur O. Sandved, and Bjorn Tysdahl, eds. (Oslo: University of Olso Institute of English Studies, 1986), 29–46, esp. 30.

13. Gaedertz, *Zur Kenntnis,* 35.

14. J. Dover Wilson, "*Titus Andronicus* on the Stage in 1595," *Shakespeare Survey* 1 (1948): 17–22, esp. 21.

15. Martin Holmes, "A New Theory about the Swan Drawing," *Theatre Notebook* 10 (1956): 80–83, esp. 80.

16. J. Le Gay Brereton, "De Witt at the Swan," in *A Book of Homage to Shakespeare,* Israel Gollancz, ed. (Oxford: Humphrey Milford, Oxford University Press, 1916), 204.

17. John B. Gleason, "The Dutch Humanist Origins of The De Witt Drawing of the Swan Theatre," *Shakespeare Quarterly* 32 (1981): 324–38.

18. Hulshof and Breuning, eds., 1939, 87–208f, and 1940, 60–99.

19. *Arnoldus Buchelius, Res Pictoriae: Aanteekeningen over Kunstenaars en Kunstwerken voorkomende in zijn Diarium, Res Pictoriae, Notae Quotidianae en Descriptio Urbis Ultrajectinae* (1583–1639), G. J. Hoogewerff and J. Q. Van Regteren Altena, eds. (The Hague: Martinus Nijhoff, 1928).

20. *Het Schilder-Boek van Carel van Mander: Het Leven der Dooluchtige Nederlandsche en Hoogduitsche Schilders,* 4th ed., A. F. Mirande and G. S. Overdiep, eds. (Amsterdam: Wereldbibliotheek N. V., 1950). The book contains some one hundred entries documenting the lives of Dutch and German painters.

21. Many of van Buchell's drawings appear in the two-volume *Commentarius rerum quotidianarum* (MS 798, Rijksuniversiteit Utrecht), commonly known as the *Diarium.* A more modest sampling of drawings by de Witt may be found in MS 1647 (Rijksuniversiteit Utrecht). The full title of the van Buchell manuscript is *Commentarius rerum quotidianarum, in quo, praeter itinera diversarum regionum, urbium oppidorumque situs, antiquitates, principes, instututa, mores, multa eorum quae tam inter publicos quam privatos contingere solent, occurrunt exempla, lectoribus pro cujusque ingenio vel utilia vel saltem non injucunda futura.* A selection from these volumes appears in G. Brom and L. A. van Langeraad, eds. As *Diarium van Arend van Buchell* (Amsterdam: Johannes Müller, 1907). Unfortunately, the edited volume does not include drawings.

22. Justus Lipsius, *De amphitheatro liber* (Leiden: Christophe Plantin, 1584). The 1585 edition, *De amphitheatro liber. In quo forma ipsa loci expressa, & ratio spectandi* (Antwerp: Christoffel Plantijn, 1585), as well as subsequent editions, also includes Lipsius's *De amphitheatris quae extra Roman libellus. In quo Formae eorum aliquot et typi,* origianlly published in 1584 in Leiden under C. Plantijn's imprint.

23. Gleason, "Dutch Humanist Origins," 332.

24. Gleason, "Dutch Humanist Origins," 329. The comment—"Putamus enim et nos habere nasum in hac Pictoria atque (ut Ciceronis verbo utar) non indoctos oculos"—appears in an abstract by van Buchell dated 17 June 1611 of a letter from de Witt in Antwerp (Hulshof and Breuning, eds., 1939, 146). The abstract, like the one following it, may be misdated, for its contents do not match those of the letter.

25. Gleason, "Dutch Humanist Origins," 329. the comment—"Et iam coacervav-eram eorum copiam copiosam, in qua erant quaedam a me delineata satis foeliciter nec invitis Gratiis"—appears in a letter dated 5 February 1614 to van Buchell from de Witt in Paris (Hulshof and Breuning, eds., 1939, 161).

26. Gleason, "Dutch Humanist Origins," 329.

27. Johan Gerritsen, "The Swan Theater Drawing: A Review," *FOLIO—Shakespeare-Genootschap van Nederland en Vlaanderen* 2.2 (1995): 33–38, esp. 37–38.

28. Gerritsen, "De Witt, van Buchell, the Swan and the Globe," opposite p. 31. See also Hulshof and Breuning, eds., 1939, 136. Curiously, in notes accompanying the drawings, de Witt places the de Vriendt monument at Antwerp's Minorite church, van Buchell at the Francisan church.

29. Other exterior views from the west by Saenredam are at the Fondazione Thys-sen-Bornemisza, Lugano (1662) and the Teylers Museum, Haalem (1636). See *Pieter Saenredam: Gezicht op de Mariaplaats en de Mariakerk te Utrecht* (Rotterdam: Museum Boymans-van Beuingen, 1987) and H. M. Haverkate and C. J. Van Der Peet, *Een Kerk van Papier: De Geschiedenis van de Voormalige Mariakerk te Utrecht* (Zutphen: Walburg Press, 1985).

30. MS 1647 was acquired at the Smissaert sale on 3 April 1906, at Doelenstraat 10, Amsterdam; it appears in the auction catalog as item 303. See "Les manuscripts héraldiques et généalogiques d'Arnoldus Buchelius," in *Manuscripts, Autographes, Albums Amicorum* (Amsterdam: Frederik Muller, 1906), 42–52. On the second copy of "The View of the Cittye of London," see Herbert Berry, "The View of London from the North and the Playhouses in Holywell," *Shakespeare Survey* 53 (2000): 196–212.

31. De Witt's letters from France and Rome, along with van Buchell's abstracts, appear in Hulshof and Breuning, eds. Although the abstracts are brief, in many cases they are the only record of letters now lost, and scholars can be grateful that van Buchell was in the habit of inventorying de Witt's lifelong correspondence with him: the earliest dated abstract is from 1586, the latest from 1622. In 1940, a year after publishing transcripts of de Witt's letters and van Buchell's abstracts, Hulshof and Breuning followed with six additional, full-text letters from the Gemeentearchief Utrecht, including four from France and two from Rome.

32. De Witt's first communication from Paris, preserved as an abstract in van Buchell's hand, is dated 13 February 1612, eight months after his last communication from Antwerp. His last communication from Paris, a letter to van Buchell, is dated 31 October 1616. The correspondence from Lyon consists of three communications to van Buchell, the earliest dated 12 December 1617 (fourteen months after his last communication from Paris), the latest dated 21 May 1618. In all, the epistolary record of de Witt's time in France consists of some twenty letters and/or abstracts of letters from Paris, over four years and four months, to three recipients—van Buchell, van der Burch, and van Ledenbergh—and three letters and/or abstracts from Lyon, over five months, to van Buchell.

33. De Witt actually names Crispiani van den Broeck, almost certainly erroneously: in 1612, van den Broeck had been dead for over twenty years, and he had no known connection to Utrecht, only Mechelen and Antwerp. Jos. J. B. M. M. Sterk, in an excellent biographical essay on de Witt and his father, "Johannes de Witt Stevens-

zoon," *Jaarboek Oud Utrecht 1974* (Utrecht: De Vereniging Oud-Utrecht, 1974): 108–62, offers a Dutch translation of de Witt's 21 June 1612 letter; in it, he substitutes "Crispijn van de Passe" for "Crispiani van den Broeck," pointing out that it was van de Passe who moved from Cologne to Utrecht ca. 1612. van Buchell clearly had a relationship with the van de Passe family, which consisted of three generations of engravers: Crispijn the elder; Crispijn the younger, Simon, Willem, and Magdalena; and Crispijn III. (Collectively, their work covered nearly one hundred years, from c. 1587 to 1678, and was done in at least four countries: The Netherlands, France, England, and Germany). Daniel Franken's catalog of van de Passe engravings, published as *L'Oeuvre Gravé des van de Passe: Catalogue Raisonné des Estampes de Chrispijn Senior et Junior, Simon, Willem, Magdalena et Chrispijn III van de Passe, Graveurs Néerlandais des XVIE et XVIIE Siècles, précédé d'une Introduction Biographique, avec des Listes Chronologiques et Alphabétiques [1881], augmenté d'un Supplément d'Additions et Corrections par Simon Laschitzer* (Amsterdam: G. W. Hissink, 1975), lists an engraving of van Buchell, done in 1614 (81, #503). In addition, following the title engraving in a Latin-text edition of *Hortus Floridas,* 1614, are two verses in honor of Crispijn the younger by A. Buchelius and Jacobus Valentinus van der Voort Med. (van Buchell's stepson) (268, #1346, III).

34. In his note to the readers of *Van 't Light der Teken en Schilderkonst,* published in 1643, Crispijn van de Passe the younger lists the masters with whom he had studied and worked, including Peter Paul Rubens, Bloemaert, and Paulus Moreelse; he goes on to say that he attended a "vermaarde Teekenschool / die op dien tijt van de voornaemste meesters wiert gehouden" (a "renowned drawing school held by the leading masters of the day"). Marcel G. Roethlisberger and Marten Jans Bok take this as a reference to the Utrecht academy. See Chrispijn van de Passe, *'t Light der Teken en Schilderkonst* (Soest: Davaco Publishers, 1973), part 1, note to readers and Introduction, p. 4; Roethlisberger, *Abraham Bloemaert and His Sons: Paintings and Prints,* trans. Diane L. Webb (Doornspijk: Davaco, 1993), 1:571; Bok, "'Nulla dies sine linie': De Opleiding van Schilders in Utrecht in de Eerste Helft van de Zeventiende Eeuw," *De Zeventiende Eeuw* 6.1 (1990): 58.

35. Steven de Witt was knighted for his defense of the fatherland on 2 May 1567, in the First Dutch Revolt. The coin and Steven de Witt's accomplishments are discussed in *Histoire Metallique des XVII Provinces des Pays-Bas, depuis l'Abdication de Charles-Quint, jusqu'a' la Paix de Bade en MDCCXVI,* trans. Gerard van Loon (The Hague: P. Gosse, J. Neaulme, and P. de Hondt, 1732), 1:95–96. Sterk reproduces three surviving versions of the coin (126–28).

36. Franken, *L'Oeuvre Gravé,* 83, #513; 96, #575.

37. De Witt's manuscript is in the Bibliothèque Nationale, Paris.

38. MS 838, fol 167 (Rijksuniversiteit Utrecht). Van Buchell also includes a biographic sketch of Axel in *Vitae eruditorum Belgicorum,* fol 267, and writes of having lodged with him in March 1588 when he was on his Italian journey. See Brom and van Langeraad, eds., 168; *Acta diurna (in itinere Gallico et Italico)* (MS 1640, Rijksuniversiteit Utrecht).

39. *Ecclesiastica Ultraiectina (1626–38),* MS 1053, fol 156 (Rijksuniversiteit Utrecht).

40. For commentary on and an excerpt from van Buchell's letter, see Brom and van Langeraad, eds. LXXVII.

"What about Our Hands?":
A Presentational Image Cluster

FRANCES TEAGUE

ARGUING that language is not essential to communicate meaning, Michel de Montaigne insisted that "movements serve as arguments and ideas," that deaf mutes use signs to talk, that lovers arrange their affairs with glances. And for the rest of humanity,

> What about our hands? With them we request, promise, summon, dismiss, menace, pray, supplicate, refuse, question, show astonishment, count, confess, repent, fear, show shame, doubt, teach, command, incite, encourage, make oaths, bear witness, make accusations, condemn, give absolution, insult, despise, defy, provoke, flatter, applaud, bless, humiliate, mock, reconcile, advise, exalt, welcome, rejoice, lament; show sadness, grieve, despair; astonish, cry out, keep silent and what not else, with a variety and multiplicity rivalling the tongue.[1]

Thus people perform meaning with their hands, as well as with their words. Montaigne's remark about deaf mutes who communicate with hand gestures has an early modern instance. In 1614, John Bulwer produced "a manual of what he called with unconscious irony the 'Naturall language of the hand,' describing the gesture appropriate to each emotion (*Chirologia* and *Chironomia,* 1644)."[2] As a teacher of the deaf, Bulwer wished to make gestures conventional, standard, offering a sort of glossary of gestural language for his pupils. "Of Bulwer's illustrations," Andrew Gurr remarks, "120 in all, perhaps 20 would not still be readily recognizable to a modern audience" (100). Whether such hand gestures were heavily stylized or naturalized, which is Gurr's topic, is less my concern than the way that such performed gesture can serve as presentational imagery. By presentational image, I mean a performed reference that acts like a figure of speech. For instance, in *The Merchant of Venice* 4.1., when Shylock holds the knife he has whetted (l. 121) and the balance to weigh the flesh (251), the actor performs a reference to the traditional image of Iustitia. Presentational imagery need not involve a property, however, as Gurr shows when he discusses "conventions of gesture" that were "the shorthand of stage presentation," such as the enactment of grief or a stock pose to indicate "love at first sight" (102–3).

218

The way that one creates meaning in performance with gestures may follow a process like that of utterance. In a 1949 essay that anticipated later work in performance criticism and the semiotics of staging, Alan Downer wrote about "the function of imagery in poetic drama," arguing that staged images function analogously to verbal images.[3] While critics have largely accepted this idea, it seems reasonable to see if it might be taken a step further by asking whether one can stage not simply images, but rather image clusters. As Caroline Spurgeon demonstrated, when Shakespeare writes about light and dark, he often adds imagery about jewels against black skin or white and black birds (*Rom, Son, MND, WT*), while the mention of flattery produces images of slobbery dogs and melting candy (*JC, 1H4, Ham*).[4] An analogous set of stage or presentational images, consistently related to one another, recur in early modern drama: repeatedly plays mention a female character's hand, sexualize it, introduce an inappropriate suitor for the woman, and then suggest that a male character's body has been maimed. I want to consider what this staged image cluster may indicate, viz., what meaning it may make and why that meaning is not expressed with language.

The central part of this cluster is a staged synecdoche or metonymy about hands that can be traced to common phrases realized physically onstage. In a verbal synecdoche, the figure of speech in which a part stands for the whole, when a woman gives her hand in marriage, she gives herself. In *The Duchess of Malfi*, this figure is realized in gesture as well as language when the Duchess and Antonio enact their handfast marriage, and the Duchess tells her new husband, "I would have you lead your fortune *by the hand,* / Unto your marriage bed" (my emphasis, 1.2.428–29).[5] A stage synecdoche, then, may explicitly link the hand of an actor portraying a woman to female sexuality. A verbal metonymy is a related figure of speech in which a word stands for the attribute of a more complex related system: thus speaking about a woman's hand in a letter refers to the way in which she writes, for her "character" is both her handwriting and her self. In a famous piece of stage metonymy, Malvolio is deceived by Maria's hand (i.e., her writing) and believes he has a chance to gain Olivia's hand (i.e., her consent to marry). It seems worth noting that in this latter synecdoche, the hand is invariably feminine: men do not give their hands in marriage in early modern culture, but seek women's hands. Perhaps that is why, in the sixteenth-century wedding ceremony, when the groom formally claimed the bride's hand by enclosing her finger in a ring, he declared, "With this ring, I thee wed; with my body, I thee worship; and with all my worldly goods I thee endow."[6] The male body gets to act as a body, then, while the female body is symbolized in that ring. In the metonymic usage, however, the hand that writes a letter can be either feminine or masculine, although a higher level of male literacy in the sixteenth and seventeenth centuries means that a woman's handwriting is more unusual and hence more worthy of comment.[7]

When one performs (instead of uttering) a synecdoche, a body part stands
for the whole person. The first scene of *The Changeling* offers an instance,
as well as a rich performative moment. Beatrice-Joanna is betrothed to
Alonzo, but in love with Alsemero; her father Vermandero has just invited
Alsemero to their castle. Beatrice drops her glove. Vermandero orders the
servant De Flores to pick it up, which disgusts Beatrice who loathes De Flores. She refuses to take the glove from De Flores and throws down the second
glove. Everyone exits and De Flores, who desires Beatrice, gloats over the
gloves.

This moment is a particularly rich one performatively because it offers so
many choices for the actors. Does Beatrice drop the glove deliberately, hoping to provide Alsemero with a love token and the synecdochic reassurance
that her hand is available despite her betrothal? Does she drop it by accident
because she is flustered by her confusing flood of emotions? If so, does her
action signal that her hand (or synecdochally her body) is available to anyone? Does she unconsciously desire De Flores, in a mixture of loathing and
lusting, and want him to have her hand and by extension her body? And why
does Vermandero order De Flores to pick it up? He may be acting as a careful
father, who does not want his daughter's hand available to all comers (or
simply to Alsemero). Or perhaps he is careless and haughty, indifferent to
that danger. What is Alsemero doing-does he make a try for the glove or does
he miss it altogether? If these questions seem to overanalyze, let me point out
that the one character who is relatively straightforward in his response to the
glove is De Flores, who leaves us with no doubt that the glove functions as
the lady's hand and that her hand is a synecdoche for her body:

> Here's a favor come, with a mischief! Now I know
> She had rather wear my pelt tanned in a pair
> Of dancing pumps than I should thrust my fingers
> Into her sockets here.

(1.1.240–43)

Arguing about other meanings for the gloves immediately becomes irrelevant: De Flores knows that the glove represents Beatrice-Joanna's body: he
uses the glove to thrust into her sockets until such time as he obtains her body
for his thrusting.

It takes much longer to describe what occurs in that moment than it would
to perform it, partly because it takes longer to list the various alternatives
among which actors must choose than it does to act upon such a choice.
Moreover, discussing what happens at that moment has far less power than
the moment itself.[8] Because that moment is memorable, it may remain in an
audience's memory and set up subsequent moments. Later, for example,
when Beatrice-Joanna promises to clear up De Flores's bad skin and places
her hand on his face, he nearly erupts in ecstasy.

> *Bea.*   Come hither; nearer, man!
> *De F.* [Aside] I'm up to the chin in heaven!
> *Bea.*   Turn, let me see;
> Faugh, 'tis but the heat of the liver, I perceiv't.
> I thought it had been worse.
> *De F.* [Aside]   Her fingers touched me!
> She smells all amber.
> *Bea.*   I'll make a water for you shall cleanse this
> Within a fortnight.
> *De F.* With your own hands, Lady?
> *Bea.*   Yes, min own, sir; in a work of cure,
> I'll trust no other.
> *De F.* [Aside] 'Tis half an act of pleasure
> To hear her talk thus to me.
>
> (2.2.78–86)

But talking thus is not, finally, what De Flores desires. To obtain Beatrice, he murders Alonzo. Once again, the sexualized meaning of hands is important to understanding what happens: after killing Beatrice's betrothed, he notices that Alonzo has a ring that he desires. To obtain it, he mutilates the corpse and cuts off the finger. The ring, like the glove, stands in for Beatrice, but belongs to Alonzo. To get the ring (and the woman), De Flores uses violence: the finger within the ring represents the man who must be removed before Beatrice is available. (I need not belabor the meaning of the ring as representative of a woman's vagina to anyone who has read *The Merchant of Venice,* nor need I say much about the finger as phallus to anyone who has driven in the States lately, but I should note that Gary Taylor's recent study *Castration: An Abbreviated History of Western Manhood* says that "the ritual amputation of a finger was practiced at least twenty thousand years B.C.E.")[9]

Stage images of hands are sexualized in *The Changeling* in ways that are clearer in performance than in reading. Yet such stage images occur elsewhere, for one can and should notice sexualized hands in other plays. We might consider once again Malvolio in *Twelfth Night* who picks up a letter, thinks he recognizes Olivia's hand, and immediately makes the most obscene joke in Shakespeare's canon. Or we can note the way that Lavinia in *Titus Andronicus* is mutilated after being raped: Demetrius and Chiron chop off her tongue and hands to prevent her telling. Here her rape is represented by the bloody stumps of her arms, a detail that is in none of the classical sources and evidently originates in early modern accounts. Finally, we can consider Hammon in *The Shoemakers Holiday,* who desires Jane the seamstress and plays the voyeur to spy on her in her shop:

> Yonder's the shop, and there my fair love sits.
> She's fair and lovely, but she is not mine.
> Oh, would she were! Thrice have I courted her,

Thrice hath my hand been moistened with her hand
Whilst my poor famished eyes do feed on that
Which made them famish. . . .

. . . .

How prettily she works! Oh, pretty hand!
Oh, happy work! It doth me good to stand
Unseen to see her.

                                                                    (scene 12.1–6, 13–15)

Hammon is a peeping Tom excited by the thought of Jane's hand. He has
touched her hand three times and exclaims in pleasure at the sight of her hand
moving up and down as she stitches. The speech is less overtly sexual than
that of De Flores with the gloves, but nonetheless, he clearly associates Jane's
hand with his sexual desire. (At other points in this play, admittedly, it is not
female hands, but feet that become sexualized.)

These examples could be multiplied, but clearly in each of these plays the
hand functions as a symbol of a woman's sexuality. Moreover, in each play
the woman's sexualized hand receives attention from a man who should not
be imagining her as a sexual object, and that character provides the second
part of the stage image cluster. De Flores and Malvolio are both servants, the
former a murderer and the latter a prig. Chiron and Demetrius are rapists, and
Hammon is a voyeur. Unwelcome suitors are not the only ones to link hands
and sexual desire in this way: Romeo, after all, wants to be a glove on Juliet's
hand, and he is unwelcome to her family only. Nevertheless, when a woman's
sexualized hand appears in an early modern play, an unwelcome suitor also
appears. Nor is that the entire image cluster.

Another feature occurs: each play includes a male body that is mutilated
or incomplete. In *The Changeling,* De Flores mutilates Alonzo's finger. In
Twelfth Night, Caesario's body is actually that of a woman, Viola. Titus Andronicus chops his own hand off. Finally, in *The Shoemakers Holiday,* Jane's
lost husband Rafe comes home from the wars crippled, which elicits the
memorable speech from Margery Eyre:

> Trust me, I am sorry, Rafe, to see thee impotent. Lord, how the wars have made
> him sunburned! The left leg is not well. 'Twas a fair gift of God the infirmity took
> not hold a little higher, considering thou camest from France. But let that pass.
> (scene 10.82–87)

Rafe's body is like those of the others, mutilated, and Margery's suggestion
that it is probably sexually inadequate as well simply continues the way that
this stage image cluster locates sexuality in moments that seem at first quite
chaste.

The principal difference between the verbal image clusters familiar in
Shakespeare's plays and this stage image cluster lies in the generality of the

stage images. While Spurgeon analyzed Shakespearean image clusters because she hoped to infer "some aspects of the poet's own experiences, tastes,
temperament, and vision of life," one cannot have the same goal in analyzing
a presentational image cluster like the one I have described.[10] The association
of woman's sexualized hand, inappropriate suitor, and mutilated man is not
found in a single playwright, but rather in several (Shakespeare, Dekker,
Middleton, and Rowley)[11] writing different sorts of plays over a quarter of a
century. These dramatists must be drawing on common cultural attitudes that
link inappropriate desire and inadequate men to women's sexualized hands.

One can speculate on the reasons for this staged image cluster, although
such speculation must, of course, remain unproven. Each of these playwrights knows both that the female sex object is being performed and that
the body beneath the woman's dress is male, that of a boy actor. Consciously
or unconsciously, the dramatist's imagination decides that referring linguistically to that male body as if it were a woman's body will not work and hence
he shifts to the cultural synecdoche of a woman's hand as a performative
device (one might even say "shorthand") to signal that the character is sexually desirable.[12] The inappropriate lover seems to be the least difficult part of
the image cluster. Because drama depends on conflict, the most dramatic version of sexual desire is inappropriate desire: sanctioned and successful lovers
do not need to talk about their beloved's body since they either have or will
have access to it. The speeches about the sexually desirable female hands are
given to suitors who will not succeed. One more element remains: the mutilated male bodies. Because an early modern woman's body was thought to
be the property of a man, her father or her husband, a woman who found
herself with an inappropriate lover might be presumed to have an inadequate
guardian. That inadequacy is marked on the protector's male body by mutilation: Beatrice's betrothed is inadequate to hold her interest, so his corpse is
mutilated and the ring she gave him is cut off his finger. Neither Lavinia's
husband nor her father can protect her: one dies and the other loses a hand.
Jane's husband Rafe loses her (quite literally) and is crippled; he only regains
her hand by regaining and remaking her shoes. And Olivia, who has no
father, no brother, no betrothed, chooses for herself and picks a girl. (In the
case of The Duchess of Malfi, which is less clear-cut, the mutilated body is
that of a dead stranger, the surrogate for Ferdinand whose hand appears in
act 4. One might argue, albeit tentatively, that Ferdinand's lycanthropia fits
the pattern.)

What then is one to make of this staged image cluster? Clearly it has meaning beyond an individual writer: it operates in works by several dramatists.
Presumably it suggests that the boy's body under a women's clothing cannot
be sexualized as his hand can be. This discomfort with the male body in turn
elicits the illicit, namely, inappropriate suitors and sexually active women.
The consequence of such sexual liberty that crosses social boundaries is the

imaged mutilation of the guardian. Because the consequences are so extreme in the plots of these plays, a thoughtful observer will want to reconsider other plays from the period that make use of women's hands and gloves. An early play in which a lady drops her glove (perhaps for the first time onstage), is *The Spanish Tragedy,* which has, of course, the requisite inappropriate suitor and maimed male body. Yet the glove itself, though clearly intended to represent Bel-Imperia, is not sexualized as Beatrice Joanna's is in *The Changeling.* One might ask how *The Spanish Tragedy* fits into this pattern of presentational imagery: does it initiate the image cluster for other dramatists or is it simply a coincidental precursor? In *The Two Gentlemen of Verona,* the mixed-up gloves in 2.1 betray Valentine's love-struck state in a play where the body of the boy actor playing his female love object is central to the plot and to its resolution. In this scene, however, the man's glove is as important as the woman's, and one might investigate what that point implies for the play more generally. In the quarto of *2 Henry VI,* the queen drops her glove and then strikes Eleanor, Duchess of Gloucester for failing to pick it up. Later, of course, the queen's inappropriately adulterous suitor Suffolk is murdered and the queen carries his head around in a bag. Yet in the folio that property has changed to a fan. Is it possible that the change to a fan is meant to diminish the audience's sense of the queen's sexual betrayal?

A larger question remains. How aware of this construct were the playwrights? At first one is tempted to say they were not at all conscious of it: this staged cluster of images sounds like the sort of idea that might exclusively occur on an unconscious level, save for an academic mind. Yet what then shall we make of an early modern playwright who seems to write with deliberate mockery about the cluster?

I want to turn to one final instance of sexualized hands, inappropriate suitor, and mutilated male body. In this case, the performed image cluster seems deliberately employed for comic effect. The would-be suitor in *The Knight of the Burning Pestle* is sanctioned by the girl's father, but the girl herself loves another who is powerless to win her father's consent. Not only is the sanctioned suitor unable to win the girl's love, but he is also a ninny, who speaks so compulsively in rhyming couplets that those who converse with him soon find themselves falling into his habit and spouting bad verse. Greeting Luce, the girl he loves, Humphrey proceeds to woo her idiotically:

> *Humphrey.* Fair Mistress Luce, how do you? Are you well?
> Give me your hand, and then, I pray you, tell
> How doth your little sister and your brother?
> And whether you love me or any other.

Luce resists his suit, but he continues to urge her:

Luce. Beshrew me, sir, I am sorry for your losses,
But, as the proverb says, I cannot cry.
I would you had not seen me!
Humphrey.   So would I,
Unless you had more maw to do me good.
Luce. Why, cannot this strange passion be withstood?
Send for a constable, and raise the town.
Humphrey. Oh, no, my valiant love will batter down
Millions of constables, and put to flight
Even that great watch of Midsummer-day at night
Luce. Beshrew me, sir, 'twere good I yielded, then;
Weak women cannot hope where valiant men
Have no resistance.
Humphrey.   Yield, then. I am full
Of pity, though I say it, and can pull
Out of my pocket thus a pair of gloves.
Look, Lucy, look; the dog's tooth nor the dove's
Are not so white as these, and sweet they be,
And whipped about with silk, as you may see.
If you desire the price, shoot from your eye
A beam to this place, and you shall espy
"F.S.," which is to say, my sweetest honey,
They cost me three and two pence, or no money.

(1.1.121–24, 139–59)

Humphrey has the whole process backward, of course. He begins conventionally enough, by declaring his love and focusing on the woman's hand in the form of the gloves that he wants to put on her hand. Yet Humphrey can hardly be said to be an ordinary wooer. To begin with, he rhymes the poor girl to death. Then he links the gloves not to her hand or body but rather to a "dog's tooth" or "a dove's" and is particularly taken by their price tag. Small wonder Luce scorns him, although she persuades him to help her elope. By his talk of gloves as a synecdoche for Luce's hand and by his agreeing to her plan, Humphrey slides from the role of sanctioned wooer into the role of transgressive suitor, displacing Jasper, the servant (and transgressive suitor) whom Luce actually loves. Once free of her father's household, Luce discards Humphrey to join Jasper, her true love and now her protector. Consequently, both Humphrey and Jasper are Luce's inappropriate suitors and her protectors. It is fitting that both of their bodies suffer: first Jasper beats Humphrey and drives him away, only to be beaten himself when the lovers are caught. Finally, however, Jasper becomes the protector whose body suffers most severely. Unable to protect his betrothed, the only way that he can regain Luce is by the ultimate bodily outrage: death. Covering himself in flour, he passes himself off as a corpse.

   In this instance, Francis Beaumont employs the image cluster that I have described, with the sexualized hand, the inappropriate suitor, and the maimed male body. Yet we laugh at each element because Beaumont burlesques the material. While such coincident stage images might be unconscious, it seems more likely that Humphrey suddenly produces the gloves in his wooing of Luce because Beaumont is at some level aware of what he is staging. Similarly, the way that Jasper uses flour to signal his body's death is a burlesqued form of the bodily suffering that male protectors undergo when this image cluster occurs in other plays. In *Knight of the Burning Pestle,* then, we have the staged image cluster complete: the gloves that represent the woman's sexuality, the repellent suitor, and the damaged protectors, but the playwright's wonderful joke is to take such standard material of the Renaissance stage and, like a good wit playing with a chevril glove, quickly turn it inside out.

Notes

1. Michel de Montaigne, *An Apology for Raymond Sebond,* trans. M. A. Screech (Harmondsworth: Penguin, 1987), 507. I presented early versions of this essay at two conferences in 2001: the Middleton Symposium at the Georgia Shakespeare Conference and the SCAENA Conference at Cambridge University. My thanks to the meeting organizers, especially Edward Esche and Nigel Wheale in Cambridge and Andrew Hartley and Richard Garner in Georgia.

2. Andrew Gurr, *The Shakespearean Stage 1574–1642,* 3rd ed. (Cambridge: Cambridge University Press, 1992), 100. Gurr includes a plate that shows some of Bulwer's gestures on 101. Thanks to Susan Cerasano for drawing my attention to this reference. See also David Bevington's *Action is Eloquence* (Cambridge: Harvard University Press, 1984).

3. Alan Downer, "The Life of Our Design: The Function of Imagery in Poetic Drama," *Hudson Review* 2 (1949): 242–63. I shall use the phrase "presentational imagery" rather than "staged imagery" in this essay.

4. Caroline Spurgeon, *Shakespeare's Imagery* (Cambridge: Cambridge University Press, 1977 reprint of 1935 ed.), esp. chapter 10. Specific passages are these: (for light-dark imagery) *Romeo and Juliet,* 1.5.41–50; Sonnet 27–28, *A Midsummer Night's Dream,* 3.2.142–45, 187–91; *Winter's Tale,* 4.4.346–51; (for flattery) *Julius Caesar,* 3.1.40–46; *1 Henry IV,* 1.3.247–50; Hamlet 3.2.52–54. I cite the *Norton Shakespeare,* ed. Stephen Greenblatt (New York and London: W. W. Norton, 1997).

5. I cite the non-Shakespearean plays from *Renaissance Drama,* ed. Arthur Kinney (Oxford and Malden: Blackwell, 1999).

6. *The Book of Common Prayer, 1559: The Elizabethan Prayer Book,* ed. John E. Booty (Charlottesville: The University Press of Virginia for the Folger Shakespeare Library, 1976).

7. On women and handwriting, see Roger Chartier, et al. *A History of Private Life: Passions of the Renaissance,* trans. Arthur Goldhammer (Cambridge and London: Harvard Belknap, 1989), esp. 115–17. A woman's hand could be represented materially in a variety of ways, as I show in "Princess Elizabeth's Hand in The Glass

of the Sinful Soul," *English Manuscript Studies* 9 (2000): 33–48. On men's hands, see Jonathan Goldberg, *Writing Matter: from the Hands of the English Renaissance* (Stanford: Stanford University Press, 1990). Robert Wiemann's *Author's Pen and Actor's Voice: Playing and Writing in Shakespeare's Theatre* (Cambridge: Cambridge University Press, 2000) is also relevant.

8. When I showed a film of the play to a class of graduate students, all of them had read and understood it intellectually; watching Bob Hoskins as De Flores thrust his fingers into the glove brought a chorus of gasps from them as they realized what the lines implied. The performance was necessary for an intelligent audience to understand the implications.

9. Gary Taylor, *Castration: An Abbreviated History of Western Manhood* (New York: Routledge, 2000), 182.

10. *The New Princeton Encyclopedia of Poetry and Poetics,* ed. Alex Preminger, T. V. F. Brogan, et al. (Princeton: Princeton University Press, 1993), s.v., "Imagery," esp. "Cluster Criticism."

11. Others include John Webster, *The Duchess of Malfi* and Francis Beaumont, *The Knight of the Burning Pestle,* discussed below.

12. Stephen Orgel, *Impersonations* (Cambridge: Cambridge University Press, 1996) has much to say about how early modern playwrights and audiences understood (or misunderstood) the boy actor's body as that of a woman.

Laugher and Blasphemy in
the Shakespearean Theater

INDIRA GHOSE

READERS of European newspapers were able to follow a curious scenario that unfolded in Austria early in 2002: the scandal raging about the cartoons of Jesus published by the well-known Austrian cartoonist Gerhard Haderer. The cartoons portray a hippyish Jesus, permanently high on incense (which contains the same chemical ingredients as hash, as Haderer takes care to explain), while his apostles, who are clearly caricatures of present-day Austrian bishops, are shown as dealers relegated the job of procuring a steady supply of dope for Christ. The miracle of Jesus walking on the sea is revealed as his little joke (he was surfing). The final image is that of Jesus enjoying a hash party in heaven with friends Janis Joplin and John Lennon. Haderer himself presents his Jesus biography (*The Life of Jesus*) tongue-in-cheek as the result of "years of historical research, meticulous scrutiny of original texts, costly research trips and innumerable analyses of incense."[1] Immediately on the book appearing a storm of protest broke loose. The Archbishop of Vienna, Cardinal Christoph Schönborn, attacked the book as "blasphemous" and an insult to all Christians, calling for a boycott of the publishers, while his colleague from Salzburg thundered from the pulpit: "One does not laugh about the sacred!"[2] Haderer has been charged with the "degradation of religious belief," which if convicted could earn him a six-month prison sentence. Reams of letters to the editor in Austrian tabloids demanded a Christian fatwa against the cartoonist. It is the sentiments bandied about in connection with this scandal, the linking of blasphemy with laughter, that is worth tracing back to the early modern period.

Attacks on the theater at this time involve a barrage of accusations ranging from incitement to disorder, sedition, criminality, idleness, the spread of disease, immorality, to blasphemy—particularly in the wider sense of irreverence toward the sacred. (The seventeenth-century jurist Blackstone distinguished between profanity—cursing and swearing—and blasphemy—holding the Bible up to ridicule.[3] I wish to focus on the range of attacks carried out by religious reformers. A broad overview of antitheatrical critique leads one recent critic to subsume them under two main keywords: eros and magic (or sex and idolatry).[4] I would argue that a third element is inextricably intertwined with these two factors: laughter.

Antitheatrical writers recurrently rage about the lascivious atmosphere at the theater. Stephen Gosson describes them as "markets of bawdry":

> Our Theaters, and play houses in London, are as full of secrete adulterie as as they were in Rome. . . . In the playhouses at London, it is the fashion of youthes to go first into the yarde, and to carry theire eye through every gallery, then like unto ravens where they spye the carion thither they flye, and presse as nere to ye fairest as they can. . . . They give them pippines, they dally with their garments to passe the time, they minister talke upon al occasions, & eyther bring them home to their houses on small acquaintance, or slip into taverns when the plaies are done.[5]

The plays themselves—particularly comedies—work to incite these passions, stimulating erotic friction through erotic banter.[6] Not only do prostitutes ply their wares at the theater, but the morals of commoners (especially women) are corrupted as well. Further, the violation of the Deuteronomic injunction against cross-dressing triggers off a variety of disorderly effects that threaten gender norms and evoke unspeakable corrupting passions: "Then, these godly pageants being done, every mate sorts to his mate, every one bringes another homeward of their way verye freendly, and in their secret conclaves (covertly) they play the *Sodomits,* or worse."[7]

All this is well known, of course, and requires no further rehearsing. One might think that a thorough cleansing of the moral of the plays and the play-house would do the job. This was not the case, however. As recent critics have pointed out, the antitheatricalist writers were not interested in reforming the theater.[8] Far more was at stake. "The real issue" according to O'Connell, "is representation."[9] What the antitheatrical critics inveigh most against is the physical, visual portrayal of the sacred. With the Reformation came the transition from an oral to a literary culture and a concomitant crisis in the relation to the image.[10] The medieval practice of incarnating the sacred in visual images (most importantly, in the principle of transubstantiation in the Eucharist itself) was now condemned as blasphemous. For reformers, the divine was invisible. Statues of saints, roods, and the like, which were venerated for their magical powers, for embodying a little piece of divine power, as it were, were the objects of the rage and fury of iconoclasts. Reforming enthusiasts went on a nationwide rampage to deface images and smash idols, setting into motion what Keith Thomas has described as the decline of magic in popular culture.[11] Iconoclastic fervor was carried into the arena of the theater in a vehement rejection of illusion, associated with deception, seduction, and above all, idolatry. The antitheatricalist writers reserved their special ire for biblical plays, where remnants of the Roman Catholic practice of venerating visual symbols of the sacred were suspected to be at work. Even though

from 1559 onward religious topics were banned from the stage, antitheatricalists continued to link theatricality to Roman Catholicism, rejecting the
power of the image as deceptive and fraudulent.

Nevertheless, we need to beware of equating antitheatricality with Protestantism or even Puritanism.[12] Early Protestants were eager to harness the seductive power of the theater for ideological purposes in moralistic interludes
and plays. A number of prominent theater enthusiasts and patrons (the Earls
of Leicester and Warwick, Walsingham,) harbored Puritan sympathies. Similarly, a notable number of playwrights were sympathetic to the Puritan cause,
ranging from Bale to Middleton.[13] Calvin's successor Theodore Beza was not
averse to cross-dressing onstage. Nor were all detractors of the stage radical
Puritans. Antitheatricalism can look back on a venerable tradition in Western
culture, as Jonas Barish has demonstrated.[14] And among the antitheatrical
critics themselves the most vocal were often moderate in religious matters,
among them Gosson and Stubbes.

What is the role allotted to laughter in the roster of crimes attributed to the
theater? For the antitheatricalist writers, laughter is conflated with the bawdy
and the idolatrous. The most influential critic of them all, Philip Stubbes,
whose book *The Anatomie of Abuses* went through four editions in two years,
sums it up succinctly in the following passage:

> There is no mischief which these plaies maintain not. For do they not norish yd-
> lenes? And *otia dant vitia,* iydleness is the Mother of vice. . . . Do they not main-
> taine bawdrie, infinit folery, & renue the rememberance of hethen ydolatrie? Do
> they not induce whordom and unclennes? . . . For proofe wherof, but marke the
> flocking and running to Theatres & curtens, daylie and hourely, night and daye,
> tyme and tyde, to see Playes and Enterludes; where such wanton gestures, such
> bawdie speaches, such laughing and fleering, such kissing and bussing, such clip-
> ping and culling. Suche winckinge and glancinge of wanton eyes, and the like, is
> used, as is wonderfull to behold.[15]

With grim irony, he advised that "if you will learn to deceive; . . . if you will
learne to iest, laugh, and fleer, to grin, to nodd, . . . to blaspheme both Heaven
and Earth," the theater is just the right place to learn these arts.

Laughter is clearly inseparable from fleering (mocking), from irrevent and
ribald mockery. Even defenders of the arts (though hardly of the theater) like
Philip Sidney define laughter as "only a scornful ticking."[16]

What is obliquely being referred to is the scurrilous humor with which
mystery and miracle plays were larded. In point of fact, medieval festive culture was saturated with ribaldry and jeering at things sacred.[17] In France, for
instance, during the Feast of Fools (28 December, to mark Herod's massacre
of children), which was organized by junior clergy, a bishop of the fools was
elected, and there was dancing in the church and the streets. In a mock mass

the clergy wore masks or women's clothes or their vestments back-to-front, played cards, ate sausages, sang bawdy songs, and cursed the congregation instead of blessing them. In England, a boy bishop was elected. While Christian theology might frown on laughter, medieval popular culture was rich in mirth. During the so-called Easter laughter the congregation was invited to laugh loudly during Mass to express their joy in the Resurrection. To this end, preachers would regularly tell obscene jokes and funny stories.

For centuries, just as regularly, reformers had been condemning scurrility in connection with the sacred. Why then did the reforming impetus gain such enormous momentum during this period? Cultural historians (in the footsteps of Peter Burke) tell us that it was the coalition between two "habits of thought"[18]—roughly subsumable under the labels of the Renaissance and the Reformation—in conjunction with far-reaching social and economic changes, such as a communications revolution (the rise of literacy) and the transition to a modern economy, linked to rapid urbanization and the commercialization of society. The paradigmatic figure for this reforming ethos was Erasmus, who was immensely influential in the movement to reform manners, as well as being responsible for having laid the egg hatched by Martin Luther.[19] Now festive rituals were condemned for precisely the reasons named above: idolatry and immorality. Erasmus pointed to the pagan roots of carnival festivity, linking the cult of Mary to the cult of Venus, and condemned all forms of misrule and mockery of the sacred as blasphemy. This wasn't exactly news for Christian theologians, but whereas the medieval policy had been to *incorporate* pagan remnants and harness carnivalesque energy by channeling it within the framework of Christian festivals (a strategy later dubbed the safety valve theory by cultural anthropologists), now reformers insisted on a strict separation between the sacred and the profane. This was not merely a Protestant phenomenon, but affected both the Reformation and the Counter-Reformation—Gian Matteo Giberti, the bishop of Verona, condemned preachers who "tell ridiculous stories and old wives' tales in the manner of buffoons and make their congregation roar with laughter," while the Puritan preacher William Perkins declared "it is not meet, convenient or laudable for men to move occasion of laughter in sermons."[20] In England, Archbishop Grindal attacked religious drama along with lords of misrule, May games, Christmas feasting, church ales, wakes, bearbaiting, cock-fighting, and dancing.

As Keith Thomas has shown, in the early modern period laughter was increasingly displaced from specific arenas: the religious, the political, the social.[21] Together with the reformation of morals, a wide-scale campaign to reform manners was instigated—once again, virtually launched by Erasmus's *De Civilitate Morum Puerilium,* first translated as *A Lytell Booke of Good Maners for Chyldren* (1532) and one of the first bestsellers in England. This movement has been magisterially charted by Norbert Elias in *The History of*

Manners, the first part of *The Civilising Process.*[22] What he demonstrates is how a new regimen of bodily control was propagated in the education of the nobility and the gentry. As Anna Bryson points out, while courtesy books abound in the medieval period, what is new is a concern with the body as the site for the inscription of status.[23] A member of the elite was distinguished by discipline of gesture and demeanor. Accordingly, jesting was to be curbed and was made subject to decorum and temperance. The classical influence is clear, linked to the humanist revival of rhetoric. But above all the reformation of manners in the early modern period needs to be seen against the backdrop of what Peter Burke has identified as an increasing distance between elite and popular culture—the withdrawal of the elite from participation in popular culture.

Thus if, as Deborah Shuger argues, the shift from premodern to modern thought is marked by the redrawing of boundaries, this is particularly true in the case of laughter.[24] Along with a separate spheres ideology that divided the sacred from the profane, an increasing gulf separated what was seen as vulgar laugher from intellectual laughter (wit).

Early modern thinkers tended to focus on the physiological dimensions of laughter (e.g., Laurent Joubert, *A Treatise on Laughter,* 1579) or have recourse to classical notions of laughter as normative, working to reinforce social norms.[25] In the long history of philosophical discussion of laughter, it has consistently been conflated with the comic. This implies a telescoping of laughter itself with either functions or stimuli of laughter. By contrast, scientific investigation of the phenomenon reveals that laughter is only tangentially related to humor. It is above all a *pleasurable* physical sensation that is linked to a sense of *community.* Laughter is mostly about social relationships, not humor.[26] This means that laughter as a cultural practice could be circumscribed by the term "mirth and merriment" (*The Taming of the Shrew*)— which brings us to the role of the Shakespearean theater at the time.

As a number of recent critics have shown, the early modern period was a period marked by the transition to a market economy.[27] Joan Thirsk speaks in this connection of the development of a consumer society in early modern England.[28] I will argue that what evolves with the suppression of popular festivity is the displacement of mirth onto what emerges as an incipient entertainment industry—the theater. Seasonal cycles of mirth are transmuted into a localized site of pleasure: carnival on a daily, albeit temporary basis. ("We'll strive to please you every day," as Feste promises in *Twelfth Night.*) Here I draw on insights from cultural anthropology, in particular Victor Turner's discussion of the transition of the liminal into the liminoid in modern industrial societies.[29] Festive occasions in premodern cultures (such as carnival) are organized around a liminal phase that is broadly characterized by misrule and topsy-turvydom, before norms are reclarified in a new stage of development. By contrast, modern societies are characterized by a rigid division between phases of work and leisure. While leisure is increasingly commercialized, the phenomena of popular culture (sports, games) take on certain aspects of carnival culture.

The link between laughter and mass entertainment is not new, of course. Erich Segal makes a similar point in connection with Plautine comedy in his book *Roman Laughter.*[30] What is new, however, is the formation of a nascent entertainment business grounded in the conditions of an increasingly effective market economy. As Michael Bristol puts it, "in a sense . . . the abstract, socially undifferentiated consumer of cultural services was the most important "invention" of the early modern theatre."[31] An important function of laughter or mirth is that of a social lubricant, defusing social tensions and purveying social harmony. And it is precisely this function one might pin down in the "happy comedies" of the 1590s. To draw a breathtakingly ahistorical analogy: a strikingly similar move is discernible in the reaction of Hollywood to the attacks by latter-day Puritans, the HUAC and McCarthyism in the 1950s. In the films produced in the period after the hearings, a clear shift takes place from reflecting social conflict toward purveying consensus and harmony.[32]

From a retrospective viewpoint it might appear that the stage and the Puritans were, ironically enough, collaborating in the project of disciplining the modern subject. Together they facilitated the demise of seasonal mirth and shaped the modern regimen of work and leisure. However, I would not wish to endorse either such a bleak, Foucauldian viewpoint, nor Adorno-like fulminations against mass culture as unadulterated escapism. While an escapist element is undoubtedly discernible, what is striking is the creation of a new community of shifting alliances unified by the experience of mirth. Without wishing to pinpoint a utopian dimension to this community, it is manifest that a new social space for pleasure was evolving that created a new form of public—a public sphere that contained a potential challenge to the monopoly of both state and church.[33]

Further, I would argue that the real struggle about the role of laughter in early modern society takes place elsewhere—in the debates about Sabbatarianism. For along with the second and third commandments (idolatry, blasphemy), antitheatricalist critics were obsessed with the abuse of the fourth commandment, the desecration of the Sabbath.

In their outpourings on the abuse of the Sabbath, antitheatricalist writers (and above all, Puritans), lump the theater with other forms of games and pastimes like wakes, bearbaiting, cock-fighting, dancing, gaming, and of course, football. Despite the injunctions against Sabbath playing during the Elizabethan reign, complaints are regularly voiced about the infringement of the law. In his discussion of "The Uses of Sabbatarianism," Christopher Hill (by no means unsympathetic to the Puritan cause) sees the Puritan stake in Sabbatarianism as bound up with an interest in maintaining the regular and continuous rhythms of modern industrial society.[34] The numerous festivals (a hundred or more saints' days a year) were seen as a disruption of regular, disciplined labor, as was increasingly required by the economic conditions of sixteenth-century England. Other concerns were their pagan roots and the disorderly conduct linked to holy day festivity. The idea of reducing holy days to the weekly Sabbath derives from the Lollards, another sect that attracted above all the industrious sort. The Sabbath was to be kept free from labor as well as recreation to allow people to indulge in spiritual labor, to scrutinize their inner selves and examine their consciences. The egalitarian implications of Sabbatarianism need to be taken into account—even domestic servants and farm laborers were considered to be deserving of a rest-day, by no means a consensus amongst employers of labor at the time. Hill points out, however, that the Puritan attack on Sunday sports should be seen as part of an attempt to impose the ethos of a modern industrial society on the nation. Whatever dents the Weberian grand narrative of a one-way street leading from Protestantism to capitalism might have taken with time, in the case of the Sabbath the Protestant ideal of serving God by industry, in combination with the attack on the idleness encouraged by holy days, was certainly conducive to productivity.[35] The reasons why the rigid enforcement of Sabbath should become such a British institution lie in the "peculiar economic and political development of England. In England commerce, industry, and an urban way of life established themselves on national scale earlier than anywhere else."[36]

It was their hostility to sports and pastimes that earned the Puritans the sobriquet of killjoys, particularly in stage caricatures, though it is worth bearing in mind that there were few more ideal scapegoats to thrash, since it might be inexpedient to pick on politically more powerful opponents. (Shakespeare as usual remains equivocal.) Nevertheless, Puritans reveal the right instinct in attacking mirth. To quote Stubbes again: "Do they not draw the people from hearing the word of God, from godly Lectures and sermons? for you shall have them flocke thither, thick & threefould, when the church of God shal be bare & emptie."[37] Quite clearly a nerve has been hit. This lament is endlessly reiterated in antitheatrical literature. The conditions of a market economy for recreation force the Puritans into purveying the sacred as just another commodity, competing for attention on the marketplace. In fact, one might see a link between the explosion of the theater into a booming entertainment industry and the increasing virulence of Puritan attacks. The same crowds that throng the theaters are the ones they wish to attract (and often do) to their sermons. Even William Perkins admits this frankly; in a sermon delivered at Sturbridge Fair in 1593, he says:

> Everybody brings hither something to be sold. This is the merchandise that I bring and set to sale unto you. Whatever commodity any of you bring it is from some

quarter of this land, but all is from the earth. But this that I bring it is from heaven and all the earth cannot yield it: and as it is from heaven, so it is of a heavenly virtue and will work that which all the wealth in this fair is not able to do.[38]

Critics have pointed out that the stage internalizes antitheatrical critique and sets about reforming itself, for instance by attacking the deception of surfaces ("I know not seems"), or by creating figures obsessively preoccupied with self-scrutiny.[39] Paradoxically, the preachers were just as influenced by the theater as vice versa. Bryan Crockett points out that "like the playwrights, the preachers employ a whole arsenal of rhetorical devices in the service of effective performance."[40] For all their inveighing against theatricality, the Puritans were heavily invested in producing a convincing show. There were star preachers who could be depended upon to draw a crowd, and printed tracts that were bestsellers. Their rituals were often derided as theatrical (read: fraudulent) by critics, particularly the public rituals of confession and exhibitions of self-scrutiny. Even their markedly inconspicuous demeanor and plain clothing bore the marks of a performative staging of antitheatricality.

To return to laughter and the theater: if one were to see laughter and mirth above all as a a form of play,[41] a ludic space governed by its own set of rules, one might come even closer to the heart of the issue: the anxiety that mirth and forms of leisure activity caused to radical religious movements like the Puritans. As Johan Huizinga defines it, "play is a voluntary activity or occupation executed within certain fixed limits of time and place, according to rules freely accepted but absolutely binding, having its aim in itself and accompanied by a feeling of tension, joy, and the consciousness that it is 'different' from 'ordinary life.'"[42] What is at stake is not merely rivalry for the same audiences under competitive market conditions. The Shakespearean theater (and above all, the comedies of the 1590s) seem to offer a separate world, a liminal space that is set apart from, and independent of, the sacred. (I do not refer the "green world" within the comedies itself, but instead to the cultural performances linked with mirth.) If, as Keith Thomas and Max Weber have argued, the transition to modernity brings with it a disenchantment of the world and the decline of magic, the theater/popular entertainment purveys a new form of magic, a dream world of make-believe where the rules of reality don't apply. What is at stake is not merely competition with the scared—it is the emergence of new imaginative worlds where the sacred becomes simply irrelevant. The final effect of the separation of the sacred and the profane is, it seems, the displacement of God. And in the final analysis it is this suspicion that haunts the Puritan attack on laughter and mirth. It is really the first commandment that is at issue—the opening up of self-sufficient, self-absorbed, rival worlds of the imagination that challenge the monopoly of the sacred.

Without entering into debates about the Reformation, whether slow or rapid, imposed from above or engineered from below, it remains indisputable that something akin to what Patrick Collinson has recently called a cultural revolution took place.[43] However, historical ironies abound. Historians such as Keith Wrightson point out that in the final analysis, the intense proselytizing effort failed—the people remained "sermon-proof" and truculently resistant. The project of reforming the people's morals led in the long run to an alienation from the church. The move to eliminate intermediaries between the people and God (saints, the Virgin Mary) led to a distancing from God and finally to a withdrawal from the sacred. For Christopher Haigh, the political Reformation succeeded, but the religious Reformation remained an unfinished project. England became "a Protestant nation, but not a nation of Protestants."[44] A convocation of ministers in 1604 complained bitterly about the indifference and ignorance of the people, although outward conformity had prevailed. Haigh concludes that religion as envisaged by the godly was too demanding for most people—a vision of religion as a spiritual experience rather than a social practice.

Conversely, laughter has triumphed all along the line. Far from being increasingly disciplined, there has been a veritable explosion of laughter. The realms that were closed down to laughter in the early modern period—the political, the social, the religious—have all been reconquered, one after another. The entertainment factor in politics has become a commonplace. If only a couple of decades ago manuals on advertising warned, "Spending money is serious business. . . . People do not buy from clowns,"[45] today almost the obverse is true—only sex rivals humor as the most effective means to sell a commodity. Companies engage clowns on a regular basis to improve managerial morale. There is a proliferation of greasy gurus whose main qualification is hailing from India running laughter therapy clubs. Even the sphere of religion has not remained immune. Evangelicals have long rediscovered the attractions of laughter. Key in the word laughter in Amazon.com and the vast majority of the books listed deal with Christian laughter. Robert Provine describes the phenomenon of "holy laughter," a movement whose main proponent is the Pentecostal revivalist Rodney Howard-Brown. At their meetings "Laughing for the Lord" is practiced, with Howard-Brown urging, "Let it bubble out of your belly like a river of living water."[46]

Which is why Cardinal Schönborn and his fulminations against the blasphemy of laughter seem a quaint, almost touching throwback to the world we have lost. Not that he can throw the switch completely. For blasphemy only hurts in a deeply religious society, not a society characterized by a dramatic decline in the number of churchgoers—true for Austria as much as for the rest of Europe. Ever since his outburst on blasphemy, the sales of the Jesus cartoons have soared. The slim volume has become an all-time bestseller. As the noninhaling (unlike Jesus), non-sex-having (at least not with that woman), ex-President of the United States would have reminded the Cardinal: it's the economy, stupid!

Notes

1. Gerhard Haderer, *Das Leben des Jesus* (Vienna: Ueberreuter, 2002), jacket blurb (my translation).

2. See *Frankfurter Rundschau,* 8 Apr. 2002, 11; *Tageszeitung,* 5 Apr. 2002, 17 (my translation).

3. Frank Kermode, *"Blasphemy: Impious Speech in the West from the 17th. to the 19th. Century,* by Alain Cabantous," *LRB* 24.2 (2002): 19–20 (cited from 20).

4. See Ioan P. Couliano, *Eros and Magic in the Renaissance* (Chicago: University of Chicago Press, 1987).

5. Stephen Gosson, *Playes Confuted in five Actions,* rpt. in E. K. Chambers, *The Elizabethan Stage* (Oxford: Clarendon, 1923), 4:218.

6. See Stephen Greenblatt, "Fiction and Friction," in *Shakespearean Negotiations: The Circulation of Social Energy in Elizabethan England* (Oxford: Clarendon, 1988), 66–93.

7. Philip Stubbes, *The Anatomie of Abuses,* rpt. in Chambers, 4:224.

8. See Huston Diehl, *Staging Reform, Reforming the Stage: Protestantism and Popular Theatre in Early Modern England* (Ithaca: Cornell University Press, 1997) and Michael O'Connell, *The Idolatrous Eye: Iconoclasm and Theatre in Early Modern England* (Oxford: Oxford University Press, 2000). Also see James R. Siemon, *Shakespearean Iconoclasm* (Berkeley: University of California Press, 1985).

9. Michael O'Connell, "The Idolatrous Eye: Iconoclasm, Anti-Theatricalism, and the Image of the Elizabethan Theater," *English Literary History* 52.2 (1985):279–310 (cited from 285).

10. See Walter J. Ong, *Orality and Literacy: The Technologizing of the Word* (London: Routledge, 1988).

11. Keith Thomas, *Religion and the Decline of Magic: Studies in Popular Beliefs in Sixteenth and Seventeenth Century England* (London: Weidenfeld and Nicolson, 1971).

12. I use the term Puritan as shorthand for zealous Protestants, bearing in mind the fact that the term is notoriously inexact. See Christopher Hill, "The Definition of a Puritan," *Society and Puritanism in Pre-Revolutionary England* (London: Secker & Warburg, 1964) 13–29.

13. Margot Heinemann, *Puritanism and Theatre: Thomas Middleton and Opposition Drama under the Early Stuarts* (Cambridge: Cambridge University Press, 1980).

14. Jonas Barish, *The Antitheatrical Prejudice* (Berkeley: University of California Press, 1981)

15. Stubbes, rpt. in Chambers, 4:223.

16. Philip Sidney, *A Defence of Poetry* (Oxford: Oxford University Press, 1966), 68.

17. See Peter Burke, *Popular Culture in Early Modern Europe* (London: Temple

Smith, 1978), and Natalie Zemon Davis, *Society and Culture in Early Modern France* (Stanford: Stanford University Press, 1975).

18. See Debora Kuller Shuger, *Habits of Thought in the English Renaissance: Religion, Politics, and the Dominant Culture* (Berkeley: University of California Press, 1990).

19. Robert C. Solomon and Kathleen M. Higgins, *A Short History of Philosophy* (New York: Oxford University Press, 1996), 161.

20. Burke, *Popular Culture,* 211.

21. Keith Thomas, "The Place of Laughter in Tudor and Stuart England," *TLS,* 21 January 1977, 77–81. Also see Jan Bremmer and Herman Roodenburg, eds., *A Cultural History of Humour: From Antiquity to the Present Day* (Cambridge: Polity, 1997).

22. Norbert Elias, *The Civilizing Process* (1939: Oxford: Blackwell, 1978).

23. Anne Bryson, *From Courtesy to Civility: Changing Codes of Conduct in Early Modern England* (Oxford: Clarendon, 1998).

24. Shuger, *Habits of Thought,* 11.

25. See M. A. Screech and Ruth Calder, "Some Renaissance Attitudes to Laughter," in *Humanism in France at the End of the Middle Ages and in the Early Renaissance* (Manchester: Manchester University Press, 1970), 216–27.

26. I draw on recent research by Robert R. Provine, the neurobiologist and leading expert on laughter from a scientific point of view, in his *Laughter: A Scientific Investigation* (London: Faber and Faber, 2000).

27. See e.g., Richard Halpern, *The Poetics of Primitive Accumulation: English Renaissance Culture and the Genealogy of Capital* (Ithaca: Cornell University Press, 1991).

28. Joan Thirsk, *Economic Policy and Projects: The Development of a Consumer Society in Early Modern England* (Oxford: Clarendon, 1978).

29. Victor Turner, "Liminal to Liminoid in Play, Flow, and Ritual: An Essay in Comparative Symbology," *Rice University Studies* 60.3 (1974): 53–92.

30. Erich Segal, *Roman Laugher: The Comedy of Plautus* (Cambridge: Harvard United Press, 1968).

31. Michael D. Bristol, "Theatre and Popular Culture," in *A New History of Early English Drama,* ed. John D. Cox and David Scott Kastan (New York: Columbia United Press, 1997), 231–48; cited from 248.

32. See Larry Ceplair and Steven Englund, *The Inquisition in Hollywood: Politics in the Film Community 1930–1960* (New York: Anchor Press/Doubleday, 1980).

33. I draw inspiration from a remark by Robert Weimann in his "Towards a Literary Theory of Ideology: Mimesis, Representation, Authority," in *Shakespeare Reproduced: The text in History and Ideology,* ed. Jean E. Howard (New York: Methuen, 1987) 265–72; cited from 272. The political implications of the creation of a new public space are looked at by David Scott Kastan in his "'Publike Sports' and 'Publike Calamities': Plays, Playing, and Politics," in *Shakespeare After Theory* (New York: Routledge, 1999), 201–20.

34. Christopher Hill, "The Uses of Sabbatarianism," *Society and Puritanism in Pre-Revolutionary England* (London: Secker & Warburg, 1964), 145–218. Also see Keith Thomas, "Work and Leisure," *Past & Present* 29 (1964): 51–62.

35. Hill, "Uses of Sabbatarianism," 154. Paul Seaver argues that the entrepreneurial spirit is more visible among post-Restoration Anglicans than among the Puritans. However, he does not deny the Puritan exhortations against wasting time in leisure. See Paul Seaver, "The Puritan Work Ethic Revisited," *Journal of British Studies* 19 (1980): 35–53.

36. Hill, "Uses of Sabbatarianism," 208.

37. Stubbes, rpt. in Chambers, 4:223.

38. I owe this quote to Jean-Christophe Agnew in his groundbreaking work *Worlds Apart: The Market and the Theatre in Anglo-American Thought, 1550–1750* (Cambridge: Cambridge University Press, 1986), 139–40.

39. See e.g., Diehl, Agnew, and Barish.

40. Bryan Crockett, *The Play of Paradox: Stage and Sermon in Renaissance England* (Philadelphia: University of Pennsylvania Press, 1995), 18.

41. See Peter L. Berger, *Redeeming Laughter: The Comic Dimension of Human Experience* (Berlin: Walter de Gruyter, 1997).

42. Johan Huizinga, *Homo Ludens* (Boston: Beacon Press, 1955), 28.

43. Patrick Collinson, "Through Trychay's Eyes," *LRB,* 25 Apr. 2002, 21–22 (cited from 21).

44. Christopher Haigh: *English Reformation: Religion, Politics, and Society under the Tudors* (Oxford: Clarendon, 1993), 280.

45. Claude C. Hopkins, one of the founders of modern American advertising, in *My Life in Advertising/Scientific Advertising* (Chicago; Advertising Publications, 1966), qtd. in Daniel Wickberg, *The Senses of Humor: Self and Laughter in Modern America* (Ithaca: Cornell University Press, 1998), 220–21.

46. Provine, *Laughter,* 136.

Reviews

The Reign of Elizabeth I, by Carole Levin. Houndmills, Basingstoke, Hampshire; New York: Palgrave, 2002. ix + 144pp. £45.00 pb £14.99

Reviewer: ILONA BELL

This refreshingly readable and meticulously researched history reviews the major social, political, and cultural issues that marked Elizabeth I's reign from 1558–1603. *The Reign of Elizabeth I* is especially suitable for students, even if they have no prior knowledge of the field, because nothing is taken for granted. It will also be useful to teachers who want to refresh their memories (who was Henry VIII's fourth wife?) with an overview of the period. It will also be invaluable to literary scholars who analyze literature as part of a larger social and political nexus and who need a reliable guide to the historical debates, complications, and discoveries that have emerged during the last half century, especially the last decade. For almost any major political, social, or historical question, this book is an ideal place to begin.

The book is designed as an introduction to Elizabeth I and her reign, and it takes pains to explain the background, the players, the institutions, and the stakes to any reader wandering into the thickets of Elizabethan history. For example, whereas most biographers and historians simply refer to the Privy Council, Levin pauses to tell the reader, in one brief, packed sentence, exactly what the Privy Council did: "it advised the ruler on policy, carried out responsibility for general administration and public expenditure, and coordinated the work of different agencies of government" (16). Levin proceeds to explain a simple fact that reveals a great deal about the way Elizabeth did business: although the Privy Council formulated opinions on all important decisions such as the religious settlement or the succession, Elizabeth preferred to consult individual members of the council separately.

Chapter 1, "Overview of Elizabeth's Life and Reign," presents all the most important events in a taut sixteen pages, and would be useful background reading for any course in Elizabethan literature. The chapter begins with the War of the Roses and Henry VII's tentative claim to the throne which Elizabeth's father inherited and strove valiantly to overcome. It reviews all six of Henry VIII's marriages. We learn, for example, that Henry's first wife, Katherine of Aragon, was "highly educated, loyal, and strong-willed. But she failed at her premiere function as Queen; she had no son who survived infancy" (6). Most readers will know that Henry's "passion" for Elizabeth's mother, Anne Boleyn, led him to break with the Church of Rome, but they may not know why the pope balked at Henry's request for a divorce: Catherine's nephew, Charles V, Holy Roman Emperor and King of Spain, was "the last person Pope Clement VII wanted to offend" (6). Henry's Parliament met for an "unprecedented seven years" which created a model of parliamentary power that continued to pose difficulties for Elizabeth throughout her reign.

One of Levin's great gifts as a historian is a capacity for narrative. Although this book conveys vast amounts of information in 150 pages, Levin's penchant for storytelling produces a sense of drama and suspense. Thus we learn that in August 1532 "Henry openly proclaimed his marriage to Anne Boleyn, who was five months pregnant at the time. Her coronation, was one of exceptional magnificence. Henry had broken with the Catholic Church and turned his whole world upside down to have a legitimate son; however the child to whom Anne Boleyn gave birth on 7 September 1533 was another daughter" (7). The remainder of the chapter traces the highlights and major crises of Elizabeth's life and reign: the improprieties Thomas Seymour, husband to Queen Dowager, Katherine Parr, took with the vulnerable thirteen-year-old Elizabeth ("he would come into her bedchamber in the mornings and tease and sometimes tickle her, sometimes slapping her on the bottom" [8]); Elizabeth's skillful evasion of danger when, after Parr's death, Seymour tried to lure the young princess into a clandestine and potentially treasonous marriage ("Elizabeth handled herself so well and carefully that she managed to extricate herself from the crisis" [9]); Wyatt's plot to assassinate Mary and crown Elizabeth, and Elizabeth's imprisonment in the tower and lingering house arrest; the remarkably smooth transition to power after Mary's death; Elizabeth's great desire to "be Queen of all the English, not just the Protestants" (14); her mutually respectful relations with her principle advisers, Burghley, Walsingham, and Leicester, and her irreparable disagreement with Grindal, Archbishop of Canterbury whom Elizabeth suspended from office, leaving the Church without an ecclesiastical leader from 1577 to 1583; the thorny problem of Mary Queen of Scots who, after marrying her husband's murderer, fled to England, where she remained under house arrest for nineteen years, becoming a focus for innumerable Catholic plots against Elizabeth until Mary was finally executed in 1587—all this and much more in sixteen tightly packed pages.

Chapter 2, "Religious Divides and the Religious Settlement," is one of the best available short surveys of the religious differences that preoccupied and threatened the reign. Many historians have argued that Elizabeth was more political than religious, and Levin basically concurs. Elizabeth was not a zealot, Levin tells us; moreover, Elizabeth took care to conceal her personal beliefs, so it is now difficult to know what she thought about disputed matters of doctrine and ritual.[1] The first major controversy of the reign shows how inextricably interconnected were politics, religion, and gender. Many members of Parliament thought Elizabeth, as a woman, should not be named "Supreme Head of the Church of England." Elizabeth listened to the objections and then finessed the question, choosing the title of "Governor" instead, thereby overcoming parliamentary resistance without yielding any actual power. The crisis and the resulting compromise illustrate the strategies Elizabeth used throughout the reign as she sought to maintain a compromise between zealous Protestants and unreconstructed Catholics. For the first half of the reign, she adopted a policy of tolerance toward Catholics as long as they attended church services. Later, when opposition from abroad and plots against her life multiplied, the government began to treat recusants more severely. Conrad Russell argues that Elizabeth "settled for churches that looked Catholic and sounded Protestant," which produced a national Church "with which no one was satisfied." Yet by the end of her reign Elizabeth had made England into a profoundly Protestant country, and religion had ceased to be a major divisive force.[2]

Chapters 3 and 4 explore England's relation with others, both on the Continent and within the British Isles. It takes considerable concentration to wend one's way through the historical morass, but by the end of these chapters the reader will understand the internal conflicts within the British Isles, between England and Scotland or Ireland, which created major problems throughout the reign, taking the lives of many men sent to fight there, making a constant drain on Elizabeth's treasury, and bringing international threats to Elizabeth's Protestant government much closer to home, thus creating a feeling of anxiety and instability that disturbed the entire reign. Have you ever wondered what Henry Sidney, Edmund Spenser, or the Earl of Essex were doing in Ireland? In just a few pages Levin explains the cast of characters, the major battles, and the persistent political anxieties that were used to justify "horrific" violence against the Irish.

Throughout the reign, England was caught up in military struggles on the Continent as well. The most chilling moment in these two chapters is the Bartholomew Day massacre which shook English Protestants to the core, making them fear that Catholic designs on Elizabeth's Protestant government could, at any moment, lead to mass destruction. Especially interesting are the parallels between England's decision to fight Catholic aggression in the Netherlands and England's own imperialist policy in Ireland.[3]

These chapters also discuss the marriage negotiations that preoccupied the first three Elizabethan Parliaments and dominated foreign policy for the first half of the reign. Levin herself tends to the belief that Elizabeth preferred not to marry, but she provides a balanced account of the courtships, both those Elizabeth never seriously considered (Erik of Sweden, the Austrian Archduke Charles) as well as the two that moved her deeply (her subject, Robert Dudley, and Francis, Duke of Anjou).

Chapter 4 ends with the major political and military challenge of the reign, the Spanish Armada. Levin quotes a good chunk of Elizabeth's remarkable speech to the troops at Tilbury, but better yet (especially for those of us who teach the speech), she explains the continual delays, the inclement weather, Drake's secret attack upon the Spanish at Cadiz which destroyed between two and three dozen of the largest ships, netted £140,000 for the queen, and delayed the actual attack by a whole year; the English fire ships that threw the Spanish force into disarray; the famous victory; the continuing "fear of

further Armadas [that] darkened the 1590s" (70). If you want more information, here as always the footnotes tell you where to go next.

Elizabeth has often been celebrated as a monarch who kept England at
peace throughout her forty-five-year-long reign, but Levin, along with a number of other recent historians, describes a country at war. In the course of the
reign, 105,000 men served in the army. The government spent £4,500,000 on
the war effort, almost £2,000,000 on Ireland alone. The war effort produced
great financial stress, social anxiety, and political unrest. Elizabeth's government faced persistent pressures to support the Protestant cause in the Netherlands; to subdue the Catholic warlords in Ireland; to maintain a balance
between Catholic power in France, Spain, and Holy Roman Empire, keeping
each in check; and to uncover and prevent plots to assassinate Elizabeth and
return England to Catholicism.

Chapter 5 analyzes the numerous plots and conspiracies that dogged Elizabeth's reign. Some like the Parry plot were exaggerated by the government
to beef up loyalty to the queen; others posed a continuing and serious threat
which was exacerbated by, and which in turn further exacerbated, anxieties
over the succession. Having herself been the object of Wyatt's plot to depose
Mary, Elizabeth was loathe from the very outset of the reign to name a successor who might become the locus for opposition against her. Hence "the
question of the succession," Levin concludes, "may have been the most sustained issue of her reign" (79).

As the final chapter, "Culture and Difference at the End of the Reign,"
shows most clearly, this is a history for the twenty-first century.

> Many of those who fought for England and their Queen were never paid and in
> the 1590s suffered a life of poverty. It was also a time when outsiders were more
> recognized and more persecuted. The 1590s was the harshest decade in the reign in
> terms of witchcraft trials, and the targets of the trial were often poorer women. The
> charge that Dr Roderigo Lopez, an Anglicized Iberian Jew, planned to poison Eliz-
> abeth in 1594 gave voice to strong anti-Jewish sentiments, and though the few Afri-
> cans in England had been brought there against their will, English anxiety over
> them caused Elizabeth to attempt to expel them in 1601, on the excuse that they
> were taking jobs away from the English who needed them. (104)

This chapter stresses the financial problems at the end of the reign. Although
the newly passed Poor Laws didn't solve the growing problems of urbanization, poverty, homelessness, or hunger, they "accomplished at least some of
their goals" and were "an early model of the modern welfare state" (108). As
anxieties about the economy, the succession, and the queen's waning powers
mushroomed in the last decade, so did witchcraft trials, largely of poor
women, though the numbers never matched those on the Continent. Levin's
discussion of Africans and Moors, some of whom had been brought to En-

gland in the nascent slave trade, should be of particular interest to teachers and students of *Titus Andronicus* and *Othello;* her comments about the community of London Jews and the Lopez trial sheds light on *The Jew of Malta* and *Merchant of Venice.* "Paralleling the delight people felt in the achievements of Shakespeare, Marlowe, and Spenser were the poor harvests, the inflation, and the general anxiety of the end of the sixteenth century" (71).

The Reign of Elizabeth I would be a useful text to assign in many Renaissance literature courses. It is an ideal way to get students to understand, quickly and efficiently, what was going on in the world so that they can understand what is at stake in a Shakespeare play or a Donne poem. There is a brief, one-page bibliographical essay at the end which tells readers where to go for additional information. The footnotes are an even more valuable treasure trove of carefully culled references to the most recent, trenchant studies of all the main political, religious, and social issues. One of the book's great strengths is that Levin is scrupulous, in fact generous, about crediting other scholars.

The Reign of Elizabeth I provides an invaluable overview of the Elizabethan period; it is an impressive accomplishment, especially given the challenges and constraints of writing a concise history of a time that was at once so glorious and so contentious. I have only a few quibbles. I would have liked to hear more about the lives of Elizabethan women, an area about which Levin happens to be very knowledgeable. In the introduction Levin makes a claim that is reiterated throughout: "Elizabeth's reign saw great cultural development that often reflected and helped interpret political events" (3). Levin has written fascinatingly about Shakespearean drama and Elizabethan history elsewhere, but this book repeatedly acknowledges without actually discussing the great cultural achievements of the period. I wish the introduction or the last chapter had included a broader, more substantial amount of Elizabethan culture, of the Shakespearean stage and the great flourishing of Elizabethan poetry. Yet thanks to Levin's efforts, the readers of this journal are now in a much better position to continue exploring the links between politics and culture. As Levin concludes, "Elizabeth's amazing personality not only shaped her own century so it is known as the Elizabethan Age, but hundreds of years later her image still fascinates us" (122).

Notes

1. Here Levin cites and agrees with Diarmaid MacCulloch, *The Later Reformation in England, 1547–1603* (New York: Palgrave, 1990).

2. Quoted from "The Reformation and the Creation of the Church of England 1500–1640," in *The Oxford Illustrated History of Tudor & Stuart Britain,* ed. John Morrill (Oxford: New York, 1996).

3. Levin attributes the comparison to William Palmer, *The Problem of Ireland in Tudor Foreign Policy, 1485–1603* (Woodbridge, Suffolk; Rochester, N.Y.: Boydell Press, 1994).

Shakespeare and the Loss of Eden, by Catherine Belsey. New Brunswick, N.J.: Rutgers University Press, 1999. Pp. Xvii + 203. Cloth $26.00

Reviewer: HARRY BERGER

For all those who disdainfully dismiss the monster called deconstruction or postmodern of post-almost-anything for its insufferable jargon, I have news: it's possible to do this kind of work in a way that is clear, instructive, and considerate of the reader. Admittedly not many who try succeed. But Catherine Belsey does, and it seems to me that the ordinary pundit in the street who's inclined to run on at the mouth or the motherboard about deconstruction should stop long enough to read Belsey's work. Since the publication of *Critical Practice* in 1980, hers has been a significant and welcome voice in literary criticism. She has shown us all how it is possible to write with extraordinary methodological and theoretical sophistication and at the same time to write clearly, gracefully, and simply. No one who acknowledges and displays the influence of the French Connection has done better in this respect. And also in another respect: Belsey demonstrates by example that criticism can go about its academic business—the business of interpreting representations and discourses—and still have political consequences, still demand the critic to examine and take a position on issues that affect our lives; issues of identity and difference, the subject of desire, the naturalization of arbitrary inequities of gender, the historical and ideological foundations of common sense, the early modern origin of family values. The appearance in 1999 of *Shakespeare and the Loss of Eden* confirms that in addition to the virtues just enumerated, her own critical practice has produced not merely a series of books but a single continuously growing and still unfolding discourse. To say that the whole is greater than the sum of the parts is not to denigrate the parts, each of which gains depth by what it contributes to and receives from the whole project. Faced with this situation, I've decided that in order to do justice to Catherine Belsey's latest book I should try to contextualize it. Accordingly, what follows consists of two parts, the first on *Shakespeare and the Loss of Eden* and the second on its place in Belseian discourse.

1.

"Through detailed analysis of the plays, Belsey presents a comprehensive exposé on the domestication of desire in marriage, parental love and cruelty, and sibling rivalry. Showing the loving family as an object of propaganda then as now, Belsey points out the unforeseen affinities between the present day and the world of early modern England. Richly illustrated and written with perception and wit, *Shakespeare and the Loss of Eden* is a significant work of both literary criticism and cultural history." So goes the advance publicity notice put out by the book's publisher, and I begin with this statement because, although it is seriously inaccurate (apart from its praise of Belsey's perception and wit), its misdescription glances usefully at three of the book's distinctive features.

First, the analyses of the plays are not detailed and aren't intended to be. *Shakespeare and the Loss of Eden* is primarily a complex meditation, partly ethical and partly methodological, on the ways in which the conflicting demands of an emergent culture of family values are represented. The second part of the title refers not to the story of the Fall per se but to the mythical invention of the nuclear family both as a sociopolitical structure of relations and as a political idea whose costs outweigh its benefits. Belsey is careful to note that her comments on particular aspects, scenes, and passages of the plays are determined by the themes the plays are chosen to illustrate: "I have chosen, perhaps arbitrarily, to isolate visual representations of the biblical story of the first family in relation to some of Shakespeare's plays, linking these in turn with other instances from the image repertory of the period" (24). This decision carries with it a danger that she doesn't fully avoid, and that I return to at the end of my review. The level of textual engagement varies widely from the very spare attention given but one scene in *Cymbeline* to the searching exploration of "the impossible dilemma"—familial, ethical, spiritual—the Ghost confronts Hamlet with. The plays are often the secondary rather than primary objects of Belsey's attention in the sense that passages and themes are discussed not so much for themselves as for the light they throw on the complexity and ambivalence of the titular theme.

Second, Belsey's "exposé" (the tabloid implications of this term are all wrong) is not "comprehensive" but narrowly and indeed productively focused on the connection "between the emergence of family values" in early modern Reformation England "and the increasing perception of the loving family as a place of danger" (23). She traces this connection through representations of the family in "Shakespeare's plays, English visual culture of the sixteenth and seventeenth centuries, and interpretations of the Book of Genesis in the period." The visual materials are drawn from illustrated Bibles, tracts, marriage chests, valances, bedposts, funeral monuments, and verbal as well as visual representations of the Dance of Death. Their common burden is that although "marriage is synonymous with a happy ending, married love is shown to give way to murderous jealousy, and sibling rivalry leads to violence and death." The troubled diachrony of "the story of the nuclear family told in these texts and images" determines not only Belsey's

selective and strategic discussions of Shakespeare but also the narrative structure of *Shakespeare and the Loss of Eden*. In each of the four chapters that
follow the methodological introduction, the selection and discussion of plays
is determined by one phase of this story as it moves "from romance [Chapter
2, featuring *Love's Labour's Lost* and *As You Like It*] through marital conflict
[Chapters 3 and 4, featuring *Cymbeline* and *The Winter's Tale*] to parenthood
[Chapter 4, *The Winter's Tale* again] and the relations between children
[Chapter 5, featuring *Hamlet*]" (xv). Since this is not only a book about early
modern domestic ideology but also a book that expressly intervenes in a current debate—Belsey's "essay in cultural history . . . is put forward as a reser-
vation about the call for the restoration of family values in our own society"
(176)—three of the four chapters containing discussions of the plays focus
on the darker aspects of the ambivalent domestic model.[1]

Third, to say that Belsey points out "unforeseen affinities" between the
present and the early modern past is at best only partially true. Although she
argues that our current sense of family values and their ambivalence originated in the culture of the sixteenth-century England and the Reformation,
her theoretical investments and critique are based on the premise of insur-
mountable historical difference. This premise underwrites an approach that
diverges from those attempted by "living history" and "conventional historiography." She begins by wittily staging her own embarrassment at the contradictions of "a heritage spectacle" in which Llanchaiach Fawr, a sixteenth-
century manor house near Cardiff, was in recent years restored and turned
into a "living history museum." Its "you are there" show puts on display
the domestic routine of a seventeenth-century family and invites visitors to
"experience" daily life as it was lived in the house during the critical decade
of the 1640s. Where the living history museum tries to revive the past in its
pastness, conventional historiography constructs narratives that translate the
"unfamiliar language" of the past into the present so as to recover it "in its
truth as an object of knowledge" (4–5). On the one hand, the scenario pro-
jected by the actors who play seventeenth-century servants forces the modern
observer "to cross the boundary in one direction" only, to enter the past in a
manner that deprives her "of any intelligible reference to the present," so
that she has "no secure place to speak from," no way to contextualize that
past representation in terms of her own interests and interpretations (3).
"Conventional historiography, on the other hand, translates the past into the
present" so that "what is lost is the pastness of the past, its otherness" (5).

Rejecting these alternatives, *Shakespeare and the Loss of Eden* aims "to
interpret, from [the standpoint of] the present, the complex, plural, contradictory character of a past culture . . . displayed" in visual as well as verbal and
fictional as well as nonfictional representations (xv). Belsey elaborates a thesis she had discussed briefly and intermittently in two previous studies, *The
Subject of Tragedy* and *Desire: Love Stories in Western Culture,* the thesis

that during the English Reformation the affective nuclear family built on "the institution of permanent marriage . . . becomes quite explicitly an ideological apparatus" through which the state strives to organize, control, and maintain surveillance over its population.[2] In the present study Belsey develops this argument in terms of three objectives.

The first is "to historicize and thus denaturalize family values" (xiv). Belsey begins by noting that during the sixteenth century the emergent English state and its local parishes sought to keep their populations in order by "encouraging people to settle in stable groups" centered in the nuclear family unit. In the same period the Reformation clergy seized on "the ideal of the affective nuclear family" (xiv) as "a new way of perfection" that would "replace the now discredited monastic celibacy. Family values became the object of intense propaganda, and of the anxiety that the reconstruction of any value system necessarily creates." We today "are the direct heirs" to this reconstruction and to the anxieties structurally built into it—anxieties partly fueled by "the proposition that there is only one proper ['natural'] way to arrange our sexual relations" (xiii).

Belsey's second objective involves a challenge to the convention "that we should interpret fiction in the light of its context" or "background." She wishes to controvert the convention by showing how Shakespeare's plays help not only to constitute but also to critique their background—how they, alongside (and no less than) nonfictional texts, "participate in the construction and affirmation of [cultural] meanings in the period," and in their interrogation (xiv–xv). The target here is the familiar iconographer's fallacy, the fallacy of moral overdetermination: "Are women enjoined to submission in the homiletic literature? It seems to follow that we are invited to condemn women who assert a position in the plays, however little support we find for this view in the fictional texts themselves" (xiv). Belsey is at her epigrammatic best when comparing the different contributions of the plays and tomb sculpture to the discourse of family values:

> Tombs show what the family wanted the world to see: the plays show what they might have preferred to conceal. The tombs are formal, ceremonial; the plays are popular entertainment. But in one sense, the plays and the monuments tell the same story. The project of the tombs is to transcend time and stabilize an ideal in a single image; the plays, by contrast, set out to sustain the attention of an audience by deferring stability for five acts. At the same time, the plays take it for granted that their audiences recognize the values against which deviations from the ideal can be measured. (95)

The third objective is to demonstrate the viability of an interpretive practice, an approach to cultural history, that avoids the linguistic obsession mistakenly imputed to poststructuralist theory, which, Belsey reminds us, privileges not language per se but rather "the signifying process." She uses the informative if not catchy rubric "history at the level of the signifier" (5) to distinguish her approach from those of living history and conventional historiography (4–5). The phrase is meant to pick out a cultural history based on the interpretation of visual and verbal representations, potential "texts" that may themselves be interpretations rather than innocent or transparent evidence of the meanings and values they signify.[3]

Belsey goes on to note that in emphasizing the opacity, the inconsistencies, the negative capability, of Shakespearean and other fictions, the approach she proposes differs from several features of the new historicism whose "commitment to cultural history" she otherwise shares: its tendency "to treat texts as relatively transparent," its reliance on functionalist models of integration borrowed from anthropological theory, and its cognate reliance on the use of the anecdote to shift attention from the diachronic instability of cultural moments to their synchronic homogeneity (18–19). A fourth difference may be added to these. She claims to have been following in the "post-Cartesian" footsteps of Foucault, Derrida, and Lacan (Foucault's "identification of the coercive potential of norms," Derrida's "analysis of meaning," Lacan's "account of the human condition," 24–25).[4] In my opinion, Derridean and Lacanian moves are more central to her interpretive practice than is the Foucauldian—or quasi-Foucauldian—orientation that characterizes much of what goes by the name of new historicism. This is because her approach to cultural history is better attuned to the precise etymological sense of the term, "anecdote"—an-ec-dota, something "not given out"—for, as she insists, "the problem of history is not the real, but our account of it, our record of its past, which is always delimited by the signifier" (12). The best that history at the level of the signifier can do is to fix the signifiable past "momentarily, provisionally, and ineffectually . . . in the present text" as a signified that is expressly "differential and differentiated"—a signified that designates as its referent something "other than it [the signified] is, no more than the lost cause of its own representation" (176).[5]

This vexed relation to the signifiable object at once designated and occulted by its signified is beautifully illustrated in Belsey's discussion of *Hamlet*. Her rhetorically and conceptually powerful conflation of images of the first murder and the Dance of Death with *Hamlet* produces uncanny vibrations. Like Death in the *Dans Macabre*, she argues, the Ghost returns from "the undiscover'd country" and summons Hamlet to lethal and self-imperiling revenge by appealing to the ethical imperatives of family values: "Whatever made us think of marriage as closure, or associate the parental relationship with the promise of security? The family is a place of pasison. . . . Family values . . . enmesh Hamlet in a web of anxiety, deceit, and death: tragedy stems from the commitment the family elicits" (173–74). Belsey prepares for this reading of Hamlet's dilemma by commenting brilliantly on the "urgent, hectic energy" (155) with which dancing Death intrudes upon life and on the way this image reflects Hamlet's longing and terror as he contemplates the alternatives that confront him: the fear of eternal punishment after death or the foreverness of nothing.

I have some minor reservations about aspects of *Shakespeare and the Loss of Eden* that I want to register now, before considering the larger project to which it contributes and by which it is informed. The first concerns Belsey's assertion, quoted in part above, that Shakespeare's plays "participate in the construction and affirmation of meanings in the period" and that she intends to treat them "alongside non-fictional texts of the period, rather than identify one as explanatory background to the other." Nonfictional texts—"accounts of the family, domestic conduct books"—"are no more neutral, . . . no more representative of their culture, than fiction" (xiv–xv). Construed as an interpretive guideline, this welcome recourse to the "fiction in the archives" approach suggests that nonfictional texts will be accorded the kind of attention—the kind of suspicious reading—elicited by fictional texts, and it leads me to expect suspicious accounts of the plays that will provide models of Belsey's accounts of the visual "texts."

It turns out, however, that the book is inconsistent on this score. In the chapters on *The Winter's Tale* and *Hamlet* the reading of the visual materials seems intended chiefly to throw light on or settle problems represented in the plays, but in the other two chapters the treatment of the plays is less fully developed, more prdictable, than that of the visual materials. Belsey succeeds impressively throughout in showing how those materials render the full complexity of the Genesis story of the Fall and the first family, and thus bring out the difficulties that the Reformers' idealizing representations of marriage and family values tend to downplay or evade. But the attention devoted to *Cymbeline* in chapter 3 is perfunctory—a bare-bones history-of-ideas episode in an otherwise rich interpretive study. To a lesser degree this also holds for the discussions of *As You Like It* and *Love's Labor's Lost* in chapter 2. In these chapters the accounts of the plays are too often limited to passages taken out of context and treated as contributions to a cultural consensus in which the dangers of the family values model are recognized.

The discussion of parenthood and *The Winter's Tale* in chapter 4 strikes a better balance, though it is marred by a curiously flat set of speculations about the light the conventions of tomb sculpture may throw on the quesiton of whether the play presents the enstatued Hermione as an effigy (116–20). The speculations nevertheless serve a purpose: they bolster the argument against the banality of the realist interpretation in which, as Stephen Greenblatt puts it, "Hermione has been sulking for sixteen years."[6] Belsey had used *The Winter's Tale* in her first book, *Critical Practice,* to exemplify the "interrogative" as opposed to the "classic realist" text: the former is "increasingly dismissive of its own pretensions to truth," and emphasizes "the incredibility of what the audience is being asked to believe."[7] Now, in revisiting the play, she considers the effects of its interrogative features on its representation of family values and concludes that the incredibility of the Hermione episode allows for a more devastating "comment . . . on family values then or now" (120).

The Winter's Tale is indeed devastating because the very extravagance of either possibility (miraculous resurrection or sixteen years of seclusion) comments on the extravagance—and thus the bad faith—of everyone's intense, awkward, and vaguely skeptical desire to end happily. Belsey's focus in *Critical Practice* was on the formal phenomenon of a text that "draws attention to its own implausibility" (101). In *Shakespeare and the Loss of Eden* the same phenomenon is shown to sharpen our sense that the positive model of family values is equally implausible: *The Winter's Tale* is about the desperate urge to enjoy the benefits and escape the unhappy truths of bad family values by turning them into good theater. The theater, Greenblatt remarks in his discussion of the same episode, "is the place . . . where those things are permitted that the authorities have ruled illicit"[8]—or, as Belsey tartly puts it, the place where "family values [can be made to] represent another instance of the triumph of hope over experience" (*Shakespeare and the Loss of Eden*, 121).

2.

Catherine Belsey's methodological consistency and rigor may not get the press they deserve because, as I note at the beginning of this review, she makes do with ordinary language that is wonderfully lucid and because she has a remarkable ability to put complex and sophisticated notions into play in economically phrased and compactly developed arguments. This presentational modesty is genuine, but it is also deceptive. Belsey is that rarest of birds, a toughminded romantic, at once a close reader and a far-seeker. For more than two decades she's been following her star on an intellectual quest that has taken her through heavy French weather into a critical clearing all her own. In this clearing she has gradually unpacked the consequences of an interpretive strategy that makes her work both unique and vitally important. The strategy consists in identifying, denaturalizing, and problematizing dominant cultural discourses, and in establishing their historical interrelatedness: the discourse of common sense in *Critical Practice* (1980), the discourse of liberal humanism in *The Subject of Tragedy* (1985), the discourse of family values in *Shakespeare and the Loss of Eden*.

Early in *Critical Practice,* Belsey defines the term I just repeated several times, the term I consider to be not only the basic building block of her approach to interpretation but also the germinal form of what she now calls history at the level of the signifier:

A discourse is a domain of language-use, a particular way of talking (and writing and thinking). A discourse involves certain shared assumptions which appear in the formulations that characterize it. . . . Ideology is inscribed in discourse in the sense that it is literally written or spoken in it; it is not a separate element which exists independently in some free-floating realm of "ideas" and is subsequently embodied in words, but a way of thinking, speaking, experiencing.[9]

Belsey argues that under so expressly post-Saussurian a definition even "common sense" is a discourse, which is to say that, far from being "the collective and timeless wisdom" it seems to be, it is "ideologically and discursively constructed, rooted in a specific historical situation and operating in conjunction with a particular social formation" (3).[10] In articulating this concept she combines a variant of the Althusserian concept of ideology with a Lacanian concept of subjectivity as "linguistically and discursively constructed and displaced across the range of discourses in which the concrete individual participates" (61). Following Lacan, she locates the conundrums of signification and representation in a double distinction, first, between the "concrete individual" and the subject of/in discourse, and second, between the signified in the discursive or symbolic order and its referent in *the real* that transcends discourse.

The second distinction gives rise to the apparition of something *an-ec-dota* that exceeds the reach of the writing, signification, discourse, or textuality it provokes, and that nevertheless leaves its mark. Lacan's term for the way the absence of the real is represented in the symbolic order is the *object petit à,* "that other element that takes the place of what the subject is— symbolically—deprived of. . . . [It is] not the object of desire but the object *in* desire. . . . Something becomes an object in desire when it takes the place of what by its very nature remains concealed from the subject."[11] Belsey had always been attentive to this correlation between excess and desire, but it became the keynote to her history at the level of the signifier in *Desire: Love Stories in Western Culture* (1994). "Desire is in excess of the organism"; in "a human life divided between the unmasterable symbolic and the unreachable, inextricable real," desire "is what remains unspoken" in discourse (5, 60). Yet far from being "given" or universal or unmediated and thus "indifferent to the signifier" (8), desire is born in the gap, the *différance,* between signs and the presences they signify but conspicuously fail to reproduce. It is "the location of resistances to the norms, proprieties and taxonomies of the cultural order" (6).

Since culture is "the regime of the signifier" and "desire is an effect of the signifier," it follows that desire "has its own political history" (5, 18, 134) and that this history can be explored at the level of the signifier. Because of four studies mentioned above consider different moments and features of this history, they compose into a single large ongoing project.[12] Belsey's interlocking expositions make it clear that common sense is the discourse of liberal humanism dehistoricized (or, more pointedly, depoliticized) and that the discourse of family values is the emergent one of liberal humanism.[13] At the same time this cultural history unfolds within the ambience of feminist critique, which is a central feature of Belsey's interpretive strategy. The story she tells is "the sad history of collaboration between liberalism and sexism which defines the western family from the seventeenth century to the present."[14] Liberal humanism may well propose "that the subject is the free, unconstrained author of meaning and action, the origin of history," but "women in Britain for most of the sixteenth and seventeenth centuries were not fully any of these things" as liberal humanism continually failed "to deliver the promised equality of access to power" (222).

In her attempt to situate the origins of this "sad history" in the early modern ideology of family values Belsey develops an ingenious but generally persuasive argument about the cultural displacement of desire. Desire in the form of romantic love was not a property of the conjugal bond in the literature and culture of the medieval romances: "both sensual and rhapsodic . . . it has as yet little to do with social institutions or political stability" (*Desire,* 108). The significant tension was not the Victorian one between adultery and marriage. Rather it centered on "the contradictory imperatives of love and honor" (*Desire,* 99). Love no less than chivalry was a secular "value" and both had distinct if conflicting "codes of appropriate behavior" (117). And if it was "dangerous and destructive" it was not "domestic" (115) because at that time the operative unit was the dynastic family instituted for reasons or functions that often demanded husbands to be older, sometimes much older, than their wives.[15]

Twelfth-century romances "show no sympathy with loveless marriages: jealous old husbands who lock up their wives deserve to lose them, and in these circumstances no guilt appears to attach to an adulterous wife" (107). This is what Belsey calls the "absolutist version of marriage" in which women are expressly reduced to "objects of exchange and the guarantee of dynastic continuity" (*Subject of Tragedy,* 192). "Part of the project of the early modern romance of marriage," therefore, was "to bring desire in from the cold: to moralize and domesticate a destabilizing passion, confining it within the safety of the loving family. Dynastic marriage must have been an anxious business, especially with so many adulterous love stories in circulation idealizing unfaithfulness" (*Shakespeare,* 81). The shift from the absolutist to the liberal-humanist version presupposed a change from the "ancestor-focused patrilineage organized around agnatic lines of descent," a structure in which women were formally and structurally (if not actually) marginalized, to the more compact and narrowly circumscribed conjugal family unit in which the position of woman/wife/mother as a kind of *secunda inter pares* was formally and structurally (if not actually) central.[16]

There was never sexual equality in any regime, of course, but the inequality of women to men and of wives to husbands became more conspicuous (and thus potentially more problematic) in a model that promised or demanded a measure of equality because it made the reciprocity of desire, affection, and romantic love normative.[17] Thus it was only when desire in the form of romantic love was captured, co-opted, *contained*, as the basis of marriage and the affective guarantor of family values, that women were formally allocated their proper place and unequal rights "in the bosom of the family."[18] But if, in the inaugural phase of this development, domestic conduct literature predictably defines and defends the ideal while evading its problems, the drama and poetry of the period are more discerning and therefore more skeptical (200–201). "Historically, this is the moment when the intensity of erotic experience is in the process of being regularized and sanctified as the basis of domestic life and family values," and so "early modern love poetry" is "less certain . . . than the Victorians [would be] about the social value of the heterosexual nuclear couple," and "may perhaps be read as indicating that true love is not, after all, quite so simple" (*Desire,* 134–35). This argument, most fully developed in *Desire,* is revisited in *Shakespeare and the Loss of Eden* when Belsey shows that although "descendants of the medieval stereotype" of the jealous husband "survive into early modern drama . . . what is new in *Othello, Cymbeline* and *The Winter Tale's* . . . is the direct connection between romantic marriage and sexual jealousy" (*Shakespeare,* 104). Shining a Freudian/Lacanian light on the equivocality of desire represented in the language of *The Winter Tale's* pastoral episode, she concludes that the play, depicts desire as "an improbable basis for the discipline that marriage is expected to entail," and that, "[a]s *The Winter's Tale* indicates, the most helpless victims of love-turned-hate are the children" (127).

Belsey's thesis about the domestication of desire enables her to show that when Shakespeare, Donne, and their contemporaries depict the cost incurred or the difficulty encountered or the bad faith betrayed by the actors in this version of the family romance, the depictions don't necessarily reflect a profound insight into human nature. Rather they spring from an ironic yet sympathetic engagement with the pressures imposed on those actors by relatively recent changes in a set of institutional discourses. Just here, however, I have a problem with *Shakespeare and the Loss of Eden.* The account of Shakespeare is one of several reflectors of or pathways into the ideological contradictions and ambivalence that characterize the institutional discourse of family values. But an "institutional discourse" existing apart from its various discursive representations in visual and verbal form is a pure schema or "ideal type," semantically specific but semiotically abstract. The notion that large-scale changes in institutional discourses can be charted at the level of the schema is a notion basic to the fields of conventional historiography and intellectual history Belsey criticizes, fields whose practitioners tend to let the

schema dominate and determine the attention they give to its various embodi-
ments at the level of the signifier. Yet it is only at this level, according to the
theory of discourse developed in *Critical Practice,* that justice can be done
to the ideological dimension of a discourse.

To make this constraint explicit, Belsey's theory requires a *meta*-compo-
nent, a discourse of discourse, that is, a discourse of the signifier. This would
include not only the "domain of [English] language-use" and the "particular
way of talking (and writing and thinking)" it makes possible but also, in the
case of Shakespeare, the domain of "[public] theater-use."[19] In *Desire,* for
example, Belsey's supple reading of Donne's Elegy XIX and other poems
dwells on the importance of the speaker's "claim to mastery of the possibilities of signifying practice" (*Desire,* 138). Because his "minute attention to
the perplexities of desire" (149) is indistinguishable from his minute attention to, his delight in, the perplexities of syntax and rhetoric, the interaction
between these two discursive registers produces a wryly reflexive performance in which the speaker parades, submits to, and mocks the intensity of his
desire. Paradoxically, Donne's poems dramatize the danger and instability of
desire ("noble and thrilling exactly in so far as it rejects common sense,"
142) at the very moment in history during which desire "becomes the basis
of a lifetime of concord" in "the modern nuclear family" (147). Belsey
deftly demonstrates how "the uncertainty of the lover" is "registered in the
indeterminacies of the texts" (146), how the conflicts of meaning and feeling
dramatized by Donne's play with the discourse of the signifier identifies
"problems that proponents (then and now) of family values centered on the
conjugal couple generally prefer to forget" (*Desire,* 149).

My problem with *Shakespeare and the Loss of Eden* is that it contains too
few passages comparable in density and "minute attention" with the readings
of Donne and other authors in *Desire.* Belsey doesn't dwell enough on
Shakespeare's engagement with the discourses of language use and theater—on his grammatical, rhetorical, citational, and metatheatrical play—or
on the way this engagement qualifies his negotiation with the discourse of
family values.[20] Admittedly, her decision to concentrate on a "multimedial"
and consensual critique of the institutional discourse of family values affected this: she chose to let the demands of the *Loss of Eden* theme determine
the extent and level of the commentary on Shakespeare. But this decision
carries the cost of what I consider to be a missed opportunity—a Lacanian
opportunity—which I'll try to describe in my concluding remarks.

In summarizing her discussion of *As You Like It* and *Love's Labor's Lost,*
Belsey first remarks that "early modern stage lovers perform an identity by
citation, impersonality, theatricality itself" (49), and then rephrases the statement in the more general terms provided by contemporary thought: "Lovers
come to reproduce the conventions of their culture by learning to enact the
identities it prescribes. We are what we are, twentieth-century psychoanalysis

maintains, in response to the gaze of other people" (50). This leads to a quick glance at Lacan's treatment of seduction, the gaze, and the dialectics of identification (50–51). Although the first sentence in the second passage I just quoted is marked as a twentieth-century (Lacanian) thesis, Belsey has just spent the better part of the second chapter arguing that this is precisely what Shakespeare's lovers are shown to do, that is, "reproduce the conventions of their culture by learning to enact the identities it prescribes." The quotation marks are in effect Shakespeare's. Her compact description of this cultural and theatrical practice is a controlled caricature, a cartoon, of the practices and motives of identification depicted in Lacanian theory. Yet a serious discussion of Lacan's views of identification and the mirror stage doesn't occur until more than two-thirds of the way through the book, and then, only briefly (137–38).

In the *Winter's Tale* and *Hamlet* chapters Belsey turns to Freud's *Beyond the Pleasure Principle* and makes excellent use of Little Ernst's *fort/da* game to suggest how children deal with, and revenge themselves on, their disappearing parents and how the plays similarly dance with, and try to resist being mastered by, their spectators and readers (103–4, 166–72). She is fascinated by, and fascinating on, the aporias of Freudian and Lacanian performances whose "interrogative" character she frequently highlights, as when she outlines the *fort/da* structure of Freud's own text, mediates it through Derrida's equally aporetic dance with it in *The Post Card,* and offers that as a model for the way *Hamlet* seductively teases and dances with its audience (169–71). The arousal of desire produced by the aporias such texts enact is both the goal and the effect of the interpretive practice Belsey embraces (or at least dances with): history at the level of the signifier. It is also the major objective of the Shakespearean and Lacanian texts. I would therefore have liked to see her attempt to consolidate her Freudian and Lacanian pictures of desire, identification, emulation, and generational dynamics into a hypothetical formulation that would precede and inform all the interpretations in *Shakespeare and the Loss of Eden.*

There is a historical rationale for this move, and Belsey touches on it when she mentions, almost in passing, why it is not anachronistic to apply Lacan's "account of the formation of identity" to early modern structures of acculturation. It is because that account, with its accent on mimetic ambivalence, aggressivity, and performativity, speaks directly to the emphasis on—and the "duality" of—"emulation" in early modern pedagogy: "admiration and imitation are hard to distinguish from their opposites, competitiveness and jealousy, so that the practice of emulation is at once valuable and dangerous, a source of instruction and a rivalry to be feared" (138).[21] It is also because Lacan commits these vicissitudes and adventures of the subject to the discourse of the signifier, which humanist pedagogy in England—with its attention divided between English and Latin, the mother and father tongues—famously worried.

The relevance of Lacanian theory to humanist pedagogy has often been noted by scholars who, in recent years, have questioned the hypothesis about the bracing efforts on masculine identity formation of Latin language study as a rite of passage into manhood—a hypothesis first put forth by Walter Ong in 1959, restated with pseudo-Lacanian variations by William Kerrigan in 1980, and accepted by Bruce R. Smith in 1991.[22] In Kerrigan's words, "Latin was the gift of a severe, if ultimately forthcoming, father. It was an initiation into the mysteries of his ways, and the ardors of . . . imitation . . . finally yielded to possession. . . . Veneration was rewarded by a new and male articulation of the ego."[23] This opinion, oddly hoisted up the flagpole of Lacanian theory, was easy to demystify when scholars looked more closely at the pedagogical sense of such mimetic ardors and at the archival accounts of or by the humanist masters who supposedly stood in as models of patriarchal authority. The revised story generated from the more context-sensitive standpoint of queer theory may be concisely illustrated by Alan Stewart's comment that "the value of the educational experience of a young man as a rite of passage or an act of institution—the making of the man—is fundamentally threatened by that experience itself."[24] It seems to me that the next move in this revisionary project is to reintroduce the context of family values in its new Belseian form and then see what happens. It also seems to me that Belsey is the critic to do it.

When I took out my copy of *Critical Practice* to begin this review I found scrawled in the flyleaf the following breathless, or grammatically untenable, puff: "no one in the past two decades or so has produced an analysis and profile of criminal practice and its place in culture with more depth of insight, lucidity of expression—unparalleled force and directness—sympathy of understanding yet critical distance." I must have written that some ten or twelve years ago and late at night. Now that I've read a much larger sample of Catherine Belsey's work and said what I have to say about it, I see no reason to change my opinion.

Notes

1. Her expressions of antipathy to the ideology of family values preached by contemporary conservative movements predate this book. For a direct and polemical statement, see Belsey, *Desire: Love Stories in Western Culture* (Oxford: Blackwell, 1994), 6: "family values, cemented by true love, legitimize oppressive state policies and inadequate social expenditure."

2. Belsey, *The Subject of Tragedy: Identity and Difference in Renaissance Drama* (London: Methuen, 1985), 145. See also *Desire,* 6, 134–35, 149–49, 158.

In *Private Matters and Public Culture,* Lena Cowen Orlin explores what happens at the interface of the domestic and political orders when the taxonomies and dichotomies of ideological prescription are skewed by their embeddedness in household "stuff," which includes not only goods and possessions but also architecture and domestic spaces. *Shakespeare and the Loss of Eden* complements Orlin's account by attending to what happens when similar prescriptive structures are skewed by their embeddedness in visual and verbal texts. It also complements Richard Helgerson's study, in *Adulterous Alliances,* of the ways in which conflicts between the literary genres of domestic drama and history (or tragedy) represent and interact with conflicts between the institutions of the household and the state. See Lena Cowen Orlin, *Private Matters and Public Culture* (Ithaca: Cornell University Press, 1994). Richard Helgerson, *Adulterous Alliances: Home, State, and History in Early Modern European Drama and Painting* (Chicago: University of Chicago Press, 2000). For Helgerson's responses to the work of Orlin and Belsey, *inter alia,* see "Murder in Faversham: Holinshed's Impertinent History," in *The Historical Imagination in Early Modern Britain: History, Rhetoric, and Fiction, 1500–1800,* ed. Donald R. Kelley and David Harris Sacks (Cambridge: Cambridge University Press, 1997), 133–58.

3. For an earlier description of this approach, see *The Subject of Tragedy,* 2–5.

4. She is anything but uncritical to her deployment of Lacanism and Derridean moves. See, for example, the powerful critique of Freud, Lacan, and Derrida in the third chapter of *Desire* (42–71). Belsey's indebtedness to the work of Julia Kristeva is chiefly evident in *Desire.*

5. Belsey's acknowledged source for this idea is Lacan's statement that the signifier "has an active function in determining certain effects in which the signifiable appears as submitting to its mark" (176, cited from Jacques Lacan, *Écrits,* trans. Alan Sheridan [London: Tavistock, 1977], 284). See also *Desire,* 55.

6. Stephen Greenblatt, *Hamlet in Purgatory* (Princeton: Princeton University Press, 2001), 203.

7. Belsey, *Critical Practice* (London: Methuen, 1980), 100–102.

8. Greenblatt, *Hamlet in Purgatory,* 203.

9. Belsey, *Critical Practice,* 5.

10. As Belsey smartly observes in *The Subject of Tragedy,* "the common sense" is etymologically akin to "the shared meanings" (9–10).

11. Jacques Lacan, "Desire and the Interpretation of Desire in *Hamlet,*" trans. James Hulbert, in *Literature and Psychoanalysis, The Question of Reading: Otherwise,* ed. Shoshana Felman (Baltimore: Johns Hopkins University Press, 1982), 15, 28. As Joan Copjec puts it, "it is necessary to *say* that the real is absented, to *declare* its impossibility. The symbolic, in other words, must include the negation of what it is not": Joan Copjec, "Vampires, Breast-Feeding, and Anxiety," *October* 58 (fall 1991): 28. A negation, or an absence, that declares itself is an example of the trope I have elsewhere described as *conspicuous exclusion.*

12. I say nothing about Belsey's *John Milton: Language, Gender, Power* (1988) because I haven't yet read it.

13. "Depoliticized" is intended to evoke the work of Roland Barthes, who is an important presence as an exemplary post-Saussurian reader in *Critical Practice* and *Desire,* though his influence is less evident in *The Subject of Tragedy* and *Shakespeare and the Loss of Eden.*

On the definition of liberal humanism and its association with common sense and sexism, see *The Subject of Tragedy,* 7–10, 86–92, 192–93, 199, 216–21.

14. *The Subject of Tragedy,* 199–200.

15. "The dignity of marriage is . . . not based on the satisfaction accruing to the couple; rather it derives from the vital social function marriage fulfills in bringing kin groups together and in preserving peace among them": so David Herlihy and Christiane Klapisch-Zuber paraphrase the view expressed in 1053 by Peter Damian in "De parentelae gradibus." See their *Tuscans and their Families: A Study of the Florentine Catasto of 1427* (New Haven: Yale University Press, 1985), 339.

16. David Herlihy, *Medieval Households* (Cambridge: Harvard University Press, 1985), 82.

17. Barbara Correll comments on this in "Malleable Material, Models of Power: Woman in Erasmus's 'Marriage Group' and *Civilty in Boys,*" *English Literary History* 57 (1990): 241–62, especially 241–42. On the pictorial evidence of the wife's changing and uncertain position in the conjugal household, see Diane Owen Hughes, "Representing the Family: Portraits and Purposes in Early Modern Italy," *Journal of Interdisciplinary History* 17 (1986): 7–38. Hughes's evidence is chiefly from Genoa and Italian merchant families, but her analysis picks out precisely the contradictions on which Belsey focuses.

18. *The Subject of Tragedy,* 192. In this liberal-humanist version of marriage women are represented as "autonomous subjects freely exercising their power to choose a husband"—an exercise putatively conducted "on the basis of romantic love"—"and becoming partners in the affective family." But, Belsey styptically continues, the plays and the domestic conduct books of the Restoration period show "women as free to choose to the extent that they are free to acquiesce," and the price they pay for the apparent upgrading of their position in the family "is their exclusion from the political," since, after 1660, "the family progressively becomes a privileged private realm of retreat from a public world increasingly experienced as hostile and alien" (ibid., 192–93).

19. Belsey doesn't historicize the discourse of history at the level of the signifier beyond establishing its roots in post-Saussurian discourse. But she could have found support for a much earlier point of origin of that discourse, and also of the discourse of the signifier that underwrites it, had she taken into account Judith Anderson's *Words That Matter: Linguistic Perception in Renaissance English* (Stanford: Stanford University Press, 1996). Anderson is concerned with what Renaissance writers, theorists, and lexicographers wanted language to do and why they thought it mattered so much. Taking as a point of departure Ian Hacking's *Why does Language Matter to Philosophy?* (Cambridge: Cambridge University Press, 1975), she argues that his emphasis on the early modern "heyday of ideas," which he distinguished from "the heyday of sentences" in modern language philosophy, should be reunderstood as a heyday of *subsentential* units of various kinds (individual words, proverbs, lexical entries, rhetorical tropes and schemes, etc.). She goes on to demonstrate how this subsentential emphasis led to the objectification of words, the increasing sense of their substantiality and weight as *things,* and she explores the effects of the emphasis not only on individual signifiers as objects of definition but also on subsentential units of *sentence,* i.e., sententiousness, and on the meaningful expressions she calls "frozen

words." Anderson attributes the cultural foregrounding of these units "in part but in *significant* part" to "print and lexicography," which contributed to the shaping of a new "linguistic universe," new verbal practices, and a new set of attitudes toward language. In everything but name, then, her account gestures toward the histories both of the discourse of the signifier and of the discourse of history at the level of the signifier.

20. Given my track record on the question of Shakespeare's theater I suppose it's strange to find me commenting on anyone else's inattention to theater. But there it is.

21. The explicit context of this remark is sibling rivalry in *Hamlet* but Belsey's discussion features displacements of rivalry from one dyad to another: from brother/ brother to son/father to nephew/uncle.

22. Walter J. Ong, "Latin Language as a Renaissance Puberty Rite," *Studies in Philology* 56 (1959): 103–24, reprinted in *Rhetoric, Romance and Technology: Studies in the Interaction of Expression and Culture* (Ithaca: Cornell University Press, 1981), 113–41; *Fighting for Life: Contest, Sexuality and Consciousness* (Ithaca: Cornell University Press, 1981), 126–39; William Kerrigan, "The Articulation of the Ego in the English Renaissance," in *The Literary Freud: Mechanisms of Defense and the Poetic Will,* ed. Joseph H. Smith (New Haven: Yale University Press, 1980), 262–308; Bruce R. Smith, *Homosexual Desire in Shakespeare's England: A Cultural Poetics* (Chicago: University of Chicago Press, 1991), 82–86.

23. Kerrigan, "The Articulation of the Ego in the English Renaissance," 285–86.

24. Alan Stewart, *Close Readers: Humanism and Sodomy in Early Modern England* (Princeton: Princeton University Press, 1997), 102. Stewart supports this generalization with the following example: "The 'breeching' of a boy was not only the entry into his education, but also his institution as a man. . . . For this major psychological event . . . to be temporarily reversed by the schoolmaster in a new form of breeching, to expose the boy for beating, can therefore be seen as a radical form of 'unmanning'" (ibid.). See also Richard Halpern, *The Poetics of Primitive Accumulation: English Renaissance Culture and the Genealogy of Capital* (Ithaca): Cornell University Press, 1991), 21–60; Mary Thomas Crane, *Framing Authority: Sayings, Self, and Society in Sixteenth-Century England* (Princeton: Princeton University Press, 1993), 77–92 and passim. In a work in progress entitled "Imitating Schoolboys" Lynn Enterline argues that Lacan's mirror-stage account of emulation has much in common with Shakespeare's critique of subject and gender formation in humanist pedagogy, and therefore that Lacanian theory can illuminate the perils of emulation and imitation in humanist pedagogy more accurately, more fully, than does the theory advanced by Ong and Kerrigan. My comments in this review are indebted to Enterline's study and I'm grateful to her for sharing it with me.

Shakespeare's Theatre of War, by Nick de Somogyi. Aldershot, Eng.; Brookfield, Vt.: Ashgate, 1998. Pp. 296.

Reviewer: CURTIS BREIGHT

The New Historicist view of state power in early modern England is increasingly untenable, as invaluable books such as Nick de Somogyi's *Shake-*

speare's Theatre of War help to reveal. We have been assailed since the 1980s with a modified version of the Myth of Elizabeth I whereby the Virgin Queen (replacing the Virgin Mary) is the focal point of power, ruling through representations and illusions, reigning by consent rather than coercion. Anyone who cares to peel away this myth will discover (as I have attempted to demonstrate in my own *Surveillance, Militarism and Drama in the Elizabethan Era,* Basingstoke: Macmillan, 1996) that so many men were siphoned off from a small yet roiling domestic population that war served as a form of social control. Nearly relentless warfare from 1585 to 1604, along with concomitant naval and other maritime operations, consumed some 200,000 men—men who might otherwise find good reasons to question the seemingly disastrous domestic and foreign policies of the English state, especially in the miserable 1590s. Population growth, widespread poverty, and expulsion from the land were among the factors creating a mobile class of "vagabonds" and other disenfranchised people who, in theory, threatened the very foundations of the state. Such people, in the minds of the Protestant new men who ran Elizabethan England, could be usefully deployed to fight the Spanish Empire, the Irish, French Catholics, and others, on numerous fronts. When a government empties out a significant percentage of its young male population (far more significant than U.S. deployments to Vietnam), coercion can look like consent. It's difficult to raise rebellion when thousands of potential rebels are already being eliminated on an annual basis.

Hence the 1980s (and later) New Historicist mantra of a weak Elizabethan government handicapped by lack of a "police force," "standing army," and surveillance apparatus is usefully and powerfully countered by a study such as Somogyi's, all the more so because the circulation of such a mantra continues to distort the scholarly and no doubt pedagogical strategies of the next generation of academics.

Somogyi's fine book "explores the relations between drama and history, and seeks to illuminate the influence of wartime on the production of Elizabethan plays" (2). Somogyi's title, however, is a bit misleading because he addresses not only Shakespearean drama but also that of Shakespeare's contemporaries. Yet the inclusion of contemporaries such as Marlowe broadens the work and strengthens the argument, and also helps to account for Somogyi's chapter titles: "Casualties of War," "The Art of War," "Theatres of War," "Rumours of War," "Ghosts of War," and "The Question of these Wars." Although he appears to have done little research in the vast manuscript archives and even the calendars of such archives, Somogyi's erudition in other primary and in secondary sources is considerable. His bibliography is nearly forty pages long (253–67 for primary sources, 267–91 for secondary), and this alone suggests just how rich the topic is. In a sense, the many military books and news pamphlets concerning war that Somogyi lists constitute a kind of new genre paralleling the rise of drama as the predominant form of literature in Elizabethan England. Armed with this kind of evidence, regardless of how empirical the study is, Somogyi can deploy the eminent historian John Hale to imply that the reality of early modern warfare cannot simply be "thought away" (2).

Although Somogyi's political perspective—in which the Low Countries are said to be seeking independence from Spain whereas Ireland is rebelling against England—is dubious, his apparent endorsement of Geoffrey's Parker's idea that the Anglo-Spanish conflict on multiple fronts (including the New World) renders the period from 1585 to 1604 a kind of first World War is right on the mark (3). Somogyi's "chief aim," then, is "to allow a series of the period's non-'literary' texts both generally and in detail to further the interpretation of its drama" (5). To his additional credit, Somogyi's first chapter captures our attention and, one would hope, our historical empathy by focusing on a multitude of references to limbless veterans—a topic rarely addressed in scholarship but now undergoing some consideration in the new discourse of disability studies (see *Disabled Veterans in History,* ed. David Gerber, Ann Arbor: University of Michigan Press, 2000). Somogyi's intention is to analyze how "Elizabethan dramatists erected about the damaged figure of the returning soldier an ideological scaffolding that enhanced both roles [of the tragic and the comic], and which sought comparison and contrast between war and revenge, valour and villainy, hero and braggart" (13). In this chapter he also sets a pattern followed regularly throughout the book, combining loads of primary citations in a discussion not centrally focused on Shakespeare but, in this case, on the anonymous *A Larum for London* (c. 1600; performed by Shakespeare's theatrical company).

In his second chapter Somogyi details what has now become a truism in a military empire such as the United States—that war, perhaps paradoxically and/or ironically, serves to advance the health of civilization through its scientific breakthroughs. There is nothing quite like militarism to motivate the kinds of discoveries that result in secondary or tertiary uses (and so forth). Thus the first ten pages of this chapter economically cover the emerging areas such as mathematics, geography, cartography, surveying, charting, geometry, astronomy, and engineering (54–64). The chapter also demonstrates how Christopher Marlowe's *Doctor Faustus, The Jew of Malta,* and *Tamburlaine* are preoccupied with such matters. Indeed, in seeking "to reveal that the common ground between those two Elizabethan archetypes, the geographer and the playwright, extended beyond any shared authorship of a 'discription of the world'" (55), Somogyi finds it expedient to analyze that first great dramatic coup of the Elizabethan stage—both parts of *Tamburlaine*—as the focus of his argument (64–88). The two parts of *Tamburlaine* are not simply an unrelenting exercise in pragmatic geography but also a delineation of contemporary military terminology, as many critics have noted yet not fully appreciated in their dismissal of warfare's centrality to late Elizabethan culture.

Somogyi persuasively argues that "the paradoxical subject of *Tamburlaine* is war itself" (72).

Since, citing Charles Wilson's *Queen Elizabeth and the Revolt of the Netherlands* (Berkeley: University of California Press, 1970; p. 10), "Shakespeare's was an 'age of siege warfare rather than of mobile warfare'" (104), it is logical for Somogyi to claim that "the 'Pitch'd *Fields*' of Elizabethan warfare drew an almost instinctive comparison with the theatre" (100). We still refer to "theatres of war," and thus Somogyi's third chapter is perhaps best epitomized by quoting a couple sentences from p. 95: "It is not that soldiers were urged to 'play Alexander . . . in the field'; rather that theatrical methods of disguise, pretence, and deceit comprised the essence of the *Stratagemes, Sleyghtes, and Policies of Warre* by which in 1539 Richard Morysine translated the title of Frontinus's influential work. 'Speak one thing to thine enemie, but doe another', advised the author of *A Myrrour for English Souldiers* (1596, C1v); 'Always faine to have good newes that your souldiers faint not' (D1r), and (most tellingly perhaps), 'He is most wise that in cases of warre can best dissemble' (D2v)." Although Somogyi draws a dubious distinction between Shakespearean and Jonsonian viewpoints (in *Henry V* and *Every Man in His Humour,* respectively) as regards the "city's wartime training grounds" (125–26)—especially by taking Shakespeare's Chorus as straightforward—this is nevertheless a very valuable chapter due to its linkages between real and fictional military theaters.

The first two-thirds or three-quarters of Somogyi's fourth chapter are less striking than its final dozen pages (perhaps since the subject matter largely involves the genre of comedy), but the end of the chapter provides a solid payoff in its interpretation of Shakespeare's Pistol as a character whose language aligns him with sufferers of shell-shock in World War I (especially 170–72, and 174). The fifth chapter deals with the mysterious or, more specifically, the spectral character of war, especially in Thomas Kyd's *The Spanish Tragedy* and Shakespeare's *Henry V.* The reality of war is difficult enough, but it becomes even more terrifying (and powerful onstage) when the uncanny is deployed.

Somogyi's final chapter focuses on *Hamlet* and how that tragedy's complex publication history in Q1 (1603), Q2 (1604–5), and F (1623) indicate that Shakespeare was heavily influenced by the last year of Elizabethan war before the onset of Jacobean peace. It is finely ironic that *Hamlet,* a play largely enshrined in stage, critical, and cinematic history as meditative and philosophical, can be interpreted as fully preoccupied with the question of the wars of the Elizabethan state. Somogyi argues for Shakespeare's "judicious revision" of Q1 preceding the play's publication "*in extenso*" in Q2 as due to wartime pressures before change of regime. *Hamlet* displays what I tell undergraduates are "military bookends" because the tragedy is literally framed by war (from Horatio's act 1, scene 1 speech on Denmark's 24/7 preparations for war to Fortinbras's palace coup and ceremonially military burial of Hamlet's corpse at the end). But even as *Hamlet* evinces war on the macro level, it also reminds the viewer/reader of war on the micro level, as Somogyi relentlessly shows. The tragedy is constructed through a veritable vocabulary of military terminology (228–32), somewhat muted in Q1 because of Shakespeare's supposed need to create a more domesticated or less militaristic play. Somogyi's distinction among the texts, as well as his overall discussion of what he takes to be the truest one, is all the more important given how Olivier's 1948 and Zeffirelli's 1990 films are constructed *sans* Fortinbras (235). Despite Branagh's distortion of militarism and its discontents in his adaptation of *Henry V* (1989), it is to Branagh's credit that he gets it right by providing an excess of Fortinbras in his epic adaptation of *Hamlet* (1996), which Somogyi ought to cite as a counterweight to the usual directorial maneuvers.

The construction of Somogyi's book is intelligent because it forces the reader to consider the entire argument, an argument that gains strength as he marshals unrelenting evidence. If this book lacks the style of a typical New Historicist paean to the poor old Virgin Queen, it provides the kind of "Bloody Constraint" (after Theodor Meron's *Bloody Constraint: War and Chivalry in Shakespeare,* Oxford: Oxford University Press, 1998) to make any open-minded reader question New Historicist substance with regard to the considerable powers of the early modern state.

Shakespeare and the Book, by David Scott Kastan. Cambridge: Cambridge University Press, 2001. 245 pp. Hardcover: $55 ISBN: 0-521-78139-6. Paper: $20 ISBN: 0-521-78651-7

Reviewer: CYNDIA SUSAN CLEGG

David Scott Kastan offers *Shakespeare and the Book* as mediation between two tendencies in Shakespeare studies: the persistent effort "to act as if the works we have read have a reality independent of the physical texts in which we engage them" (3) and a pervasive commitment in the academy to a "stage-centered" pedagogy. Neither of these, according to Kastan, can satisfactorily engage Shakespeare's play texts as anything other than the object of our own desires. The first tendency, which has so strongly influenced a century of Shakespearean textual studies, engages the text as something that never really existed but is instead "an ideal text of an author's intentions that no materialization does (or can) bear witness to" (3). Shakespeare in performance functions similarly as the projection of desire: "In the theatre Shakespeare escapes historicity, becoming for every age a contemporary playwright, and arguably its most important one" (7). The alternative Kastan poses is not to eliminate altogether a performative approach to Shakespeare

studies but to give equal weight to the printed text in all its varied historical
interations as equally central to understanding Shakespeare and his plays. He
would have us recognize that

> text and performance are . . . not partial and congruent aspects of some unity that
> we think of as the play, but are two discrete modes of production. Performance
> operates according to a theatrical logic of its own rather than one derived from the
> text; the printed play operates accordng to a textual logic that is not derived from
> performance. . . . Neither is more or less authentic than the other, for there is no
> external reality, apart from the texts and the performances themselves, that can pro-
> vide a standard against which that authenticity might be measured. (9)

If a considerable body of critical interest has centered on recovering the performative aspects of Shakespearean drama, *Shakespeare and the Book* presents an alternative by offering a concise history of the material books of
Shakespeare's plays. In doing so, it traces the role the printing house has
played in constructing Shakespeare as perhaps the quintessential national (international?) author.

Chapter 1, which locates the printing of Shakespeare's plays in the materialistic interests of sixteenth-century printers, introduces Kastan's central
theme, that "print falsifies even as it recalls the records," which means that
"the text, like the past is never available in unmediated form" (15–16). This
chapter counters all the efforts of the "new bibliography" to locate the ideal
texts of Shakespeare's pure intention and discriminate them from all the bad
and "pirated texts." Instead, Kastan presents us with Shakespeare the playwright, who, unlike some of his peers, was indifferent to print in a city where
printers and publishers printed plays "because they could"—because they
could be printed inexpensively in quarto format, because performance created a market (however small), and because legal rights in a text belonged to
the stationer who published it and not to an idealized "author." Here Kastan
brings together his solid editorial knowledge of Shakespeare play-quartos
with an informed understanding of the material conditions of London printing at the end of the sixteenth century to dispel any illusions anyone might
still hold about Shakespeare's authorial intentions. The second chapter's account of the first folio's production shows what happened to "Shakespeare"
when printers and publishers discovered that a playwright's (the playwright's?) name could be used to sell a more expensive folio edition. This
chapter recounts the now familiar story of Heminge and Condell's achievement "of creating Shakespeare as the author he never was or wanted to be"
by claiming that theirs is the authoritative text in which plays are "Truly set
forth according to their first ORIGINALL" (71). In the process of accounting
for how the first folio was compiled, this chapter nicely restores the reputation of the Jaggards, père et fils, and makes a persuasive claim for *Henry VIII*

as Shakespeare's own. In what one might best describe as a study of the textual effects of bardolatry, the third chapter offers a useful history of Shakespearean editions from the second folio, through Augustan adaptations, to the conscientious efforts of eighteenth- and nineteenth-century editors to recover and restore Shakespeare's plays by consulting earlier editions, to Bowdler's *Family Shakespeare*. While offering little scholarly justification for Edmund Malone's and W. W. Greg's obsessive desires for the ideal Shakespeare, it does help explain them. Finally, while the first chapter explored the vagaries of Shakespeare's plays finding their way from the stage to the page, the last accounts for their flight from printed text to hypertext. This chapter, while reminding its readers of the multiple electronic forms in which Shakespeare's texts appear as well as the means by which they may be mediated, affords Kastan the opportunity to reflect on the general materiality of Shakespeare's texts—indeed of any texts. According to Kastan, the new electronic technology demands that we realize that texts of Shakespeare's plays are not self-sufficient—that they demand mediation—that all texts demand mediation: "What is perhaps most unnerving about electronic texts, then, is not merely that they are virtual but that they are no more virtual than any other text we read" (116). This, Kastan maintains, takes us to the heart of our critical understanding of literature—whether it is some ideal that no material manifestation can fully realize or whether it is something knowable only in its "specific material modes of existence" (118). Kastan embraces the latter, and in doing so, makes a case for embracing electronic texts of Shakespeare because they are no less authentic than any of the textual spaces in which Shakespeare's plays have been represented. The advantage of hypertext is that it can enrich scholarly study of the plays because it can represent simultaneously (or almost so) multiple states of the text.

A timely work, *Shakespeare and the Book* appears as substantive efforts are being made in scholarly circles to define the disciplinary nature of the "history of the book" and assess its importance. For several years more and more sessions at scholarly conferences—especially in Renaissance studies—have been dedicated to the material book, print culture, manuscript culture, and the history of reading, and recently these topics have become subjects of entire conferences at universities and academic institutions like the Folger Shakespeare Library, the Newberry, and the Huntington. Indeed, *Shakespeare and the Book* emerged from such a scholarly setting, Kastan having been invited to University College, London, to deliver the Lord Northcliffe Lectures, intended by Lord Northcliffe Professor, John Sutherland, to remedy "scholarly ignorance about book trade and publishing history technicalities" (xi). The invitation was well deserved. In recent years at Columbia University Kastan has shepherded a generation of excellent young scholars through doctoral dissertations on the history of the book in Renaissance England, and he is currently a general editor for the Arden Shakespeare. *Shakespeare and the*

Book bears the substance and form of this initial conception. Having once addressed a lecture audience's varied scholarly interests, this book continues to speak to readers with diverse levels of expertise in trade and publishing technicalities, as well as those who are familiar with textual theory and Shakespearean textual studies. The lecture format's constraints, however, appear to have led to the book becoming somewhat (and perhaps necessarily) reductive in its treatment of critical and editorial theory. The book's four chapters, presumably once each a single lecture, weave together multiple threads of scholarly investigation into Shakespeare studies, critical theory, theatrical practice, publishing, printing, trade relationships, and textual and bibliographical studies, to produce four finely crafted and beautifully written essays that are at the same time erudite and accessible. As such, this should prove especially useful in the classroom. *Shakespeare and the Book* offers an account of the editions of Shakespeare's plays, and a rationale for editorial practices, that is just as accurate—and eminently more readable—than the textual histories that appear in any of the current complete editions of Shakespeare's plays. (This should prove especially useful for a class that focuses on only a few plays using individual editions and still includes textual study.) Outside the classroom, for the Shakespearean scholar whose work has not been immersed in textual studies or the history of the book, or for the scholar of book history who has not considered its implications for Shakespeare studies, this book offers at the very least a useful synthesis, and at its best, astute and sometimes provocative formulations. There will be, however, a handful of scholars—those who have presented and heard conference papers on Shakespeare and print culture, on Shakespeare and the history of the book, or on Shakespeare and authorship—who will find some matters in *Shakespeare and the Book* somewhat familiar. This attests to the scholarly vitality and cross-fertilization attending to the history of the book at academic conferences. Many of the scholars who find familiar ground in Kastan's work are surely anticipating their own forthcoming publications in the field and will appreciate having Kastan as their peer. To the few whose work passed through the press concurrently with Kastan's, as per his "Acknowledgements," Kastan conveys his thanks (xii).

Pure Resistance: Queer Virginity in Early Modern English Drama, by Theodora A. Jankowski. Philadelphia: University of Pennsylvania Press, 2000. Pp. 283. Cloth $46.50.

Reviewer: VIVIANA COMENSOLI

Theodora Jankowski's aim in *Pure Resistance: Queer Virginity in Early Modern English Drama* is twofold: in part 1 she considers, in the context of contemporary queer theory, the history of the European discourse of virgin-

ity, beginning with its grounding in early pre-Christian asceticism and its development in Roman Catholic traditions, through to its modifications during
the Protestant Reformation; in part 2 she compares stage representations of
dissident and orthodox female virginity, focusing on plays performed in England primarily in the public theatres between 1590 and 1670. The book contributes significantly to the project of "queering the Renaissance,"[1] as well
as to the growing scholarship on premodern social constructions of virginity
and the intersection of Renaissance sociocultural discourses with stage representations of the gendered (female) body.[2]

In the introductory chapter, "Queer(y)ing Virginity: Virgins, Lesbians, and
Queers of all Types," Jankowski explores the term "queer" in relation to
contemporary queer and feminist theory and suggests that the early modern
condition of virginity can be deemed "a queer construct" (15). Acknowledging that "there were no early modern heterosexuals, homosexuals, lesbians,
gays, or bisexuals," and "no early modern queers," Jankowski argues that
queer theory nevertheless permits a consideration of the position occupied by
women who chose virginity over marriage in Reformation England "as a
queer space" (6). She defines the term "queer" as an inclusive category that
permits the exploration of "issues of sexuality that are not restricted to the
binary axis of homo- versus heterosexuality" (7) and that encompasses "a
multitude of sexual, gender, and/or erotic positioning" (10). In her survey of
some of the most influential contributors to contemporary queer theory
(among them Alexander Doty, Teresa de Lauretis, Sue Ellen Case, Eve Sedgwick, Arnold Davidson, Monique Wittig, and Marilyn Frye),[3] Jankowski
notes her particular debt to Doty, who has argued that "queerness should
challenge and confuse our understanding and uses of sexual and gender categories,"[4] and to Sedgwick, for whom "queer" refers, among other things, to
"the open mesh of possibilities, gaps, overlaps, dissonances and resonances,
laps and excesses of meaning when the constituent elements of anyone's gender, of anyone's sexuality aren't made (or *can't* be made) to signify mono-
lithically."[5] Identifying the "non-normative" gender position of female
virginity in early modern England, Jankowski argues for a queer virginity
that disrupts conventional categories and inevitably fractures "the regime of
heterosexuality" (10).

In part 1 of the book Jankowski begins by focusing on gender in pre-Reformation Europe as constructed not only in terms of the male/female binary
but also in relation to "the theological virgin/not-virgin" distinction (10).
Most early Christian and Roman Catholic women who chose permanent virginity, she argues, cannot be considered queer; in effect, they "did not need
to be queer" since medieval Europe promoted a fluid sex/gender system that
allowed "a socially/cultural/theologically acceptable place for female (and
male) virgins" (74). Medieval women were deemed to be "as capable as men
of maintaining their physical integrity," and each gender was permitted to

choose virginity as an "acceptable alternative to marriage" (10). The flexibility accorded virginity was pronounced in pre- and early Christian ascetic movements, which were radical in their views of gender relations and inclusive in their theological doctrines. Jankowski consults texts from various ascetic traditions, with an emphasis on the Gnostic scripture, in which "the ascetic space of virginity" granted to women also conferred on them the social and spiritual autonomy that in the orthodox church was granted only to men (39).[6] As further evidence of the plurality of the early Christian and medieval discourse of virginity, Jankowski cites three important developments: 1) the choice available to medieval women either to marry or join a celibate religious order; 2) the absence of prohibitions concerning previous sexual activity for widows, widowers, or unmarried individuals wishing to join a religious order; and 3) the existence of "communities of unmarried— but not necessarily never married—Beguines and married or single Third Order members" that promoted ambiguous religous/secular "living and working arrangements" (11). Jankowski's argument for the fluidity of the medieval sex/gender system and the flexibility of the space occupied by female virginity is often compelling; in her suggestion, however, that the medieval sexual economy ultimately allowed virginity "the potential to destabilize the categories of sex and gender" (11) she does not explore the extent to which the social sanctioning and regulation of virginity in the Middle Ages limited its destabilizing potential.

In her discussion of the sexual economy of early modern England, Jankowski notes that virginity was not venerated because it was no longer regarded as a permissible permanent choice for women. Whereas Roman Catholicism had sanctioned and even encouraged perpetual virginity, early humanist and Protestant discourses strongly promoted the idea of "the necessity and the inevitability of marriage" and the value of virginity solely as a "premarital condition" for women (90). Jankowski contends that one of the chief reasons for the differences between Catholic and early modern constructions of virginity is that "Protestant social organization did seem ultimately to lead to, or benefit from, the bourgeois family structure" that in England evolved chiefly as a consequence of changes in the economy "independent of religious reformation" (75). These changes resulted in the "fetishization of female premarital virginity" (83) and its signification as "an erotic stance" that conferred on virgin women a distinct spiritual and social status (113). Women who chose to remain virgins were thus claiming "an officially unnamed position that was both dissident and highly resistant," for which they were considered threatening to the Protestant sex/gender system (113). In a society like early modern Protestant England, where gender was constructed according to a rigid binary, argues Jankowski, dissident positions like female virginity must be viewed as queer, the position occupied by queer virgins functioning "ostensibly [as] that of a third gender, neither dominantly male nor subserviently female" (34).

Although provocative, Jankowski's paradigm of a "third gender" that defines as transgressive and therefore queer all early modern women who lived their lives as virgins approaches a monolithic view of virginity. The paradigm, moreover, does not take into account the condition of male virginity in Protestant England. Historians and sociologists of religion generally concur that medieval and early modern representations of virginity are, as Kathleen Kelly and Marina Leslie observe, "gendered—or coded—as female, even when male virginity is ostensibly the subject";[7] Jankowski accepts this codification without exploring how female virginity was conceptualized differently from male virginity in Protestant discourses, restricting her definition of virginity to women who are not "sexually active with men" (10). A discussion of the differences between female and male virginity could have been especially useful in the context of the queerness of female virginity that Jankowski locates in the early modern period. Was transgressive virginity in Protestant England gender-specific so that only women who renounced marriage and chose virginity as a permanent condition functioned as queer, or were there circumstances in which male virginity may also be considered a queer sexual practice?

Jankowski does, however, provide an engaging discussion of early modern "queer virgins" as women who disrupt the sex/gender hierarchy "*not* by trying to be men, but by *not being* 'women'" (12). She contrasts two early modern cultural icons—Joan of Arc and Elizabeth I. In early modern English representations of Joan of Arc, such as Shakespeare's Joan la Pucelle in *1 Henry VI,* Joan's virginity poses a threat to social stability. Joan's behavior is transgressive not only because Joan's military life is unacceptable in a woman, but more significantly because her permanent virginity creates an opposition to the cultural stereotype of the quiet young virgin whose destiny is marriage. "As a perpetual virgin," Jankowski argues, Joan "was easily viewed as a monster. But she was more than that. She was queer" (4). Jankowski's comparison of Joan of Arc's virginity with that of Elizabeth I demonstrates that the function of Elizabeth's virginity was to promote the Protestant sex/gender system. On one hand, Elizabeth's conflicting position of "anomalous Virgin Queen *and* eternally desired love object" defined her virginity as a signifier of her nonwomanhood (13); on the other hand, Elizabeth's virginity was a condition applicable only to her, and functioned as a marker of the profound distinction between the queen and all other Englishwomen, for whom companionate marriage was the ideal earthly goal. Jankowski's otherwise illuminating analysis of Elizabeth's separateness from other women leads to a categorical claim for early modern female virginity as always already transgressive: "the condition of virginity, especially during Elizabeth I's reign, could not be anything but a queer construct" (15).

While the anomaly of Elizabeth's virginity upheld the Protestant sex/gender system, Elizabeth's court, "as a venue for the drama," had the potential, Jankowski suggests, to interrogate dominant ideologies of virginity and cast them as "at best curious, at worst dangerously queer and in need of recuperation" (27). An example of an Elizabethan court play that inscribes a radical discourse of virginity is John Lyly's *Gallathea* (1592), in which the dissident love of the virgins Gallathea and Phillida invites the spectator to question the restrictiveness of patriarchal constructions of sex and gender. The play allows for the "distinctly queer" definition of the virgin woman as one who resists the heterosexual, reproductive economy, choosing instead female friendships that permit this resistance by gesturing toward "woman-woman desire" (26). Given the comprehensiveness of Jankowski's analysis of virginity in the Elizabethan court, it is surprising that she does not discuss its function in the Jacobean and Caroline courts, even though a number of the plays she goes on to analyze were written during the reigns of James I and Charles I. Questions that her analysis invites include how the cultural capital of Elizabeth's virginity, together with Elizabeth's appropriation of the cult of the Virgin Mary in her identification as "a miraculous virgin mother to her people" (124), was counterbalanced by James's identification as father of the English people, and why by midcentury virginity increasingly became viewed as a valuable commodity.

In part 2 of *Pure Resistance* Jankowski discusses a number of plays written for the public theaters in light of how they represent conventional and queer virgins. Her focus on the drama is based on the early modern theater's close links with social and cultural traditions and discursive practices, both popular and élite. The public theater was multivocal in that it was both a means of state control and a social space where subversive ideas could be promulgated to diverse members of the population. State censorship focused for the most part on challenges to the government or to established religious institutions; it was not as concerned with threats to social structures. Although Jankowski's suggestion that the theater was, therefore, perhaps the only space where questions concerning ideas about virginity could be scrutinized and challenged is debatable, she offers a comprehensive and illuminating discussion of how female characters enact a negotiation between actual early modern Englishwomen and attitudes toward female behavior that belong to the playwright's "cultural/social/gender location" as well as to that of the contemporary critic (114).

Jankowski's detailed and provative readings of canonical and noncanonical plays will be useful to teachers and students of early modern drama. She identifies three types of virgins on the English Renaissance stage: "dutiful" ("queer"), "challenging" ("queerer"), and "resistant" ("queerest") (115).[8] Queer virgins are ideal virgins (for example, Helena in *All's Well That Ends Well* and Marina in *Pericles*) because they preserve their virginity for their husbands, but "the power" inherent in their virginity exposes the "potential for queerness of *all* virgin women characters" (28). Helena is a poor, unemployed woman who stakes her virginity and her life upon the cure for the king's fistula, the "miraculousness" of her remedy, inherently associated with her virginity, winning her economic independence (132). And Marina arrives at the realization that her survival is ultimately determined by the value of her virginity "in the marketplace" (134). Queerer virgins uneasily defer to the patriarchal sexual economy through a variety of options: by insisting on their choice of husband (Hermia in *A Midsummer Night's Dream*), by refusing to submit to the conjugal rights of marriage (Kettreena in Francis Quarles's *The Virgin Widow* [c. 1640]), by renouncing marriage (Beatrice in *Much Ado About Nothing*), or by sustaining a strong emotional bond with "a former 'lesbian' lover" (Emilia in *The Two Noble Kinsmen*) (28). The queerest virgins repudiate marriage and the sexual economy, rejecting the patriarchal sex/gender system (Isabella in *Measure for Measure,* Moll Cutpurse in *The Roaring Girl,* and the women of Lady Happy's utopian society in *The Convent of Pleasure*). Jankowski's analyses of a wide range of plays in which male dramatists consistently portray both transgressive and orthodox female behavior suggest that the playwrights were consciously contributing to competing discourses about women that were circulating in early modern England and that had originated in the *querelle des femmes.*

Jankowski's hypothesis that female virginity in early modern England occupied "a queer space" that disrupted the otherwise rigid sex/gender system (8) yields important insights into the sociocultural representations of female resistance. The book also provides a valuable corrective to the insufficient attention that has been paid in queer studies generally to virginity, chastity, and celibacy as queer sexual practices. Jankowski's definition of early modern queer virginity, however, is so inclusive that some readers will, at times, resist it. The diverse group of virgin women and virgin female characters of the early modern period may not ultimately constitute a "third gender"; they are, nevertheless, well served by the study that Jankowski has undertaken in *Pure Resistance.* The book will provoke further inquiry and will be of interest to scholars of early modern drama and culture, as well as to those working more broadly in the areas of queer theory, feminist criticism, and the history of gender and sexuality.

Notes

1. The pioneering works include Alan Bray, *Homosexuality in Renaissance England* (London: Gay Men's Press, 1982); Jonathan Dollimore, *Sexual Dissidence: Augustine to Wilde, Freud to Foucault* (Oxford: Clarendon Press, 1991); Gregory W. Bredbeck, *Sodomy and Interpretation: Marlowe to Milton* (Ithaca: Cornell University

Press, 1991); Valerie Traub; "The (In)significance of Lesiban Desire in Early Modern England," in *Erotic Politics: Desire on the Renaissance Stage,* ed. Susan Zimmerman (New York: Routledge, 1992), 150–69; and Jonathan Goldberg, ed., *Queering the Renaissance* (Durham: Duke University Press, 1994).

2. Among the studies of representations of virginity in the early modern period, Kathleen Coyne Kelly and Marina Leslie's collection of essays *Menacing Virgins: Representing Virginity in the Middle Ages and Renaissace* (Newark: University of Delaware Press, 1999) deserves special mention. *Menacing Virgins* delineates medieval and early modern cultures' ambivalent depictions of virginity from a variety of critical and theoretical viewpoints and in relation to various disciplines, whereas *Pure Resistance* provides a queer and feminist perspective on the early modern construction of virginity and its representation on the English Renaissance stage. Unfortunately, the close publication date of *Menacing Virgins* and *Pure Resistance* prevented a dialogue between them.

3. Alexander Doty, *Making Things Perfectly Queer* (Minneapolis: University of Minnesota Press, 1993); Teresa de Lauretis, "Queer Theory: Lesbian and Gay Sexualities: An Introduction," *differences* 3.2 (1991): iii–xviii; Sue Ellen Case, "Tracking the Vampire," *differences* 3.2 (1991): 1–20; Eve Kosofsky Sedgwick, *Tendencies* (Durham: Duke University Press, 1993) and *Epistemology of the Closet* (Berkeley: University of California Press, 1990); Arnold Davidson, "Sex and the Emergence of Sexuality," in *Forms of Desire: Sexual Orientation and the Social Constructionist Controversy,* ed. Edward Stein (1990; reprint, New York: Routledge, 1992), 89–132; Monique Wittig, "The Straight Mind" (1980), in *The Straight Mind and Other Essays* (Boston: Beacon Press, 1992), 21–32; Marilyn Frye, "Willful Virgin *or* Do You Have to Be a Lesbian to Be a Feminist?" (1990), in *Willful Virgin: Essays in Feminism, 1976–1992* (Freedom, Calif.: Crossing Press, 1992), 124–37.

4. Doty, *Making Things Perfectly Queer,* xvii; quoted in Jankowski, 6.

5. Sedgwick, "Queer and Now," in *Tendencies,* 8; quoted in Jankowski, 8.

6. Jankowski's analysis of the construction of virginity in pre-Christian ascetic movements complements Susanna Elm's 1994 revisionist historical study *"Virgins of God": The Making of Asceticism in Late Antiquity* (Oxford and New York: Oxford University Press, 1994). Elm considers the fluctuating constructions and the institutionalization of ascetic and monastic female virginity, as well as the economic security and self-determination that women in late antiquity sometimes derived from those constructions. Elm's book, however, is surprisingly absent from Jankowski's discussion.

7. Kelly and Lesie, introduction, *Menacing Virgins,* 16.

8. "Queer," "Queerer," and "Queerest" are the titles of chapters 4, 5, and 6 respectively of *Pure Resistance.*

Playing Companies and Commerce in Shakespeare's Time, by Roslyn Lander Knutson. Cambridge: Cambridge University Press, 2001. Pp. x + 198. Cloth $54.95.

Reviewer: W. DAVID KAY

Roslyn Knutson has previously written about the relationship between the Elizabethan repertory system and commercial tactics in *The Repertory of*

Shakespeare's Company: 1594–1613 (Fayetteville, 1991), in her essay on "The Repertory" in John D. Cox and David Scott Kasten's *A New History of Early English Drama* (New York, 1997), and in "Shakespeare's Repertory" in Kastan's *A Companion to Shakespeare* (Blackwell, 1999). Her latest study, which revisits some of the same issues while broadening her treatment to include other aspects of rivalry and commercialization in the period from the 1580s to about 1606, has both a positive and a negative valence. Positively, she argues in chapters 2 and 3 on "Players and Company Commerce" and "Playwrights, Repertories, and the Book Trade" for a model of professional interaction that stresses community and cooperation, on the analogy of the guild system. Elizabethan players, she suggests, formed an acting fraternity reinforced by a network of interpersonal ties and sustained by economic self-interest, despite the divisive effect of occasional quarrels. Although they did not have institutional structures like a Court of Assistants to resolve disputes, they nevertheless evolved informal guidelines for conduct, such as respecting the playing rights to the repertory of other companies. Rejecting narratives that emphasize the antagonism of the Burbages and Alleyns or the exclusive rivalry between the Admiral's Men and the Chamberlain's Men in the middle and late 1590s, Knutson stresses instead the surviving evidence for a multiplicity of troupes, joint performances, shifting coalitions of players, and the shared use of theaters. To counter the tendency to blame the break-up of playing companies on interpersonal conflicts, she points out that players of various troupes often lived together in the same neighborhoods, intermarrying with other actors' daughters or widows and leaving bequests to former associates in companies other than their own. Similarly, she agrees with Susan Cerasano in interpreting the move of the Admiral's Men from the Rose to the Fortune in 1600 not as a flight from competition with the Chamberlain's Men, but as an imitative effort to upgrade their theatrical facilities as the Chamberlain's Men had done at the Globe, with the added advantage of relocating so that theatergoers would not have to cross the Thames in wintertime.[1]

Knutson's view of the acting companies' relationships with playwrights and printers also stresses collaboration. "The playing companies," she states, "relied on a cooperative workforce of playwrights who could readily supply scripts on popular topics in fashionable genres that were marketable on stage and, when some advantage to the companies presented itself, at the bookshop" (49). Accordingly, she emphasizes the independent initiative of the writing syndicates that sold plays to the actors, though she does acknowledge that companies tried to secure the exclusive services of playwrights through contracts restricting them to a particular troupe or playhouse for certain periods of time. The theatrical repertory, Knutson argues, was "a company's most potent commercial instrument" and showed such commercial features as "the duplication of popular subject matter, the extension of that matter

into sequels or serials, and the expansion of a popular figure into a spin-off"
(56–57). At the same time, Knutson views "the proliferation across company
lines of plays on similar subjects" as the common pursuit of commercial advantage, thereby downplaying competition even between the adult and children's companies, which, she points out, both staged such genres as the
revenge play, pastoral comedy, and the comedy of humors (56). Following
Peter Blayney, she also revises the view that theatrical troupes were continually on the defensive against rogue publishers, proposing instead that they
themselves may have printed their plays as a way of advertising the quality
of their playing or the status of their patrons.[2]

Knutson's analysis of the relationships between players, acting companies,
theater owners, and publishers is a useful reminder that in the fluid world of
the Elizabethan theater professional ties were not limited to an actor's immediate fellows and that even theatrical competitors could sometimes act coop-
eratively in the pursuit of their commercial interests. At the same time,
Knutson's view of relationships is unusually rosy, perhaps reflecting her own
good nature, which leads her to ignore the friction generated by competing
economic interests when troupes organized on the patronage model of noblemen's servants began to play in the highly capitalized theaters of the developing London theatrical industry. After all, the fact that much of the evidence
we have about the workings of Elizabethan theatrical troupes and playhouses
comes from lawsuits is evidence that playwrights, acting troupes, and theater
owners were not always on good terms with each other. Even in that most
stable of companies, the King's Men, some of the sharers in the acting company petitioned the Lord Chamberlain in 1635 for the right to obtain an interest in the company's theaters from those of their fellow sharers who were
also householders.[3] In turn, the growing economic leverage of theater owners
threatened to transform the sharers of acting companies, the traditional employers of playwrights and hired extras, into employees of the investors who
controlled their playing space. Knutson argues that "the marketing strategy
by which a playhouse owner had a stake in more than one theatrical operation
suggests an expansion through cooperative ventures rather than through settled rivalries and theatrical wars" (37), and this claim gains some support
from James Burbage's agreement to share the profits of The Theatre and The
Curtain with the latter's owner Henry Laneman. But "cooperative" ventures
could also be used to corner a larger share of the market or to restrain competition, as in the agreement by which the Chamberlain's Men joined with
Philip Rosseter, part-owner of Whitefriars, to pay Edward Peers, the choir-
master of Paul's, to keep the theater at Paul's closed.[4] Theatrical investors
like Francis Langley and Christopher Beeston were often at odds with the
troupes who rented their playhouses, and Beeston went further than earlier
managers by demanding control of the actors who played for him and ownership of their playbooks.[5] Although compensation for playwriting increased

over time and seems generally to have been somewhat higher than that received by authors of prose pamphlets, fees governed by market principles rewarded rapid production rather than studied art—a point made satirically by the anonymous authors of *Histriomastix*. There the scholar-poet Chrysoganus requests—and is refused—ten pounds for a play by a popular troupe of actors, Sir Oliver Owlet's Men, who prefer the doggerel of the company's balladeering playwright Master Posthaste, a satiric portrait of Anthony Munday.[6] Even well-paid playwrights like the Caroline poet Richard Brome could experience financial distress when playing was interrupted if they were limited by an exclusive contract like that binding Brome to Queen Henrietta Maria's Men in 1640.[7] From its early days, then, the Elizabethan commercial theater was the site of ongoing conflicts over how its profits should be shared, and Knutson's fraternal model of theatrical relationships does not fully account for the tensions among the various parties.

"Commerce," however, remains a largely unquestioned value in Knutson's discourse. Although she has called elsewhere for theater historians "to explore the repertory as a perspective on the economics of playing, cultural attitudes, and commercial relations in the playhouse industry" (Cox and Kasten, 462), her treatment of these interrelationships here has been condensed rather than expanded, leaving many questions unexamined. In her brief discussion of Henry Chettle, for example, she objects to those who call him "a hack for writing prolifically" and argues that "Chettle should be judged by his contributions to the commerce of the Admiral's Men, which are measurable by the volume of his work and its diversity in subject matter and genre" (54). Putting aside the question of whether a "hack" is not, after all, simply a more derogatory term for someone who can turn out a diverse and voluminous body of formulaic writing to meet commercial demands, one wishes that Knutson would follow up this claim by showing how Chettle's works illustrate the dramatic appeal and social significance of commercial theater. What, one might ask, were the theatrical qualities that Elizabethans sought in a commercially successful show, and what were the constructive and poetic skills that contributed to Chettle's success? What is culturally significant about the genres in which he chose to work? Why might he have chosen those genres at that particular time? What latent appeal might they have held for his audiences? How, in other words, might a study of Chettle's output give us insight into Elizabethan popular culture and the theaters that catered to it? There has been increasing discussion in recent years of chapbooks, news pamphlets and ballads aimed at the mass market, some of it specifically concerned with the remarkable durability of such fictions and their impact on the drama.[8] The time would seem to be ripe for studies that might relate the records of Elizabethan commercial theater to the larger issues that cultural studies scholars have been raising. Unfortunately, that does not happen here, despite Knutson's insistence that commercial theater should not be lightly dismissed.

Knutson does, however, want to dismiss the "Stage Quarrel" or "War of the Theaters" that pitted Jonson against Marston, Dekker, and Shakespeare beginning sometime in 1599 or 1600. She devotes over half her book to a negative reevaluation of the subject, with the stated purpose of "dismantling the narrative that has supported a model of theatrical wars" (76). "By focusing on playwrights and their quarrels," she objects, "the War of the Theatres . . . does not encourage inquiry into the politics of company commerce" (15). She also complains that the indeterminate dates of the plays involved make it impossible to determine when the quarrel began or ended and that its narrative is "a closed field of privileged occurrences" which excludes other significant events such as the competition for patronage implied by the Oldcastle plays in the repertories of the Admiral's Men and the Chamberlain's Men (19). More specifically, she argues first of all that *Histriomastix,* often viewed as having initiated the War of the Theaters, could not have been performed at Paul's because of its extensive doubling requirements and that it could not have been written by John Marston as usually assumed because its metrics have none of the roughness characteristic of his earliest poetry in *Certain Satires* and *The Scourge of Villainy.* Secondly, she contends that the reference to an "inhibition" which "comes by means of the late innovation" in the Q2 text of *Hamlet* alludes to King James's coronation (the "innovation") and the subsequent closure of the theaters because of the plague and that the expanded version of this "little eyases" passage in the 1623 Folio "is a response . . . to actions by the Children of the Chapel in 1606 or shortly thereafter" (104). Thirdly, she argues that despite the parody of the popular repertory in *Poetaster* the play's theatricality "suggests Jonson's grudging admiration for the commercial stage" (130–31) and that the frequent allusions to the commercial repertory in Dekker's *Satiromastix* form "a defense of pulp drama": "Dekker, recognizing Jonson's gambit of jesting with popular repertory materials, seized the advantage: he used the text of *Satiromastix* to remind playgoers of the reportorial diversity in subject and kind that had been drawing them to playhouses since the 1570s" (137).

Now it is certainly true that past attempts to explain the War of the Theaters in terms of the rivalry between the adult and children's troupes are an oversimplification and that claims about the prevalence of satiric caricatures in plays of the period were wildly exaggerated by Victorian critics.[9] In my opinion, even the current standard account as summarized by Cyrus Hoy and Tom Cain and recently elaborated at greater length by James P. Bednarz in *Shakespeare and the Poet's War* overstates the case for personal satire by claiming that Hedon and Anaides in Jonson's *Cynthia's Revels* are intended as portraits of Marston and Dekker and that the cuckolding of Brabant Senior in Marston's *Jack Drum's Entertainment* refers to some episode in Jonson's experience.[10] Equally unconvincing are the efforts to link Malvolio in *Twelfth Night* or Ajax in *Troilus and Cressida* to the "purge" that the Cambridge undergraduate authors of *The Return from Parnassus, Part II* describe Shakespeare as administering to Jonson. In neither case do the details of their characterization match Jonson's known behavior closely enough to make identification with him likely.

Still, there is ample evidence that conflicts among dramatists did find expression in print and on the late Elizabethan stage, and it is puzzling that Knutson expends so much energy in denying the importance of such quarrels when they were compounded by artistic differences. Moreover, many of the arguments she makes simply do not persuade. For example, while it may in the strictest sense be true that Marston "left no evidence of a quarrel with dramatists beyond that fashioned by scholars from interpretations of his canonical and attributed playtexts" (18), Jonson's statement to William Drummond that "he had many quarrels with Marston: beat him, and took his pistol from him; . . . The beginning of th[e]m were that Marston represented him in the stage"[11] certainly invites such interpretations of the poet figures in his plays, whose qualities do correspond at many points with Jonson's. Knutson's doubling charts may show that *Histriomastix* is unlikely to have been produced at Paul's, but they do not eliminate the possibility that Marston could have had a share in writing it for the Middle Temple, and her argument that it lacks the frequent enjambment characteristic of his early poetry overlooks the fact that Elizabethan verse satire was purposefully written in a rough and elliptical style as a matter of decorum. And regardless of its authorship, the opposition in *Histriomastix* between a scholarly poet writing for an elite audience and a traveling troupe of players identified with the popular repertory of the 1580s ought to be of interest to any investigator of the developing commercial theater. Knutson's belief that the Q2 version of the "little eyases" passages in *Hamlet* must have been written not long before its publication in 1604/5 ignores its unique reference to "the humorous man" ending his part in peace—almost certainly a reference to Macilente in Jonson's *Every Man Out of His Humour,* performed in the fall of 1599—which would have been most clearly understood around 1600 when the play's celebrity was at its height. Likewise, her suggestion that the Folio version of the passage belongs to 1605–6 has already been effectively answered by James Bednarz's demonstration that its mention of boy actors who "exclaim against their own succession" to the acting profession seems to allude specifically to the criticism of the Chamberlain's Men by the Children of the Chapel in *Poetaster,* thus inviting a date closer to the latter's production in 1601.[12] Her alternative reading of the reference to the children being "most tyrannically clapped for" as a statement about political censorship (would the King's Men dare to call their master tyrannous?) and her belief that Hamlet's question, "Do the boys carry it away?" refers to the Children of the Revels' impending fall controvert her own earlier discussion of the Q1 version as a complaint against the tyranny of "a shallow public" that has "kings and players alike" at its mercy (110).

That Knutson would spend so much space arguing these relatively minor points is particularly disappointing because, as she herself recognizes, a narrative of the stage quarrel "needs to include the personality, literary style, and theatrical ideology of the dramatists, for the significance of each battle depends on the opinions they supposedly had of one another and their eagerness to parade these opinions on the stage" (18). What really seems to have prompted the War of the Theaters or the "Poets' War," as James Bednarz has more accurately termed it, was Jonson's assertion that his plays possessed distinctive literary value, thereby producing a backlash from fellow playwrights for the private theaters like Marston, who thought a more modest approach to their elite audience was in order, and from commercial dramatists like Dekker, who tried to deflate Jonson's posturing by reminding him of his own beginnings as a member of Pembroke's Men and as a collaborative scriptwriter. As I have tried to show briefly elsewhere, Jonson carried on a running battle with the commercial stage throughout his career, evolving a unique strategy of appropriating popular dramatic models not only through parody, but also to contrast his own satiric treatment of them with their conventional forms. At the same time, his publishing practices highlighted his literary pretensions as well as the theatrical auspices of his plays.[13] Jonson's artistic program, of course, was no guarantee of great drama. His reputation today still rests largely on the strength of his middle comedies, while Shakespeare's emergence as the most enduring and versatile of Elizabethan dramatists proves that there is much to be said for the theatrical skills of the playhouse "scribes" whom Jonson ridiculed. Knutson's expert knowledge of the commercial repertory system would make her uniquely qualified to present her own perspective on the underlying conflict between Jonson's authorial model of dramatic production and the commercial model of collaborative authorship that caused the Poet's War, but for some reason she loses sight of this significant issue here.

Notes

1. S. P. Cerasano, "Edward Alleyn: 1566–1626," in *Edward Alleyn: Elizabethan Actor, Jacobean Gentleman,* ed. Aileen Reid and Robert Maniura (London, 1994), 11–31.

2. See Peter W. M. Blayney, "The Publication of Playbooks," in *A New History of Early English Drama,* ed. John D. Cox and David Scott Kastan (New York, 1997), 383–422.

3. See Gerald Eades Bentley, *The Professor of Player in Shakespeare's Time:*

1590–1642 (Princeton, 1984), 53–57, and the related documents in Glynne Wickham, Herbert Berry, and William Ingram, eds., *English Professional Theatre, 1530–1660* (Cambridge, 2000), 221–28.

4. See *English Professional Theatre,* 318–19, 519.

5. For Langley, see *English Professional Theatre,* 442–46 and 464–85, and William Ingram, *A London Life in the Brazen Age: Francis Langley 1548–1602* (Cambridge, Mass., 1978), who describes "the punitive bonds, the lawsuits, the constant harassment and threat of arrest" to which Langley subjected the players (285); for Beeston, see Bentley, *Profession of Player,* 156–64, and *English Professional Theatre,* 623–34.

6. Payments for playwriting ranged from £6 in the 1590s to £20 or more by 1640. For Posthaste as a caricature of Munday, see David Mann, "Sir Oliver Owlet's Men: Fact or Fiction," *Huntington Library Quarterly* 54 (1991): 301–11, and James P. Bednarz, *Shakespeare and the Poets' War* (New York, 2001), 93–96.

7. See *English Professional Theatre,* 650–51 and 657–64.

8. See Margaret Spufford, *Small Books and Pleasant Histories: Popular Fiction and Its Readership in Seventeenth-Century England* (Athens, Ga., 1981); Tessa Watt, *Cheap Print and Popular Piety: 1550–1640* (Cambridge, 1991); Barry Reay, *Popular Cultures in England: 1550–1750* (London, 1998); Peter Lake with Michael Questier, *The Antichrist's Lewd Hat: Protestants, Papists and Players in Post-Reformation England* (New Haven, 2002); and Lori Humphrey Newcomb, *Reading Popular Romance in Early Modern England* (New York, 2002).

9. See Frederick Gard Fleay's assertion that "any criticism of any play bearing as date of production one of the three years 1599 to 1601 which does not take account of this, for the time, stage absorbing matter must be imperfect and of small utility," *A Chronicle History of the London Stage: 1559–1642* (London, 1890), 119.

10. See Cyrus Hoy, *Introductions, Notes, and Commentaries to Texts in "The Dramatic Works of Thomas Dekker"* (Cambridge, 1980), 2:179–97; Tom Cain, ed., Ben Jonson, *Poetaster,* The Revels Plays (Manchester, 1995), 28–36; and Bednarz, op. cit., passim. Brabant Senior does dismiss contemporary writers with a haughty superiority somewhat like Jonson's, but Jonson bragged to William Drummond of his affairs with other men's wives, while affirming that his own was "a shrew yet honest" ("Conversations," ll. 208, 238–40, in *Ben Jonson,* ed. Ian Donaldson [Oxford, 1985]).

11. "Conversations," ll. 235–37.

12. See Bednarz, *Shakespeare and The Poet's War,* 231–51.

13. W. David Kay, "Ben Jonson," *A Companion to Renaissance Drama,* ed. Arthur F. Kinney (Oxford, 2002), 464–81.

A Dictionary of Stage Directions in English Drama 1580–1642, by Alan C. Dessen and Leslie Thomson. Cambridge: Cambridge University Press, 1999. Pp. xvi + 289. Cloth $69.96; paperback $24.95.

Reviewer: WILLIAM B. LONG

To what kinds of offstage sounds can "noise" refer in stage directions? About how often does this term occur in the plays of the period? What about specific examples of usage? What was it that players were expected to do when instructed to "pass"? Exactly what are "permissive stage directions"? Everyone remembers the drunken porter, but where can other examples of knocking be found in plays of the period and under what conditions? "Great" would seem an easy term to define, but what did it signify when used in stage directions? Are there usages of "tents" other than in *Richard III?* Where can one find specific calls for the use of "cloaks"? And what about the intriguingly complicated problems of calls for "banquets"? Besides *The Tempest,* where can these be found and under what conditions? Answers to these and countless other questions pertaining to what happened on Elizabethan-Jacobean-Caroline stages await the users of this fascinating and enormously useful volume.

For many years, Alan Dessen has been educating students and the professoriate about how Elizabethan playwrights, players, and stages worked. Many hundreds have been helped greatly by *Recovering Shakespeare's Theatrical Vocabulary* (1995), *Elizabethan Stage Conventions and Modern Interpreters* (1984), *Elizabethan Drama and the Viewer's Eye* (1977), as well as many shorter works. Here he teams with Leslie Thomson for something almost completely different. As the title correctly describes, this is not a narrative *explicatio* as in the past, but an alphabetical listing of terms, explaining what they mean, how they are used, and adding copious instances from plays as documentation. Rarely has the access to the results of a huge amount of labor been so easy. No longer will teachers or critics or editors or directors have any excuse whatsoever for lack of information about and/or blundering interpretations of stage directions and stage practices.

Teachers of and researchers in the drama of the period most often are far, far more familiar with the works of William Shakespeare than with those of his predecessors, contemporaries, and successors. In spreading their net over the entire corpus of plays produced professionally between 1581 and 1642 and in focussing "on the shared theatrical language linked to the professional theatre in London" (xi), Dessen and Thomson also have facilitated much needed access to the workings of plays far too often either slighted or ignored entirely.

In their "Introduction," Dessen and Thomson rehearse the significance of stage directions for the understanding of the plays and their performance and explain their reasons for constructing their work as they have. "[O]ur goal is to isolate and define the terms actually used by playwrights and theatrical personnel in this period as reflected in our database" (xii).

In choosing texts from which to draw our citations we have tried to combine accuracy, efficiency, and accessibility. . . . [O]ur database has been compiled from the early printed texts, not from modern editions, so that documentation within the entries *could* have been linked exclusively to those most authoritative first versions of the plays. To have done so, however, would have made it difficult for users of this dictionary (many of whom will not have access either to the originals or to repro- ductions of them) to find items they might wish to pursue. We have therefore sought when possible to draw citations from editions that reproduce accurately the original stage directions and are accessible in many libraries. . . .

Since Shakespeare is almost always read in modern spelling, we have modern- ized the spelling of all passages drawn from old-spelling texts. In addition, to avoid obvious inconsistencies we have regularized the use of italic and roman type in the presentation of stage directions and have also expanded abbreviations and contrac- tions—although for the most part we have retained the original capitalization, punc- tuation, and spelling of proper names. Any minor distortions caused by such changes are offset by the added ease for readers and, in symbolic terms, by the presentation of Shakespeare and his contemporaries as orthographic equals—as op- posed to "modern" Shakespeare versus "primitive" Heywood. (xiii)

Thus all users are carefully instructed as to what they will find and the reasons for the choices made. These decisions are both sensible and easily defensible. They also are easily contestable. The differences lie in the audi- ence aimed for and in a stronger acceptance than this reviewer can muster for allowing any changes whatsoever to the originals as found ("warts and all"). Dessen and Thomson are well aware of the problems and quicksand pits awaiting users of stage directions. Fully understanding the problems, they present a compromise.

However, for the bibliographer as well as for the scholar who will accept only late sixteenth- early seventeenth-century spellings or, indeed, only pho- tographic reproductions of early manuscript and printed stage directions, or for those who wish to know every occurrence of even the more common di- rections, there will be inevitable disappointment here. Such demands are be- yond the scope (and no doubt, budget) of this volume. The seeker after original appearances, although certainly immensely aided by this volume in locating the directions, will have to seek the originals him/herself.

There is a further corollary to what this compilation does not contain. Those familiar with manuscript plays, particularly those that have been used in the theater, know that the place on the page where the directions occur (centered, left margin, right margin, highlighted by over and/or underscoring lines, amply spaced, almost buried in speech headings) often provides a clue to who inscribed it (whether a playwright, a scribe, or a theater bookkeeper). In addition, anomalous placings of directions occasionally are repeated from stage manuscripts in later manuscript copies of plays not made for stage use, and even in printed copies set from a manuscript that had passed through playhouse use. There is, not unexpectedly, no indication of place-on-the-page origin of directions in this volume. In other words, Dessen and Thomson have not done the bibliographers' work for them; but they have told them where to look for many, many items. As in other cases, only meticulous poring over (often not very distinct) inscriptions will find the pearls.

But certain misgivings notwithstanding, surely at this point it is obvious that any serious student of Elizabethan-Jacobean-Caroline drama needs to hand a copy of this book, now happily available in paperback.

Shakespeare and the Arts of Language, by Russ McDonald. Oxford Shakespeare Topics. New York: Oxford University Press, 2001. Pp. x + 211. Cloth $39.95, paper $18.95.

Reviewer: MARGARET MAURER

Russ McDonald's book on Shakespeare's language states its governing assumption right away: "My conviction that the study of language is central to the understanding and appreciation of Shakespeare's work informs every page of this book" (1). McDonald does not waste any time either saying why this is so, but there may be some merit here in spelling it out: "Shakespeare," such as he or it is, is fundamentally the printed words of texts written in the slightly archaic language we call early modern English. However narrative retellings or productions of his plays on stage or film may finesse the issue of how it is we understand a given Shakespearean play by conveying interpretations of that language, the words of the printed text remain to challenge that reading. Whatever it is for Hamlet, when it comes to *Hamlet,* the play is not, after all, the thing; *Hamlet*'s text is (or, in the case of *Hamlet,* the texts are). Ask your students, and they will tell you (maybe appreciatively or maybe resignedly or desperately): Shakespeare is "words, words, words."

So a central task in the teaching of Shakespeare is to convey the beauty and complexity of Shakespeare's language. It is a formidable undertaking, and *Shakespeare and the Arts of Language* can be a useful beginning for a teacher who decides to take on the challenge directly. McDonald writes beautifully, he has a good eye for the vivid example, and his panache in displaying his scholarship with a light-handed flourish is a delight:

> [I]n preparing his textbook *The Arte of Reason, rightly termed, Witcraft,* the logician Ralph Lever sought to protect his discourse from foreign contamination, refusing to import even with modifications the Latin terms appropriate to the discipline. He thus devised native substitutes, such as *witcraft* for "logic," *endsay* for "conclusio," *ifsay* for "propositio conditionalis," and, perhaps best of all, *saywhat* for "definitio." (15–16)

A sentence like that last one will disarm all but the most impatient reader.

McDonald also has an elegant way of naming figures and defining them in the context of examples as they occur in his argument; that is, he presumes the intelligent attention of his readers without harassing them. It is a strategy that will whet the interest of those disposed to go further and give those less committed to the details of the project a good feeling for it nonetheless. And he is continually sensitive to the problem of determining how best to talk about the poetical effects he notices: do they characterize the speaker or are they a function, more broadly, of the play's conceit? is there a danger of going too far in appreciating puns or other forms of verbal wit? most pervasively of all, can we determine Shakespeare's attitude toward language as a human faculty for good or ill?

A brief introductory chapter takes up some of the inhibitions to studying the arts of language. It is a pleasure to be reminded of Sigurd Burckhardt's taming of linguistic analysis to the task of describing what poetry does: it "drive[s] a wedge between words and their meanings, lessen[s] as much as possible their designatory force and thereby inhibit[s] our all too ready flight from them to the things they point to."[1] McDonald connects students' impatience with formal analysis to this demand that poetry makes of us to look *at* rather than *through* the verbal medium. He also notes that many strains of recent criticism collaborate with this impatience, "devoting [themselves] especially to social or cultural meaning . . . so much so that the materiality of the medium [words] is often neglected entirely" (3).

As if to illustrate this point, the front matter of *Shakespeare and the Arts of Language* lists the published and forthcoming titles in the Oxford Shakespeare Topics series to which this book belongs. McDonald's book takes its place in the middle of the alphabetical-by-author listing of fourteen titles, between *Shakespeare and Race* (Ania Loomba) and *Shakespeare and the Bible* (Steven Marx). In other words, the many crucial pedagogical uses to which Shakespeare is now put will not allow McDonald's book any particular priority, though it is to be hoped that many students will get to it sooner or later. Fortunately, however, because McDonald aligns himself with Catherine Belsey and Patricia Parker in believing in the possibility of an "historically grounded study of language and culture, one that takes seriously the 'matter' of language as a part of the 'material Shakespeare'" (4), his insights into Shakespeare's verbal art are informed by the concerns of other approaches to early modern literature.[2]

And it is with historical matter that this book begins. In his first chapter, McDonald offers a short discussion of early modern English, its vocabulary, syntax, grammar. Several crucial elements are covered: the rise of English (a vernacular language in contrast to Latin), including how the Reformation (with its emphasis on translation of the Scriptures into vernacular languages) and the advent of printing with movable type (whereby books in that vernacular were produced in quantity) contributed to this ascendancy; the receptiveness of English to neologisms; the fluidity of spelling, pronunciation, and grammar in early modern English as compared to modern English; and, finally of course, the predilection, among Shakespeare and his contemporaries, for artifice in language.

The exclusive emphasis on early modern English as the enabler of Shakespeare's linguistic virtuosity does, however, lead to problems. Maybe the emphasis is strategic, its point being perhaps to impress readers, particularly student readers, that Shakespeare's language is closely related to their own. And it is does, to an extent, accurately reflect an argument made in Shakespeare's day. Early modern writers gloried in the capacities of their native tongue, sometimes with self-conscious extravagance, as Sir Philip Sidney does when he asserts the superiority of English "before any other vulgar language I know" for matching the subtle effects of classical versification and surpassing the achievements in verse of other languages.[3] But this chapter does, in its paean to Shakespeare's language, omit a point of considerable historical and interpretive significance. As a boy, Shakespeare looked *at* the language of great literature before he looked *through* it because he was schooled in a language other than his mother tongue. The figures that George Puttenham, Henry Peacham, and Thomas Wilson illustrated in English in their popular books were figures he first learned and probably practiced in Latin. Latin literature and the Latin language itself significantly inspired all the writers McDonald names as making up what he calls the "golden" age of poetical achievement (31).

McDonald knows this, but in the working out of his argument something more like its opposite is implied. Oddly, in a book on Shakespeare and the arts of language, Ovid is followed by a single page reference in the index, and Vergil is not there at all.[4] Shakespeare's English is romanticized as a primitive, supple instrument, in contrast to Latin:

> Unlike Latin, in which the order of parts of speech was mostly fixed, or present-day English, in which the vast majority of sentences begin with the subject followed by the verb and then the object, early modern English afforded a number of structural alternatives. Writers could vary the position of key words and thereby achieve a particular effect without sounding stilted or confusing. Donne's famous injunction "Send not to know for whom the bell tolls," based as it is on the inverted alternative to "Do not send," efficiently conveys the power of the inversion. Lady Macbeth, likewise, breaks up the disastrous banquet with "Stand not upon the order of your going, / But go at once" (3.4.118–19). (22)[5]

Such a misleading assertion seems of a piece with McDonald's need to insist that Shakespeare is "unparalleled" (1) in his command of his verbal medium, an "unparalleled poetic imagination working in a receptive theatrical culture" (5). Without arguing that Ovid (whose soul Francis Meres said animated the body of the glover's son from Stratford) had a command of his medium equal to Shakespeare's, it must still be said that word order is not fixed in Latin compared to English, early modern or otherwise.

As a more highly inflected language, Latin has a grammar that will accommodate considerable variation from what grammarians call its regular word order; and in grammar school, a sixteenth-century boy would have memorized to admire what Livy and Cicero, Ovid and Vergil did with word order to create variation and emphasis. In a way that seems figured in his late play *Cymbeline,* Shakespeare's verbal art owed its being to two languages colliding in his extraordinary brain. The many examples of other poets then and since who have gone to foreign languages to seek out new rhythms and figurative devices should encourage us not only to try to appreciate more precisely how this alchemy works but also to hold Shakespeare up to our students as an example of the imaginative rewards that follow on the required study of a strange tongue.[6]

In his introduction, McDonald forecasts two chapters to address the "historical discussion of early modern English"; but by his second chapter, he is on to the main business of his book. "Shaping the Language: Words, Patterns, and the Traditions of Rhetoric" is really an overview of "Shakespeare's adoption of these basic rhetorical instruments" (1). This chapter traces a developmental arc that is then presumed through the rest of the book, from "Pleasure in Patterns" (38) in the early plays to "Rhetoric Revised" (43) in the great ones of the middle period to "Artifice Again" (47) in those written at the end of his career.

Perceiving these shifts will repeatedly as well as ultimately return McDonald to the problem of what Richard Lanham once called the "'Q' Question": "Is the Perfect Orator . . . a good *man* as well as a good orator?" McDonald, in his emphasis on Shakespeare deploying rhetoric in the structures of his plays, frames the question this way: does rhetoric serve truth? And his book is predicated on what Lanham would call "the strong defense." Lanham quotes Donald McCloskey because he puts the case so, well, so wittily: "Figures of speech are not mere frills. They think for us. . . . Virtuosity is some evidence of virtue."[7]

McDonald says the language of Shakespeare's plays, disposed across various characters in interaction and conflict with one another, "encourages in his audience a receptiveness to multiple points of view, a refusal of absolutes, an awareness of the competing claims of incompatible interpretations" (49), and this makes his plays "endlessly fascinating, debatable, and—what would have meant most to Shakespeare the theatrical shareholder—revivable" (50). McDonald makes no larger claim explicitly, but one is implicit in the conviction with which he addresses his subject. Learning to appreciate how Shakespeare's complex verbal structures operate is a way for students of Shakespeare to engage with the rhetorical tradition that stimulated him and have access, at least in some measure, to the complex and liberating ideas that can be expressed if not actually enabled by increased verbal facility.

The main part of this book consists of five chapters that discuss Shakespeare's verbal art. Anyone who has read more than one analysis of the schemes and tropes of classical rhetoric or even anyone who has ever tried to analyze a single poem by naming the rhetorical figures it can be seen to employ will appreciate the organizational challenge posed by this project. McDonald decides on four (or five) categories and disposes them across five chapters. They might be named imagery (apprehended locally and then apprehended in larger patterns), meter in poetry, rhythm and figurative language in prose, and wordplay.

Imagery, of course, is an unsatisfactory word for the whole panoply of figurative devices that Shakespeare's plays can be seen to employ. McDonald begins chapter three with comments on the linguistic and philosophical issues raised by the term *imagery*, placing it in relationship to other more obviously technical terms like *metaphor* and *trope*. With the word under erasure, he then proceeds practically, starting with "the pleasures of the picture" and moving on to metaphor and then to an analysis of metaphorical passages that are also shaped by other figurative devices like oxymoron. Chapter 4 interrupts this progression at the start to consider how Shakespeare's imagery was studied with increasing sophistication throughout the twentieth century, and then continues in exemplary fashion to consider networks of images in particular plays and the recurrence of images across plays in symbolic patterns. The movement of these two chapters ends with a consideration of the interpretive issues that arise when these larger patterns are noticed. Such a schematic description of the organization of these two chapters belies, however, the pleasures and profits of reading them. McDonald moves easily from a particular point to the larger critical problem his analysis of it might raise.

In chapters 5 and 6, he takes up figures associated with the sound of language, first poetry (5) and then prose (6). In chapter 5, McDonald does not bother much with the basics (he defines pyrrhic, 98, and spondee, 99; but iambic pentameter is not actually described until the beginning of the next chapter, 109); nor does he add here what is left out of chapter 1, some discussion of how early modern vernacular poets debated the value of certain formal characteristics of English poetry (like rhyme and the iambic line). The chapter is, as it advertises itself by its title, a discussion of "Shakespeare's Metrical Development," demonstrating how the iambic pentameter line is loosened from early to middle to late plays. McDonald's analysis is subtle and yet clear, admirable in particular examples and yet also serving a larger argument that the "development from metrical simplicity to sophistication recapitulates aurally the thematic and tonal complication" (89) that evolves through Shakespeare's dramatic works.

Chapter 6 discusses the rhetoric of the prose in Shakespeare's plays. Here we do get some background in the changing fashions in prose style (the Ciceronian-Senecan controversy). The treatment of "the major syntactical structures and verbal flourishes that the dramatist employs" (109) is also technical, with figures (parataxis, hypotaxis, ploce, epizeuxis) illustrated and commented on as they appear in passages from many of the plays. McDonald seems to be having a lot of fun in this chapter (of Justice Shallow, "This is *epizeuxis* if ever there was *epizeuxis,*" 121); and it is fun to read in the way that mastering some bit of any arcane system can convey pleasure in the doing of a thing purely for its own sake. The chapter includes as well an intelligent discussion of how the shifts between prose and verse can be seen to be interpretively meaningful and a consideration of the tricky question of the extent to which the use of prose might be an element of characterization.

With the discussion in chapter 7 of what McDonald calls "double talk" the focus is on figurative language that serves up multiple meanings, creates ambiguity, undermines emotional force, and sometimes even belies the meaning it ostensibly conveys—in other words, wordplay that is often dismissively described with the catch-all term *pun*. At this point, McDonald is plumb up against the issue that implicated poets along with dicers and jugglers and players in the Puritan attack on all sorts of licentious excess for not serving a clear godly purpose. McDonald's discussion of Puritans occurs in chapter 4 in a brief, good section, "Imagery and Culture" (85–88) at the end of his two-chapter discussion of imagery—right before, in other words, the chapters that focus on sound and verbal patterns. Chapter 7, then, is a discussion of some ways that poets and those who appreciate them defend their interest in the extreme cases of cleverly disposed language. Defending involves setting out the limits of what is allowed, justifying, the way margins are justified by being brought into line.

McDonald surveys "Elizabethan and Modern Theory" about wordplay (138–42) and then mounts his own defense, describing how puns convey conflict and emotion (the "amorous tussling" of Kate and Petruchio or Olivia and Cesario, 144–45), allow the disempowered to subvert authority, or represent duplicity. An assumption of this chapter's argument is that appreciation should wait on interpretation. Early in this chapter, McDonald notes that the first-century Roman rhetorician Quintilian urges the orator to restrain his impulses toward ambiguity; and while McDonald himself sees value in more of it than Quintilian would allow, he, too, has his limits, which he prescribes not for the writer but for the reader:

> Modern readers should be careful not to overlook bawdy implications when the speaker or situation calls them to the surface. Likewise, modern readers should not read sexual innuendo into words, even those liable to sexual interpretation, when the speaker or situation forbids or discourages such meaning. Sometimes a cigar is just a cigar. Context is everything. (147)

Good sentences and well-pronounced, though Humpty Dumpty's analysis of how language works should caution us from trusting that appeals to context can finally resolve anything.[8]

Yet overall it is a strength of this book that McDonald does not shrink from the mastery that his writing it requires him to assume. In the book's final chapter, "Words Effectual, Speech Unable," he takes on the responsibility of summary judgments. It is a comprehensive discussion, but attention to particular plays (*Romeo and Juliet, Henry V, Othello*) makes it useful for its method as well as its assertions. Another strength is that McDonald does not burke the evidence to find patterns he can easily describe: "The truth is that in almost every play Shakespeare's view of language and its possibilities is mixed" (165), though in groups of plays (comedies, histories, tragedies, tragicomedies) one can find the dominance of one attitude or another. After all, the most important quality of McDonald's authority is that it is solidly based on a finely tuned sensitivity to the workings of Shakespeare's verbal art, a sensitivity that this book seems written to share.

Notes

1. "The Poet as Fool and Priest: A Discourse on Method," in *Shakespearean Meanings* (Princeton: Princeton University Press, 1968), 24.

2. McDonald quotes Parker, *Shakespeare from the Margins* (Chicago: University of Chicago Press, 1996), 1.

3. McDonald does not refer here to Sidney's *Apology for Poetry,* but his argument resembles it: "I know some will say it [English] is a mingled language. And why not so much the better, taking the best of both the other. Another will say it wanteth grammar. Nay truly, it hath that praise, that it wanteth not grammar: for grammar it might have, but it needs it not; being so easy of itself, and so void of those cumbersome differences of cases, genders, moods, and tenses, which I think was a piece of the Tower of Babylon's curse, that a man should be put to school to learn his mother-tongue. But for the uttering sweetly and properly the conceits of the mind, which is the end of speech, that hath it equally with any other tongue in the world; and is particularly happy in compositions [compounds] of two or three words together, near the Greek, far beyond the Latin, which is one of the greatest beauties can be in a language." This, followed by a discourse on the superior capacities of English for various forms of meter and rhyme, is an exercise in chauvinism that Sidney seems embarrassed by and abruptly abandons: "I find already the triflingness of this discourse is much too much enlarged." I am quoting from Forrest Robinson's edition of the *Apology* (Indianapolis: Bobbs-Merrill, 1970), 85–87.

4. If a reader of McDonald's book did not know that English grammar schools were called grammar schools because they taught Latin grammar, he could learn it from this book only from a single dependent clause introducing a sentence that emphasizes the ascendancy of English: "Although Latin was still the focus of a young man's education in the grammar schools, many thousands of people were taught to read English in dame schools or petty schools" (13). McDonald makes a more extended comment on Shakespeare's schooling in chapter 2 of his *Bedford Companion*

to Shakespeare: An Introduction with Documents, 2nd ed. (New York: Bedford/St. Martin's, 2001), 36–78.

5. McDonald misquotes Donne here (Meditation 17), as he does again when he comments on the puns in "A Hymn to God the Father" (138). Such errors are trivial and easily corrected in reprinting, but in this case the slip brings up a further point. Donne wrote "never send to know for whom the bell tolls," a use of the word *never* with the imperative that the Oxford English Dictionary suggests is something of a stylistic innovation. The first use recorded is also from *Macbeth,* "never shake / Thy gory locks at me" (3.4.49–50).

6. See chapter 1 of Jonathan Bate's *Shakespeare and Ovid* (Oxford: Clarendon Press, 1993), especially p. 8, on which Bate analyzes Shakespeare's adaptation of the passage in *Metamorphoses vii* that is the basis of Prospero's speech in 5.1 of *The Tempest.*

7. I am quoting from the essay "The 'Q' Question" as it appeared in the *South Atlantic Quarterly,* 87 (1988):653–700, especially 653–54 and 669; but Lanham also incorporated it into his book, *The Electronic Word: Democracy, Technology, and the Arts* (Chicago: University of Chicago Press, 1993), 155–94, prefaced by a one-page explanation of its genesis (it is actually a series of book reviews) and its relationship to the argument of the book. McCloskey's statements come from *The Rhetoric of Economics* (Madison: University of Wisconsin Press, 1985).

8. In *Through the Looking Glass,* Alice and Humpty Dumpty discuss how the meanings of words are negotiated in conversation, with Humpty Dumpty observing that the question of what a word can mean is a question of "which is to be master— that's all." Lewis Caroll, *Through the Looking Glass* in *The Annotated Alice,* with an introduction by Martin Gardner (New York: Bramhall House, 1960), 269.

Shakespeare and Religions, ed. Peter Holland. *Shakespeare Survey* 54 (2001). Pp. x + 372.

Reviewer: ROBERT S. MIOLA

This hefty contribution to the annual series, *Shakespeare Survey,* reviews the year's work in Shakespeare production and studies, offers international perspectives on reception and translation, and gathers together a cluster of articles on its theme, "Shakespeare and Religions." Leaving my own essay in this volume to reviewers so inclined, I shall focus here on the rich contributions and important disagreements of the other essays.

Surveying professional productions in the British Isles (1999), Niky Rathbone (283–96) writes terse but engaging notes: one *Macbeth,* for example, featured "Ikrainian transvestite witches on stilts and techno/house music"; another, "witches depicted as Newcastle girls on a night out" (288). Michael Dobson (246–82) expatiates more fully on selected performances in 2000. Tom Courtenay, for example, played Lear's wrath "less as titanic than as comically inappropriate" (249); in the awakening scene, however, he was "able to rivet the auditorium with no movement of his head or body at all but just an impression of his eyes coming into focus and widening again, in a disbelieving recognition that quickly faded into the conviction that he was already dead" (250). In the closet scene Simon Russell Beale's Hamlet "found himself between Gertrude and the Ghost, touching both of them, poised yearningly between this world and the next. For a tiny second this family triad was and was not reunited, and Russell Beale's expression eloquently conveyed his sense of all that had been lost" (260). As these examples illustrate, Michael Dobson brings theatrical acuity and learning to his task. He also places the plays in the context of RSC history, evaluates actors in light of their previous work, and enlivens the whole with the wit we have come to anticipate from this slot in the *Survey:* "The designer in question was Kaffe Fasset, best known for his work in fashion and fabrics, so that while the Sheffield and Royal Exchange casts went to Arden to get in touch with material realities, Doran's discovered only the realities of material. His was a production in which the text struggle for attention throughout against the textiles" (271).

The three criticism reviewers also write thought-provoking and elegant essays. Surveying the work on Shakespeare's life, times, and stage, Leslie Thomson (329–43) notes the continuing interest in social contexts and the implicit connection (not always realized) to archival research. Occasionally applying the lash, she awards the laurel to such works as Janette Dillon's *Theatre, Court and City, 1595–1610,* which replaces the old court/city binary with a more fluid model of negotiation and exchange, R. B. Graves's *Lighting the Shakespearean Stage, 1567–1642,* which quite literally asks how an audience would have "seen" a play, and Daniel Fischlin and Mark Fortier's anthology, *Adaptations of Shakespeare,* which gathers in one place scarce and inaccessible drama. Reasserting the primacy of text, Eric Rasmussen (343–58) casts a meticulous eye on recent studies and on eight critical editions of Shakespeare. He records every error of transcription and collation (!), generously appraises the introductions and notes, and sets each edition in the context of larger issues in textual theory and practice. Edward Pechter (297–329) ably ranges over numerous critical studies for professionals and nonspecialists, all the while ruminating on a central practical and philosophical question, "What is the point?" He renews debate with Margreta de Grazia by asking whether critics must abandon the search for meaning, whether the specter of Hegelian teleology can ever be put to rest. Humorously, he responds to Gail Paster's identification of *cultural theory* as the most important advance for the next century: "maybe the 'sociological approach' will come not simply to dominate a single journal but constitute the whole field full of Shakespearian folk. If this happens it's curtains for me; I'm gone, I'm history" (325). Pechter's whimsical coda intends to reveal the personal investment in our enterprise, scholarship, and to object to exclusive forms of current politico-critical orthodoxy. The diversity and quality of many current studies, he himself concludes, along with the religious interest here (one might add), should allay the fear of extinction.

Shakespeare Survey 54 validates the editor of *Shakespeare Quarterly*'s prediction about cultural theory in at least one important respect: it features seven clear accounts of Shakespeare received, appropriated, and translated in varying cultures. David Garrick, for example, his Huguenot ancestry notwithstanding, revered the Bard as Catholic icon in the 1769 Stratford Jubilee (Dávidházi, 46–56). The tercentenary of Shakespeare's birth (23 April 1864) occasioned other intersections of religious ritual and literary celebration: Richard Chenevix Trench and some Victorian clerics "asserted that Shakespeare's genius was the gift of God and each sought to use that assertion to reject current evolutionary ideas" (Foulkes, 80–88, 88). A scant one hundred years, then, marks Shakespeare's journey from the temple in Garrick's Hampton garden to the Victorian parlor debate about Darwin's monkey. About the same time of these debates Shakespeare played an active role on both sides of Anglo-Irish politics; Tresham Gregg's 1872 play, *Queen Elizabeth; or the Origin of Shakespeare,* portrayed him as God's reward for the Reformation and urged Victoria to champion Protestantism in Ireland. Contrarily, Conal O'Riordan's play, *Shakespeare's End* (1912), depicted Shakespeare as a symbol of the English Protestant exploitation of Ireland; the poet dies in misery, having learned from an Irish Jesuit the folly of his and England's colonialism, materialism, and Protestantism (Franssen, 71–79).

Across the seas Shakespeare appears in strange garb and even stranger roles. In Japan, where suicide has different valences, Hamlet kills himself to atone for killing his uncle: the self-slaughter does not defy an everlasting canon but accesses ancient heroic codes (Kishi, 108–14). In twentieth-century Russia Stanislavsky's mystical prince, struggling to relieve suffering, yields to simpler representations after 1917. Successive attempts to present materialist fables diminish the supernaturalism of *Hamlet* and lead to post-revolutionary heroes, men of action struggling with the forces of history, men who do not dither about with compunctions or melancholy introspection (Sokolova, 140–51). In Mexico *Hamlet* appears onstage in P'urhepecha, an indigenous language, in an adaptation that derives from several Spanish translations of the play and oral traditions. The P'urhepecha Hamlet never berates himself for inaction and despair, nor does he experience any religious disillusion or confusion; in grief and anger, he waits to achieve justice (Modenessi, 152–64). Strange, indeed. But no stranger than Ithiel, i.e., Othello, in Isaac Salkinson's 1874 Hebrew translation. Salkinson isolates Ithiel (Proverbs 30:1; Nehemiah 11:7), meaning "God is with me," by giving him a Hebrew name and by surrounding him with Venetians who carry Gentile names. The resources of Hebrew language and traditions transpose Othello's alienation and his drama onto a biblical grid: Doeg (1 Samuel 21–22; Psalms 52), i.e., Iago, echoes Judges, Isaiah, and Ezekiel, thus widening and deepening the scope of his evil; the reconstituted willow song here evokes the willows of Babylon (Psalms 137), thus linking the lament for lost love "to the archetypal mourning for the lost homeland and to the nationalist sentiment of the nineteenth-century Jewish enlightenment" (Scolnikov, 182–90, 189). Every linguistic translation is a cultural reimagining, these rewarding essays demonstrate, a deep foray into an alien *mundus significans.*

The concern with religion that haunts and inflects each cultural adaptation appears centrally in nine other essays, most of which first aired at the International Shakespeare Conference in Stratford, August 2000. These essays constitute the conflicted heart of the volume and its most important contribution to current critical discourse.

On one side of the aisle is Peter Milward, SJ, whose "Religion in Arden" (115–21) sees the hidden Catholic life of the poet in his work, specifically in *As You Like It.* Milward suggests that the sylvan setting of the play evokes the English forest of Arden and the family name of Shakespeare's mother, Mary Arden, both of which had associations with the old faith. Noting that Shakespeare's application for a marriage license names "Anne Whateley of Temple Grafton," rather than her hometown of Shottery, Milward speculates that Temple Grafton might have been the place of their wedding. Furthermore, he argues, the old Marian priest of Temple Grafton may appear several times in Shakespeare's fictional Arden, in several references to religious men and, most important, in Jaques's reference to "a good priest that can tell you what marriage is" (3.3.77–78). Milward goes on to suggest a "comparison" between Duke Senior and the exiled William Allen, and, wholly subscribing to the "Lancastrian thesis" that places Shakespeare in the recusant Hoghton household,[1] asks whether young Shakespeare might have met Campion there and received from him lessons in dramaturgy, not to mention the *Spiritual Exercises* of Saint Ignatius. There are far too many suggestions and speculations in this argument to persuade any but the already converted.

Since Milward's thesis and approach appear frequently these days, often in less able hands, they are worth a moment's reflection. First of all, as regards Shakespeare's biography, possibilities do not achieve promotion to probabilities, much less to certainties, by being presented in bold face, in louder volume, or in tandem with other possibilities; they change only by the introduction of new evidence, of which there is precious little. Second, the Catholic church has long believed in "baptism by desire" but not, so far as I know, in "baptism by association." Even if Catholics number among Shakespeare's schoolmasters, friends, or family members, they do not, *ipso facto,* provide any evidence about his particular religious persuasion. Third, the practice of treating Shakespeare's works as evidence about his life and beliefs seems always to reveal more about the investigator than the investigated. One can easily find as many anti-Catholic passages, moments, and characters, as pro-Catholic. Critics might spend their time more profitably in giving voice to silenced Catholic figures, as Milward has in his impressive two volumes on religious controversies, and to exploring the religious conflicts that constitute the early modern cultural moment.

Several essays in this volume undertake such exploration. Gary Taylor (13–30) surveys theatrical representations of the divine, observing that the lying theater represented the ineffable, unimaginable divinity often in the form of pagan deities. Eighteen such deities furnish 210 characters in seventy-six different plays. Taylor illuminates especially Middleton, Jonson, and late Shakespeare, well noting the concentricities of theatrical practice and the Catholic iconic imagination. In *Cymbeline,* for example, Jupiter, "as Catholics would expect, responds to the intercession of dead souls" (24). What is absent from *King Lear,* but present in the other late plays of Shakespeare?, he asks. "Ceremony, ritual, intercession: altars, candles, statues, priests, nuns, hallowed and hallowing music, all the meaningless synechdoches condemned by Calvinists as meaningless idolatrous fetishes, but revered by Catholics as necessary mediators between the human and the divine" (25–26). Perhaps that is why the gods are silent. Jeffrey Knapp (57–70) also surveys a number of plays to investigate theatrical representations of the divine. He suggests that the theater itself functions as a holy space, one that "could spiritually unite audiences through a shared examination of human 'frailty'—especially erotic turmoil" (69).

Peter Lake (165–81) well argues that *Measure for Measure* refigures the popular murder and repentance pamphlets, exploring their moral assumptions and framing conventions. Against expectation, sinners only fall part way, the minister is a fake who converts no one, and there is no real repentance. The play also criticizes Puritan pretensions to godly rule in Angelo, and the similar pretensions of Jacobean absolutism in the Duke. Richard C. McCoy (122–39) richly analyzes *Hamlet* in light of debate over funeral rituals and the rites of memory. The prince and his ghostly father variously enact and fail to enact the rites of remembrance and sacramental conjunction precisely at issue elsewhere in the culture. Less persuasively, Donna B. Hamilton (89–99) contends that Anthony Munday's religious convictions merit reexamination and Tom McAlindon (100–107) finds precedent for Falstaff's wit in accounts of Oldcastle's examinations.

On the other side of the aisle from Peter Milward is the first essay of the volume (and the first plenary address of the Stratford Conference), David Daniell's "Shakespeare and the Protestant Mind" (1–12). Daniell, to whom we are indebted for his work on Tyndale and the Bible, starts out by saying that Shakespeare's poems and plays provide no evidence about "whether he was Protestant or Catholic" (2); he goes on to argue, however, that Shakespeare and Elizabethan literature owe directly to Protestantism, especially to its crowning achievement, the English Bible. Daniell cites musical and moving passages from Tyndale to provide a context for plain and Saxon moments in Shakespeare: "Pray you, undo this button," or "I am dying, Egypt, dying" (8). The parallels, general rather than specific, lead Daniell to extol "Protestant subjectivity," which he associates with William Tyndale: "always subjective in responses to the work of the gospel . . . he [Tyndale] allows nothing to stand between the suffering soul and God" (10). This discourse ends in the following conclusion: "Shakespeare met suffering people, registered in the ordinary language of the people, in the texts of the Gospels in English, ultimately Tyndale's English. He interiorised their suffering, and put them on his stage. This is a great bequest of Protestantism" (12).

Such an argument and conclusion reflect conventional wisdom and, as such, embody the impacted misunderstandings that have long dominated literary and historical criticism. Daniell does not trouble to know which pope excommunicated Elizabeth in 1570: it was not Gregory XIII (as he says, 2) but Pius V, who organized the victory over the Turks at Lepanto about the same time, an involvement in temporal affairs that Elizabethans celebrated (while ignoring the papal role) almost as vigorously as they denounced the excommunication. That minor slip would hardly be worth notice, did it not reflect typical blindnesses to the facts of Roman Catholic history, of which I shall address three widespread manifestations here. First, Daniell explicitly takes a Foxian view of the past, reverencing that Protestant history, expressing sorrow at "the culling of the best minds: John Frith, Robert Barnes, William Tyndale, Thomas Cranmer, Nicholas Ridley, Hugh Latimer, and dozens more. Laments for Jesuits executed bloodily . . . have to be set in the context of the many hundreds of Lollards and Protestants burned alive not long before" (4). Do they really? From the Catholic point of view the context was far wider. Maryrologies like those of John Wilson and Thomas Worthington presented not a Protestant national history but a history of the suffering Church militant here on earth, beginning with the executions of Saints Steven, Peter, and Paul and extending through the murder of the faithful in England. Catholics like Thomas Stapleton and Robert Persons charged Foxe with numerous errors. Thomas Alfield, William Allen, John Gennings, and others contributed their own moving accounts of Catholic resistance to barbaric torture. But a one-upmanship of grisly arithmetic is not the work of the intellectual historian. Both sides committed atrocities; both sides lost men and women. The true historical context must include Thomas More as well as William Tyndale, John Fisher as well as John Frith, Edmund Campion as well as Thomas Cranmer, Margaret Clitherow as well as Anne Askew.[2]

Second, equally distorted is the narrative of biblical translation as an exclusively Protestant achievement over Catholic opposition, a narrative which here, as usual, depicts reformers as objective textual theorists and Catholics as superstitious reactionaries ("The original Greek was forgotten." The correction of errors in the Vulgate "caused scandal in the Church." Protestants were astounded that accurate translations of God's word from the original

Greek should be declared blasphemous," 6). Leaving aside for the moment the tendentious question of what constitutes an "accurate translation," on which see the More-Tyndale debate for starters, and the numerous discrepancies among Protestant versions, we may recall a few historical facts. Pope Damasus originally commissioned Jerome to determine which readings *cum greca consentiant veritate,* "would agree with Greek truth."[3] The early modern textual reformers Lorenzo Valla and Desiderius Erasmus (both Catholics) saw themselves as continuing, rather than controverting, Jerome's great work. As papal secretary, Valla collated Greek manuscripts to correct the Vulgate, arguing that accidents determined the substance of many readings. The *indoctus librarius,* "unlearned bookman," *negligens scriptor,* "careless scribe," and *indocti grece lingui,* "those ignorant of Greek," had disfigured the text, like a river grown muddy and torpid with the refuse of a thousand years.[4] Inspired by Valla, Erasmus recognized that errors and impossibilities clouded the received Latin text. Furthermore, the Greek manuscripts were legion and represented translations (Christ originally spoke in Hebrew or Syriac). Producing successive versions of a collated Greek New Testament and Latin translations, Erasmus enjoyed the support of the leading Catholic English intellectual, Thomas More, whose letters to Dorp and Batmanson confirm the value of careful reference to Greek manuscripts, constant revision, and a plurality of translations.[5] And he was accompanied if not anticipated by Cardinal Ximénes de Cisneros, whose Complutensian Polyglot printed the Old Testament in Hebrew, Latin, and Greek, a Greek New Testament, and study aids, including a Hebrew and Aramaic dictionary. The Council of Trent renewed the call for correction and revision of the Vulgate. The King James translation of the Bible incorporates readings and phrasing from the Catholic Rheims edition.[6] All this suggests how simplistic is the canard about Protestant philology and humanist print culture battling against Catholic conservatism and textual superstition. Witness Jaroslav Pelikan's magisterial judgment: "the 'Reformation of the Bible' was a part of the Catholic Reformation and not only of the Protestant Reformation."[7]

Third, Daniell's dithyrambic claims for "Protestant subjectivity" and interiorization, which echo throughout current critical discourse, simply cannot stand. Protestants and Catholics read older classics like Augustine's *Confessions* and Thomas à Kempis's *Imitation of Christ,* as well as the work of the Spanish mystic Teresa of Avila. Tridentine giants like Robert Bellarmine, Luis de Granada, and Francis de Sales wrote well-read devotions and instructions for attaining inner peace and holiness. Continental Catholics wrote meditations and detailed programs for "mental prayer," including exercises for the imagination, the intellect, and the heart. The works of Antonio de Molina, Alfonso Rodriguez, Luca Pinelli, Luis de La Puente, Gaspar Loarte, and Fulvio Androzzi, for example, achieved numerous translations and adaptations in English. Ignatius of Loyola's *Spiritual Exercises* formed the basis of Robert Persons's *First Book of the Christian Exercise,* which a Yorkshire minister, Edmund Bunny, republished in 1584 as *A Christian Directory,* after excising objectionable passages. This essentially Catholic devotional manual went through twenty-four Protestant printings. In the time of persecution there was, of course, a strong Catholic literature of consolation. John Fisher's *Consolation,* Thomas More's *Dialogue of Comfort,* and Robert Southwell's *Epistle of Comfort,* for example, variously comfort the afflicted and confront the problem of human suffering. Catholics as well as Protestants suffered; Catholics as well as Protestants prayed, reflected, and expressed their thoughts and feelings.

Whatever one decides on the spectrum of questions and issues raised here, one cannot ignore *Shakespeare Survey* 54. Peter Holland's millennial volume indicates a prominent new direction in Shakespeare criticism, the exploration of early modern religions as cultural phenomena and as spiritual experience. This volume will play an important role in the shifting shapes that discussion will take in the future.

Notes

1. E. A. J. Honigmann revived this earlier idea with his investigations, *Shakespeare: The "Lost Years"* (Manchester, 1985, rev. 1998).

2. Helpful general discussions include those of John R. Knott, *Discourses of Martyrdom in English Literature, 1563–1694* (Cambridge, 1993); Peter Lake and Michael Questier, "Agency, Appropriation and Rhetoric under the Gallows: Puritans, Romanists, and the State in Early Modern England," *Past and Present* 153 (1996): 64–107.

3. Valla quotes at length Jerome's letter to Pope Damasus in the preface to his *Collatio Novi Testamenti* (wr. 1477), ed. Alessandro Perosa (Florence, 1970), 3–4 (3). On Jerome's reputation and influence, see Eugene F. Rice, Jr., *Saint Jerome in the Renaissance,* 2nd ed. (Baltimore, 1988).

4. *Quid mirum si rursus post mille annos . . . his rivus nunquam repurgatus aliqua in parte limum sordesque contraxit?* For this and the other quotations, "Preface," *Collatio,* 9.

5. Responding to Dorp, Thomas More observed that *codices latinos nihilo minus atque olim e graecis esse corrigendos,* "the need to correct Latin texts from the Greek is as great as it was in Jerome's day," *Complete Works,* vol. 15, *In Defense of Humanism,* ed. and trans. Daniel Kinney (New Haven: Yale University Press, 1986), 84–85. More advocated a plurality of translations when he responded pointedly to Batmanson's objection that multiple versions would confuse the reader: *Istud quidem verum est, si lector plane sit stipes, qui nec ingenium adferat secum, nec iudicium. Alioqui si mentem habeat, e variis transferentium versionibus facilius multo possit, ut Augustinus ait, verum quid sit elicere,* "That is undoubtedly true if the reader is simply a blockhead without any intelligence or judgment of his own. Otherwise, if he does have a mind, he will find it much easier to elicit the true sense out of a variety of translations, as Augustine says" (15:250–51).

6. James G. Carleton, *The Part of Rheims in the Making of the English Bible* (Oxford: Clarendon, 1902).

7. Jaroslav Pelikan, *The Reformation of the Bible/The Bible of the Reformation: Catalog of the Exhibition by Valerie R. Hotchkiss & David Price* (New Haven: Yale University Press, 1996), 13.

Shakespeare's Noise, by Kenneth Gross. Chicago: University of Chicago Press, 2001. Pp. x + 282. Cloth $42.00.

Reviewer: JOAN OZARK HOLMER

Learned, allusive, associative, imaginative, inquisitive, subtle, personal, and provocative are some of the essential qualities that characterize Kenneth Gross's wide-ranging analysis of transgressive language in his multifaceted—linguistic, historicist, psychoanalytic, and performative—approach to the "noise" (the work of "wounding" words) in five of Shakespeare's plays: *Hamlet, Measure for Measure, Othello, Coriolanus,* and *King Lear. Shakespeare's Noise* interrogates the risky business of speaking and hearing in dramatic worlds filled with suspect noise and scandals. Using the word "noise" as a broad category to explore a variety of forms of ill-speaking, Gross attempts to unravel the vexed associations of "slander" and "rumor" as the powerful species of disorderly language that energizes the space of discourse on Shakespeare's stage. In what Gross sees as the paradoxical love/hate relationship we humans have with verbal abuse, he maintains that such violent words take on a life of their own in shaping both character and action in Shakespeare's plays. "One scandal" (2) for which Gross ingeniously argues is that damaging words and their complex transformations function as both a blessing and a curse; the pain of such "bad" language is often surprisingly good in revealing "the ambivalent springs of human identity in Shakespeare" (2).

The author's almost eerily keen ear for the interplay of language, syntax, and grammar informs a *sprezzatura* of style in his witty, even eloquent, use of words that captivate the reader as one of this book's memorable strengths. Consider for *Hamlet:* "The ghost's story is a dead king's poisonous word about the way words can poison kings" (28). One of its main weaknesses, on the other hand, involves a tendency to overplay the thesis, straining to make some evidence fit the verbal rubric of noise—rumor, slander, and curse—while overlooking evidence that might complicate the argument. For example, Gross claims that Hamlet as "defamer" is "the "play's chief slanderer and rumormonger" who "converts all language—all public truth, all official utterance or ceremony, and all gestures of affection—into slander, abuse, mockery, contempt, and curse" (15). Such an interpretation, however, neglects Hamlet's antidefamatory correction of Horatio's self-slander of truancy (1.2.170–73).[1] Although Gross senses Hamlet's "generosity" in welcoming others (16), such repeated acts of verbally gracious courtesy on the prince's part reinforce his reprimand of Polonius's ruder reception of the actors (2.2.529–32).

A lucidly concise, yet fairly thorough, introduction and a coda that reprints the author's earlier published theory of "the imaginary theater" as "the real theater" (195) frame the six chapters that Gross has generously dedicated to his "students." Intellectually sophisticated students these must be to appreciate fully what this book accomplishes because scholars, critics, and actors will also benefit immensely from the meditative insights about the shaping power of Shakespeare's wordplay. In terms of organization, however, it is baffling why Gross's pivotal second chapter ("The Book of the Slanderer") that historically contextualizes the study of vituperative language in Shakespeare's era is not placed first to forestall troubling questions for the reader about crucial definitions and ideas. For example, "slander" appears in the introduction (2) and chapter one (17, 19), but aside from etymological notation—English "slander" shares the same root as "scandal" which means "trap" or "stumbling block" from the Greek *skandalon* (2)—"slander" in its legal and linguistic nuances is not defined until chapter two. In the course of his text, however, Gross significantly revitalizes for us the word "noise" by reintroducing some of its meanings, now obsolete in English, such as "rumor," "slander," "scandal," and "quarrel."

Observing that a *rumor* in Latin is "a noise," and the Latin *fama* can mean a rumor or a noise (2, 12), Gross grounds his investigation of Shakespeare's defamatory speech in "The Rumor of *Hamlet*" (a reprinted piece) through questions about the interrelation of slander and rumor. Rumor, as a kind of double-edged sword, works for Hamlet as a "tool" or "a defensive mask" enabling Hamlet's "covertly slanderous utterance" (3) and also works against him as a verbal enemy given the circulation of vicious rumors at court. In his emphasis on Hamlet's slanderous "way of speaking" (12), however, Gross tends to delimit Hamlet's "ways" of speaking so that, despite three brief mentions of Hamlet's antic disposition (23, 27, 32), no attempt is made to discriminate between how Hamlet speaks when wearing that adopted mask as opposed to when he doffs it, such as in his prudently honest directions to Horatio to help him justly judge Claudius's reactions to the play (3.2.75–87). The linkage of Hamlet and the ghost through rumor and slander so that Hamlet becomes "a version of the ghost" (27) depends in part on an exaggerated view of the ghost's story as "the poison of a slander" (27) or "harrowing rumors" (204). The ghost's story reveals a scandal that is proved to be not a slander but a true report, one which is hard to receive as rumor because the tale never circulates as common talk but rather remains a secret that Hamlet shares only with Horatio who ultimately must unfold its truth to the "yet unknowing world" (5.2.379). Gross, however, works very inventively with the play's quibble on "mole" (29) and the language of poison, ear, tongue, and ghost.

In his book's foundational second chapter Gross studies how slander affects "Renaissance ideas about the nature of language, the nature of human identity and interiority, the nature of political authority, and the work of the law" as well as slander's "impact on the idea of the theater" (34) so that the theater "became a version of Ovid's or Chaucer's House of Rumor" in the expansive scope it allowed to "looser forms of language, even as it absorbed more stable languages to that looseness" (64). While one may hesitate to share fully in Gross's sweeping vision of slander as "less a concrete way of speaking than an atmosphere, something 'in the air'" (34), deep gratitude must be voiced for the author's subtle exploration of a range of texts that clarify the Renaissance fascination with damaging words, texts such as Alciati's *Emblemata,* Castiglione's *The Courtier,* Calvin's *Sermons on Job,* Vaughan's *Spirit of Detraction,* Allestree's *Government of the Tongue,* Coke's *De libellis famosis, or of Scandalous Libels,* Spenser's *Faerie Queene,* Jonson's *Poetaster,* and even a letter by the earl of Essex to Queen Elizabeth. All readers will benefit immensely from Gross's contextualization of the theatricality of slander, elucidating how and why slander "is a monstrous thing that produces monsters" (66).

In *Measure for Measure* Gross focuses chiefly on what he finds to be the "Machiavellian activity" (81) of the Duke of Vienna in what he "hears and doesn't hear, what he asks others to hear, what he silences" (69). Finding the Duke resistant to troubling self-doubt, Gross breaks new critical ground in analyzing the figurative deafness of the Duke (79), especially regarding psychologically and morally unsettling cries, like Claudio's vision of life after death and Isabella's harsh response to Claudio's request that she yield to Angelo, cries that violently react to what the speaker finds unbearable. Very intriguing inquiry, especially a new context for interpreting Lucio's self-description as a sticking "burr" (76–77), informs Gross's reading of Lucio as "Shakespeare's ironic avatar at the heart of the drama" (77) who functions as the Duke's "ironic mirror" (75) in reflecting inwardness that the Duke denies. We, however, may want to limit the degree to which the rumormonger Lucio, essentially "a clown figure" who exposes others (75), serves as "a comic mouthpiece for both psychological and political truth" (3) in light of Gross's awareness (75) that the character list of the First Folio identifies Lucio as "*a fantastique*" because that description is followed with the line, "*2. Other like Gentlemen,*" that is, the play features three "fantastics."[2] The first impression a viewing, as opposed to a reading, audience gains of Lucio contextualizes him with two other men cut from the same cloth, as their wordplay on fabric suggests, in the play's second sense of ribald raillery that turns into a game of slander swapping.[3] Lucio may shed some light on the Duke, but his lightheadedness as "a fantastic" perhaps also recalls Ben Jonson's caveat: "Wheresoever manners and fashions are corrupted, Language is. It imitates the publicke riot . . . and the wantonnesse of language [denotes] a sick mind."[4]

Gross counterpoints G. Wilson Knight's evocation of "'the Othello music'" with a study of what he calls "the *Othello* noise, or the *Othello* babble" (120). Acutely aware of the literal and figurative dimensions of blackness in *Othello,* he insightfully contributes to our understanding of this play's imagery of denigration, coupling the play's "concern with blackening faces" to its "concern with blackening names" (105). The Renaissance idea of slander as depending on "something like what we would call 'projection'" (41) informs Gross's penetrating study of the psychological effects, moral pitfalls, and uncanny fantasies that abuses of speech manifest in *Othello.* He exposes particularly well Iago's masterful manipulation of his own as well as Othello's language to produce "monstrosities" (113). In light of this book's title, Iago's rumors seem ironically noiseless since we hear no one who circulates the rumor of his cuckoldry other than himself. For Iago, the play's "discourse monster" (109), one suspects that his "own thoughts . . . are composed mainly of uncertain, half-plausible rumors that circulate in his head and that he reports to himself and to us" (108). Given Gross's emphasis on the pervasiveness of slander—"slanders become the stuff of what everyone says" (66)—what does one make of the fact that it is surprisingly a woman, Desdemona, who proves the telling exception to such a rule, one whose inner goodness Iago cannot transform into evil although he can make it *appear* so? Despite Desdemona's sensible questions regarding "to whom" and "with whom" she is supposed false (4.2.40) and her outright denials that she is not a strumpet or whore, proclaiming that Othello does her "wrong" (4.2.81–86), Gross curiously finds Desdemona in the brothel scene "not in a position to answer Othello's words" (119) that "defeat entirely her ability to make sense of what he says" (122). Isn't it rather Othello who unfortunately doesn't answer Desdemona so that the general's accusation remains too general in withholding the specific name of Cassio until too late? Nonetheless, responding to what he hears as Desdemona's "reticence" (123), Gross imaginatively interprets how Desdemona's willow song can be read as her "delayed" (123) yet "visionary, rather than hallucinatory" (125), response to Othello's accusations.

In *Coriolanus* "the combative atmosphere surrounding words" (138) pits the noisy theaters of battlefield and city against each other, producing a fierce "war of tongues" (131) in which the hero's vituperative "rage undoes him" (133), despite his proven military virtue and "the profound political intelligence that sifts through his rages against *fama*" (143). Aware of fame's destructive power and loathing public praise "as if it were, in truth, a form of abuse or slander" (141)—the contaminating tongues of others as opposed to his own—Coriolanus fights against his perceived enemy of "voices" (139) through "a private language of heroism . . . about which the play gives us few clues" (142). "War noise" (131) becomes the clue Gross discovers for the perplexing attitude of this protagonist who echoes the wounding deeds of war in his self-wounding speech of vituperation, taking from "the noise of war a kind of moral candor and freedom" (146) that defeats the public's rude breath. In his analysis of the play's great crisis, Volumnia's undoing of Coriolanus's "hardness" (153), Gross concludes that "the loss of the power to make war is, for Coriolanus, the loss of almost everything" (157). When the Volscians finally bait the hero, he attempts to recover that power as he "turns the courtroom into a version of a battlefield" (159), and taunting the truth of Volscian history, "Coriolanus for the first and only time ferociously embraces his own public fame" (160).

Recognizing that cursing constitutes a more direct form of violent speech than slander or rumor and that it infects both curser and cursed, Gross enlarges the concept of curse from a specific type of "utterance" to include the sense of "a habitation" or "a state of being" (162) as he expertly untangles the transformations of curse in *King Lear.* Although Edgar in the guise of Mad Tom never curses, this "'cursitor'" or homeless wanderer (182) becomes "the one onstage to answer Lear or give new form to his curses" (182), answering in "babble" (184) that Gross parses through a superb sensitivity to its sound and sense echoes. Instead of curse, "what emerges in Tom's speech, heartrendingly, is blessing," but his blessings have "no power against the . . . violence of Lear's daughters" so that blessing is "keyed to despair" (185). But doesn't Edgar also succeed in suiting deeds to words? Although Edgar can't prevent the blinding of his father, by becoming Gloucester's "guide" he enacts blessing because he "sav'd him from despair" (5.3.191–92). With an almost poetic prose Gross focuses the ending of this chapter on Lear and Cordelia, having moved us to appreciate "the grammar of curse and blessing" (186) that newly inflects our understanding of how this tragedy still moves us.

This volume contributes to recent studies of "bad" language important for enlarging our understanding of English medieval and Renaissance drama.[5] For me, the author's engagingly confidential tone, his sustained sense of paradox, his pervasive concern with epistemology, his agile angling for possibilities, and his performative experience of these plays all enhance his subtly dark-edged postmodern readings of "the wounding presence of the word" (200). If we have ears to hear, Kenneth Gross records Shakespeare's noise in a critical register that sounds truly symphonic.

Notes

1. All citations from Shakespeare's plays are to *The Riverside Shakespeare,* ed. G. Blakemore Evans, 2nd ed. (Boston, 1997).

2. See *The Norton Facsimile: The First Folio of Shakespeare,* ed. Charlton Hinman (New York, 1968), 102.

3. In sixteenth-century discourse "a fantastic" is a primarily derogatory epithet, signifying someone with wildly fanciful notions and/or given to fancy dress (a fop). See *Oxford English Dictionary,* "Fantastic," *sb.* B.1. and 2. George Puttenham interestingly uses the precise term *"phantastici"* (or "fantastics") to refer negatively to those whose "phantasie" is "disordered" as opposed to those who use this beneficially inventive faculty in "due proportion" as do "all good Poets . . . all Legislators Polititiens [*sic*] & Counsellours of estate." According to Puttenham, if "the phantasticall part of man" is "disordered," then it breeds "monsters in mans imaginations, & not onely in his imaginations, but also in all his ordinarie actions and life which ensues." See George Puttenham, *The Arte of English Poesie* (1598; reprint Menston, 1968), 15. Sir Philip Sidney also uses the Greek for the adjective "phantastike" to signify the abuse of man's wit (i.e., "to infect the fancy with unworthy objects"). See *Sidney: A Defence of Poetry,* ed. Jan Van Dorsten (Oxford, 1966), 54, 97.

4. Ben Jonson, *Timber: or, Discoveries,* in *Ben Jonson,* eds. C. H. Herford, Percy and Evelyn Simpson (Oxford, 1947), 8:593.

5. See also, e.g., Lynn Forest-Hill, *Transgressive Language in Medieval English Drama: Signs of Challenge and Change* (Aldershot, England, 2000).

Colonial Women: Race and Culture in Stuart Drama, by Heidi Hutner. Oxford University Press, 2001. Pp. viii + 141. Cloth $35.00

Reviewer: **MARGARET THICKSTUN**

In this slim but packed volume, Hutner expands recent critical discussion of women and colonial discourse by looking at drama from Shakespeare to Behn that represents colonial contact. She demonstrates the ways in which seventeenth-century dramatists "present the colonial project as a justifiable repression of the native woman in a safe setting—the English theater—where audiences may be observers of both the exotic and the familiar at the same time" (17). But Hutner also argues that performance practice in the Restoration, where white women played women of color but without stage make-up, "destabilizes the spectacular attempt to legitimate the colonial project. Crucial to the fear of the native woman and her culture is the concern of the English going native, especially white English women—and that is precisely what these players do" (18). In order to allay both anxieties—anxiety about colonization and sexual relationships with native women but also about social instability at home—these dramatists repeatedly stage performances in which the native woman, or the European woman gone native, "falls in love with the white man and willingly gives herself to him and converts to Christianity" (4). As Hutner argues, "in giving herself to her white lover, her 'savage' culture is justifiably dominated and tamed by the Englishman. Moreover, in dominating the native woman, the English colonizer not only 'saves' the heathen by Christianizing and civilizing her, but guards himself against becoming a rebellious and chaotic other. In 'saving' her, he restores and 'saves' himself" (4).

Hutner's discussions of these plays are set within a rich consideration of history and politics, both relating to the content of the plays and to the social context of their composition and production. Prior to addressing the plays themselves, Hutner provides a detailed discussion of social structure and women's political power among tribes on the North American coast, arguing that "coastal Algonkian matrilineal and matrifocal cultures greatly threatened the cultural and political values of English male self-definitions in the early contact period" (12), a threat that exacerbates anxiety about social control in English society and about white female unruliness and power. She also addresses the different cultural attitudes toward interracial relationships of the Spanish, who intermingled freely with native and African women, and the English, who, after a brief flirtation with the idea of Pocohantas, did not. Hutner traces the shifting attitudes toward racial mixing in Virginia, from early expectations that miscegenation would lead to "the peaceful acquisition of land and property and for controlling indigenous people" (8) to a policy of apartheid and displacement that, by 1662, banned interracial sex and disenfranchised the mixed race children of women of color. She identifies as the trigger for this shift the arrival of African women in the colony "just when the disparity among white females and white males was nearly leveled" (14). Unlike in the Spanish-controlled colonies, and in the English Caribbean, where Europeans who wished to be sexually active had to choose from among women of color, white men in Virginia could choose between white and African women as potential sexual partners and were first encouraged, and then constrained, toward the former.

Continuing this deep attention to historical contexts, Hutner places Shakespeare's *Tempest* and John Fletcher's *The Sea-Voyage* in relation to the Pocohantas myth, and both Dryden's and Howard's *The Indian Queen* (1664) and Dryden's *The Indian Emperour* (1665) in relation to the history of Malinche, Cortes's interpreter during his Mexican campaign and sometime sexual partner. For her discussion of *Behn's The Widow Ranter, or The History of Bacon in Virginia,* Hutner presents a full overview and critical analysis of the events leading up to Nathaniel Bacon's rebellion in 1675–67 and the class, racial, and generational politics involved. But she also places these plays and others in the context of politics back in England, so that her discussion of Restoration adaptations of Shakespeare's *Tempest*—Dryden's and Davenant's *Tempest,* Duffet's *The Mock Tempest,* and Durfey's *The Common-Wealth of Women*—maps increasing anxiety about the ability of patriarchal figures to exercise power in a time "when the politics of monarchial authority were most violently destablized" (19). Similarly, in preparing to discuss the Dryden plays, Hutner first analyzes two dramas by Davenant, *Cruelty of the*

Spanish in Peru (1658) and *The History of Sir Francis Drake* (1659), that set
Spanish expansionism and greed against English adventurers who claim instead to seek fame, honor, and justice while asserting the superiority of the
English navy. Interestingly, *Cruelty* and *Drake* are the only plays permitted
to be performed under Cromwell's rule because, Hutner points out, they supported in his anti-Spanish campaign.

Dryden's plays, Hutner argues, approach the Spanish colonial drama quite
differently from those written either before or during the civil war because of
a new political context: a newly restored monarch who had received succor
from Spain, and renewed interest in colonial expansion as a means to unify
the kingdom. In these plays, "English politics are symbolically grafted onto
the Spanish and native wars" (75) as no "English" character appears. Similarly, "the heroic values of love and honor . . . mystify the aggressive and
acquisitive nature of European colonialism" (77). Instead of being destroyed
by aggression and greed, native women and native cultures are either destroyed by sexual desire or subordinated to white men through it. The plays
effect a double distancing, displacing onto native women the "responsibility
for the evils of colonialism" (66) and onto the Spanish conquistadors responsibility for exterminating indigenous peoples.

With *The Widow Ranter,* Behn again shifts the terms of the colonial drama,
setting her play not in Mexico among Spanish conquistadors but in Virginia.
In this play, then, the issues of interracial attraction and struggles of cultures
and social classes can be played out by English agents. On the whole, however, I found this chapter anticlimactic. The discussion of the play was quite
brief—ten pages of background to a scant eight pages about the play itself.
While the discussion of the other plays is thorough enough that a person who
has not read them recently, or in some cases perhaps not at all, attains a clear
grasp of plot, characters, and issues, the discussion of *The Widow Ranter*
assumes a reader deeply familiar with a play Hutner admits "has been com-
paratively overlooked" (89). This brevity is especialy frustrating in light of
Hutner's claim that *The Widow Ranter* both "participates in and reproduces
a colonial discourse which promotes imperial expansion" (91) and depicts
the native woman as "a victim of the sociopolitical conflicts within the Virginia colony and of the mercantilist economy of English colonial expansionism" (90). This claim might seem complex enough, but Hutner also argues
that the play represents Behn's nostalgia for "the prelapsarian world of pre–
civil war England" (91) and "a golden age of royal and divine authority"
(91) under a Stuart monarchy that is in the process of collapsing. It all goes
by too fast, including the discussion of the title character's cross-dressing.

Colonial Women amply defends its thesis that the patent nostalgia in dramas of colonization for a pre–civil war golden age "demands an account of
the historical events that preceded it—specifically, England's efforts in the
seventeenth century to establish profitable colonies in North America" (5). I

did find by the end of the chapter on Dryden that I had lost sight of the fact that these are theatrical productions, not simply stories, and wish that Hutner had reverted more frequently to the questions of representation on the stage that open the book so evocatively. On the Restoration stage, she points out, "women could play women but women could not wear black face. The other woman looked white, yet she was supposed to be of color" (16). And that other woman was, always, Native American: if "the dramatic portrayal of the New World as a submissive and willing female body assuages white masculinist anxieties about colonization, about the exploitability of America for its resources, about women, and about the stability of patriarchal authority" (5), the absence of African women, Hutner argues, "rests ambivalently on an axis of desire and aversion. . . . they serve as a reminder of forbidden desire, of loss, of absence, of human brutality that must be denied, forgotten, or explained away" (15). Surprisingly, Hutner makes this absence most clearly felt in her discussion of Shakespeare's *Tempest,* the earliest of the colonial plays.

In all, this study is rich, sophisticated, dense, and ambitious. It is a book one might in fact wish to be longer, to spell out its claims more fully, to lead its readers more carefully through some of its analysis. Specialists will appreciate its sweep and the range of Hutner's theoretical and historical learnedness; undergraduates could certainly read chapters from it with pleasure and profit.

Quoting Shakespeare: Form and Culture in Early Modern Drama, by Douglas Bruster. Lincoln and London: University of Nebraska Press, 2000. Pp. 268. Cloth $50.00.

Reviewer: **BRIAN WALSH**

An excerpt from Emerson expressing that "there is no pure originality" prefaces Douglas Bruster's *Quoting Shakespeare: Form and Culture in Early Modern Drama.* Bruster's book argues this point in the context of Renaissance drama, seeking to recuperate source study as something more than sterile antiquarianism by looking for the implications of literary indebtedness. For Bruster, source analysis reveals not just where authors get their ideas, but more crucially how they receive and retransmit those ideas. Texts are created out of extant works and their constituent words, plots, and attitudes. Close consideration of the sources from which early modern dramatists drew inspiration to create their texts gets us closer to the material realities of composition. Bruster might then have looked to Shakespeare in choosing his book's emblem, for as Lear says, "Nothing will come of nothing."

Quoting Shakespeare is refreshing in its ambition to suggest a new way to prosecute an old method. Source work is certainly a primal element of English literary studies, but one that is often given little cachet in a profession that values interpretive flair. What is exciting about Bruster's premise is his notion that the two need not be seen as exclusive. As Bruster would have it, source study is more than dulling, archival grunt work, but rather the productive first step in the process of interpretive analysis. Bruster opens his book with an impressive introductory chapter, "Quoting Shakespeare," in which he unfolds his approach to the "quotation" of Elizabethan playwrights. Quotation in Bruster's sense is Janus-faced, looking forward as well as backward: the book's title is meant to be read both as the act of quoting by Shakespeare and his contemporaries and as the fact of their being subsequently quoted. Significantly, by "quotation" Bruster does not mean a narrow iteration of particular words or phrases. Rather, quotation "stands midway between imitation and citation," and can be defined for the purposes of the book as "the incorporation, in a text, of discrete elements from outside the text, with or without acknowledgment" (4, 16). Renaissance drama (although it is the implied thesis of this book that all literary texts could be viewed this way) is thus described by terms like *"bricolage,"* "pastiche," "worldly," and "thick." Bruster uses these terms to suggest the ways in which the period's drama bore a relation—or, in his words, was "tethered"—to the world.

Such a critical move might sound familiar, but Bruster explicitly seeks to differentiate his approach from New Historicism. New Historicism has been a popular, if not dominant, critical methodology in early modern studies for the past twenty years, and it seems safe to say that a resistant criticism of it has been in vogue for almost as long. Countless books, articles, and reviews over the last two decades have attempted to undermine some basic principles of New Historicism, or at least express skepticism toward its sometimes predictable, even template-like prosecution. Such critiques often proceed from a reactionary political position that sees a liberal political bias to New Historicism, and can in themselves become as formulaic and partisan as New Historicism is accused of being. Bruster here offers one of the sounder and more original assessments of New Historicism's shortcomings that I've seen, giving what might amount to more of a qualification than an outright critique. For Bruster, New Historicism is limited by its emphasis on synchronicity, summed up in phrases such as "intertextuality" or Stephen Greenblatt's "circulation of social energy." Bruster argues that to approach the English drama as *synchronic* with its wider culture, usually by pairing literary texts with corresponding slices of contemporaneous culture, obscures the value of a *diachronic* approach that understands plays in relation to their antecedents.

Bruster is less interested in an "exchange" model of cultural production than in a more linear model of borrowing from prior sources. The reorientation Bruster envisions would force critics to understand the composition of early modern drama chronologically, as a material development in which playwrights read and heard other plays and stories which they reshaped into their own works. In a sense, certainly, this is an elementary point. Nothing

indeed comes from nothing. But Bruster's initial chapter carries force precisely because this very elementary point is often underappreciated in literary criticism. Bruster does not claim his method to be radical; he must ultimately admit that his approach is not substantially in conflict with New Historicism. Rather, the book seeks to illuminate some blind spots of prevailing historicist and materialist methodologies.

Source study has always played some role in the study of Renaissance drama, normally as "background" material of anecdotal interest more than anything else. Bruster essentially argues to "defamiliarize" source study and infuse it with the power to reveal the attitudes and frames of mind that shaped the works of Shakespeare and his contemporaries. Or, in Bruster's words, shaped the "positions" of those works. "Positions" for Bruster are "relational," and involve "orientations, assumptions, and points of view" (6). The palpable influence that is traceable through quotation can be interpreted in terms of the way in which that influence is positioned. For Bruster, a play might quote an earlier text not through exact or similar words, but through a derived posture. This is a key element to Bruster's work, as the majority of his case studies are ultimately more concerned with how playwrights adopt and refashion ideas than with instances of direct quotation as it is generally understood. In this sense, Bruster comes close to, without ever explicitly engaging, the language of contemporary performance theory and its emphasis on the "repetition and revision" of performative forms.

The book offers five chapters in addition to "Quoting Shakespeare," devoted to a genealogy of Marlowe's "The Passionate Shepherd"; the construction of authority figures in Shakespearean comedy; the *Tempest* and a material history of Shakespeare's professional relationships; the language of madwomen; in particular the jailer's Daughter in *The Two Noble Kinsmen;* and the appropriation of the English Renaissance in America between the world wars. The eponymous first chapter is the strongest and most pointed section of *Quoting Shakespeare.* While there is much that is valuable in the rest of the book, Bruster is not consistently able to lend his readings the same kind of energy and clarity that he displays in outlining his approach. As with the application of any method, Bruster's putative framework is simply unable to lend utter coherence to his objects of analysis, but stands rather as a set of ideas that loosely enable the study to proceed.

Bruster's chapters on Marlowe's Shepherd poem and agency in Shakespearean comedy work best within his interpretive framework. The chapter on Marlowe offers a compelling reading of "The Passionate Shepherd's" significations that complicates any sense of it as a simple piece of amatory invitation. Bruster conjectures that Marlowe's poem was widely read as suggestive of the threat of sexual violence by the solipsistic speaker. In a clever double move, Bruster builds this argument by looking first at some potential sources for Marlowe's work, and then to how the poem itself was read in the period. Based on the way "The Passionate Shepherd" was imitated in a variety of subsequent works (including Jonson's *Volpone* and Donne's "The Bait"), Bruster concludes that the Shepherd's words seem to have been seen as an ultimatum more than an invitation, a precariously idealized portrait of amatory bliss on the verge of aggression if the speaker is denied. The following chapter on Shakespearean comedy offers a similarly original and neat argument about Shakespeare's use of classical sources throughout his comedies, namely Plautus. Bruster argues that Shakespeare remakes the "playwright" figure of Plautine comedy from a lower class servant to a controlling aristocrat, exemplified by the likes of Duke Vincentio in *Measure for Measure*.

Both of these early chapters offer valuable insights, but both are encumbered by repetitive iterations of their premises and some unnecessarily involved feints toward contextualization. In the chapter on comedy, for instance, Bruster goes to great lengths to establish the principles of poet as "maker" as central to Renaissance literary theory. As relevant as this point is to the book's larger aims, it is hardly news, and Bruster's invocation of it here obscures some of his more particular points about Shakespeare's plays. And, oddly, he fails to interrogate the tension between the image he builds of the *poeta* as one who makes out of nothing, and his own larger premise on the indebtedness of all artistic creation.

Dwelling on significant points longer than necessary is a problem elsewhere in the book. In his chapter on *The Tempest,* Bruster offers an ingenious, noncolonialist reading of the play that posits the theatrical world in which Shakespeare worked as the play's underlying context. Addressing the old saw that Prospero is a playwright figure, perhaps even a stand in for Shakespeare himself, and that the play is about theater, Bruster asks "Which theater or theaters? And who and what in those theaters may have shaped the play?" (118). He argues that the relation between Prospero and Caliban is a figure for the relation between playwright and unlicensed actor, in particular the clown. Using Hamlet's admonishment to the players to rein in their clowns as a context, Bruster sees Prospero's obsession with authority as a working through of Shakespeare's own issues with Will Kemp, the famous clown of Shakespeare's company who departed for unknown reasons in the late 1590s.

This is very interesting conjecture, and Bruster's lucid argumentation makes it even somewhat compelling. But of course it is supported by no direct evidence, and resides on at least one very problematic assumption: that Hamlet's annoyance with clowns who speak more than is set down for them also represents Shakespeare's views, an insupportable notion. Bruster makes an equally clever but even more tenuous claim about the relation between the Blackfriars theater space and *The Tempest*. He argues that the conflict between sailors and nobles that opens the play is a comment on the playwright's resentment of gallants who sat on the stages of indoor theaters and judged the productions. Once again, Bruster gives an ingenious conjecture that is bolstered by very fleeting evidence. For all the chapter offers in terms original insights, it is very short on convincing evidence and thus seems drawn out beyond what it can feasibly demonstrate.

Methodologically, this chapter also presents some problems. Bruster here departs from his original design to analyze the "books" read by playwrights and ventures into a more amorphous idea of the influence of professional context. The chapter is titled "Quoting the Playhouse" and, the latitude of Bruster's definition of quotation aside, this sort of analysis seems at times more traditionally materialist and New Historicist than the author admits. The following chapter on the language of madwomen is most valuable for showing what an amazingly weird and powerful figure the Jailer's Daughter in *The Two Noble Kinsmen* is. Bruster offers a quasi-feminist analysis of her, arguing that the traditional forms of language ascribed to madwomen in early modern drama work to demonstrate their alienation from patriarchal social contexts. Bruster then reverts to another somewhat New Historicist sounding thesis: the representation of the Jailer's Daughter's speech helps to show "the increasing separation of court and city from the country" (170), a perfectly legitimate claim, but again one that seems to have strayed somewhat from the book's putative concerns.

Bruster's concluding chapter on the appropriation of Renaissance England and its authors by Americans in the 1920s and 1930s is a joy to read. Bruster contributes to a growing body of work by such scholars as Michael D. Bristol and Richard Burt on the sometimes astonishingly variegated uses to which Shakespeare has been put in the last hundred years or so. Bruster's claim is essentially that American cultural diffidence in the early twentieth century inspired an interest in drawing on the English Renaissance as a way both to demonstrate and spur the growth of intellectualism and culture in the United States. This is evident in the creation of the Folger Shakespeare Library and even in the invocation of the word "Renaissance" by scholars of American literature to describe the great nineteenth century works of American authors. While this chapter, like the two before it, feels somewhat superficially connected to the project as a whole, it is nonetheless a genuinely fun and informative history of the rich and strange ways that Shakespeare and his contemporaries attained currency in both elite and mainstream culture in the United States.

Source study is always undermined to some degree by the problem of partiality. It is simply impossible to identify with absolute certainty where playwrights, particularly Shakespeare, derived all their ideas. It is this partiality that makes suspect Bruster's use of a definitive sounding word like "tethered" to describe the relation between early modern drama and its sources. But it is also this partiality that allows Bruster to conceptualize quotation in the bold and imaginative ways that he does. Despite my quibbles, *Quoting Shakespeare* is a fine book. Wonderfully written in clear, thesis-driven prose, it has local moments of inspired close reading and argumentation that more than make up for the flaws I see in it as a whole. The introductory chapter especially deserves to be read by scholars who, bored with current critical trends, are in search of new and refreshing ways to approach early modern literature. While I find some of this book to be tenuous in its claims and have criticized it for failing to be fully consistent with the principles Bruster suggests in his introduction, I should also note that what I find wrong with the book might be exactly Bruster's point. The creation of great literature itself is messy, and is produced through conjectural, even incoherent acts of splicing and appropriation. Bruster suggests one way to get a handle on Shakespeare and his contemporaries is to tune our ears to the occasional clear tones evident in the cacophonous din of their disparate sources where, to quote Bruster quoting Humphrey Bogart's character in *The Maltese Falcon* quoting Shakespeare, these early modern dramatists found "the stuff, er, that dreams are made of."

Theatre of the Book, 1480–1880, by Julie Stone Peters. Oxford: Oxford University Press, 2000. Pp. xii + 404. Cloth $99.00.

Reviewer: GEORGE WALTON WILLIAMS

This substantial study examines the "entangled histories of print and . . . stage" (2) through five centuries of those histories—or, indeed, six or seven, as the epilogue addresses the confrontation of stage by cinema—describing the relationship between print and the stage "that would help create the theatre" for which the playwrights wrote (5). It ranges widely over the traditions of Western Europe: the riches of Spain, France, Italy, and, later, Germany are laid before us. By this means Professor Peters attempts to correct the insular perception of the dominance of Shakespeare and his contemporaries; for her, this attempt is "most important" (3), and certainly one of the many virtues of this study is the corrective it offers to those scholars of the English-language tradition who have satisfied themselves in thinking that the sun rose and set on Shakespeare, glimmered occasionally on other English dramatists, but scarcely could be seen through the clouds of the Continent. The backwardness of the English may be shown specifically by the fact that Tasso's *Il re Torrismondo* in the first year of its publication, 1587, was printed in ten editions (6, 317), by which date no English dramatist and no play had had more than four (and that not a vernacular play but a translation, Seneca's *Troas* [Greg, *Bibliography,* no. 28]); the plays of Terence—in Latin and the vernaculars—"had appeared in some 650 editions by 1600" (6, 317), only ten of which had been printed in England (*RSTC*). The richness of the continental material is the glory of the volume, for Professor Peters moves with assurance through all the literatures and (modern) languages of Western Europe, illustrating her arguments with full quotations from the "other" dramatic and theatrical tradition. (For a discussion of the English tradition, see Douglas Brooks's *From Playhouse to Printing House,* also reviewed in this issue.)

That prodigality of quotation does produce an uneasiness, however; for a deliberate decision was made, we are told (11), to present all the foreign language quotations in English translations (often Professor Peters's) with the originals in the rear of the volume. Reading and confirmation would have been easier—pagination more troublesome perhaps—if those originals had been placed at the foot of the pages. The translations themselves are smooth and graceful, but one is surprised sometimes: "ten volumes . . . will not an actor make" imposes an English turn of phrase foreign to "Préville's" French (289, 434). Quaintly enough, "lévite commode" rendered suitably as a "comfortable . . . gown" is described as having "extremely low *décolletage"*—a foreign word for which no translation is offered (258, 426). (That observation, incidentally, is one of several phrases in the text that would seem to call attention unnecessarily to an erotic interest; to these gendered eyes the neckline of this gown is no more unusual than many such that characterized that age—or, indeed, characterize this.) Printing conventions introduced into the English translations such as brackets (149) or the ellipsis just quoted, would seem to be unnecessary or inappropriate.

A particular awkwardness occurs in the habit of translating (or not) the titles of continental plays: Molière's *Le Malade imaginaire* (so called on p. 59) is also the *Imaginary Invalid* (on p. 139); Goldoni's *Le Donne Curiose* is *The Curious Women* (64); Gengenbach's *Totenfresser* comes across as *Feeder off the Dead* (27). Such translations of play titles are a little disconcerting; they seem out of place when the titles of collected editions are always given in the original *Oeuvres, Delle commedie,* or *Werke.*

This is perhaps to protest too much, to be too finicky, but the volume is so rich in theatrical and dramatic quotation from sources in the other traditions, that quotations in translation make a large part of the argument on almost every page. The reduction to uniformity is helpful in many ways, but the various tempers of the many originals—the "important nuances"—are, as the author admits, lost in the process (11).

Professor Peters has undertaken an exciting challenge: to demonstrate. First, what happened when "half-improvised farce, costumed civic festivals, biblical stories enacted on platforms, the songs of court poets, and the dancing of mummers were confronted by print—by a drama conceived in the fixed and silent forms of the text" (1), and then to show how these sorts of public activity over the ensuing centuries responded to and contributed to the spread of theatrical culture as manifested in the printed word and on the stage. But the printed book served another function: illustrations. As images of scenes and of (supposed) classical theaters increased in number in printed books, so at the same time, theatrical playing places and stages came into being across Europe. Purpose-built theaters appeared in Spain and in England in the same decade of the sixteenth century. The challenge of describing these interrelationships is engaged impressively in this study.

The volume consists of five sections. The first, "Printing the Drama," is a chronological narrative from 1480 to 1880—"Experimenting on the Page," "Drama as Institution," "Illustrations, Promptbooks, Stage Texts." Thereafter, the sections tend to be focused thematically. "Theatre Imprimatur," the second section, explores the contribution of the printed text to the shaping of the identity of the theater, particularly to the creating from the traditions of medieval drama a new sense of a theater where actors performed, not ad lib, but "from the book." This section also notices the tension between the authority of critical rules and the freedom exercised by the popular and not overly literate audiences. "The Senses of Media," the third section, addresses the presence of the body onstage, the gestures appropriate to the various emotions (157)—a familiar tradition—and the teaching of pronunciation, especially stage pronunciation, by a book—not so familiar. "No perfect Dictionary . . . hath hitherto been made that the true order of pronunciation might be taught," boasts Robert Robinson in his *Art of Pronunciation* (1617) (161). Gérard de Vivre included in his printed plays (1577) signs of pauses and "inhalation" ("une reprise d'haleine"), and Ben Jonson lamented the absence of any notations to indicate the accent, "most needfull to be added" (159). One chapter, "Framing Space," concerns the illustrations of stage performances in books. In a remarkable illustration from *Sechs Comoedien Publij Terentij Aphri* (Frankfurt, 1568), the plot of *The Woman of Andros* is figured in an illustration by lines drawn between all the characters, showing how they are related: the lovers Pamphilus and Glycerium are connected by a line, another line connects Glycerium and Pasibula to indicate that they are the same person (181–82). The fourth section, "The Commerce of Letters," discusses the question of 'Who owns the play?' with a fascinating examination of the "rights" to the text and to the performance. The question of ownership and plagiarism which Alphra Behn raised in the "Post Script" to her *The Rover* (1677) we have with us still, as the success of a recent film has demonstrated. Mrs Behn's perception remains apt: "That I have stolen some hints from [an earlier work], may be a proof, that I valu'd it" (220). The final section, "Theatrical Impressions," includes Hazlitt's response in reading *Midsummer Night's Dream* and then seeing it, provoking the now famous critical distinction made between the book and the performance. "That which [on the page] is merely an airy shape, a dream, a passing thought, immediately becomes an unmanageable reality [on the stage]. . . . There, poetry [is] incapable of 'sufficiently qualify[ing] the impressions of the senses,' which

[rain] down upon the spectator" (294). Hazlitt experienced the problem when the sense of sight managed to overpower the sense of hearing, and the more trustworthy of the senses, as noted below, could not be received in the downpour.

The epilogue takes us bravely into the future, still relating the mechanical to the spirit of the theatrical. In this continuum, print is replaced by electrical wonders, just as, in the parallel of a delightful anecdote, the musician is replaced by the phonograph. Bernard Shaw rejoiced in 1915 in "what the film would bring— 'Think of the gallops, the sousings in real rivers, the boatings on real salt waves'" (311). But the theatrical—which some saw as dead before the onslaughts of the cinema—refused to die. The living stage is alive and well in the metropolitan centers covered by this volume and in countless provincial theaters everywhere. There will always be humans who wish to perform, who prefer standing on a stage before a live audience to sitting in a dark place before a mechanical display of someone else. The solution to the problem, as Professor Peters tells us, in a world where "the number of cinemas doubled, the number of theatres halved" (310) has been the "cinefication" of the theater, equipping the theater "with all the technical refinements of the cinema." "The theatre was to continue to transform itself: capturing the crowd with its own . . . mechanized bodies, and its own hypnosis of light and sound; bringing the human organism fully into the electric century" (316, 312). The truth of that perception is indeed before us in Trevor Nunn's extraordinary production of Tom Stoppard's *The Coast of Utopia* (Royal National Theatre, London, Summer 2002), where the electric cinefication produces specifically "sousings in . . . real salt waves." Shaw would have been dazzled.

In the array of its cosmopolitan survey, the volume produces some interesting particulars. In forming the critical opinion of a play at the Comédie française as late as 1770, the audience standing in the pit, "n'y ayant point de femmes," gave its judgment "masculine and firm," while the "quarrelsome (feminine) boxes" gave judgment ruled by caprice (246, 421). That the audience was divided, not only by means but by gender, so late as 1770 in France is noteworthy. There is a fascinating discussion of the conflicting merits of the senses of hearing and seeing. A play heard from the stage is very different from a play read from the page. "The ear, closer to the intellect than the eye, was generally perceived as safer than the eye" (153), a principle understood as far back as Aquinas: "auditu solo tuto creditur" ("Adoro Te"). At the same time, as other critics held, sounds "could . . . be dangerously seductive," inveigling the judgment of the audience (151).

The volume cites a most interesting debate between the Abbé D'Aubignac and Corneille: the Abbé objecting that the playwright had failed in his duty by not providing in the dialogue what the scene painters and performers ought to do (marginal directions "were a form of printed 'telling' improper in a genre made of 'showing' "); Corneille defending his habit of providing full stage directions in the margins for the benefit of readers and provincial players, and arguing that placing directions extratextually in the margins removed from the text of the dialogue the "burden" of providing instructions for "the lesser actions" ("les menues actions"). "Speeches did not have to contain instructions for action; . . . [marginal stage directions could] alert [actors] to what they have to do. . . . [They would do] strange things if we did not help them out with these notes" (174, 401).

One hesitates to find fault with so richly detailed, informative, and wide-ranging a study, but one must object to what would seem to be a misquotation, *"Menuscripts"* from Humphrey Moseley's letter "to the Readers" in the Beaumont and Fletcher folio of 1647 (p. 52; an error anticipated as a bracketed insertion into the passage [p. 43]; [the passage is found on A4v not on A3v (p. 347)]); and one can register only dismay that in a study bristling with expertise in modern languages a volume from the Oxford University Press would print *"reductio ad absurdam"* (219) and—worse yet—*"in memorium"* (50).

There are 312 pages of text, 130 pages of notes, 41 pages of Works Cited. There are 60 illustrations—title pages, woodcuts, engravings—thoughtfully chosen and exactly placed in the text; they are taken from books of plays and so bear directly on the argument. They are essential to that argument.

The Politics of Carnival: Festive Misrule in Medieval England, by Chris Humphrey. Manchester: Manchester University Press, 2001. Pp. xiii + 113. Cloth $59.95, Paper $19.95.

Reviewer: MICHAEL A. WINKELMAN

Carnival, the farewell to the flesh, is more, far more, than just a party. From the fleshpots of Rio to Mardi Gras in New Orleans, and stretching back to early modern France and merry old England, Carnival is also a hotly contested site of scholarly disputation. With *The Politics of Carnival: Festive Misrule in Medieval England,* Chris Humphrey enters the fray. In his *libellum* he proposes a new approach to studying these phenomena and offers two case studies to demonstrate his methods. While not exactly groundbreaking, his book has many strengths. The overview of the critical battle lines, the clarity of his presentation, the examinations of two specific social dramas, and not least the brevity of his tome (exactly one hundred pages of text), make *The Politics of Carnival* an engaging contribution to the field, and worth reading.

There are four chapters:

1. Social protest or safety-valve? Critical approaches to festive misrule
2. A new approach to the study of medieval misrule
3. Seasonal drama and local politics in Norwich, 1443
4. Summer games at Coventry in 1480

As the chapter titles indicate, the first half attempts to work through issues surrounding interpretation at the current time. Humphrey writes in a jargon-free way (although some of the dialectical Middle English transcriptions could have been glossed, e.g., "trought" [truth?], 64), and he carefully differentiates between "Carnival"—the holiday before Lent, "carnival" being the term used by other scholars to denote general medieval festivities—and his preferred term "misrule" for a wide set of festive practices (3). The inclusion of a table with seasons and feasts for medieval English misrule is another clarifying detail (4).

Humphrey's work clearly derives its spirit from Mikhail Bakhtin. He provides the epigraph, a statement that "The problem of carnival . . . is one of the most complex and most interesting problems in the history of culture." And he reappears in the preface, the introduction, chapter 1, the conclusion, and elsewhere. Via *Rabelais and His World* and *Problems of Dostoevsky's Poetics,* Bakhtin has of course become a byword for scholarly examinations of the carnivalesque, and the argument of *The Politics of Carnival* reveals Humphrey to be an eager acolyte.[1] Yet to his credit, Humphrey is not simply imposing Bakhtinian readings on disputes in medieval towns. Furthermore, while extolling the Russian scholar's importance to his line of inquiry, Humphrey also acknowledges his "poor substantiation at the level of the historical evidence" (29). Instead he is exploring "the problem of carnival" that Bakhtin brought to the attention of the academic world. Bakhtin posited that

> the entire theatrical life of the Middle Ages was carnivalistic . . . it could be said (with certain reservations, of course) that a person of the Middle Ages lived, as it were, *two lives:* one was the *official* life, monolithically serious and gloomy, subjugated to a strict hierarchical order, full of terror, dogmatism, reverence, and piety; the other was the *life of the carnival square,* free and unrestricted, full of ambivalent laughter, blasphemy, the profanation of everything sacred, full of debasing and obscenities, familiar contact with everyone and everything. Both these lives were legitimate, but separated by strict temporal boundaries. (31, emphasis in original)

Humphrey makes the important point that though Bakhtin and his followers have rather "nostalgically represented" medieval carnival, misrule and transgression did in fact occur, at the Feast of the Boy Bishop, the Feast of Fools, Hocktide, May Day, and elsewhere. This brings us to the fish Humphrey wants to fry: he hopes to move beyond the prevailing theories that festive misrule is either subversive or a "safety valve," in order to promote more nuanced analyses based on specific evidence. The first two chapters take up such hermeneutic questions in depth.

The opening chapter reviews recent work on medieval carnival and finds fault not only with each of the two predominant perspectives, but with their central dialectic as well:

> arguments about misrule have been put in rather exclusive terms; either misrule works like a safety-valve, and the status quo is restored after a period of temporary inversion, or it is seen as the expression of class antagonism or gender politics. There is not much scope for views in between. (20)

As pathbreaking as these cultural materialist and Bakhtinian-inflected questions have been, it is about time to jump off the "safety valve" bandwagon. The author states:

> generalisations about the role of misrule tend to hinder rather than help our interpretation of it. Therefore, the more that we can see performances of misrule as meaningful in their own right, rather than just having the same effects over and over again as predicted by an abstract model, the more sensitive we can be to the subtleties and intricacies of the evidence that we study. (13)

A good metaquestion moves the book to methodology: "Why medieval people should want to get involved in such activities in the first place, that is, the motivation behind misrule" (27). It's not completely answered and perhaps it can't be; nevertheless Humphrey examines two specific situations, which at least provide satisfactory initial responses.

The next chapter proposes "a new approach," a more precise, credible way to move from evidence to interpretation (38). Humphrey's worldview is not completely free from a priori models—such a perspective would be chaotic, to say the least—but his ideas about urban culture in the fifteenth century, which are in tune with recent social history, create open space for insightful analysis. Two good notions undergirding this system are "the idea of symbolic inversion" (41), and the "politics of interpretation" by which interested parties might

> wilfully misconstrue misrule, either by trying to pass off their obviously antisocial actions as "harmless fun," or by claiming that someone else's benign pursuit was in fact a flagrant moral outrage: transgression is most certainly in the eye of the beholder. (43)

Less clear in Humphrey's argument are the undertheorized treatment of misrule as "performance" (39), and a question that is passed over: when does festive misrule become riot and rebellion? What are the boundaries of transgression? Overall, however, chapters 1 and 2 stimulate interest and under-standing by challenging prevailing patterns of (mis)reading and holding interpretation closely to evidence.[2]

The second part of the treatise puts theory into practice with two chapters exploring fifteenth-century urban unrest. In both cases, the imputed trans-gressions of commonfolk who apparently utilized specific holiday occasions to vandalize church property were recorded by the municipal authorities. These records provide Humphrey with solid evidence to work with. In both cases, the misbehavior or excessiveness stems, as far as we can tell, from disputes between powerful ecclesiastical landowners and layfolk who felt that their traditional rights were being infringed upon. In Norwich, merchant John Gladman, "corowned as kyng of Cristmesse," led a premature Shrovetide procession through the city on 22 January 1443 (64). Three days later, fol-lowing a town assembly, thousands briefly besieged St. Benet's abbey. Hum-phrey argues that these episodes relate to an ongoing conflict between city and priory over Norwich's new mills on the River Wensum, which allegedly interfered with those of the priory (68). The powerful earl of Suffolk, Wil-liam de la Pole, was invited to arbitrate, and he decided in favor of the abbot and "disaffected former office-holders" against the mayor and council (68). By January 1443, things boiled over into Gladman's Insurrection. The results were rough for Norwich: "the destruction of the city's mills, the imprison-ment of the mayor and the loss of the city's liberties and franchises" (77). Over the next several years, however, Norwich resettled matters more favor-ably. The author does more than merely contextualize this disturbance; he also offers an astute analysis of the riotous parade, worth quoting at length:

> Gladman's riding highlighted the opposition between the end of the Christmas season and the beginning of Lent; in the procession the figure of Lent followed after the King of Christmas. This image would have had an especially topical meaning in the context of the city's disputes with a number of local ecclesiastical institutions. As Lent was a period of fasting, the personification of Lent this early in the year may have helped to focus anxieties about how the city would be supplied with food in the future, given the impending destruction of the city's mills. . . . The fact that Lent was at the rear of the procession, symbolising that 'sadnesse shuld folowyn and an holy tyme,' had more than just a seasonal meaning in this context; it was a symbolic expression of the city's predicament, and perhaps also an incitement to take action to forestall these consequences. . . .
>
> The appropriateness of its imagery was not the only tactical feature of the Shrovetide format. A further advantage which it offered was that if a defence of the incident became necessary, the participants could always argue that their actions were entirely harmless, just play and nothing else. (74–75)

This strikes me as a very apposite close reading. The writer acknowledges that fifteenth-century meanings cannot be fully recovered, but here he makes good sense of the evidence.

We revisit church/citizen tensions in chapter 4, this time in Coventry in 1480, where citizens deforested abbey lands (wood and greenery were customarily gathered from private or common lands for festivals). Conflicts between city councilmen and VIPs over commons' pasturage also contributed to the imbroglio. The prior registered a complaint that "the people of the cite yerely in somer throwen down and beren away the underwode of the seid priour, and birches, holyes, ooke, hawthorn and other at Whitmore Parke and his other closez, and breken his hegges to his hurtes yerely Cs'" (90). Coventry's defenders, and information from other cities, allow the author to hypothesize that in this case, the prior may have revoked a customary tolerance due to recent overharvesting; this overharvesting, however, may have been the townsfolk's response to overgrazing on the commons by those with "big flocks and the influence to get what they wanted" (89). The town's government claimed that custom sanctioned tolerance:

> yf eny undisposed creature offend to the contrarie ayeynst their will, no defalt therin oweth to be ascryved in them, remebryng that the people of every gret cite, as London and other citeez, yerely in somur doon harme to divers lords and genty-les havyng wods and groves nygh to such citees be takyng of boughes and treez. And yit the lords and gentils suffren sych dedes ofte tymes of their goode will. (92–93)

Read in terms of vigorous debate over enclosures and local traditions, it makes sense for Humphrey to say that:

> the customarily-tolerated encroachment in question was a negotiated compromise arrived at locally and at a particular historical moment; as such, it was open to change, whether through a shift in attitude on the prior's part or because it was exploited by some of Coventry's inhabitants. (92)

He goes on to find that the breaches had some positive effects on town life in the long run.

Humphrey has acquitted himself well with this, his first book. His clear presentation and discussion of methodology, for instance, can and should serve as a model for advanced undergraduate readers.[3] The specific cases bring together church history, conflicts between different jurisdictions, law and ritual, and even archives-as-culture, and so should appeal to various late medieval scholarly constituencies. He also reaches out in his conclusion to our "modernist counterparts" and to those probing popular culture's role in inciting social change, a worthy contemporary topic for dialogue (100).

It would not be right to call *The Politics of Carnival*'s enviable brevity a fault per se, yet I would like to touch on some of its nonfatal limitations. The opening chapters are helpful, but a more aggressive interrogation of some mindless cookie-cutter scholarship might have strengthened his argument somewhat (though his reluctance to bash individual critics is definitely under-standable). More seriously, the similarity and relative homogeneity of the two episodes in chapters 3 and 4—both well-documented short-term transgressions growing out of annual rites—would seem to limit the book's methodological reach. It would have been intriguing had the author treated a dramatic text which stages festive misrule—the Towneley *Second Shepherds Pageant* would have been a particularly rich selection—to see if a profitable context could be argued for by Humphrey's means. Another literary representation, "The Miller's Prologue," the peasants' revolt within *The Canterbury Tales,* might also work. Moving outside of medieval England, Humphrey's cover illustration, *The Fight between Carnival and Lent* by Pieter Brugel the Elder, would be yet a third avenue for analysis. Judging by the bibliography, Chris Humphrey is probably a fresh young scholar; we may all hope that this study helps get him a benefice so that he can continue to produce insightful scholarship.

Notes

1. More on Bakhtin's life and working conditions might have been worthwhile. See p. 29, notes 34 and 35, for tantalizing hints about him.

2. The one major anthropologist not cited is Clifford Geertz.

3. I did, however, notice the following typographical errors: "of questions of" (first "of" superfluous) (5); "individual wagons cycles" (16); "a more thoughful to misrule" (word such as "approach" missing) (21); "terms . . . tends," "individual . . . them" (agreement) (43); "then" for "them," (55); "very" for "vary" (60); and "that . . . that" (first "that" superfluous) (68).

Index